LEARNING CENTER ACTIVITIES FOR THE FULL-DAY KINDERGARTEN

ABBY BARRY BERGMAN

illustrated by Carrie Oesmann

**THE CENTER FOR APPLIED
RESEARCH IN EDUCATION**
West Nyack, New York 10995

© 1990 by

THE CENTER FOR APPLIED
RESEARCH IN EDUCATION

West Nyack, NY

10 9 8 7 6 5 4 3

Library of Congress Cataloging-in-Publication Data

Bergman, Abby Barry,
    Learning center activities for the full-day kindergarten / Abby
Barry Bergman: illustrations by Carrie Oesmann.
        p.   cm.
    ISBN 0-87628-512-4
    1. Full-day kindergarten.   2. Kindergarten—Curricula.
3. Kindergarten—Activity programs   4. Classroom learning centers.
I. Center for Applied Research in Education. II. Title.
LB1180.B47   1990
372.12′424—dc20   90-40503
                                                            CIP

ISBN 0-87628-512-4

**THE CENTER FOR APPLIED
RESEARCH IN EDUCATION
BUSINESS & PROFESSIONAL DIVISION**
A division of Simon & Schuster
West Nyack, New York 10995

Printed in the United States of America

This book is dedicated to
the kindergarten child
and to
the kindergarten child in all of us

ACKNOWLEDGMENTS

The preparation of a meaningful book in the field of education is hardly a solitary enterprise. Over the years I have benefited from the ideas and encouragement of friends and colleagues. Among the friends who have provided support, suggestions, and inspiration are Lilith Budman, Mark Flanzraich, Constance Kehoe, and Kathryn Kosek. I have benefited from the reactions and advice of the educators at the Ralph S. Maugham School, most notably Shirley McPhillips, Michaele Salmon, and Patrick Westcott. Discussions with my college advisor, friend, and science educator Willard J. Jacobson have proven invaluable.

I thank Winfield A. Huppuch, vice-president at Prentice-Hall, for his vision and encouragement. I express sincere appreciation to Zsuzsa Neff production editor, for her patient assistance and wise judgments every step of the way. Our humorous meetings passing manuscripts on parkways added an unpredictable element. Development editor, Diane Turso also provided important suggestions and assisted in the acquisition of the art work.

And finally, I owe a great debt of gratitude to my wife Rose and son Jonathan, who have understood why I had to miss an occasional soccer or baseball game because I was trying to juggle the demands of my daily professional responsibilities along with the preparation of this book.

ABOUT THE AUTHOR

Abby Barry Bergman received his Bachelor of Arts degree from Hunter College of the City University of New York, his Master of Arts and Master of Education degrees from Teachers College, Columbia University, and his Doctor of Education degree from Columbia University.

Dr. Bergman has been involved with education for over twenty years, during which time he has been a kindergarten teacher, a teacher in a pilot prekindergarten program, an administrative intern for elementary curriculum, and a school principal. Since 1982, he has been principal of the Ralph S. Maugham School in Tenafly, New Jersey, an elementary school in a nationally reputed "lighthouse" school district.

Dr. Bergman is also an independent consultant in educational product development and evaluation. He has coauthored two books in the science education field and has written several professional articles, pamphlets, and curriculum guides.

CONTENTS

CHAPTER 5   IN THE WRITING CENTER   89

CHAPTER 6   IN THE LISTENING CENTER   109

CHAPTER 7   IN THE MATHEMATICS CENTER   125

CHAPTER 8   IN THE SCIENCE CENTER   195

CHAPTER 9   IN THE MUSIC CENTER **227**

CHAPTER 10   IN THE ART CENTER **241**

ABOUT THIS BOOK

In recent years, kindergarten teachers have experienced "curriculum overload" as increasing demands, mandated workbooks, and commercially packaged materials have crowded their programs. Happily, the growing popularity of full-day kindergarten has allowed teachers to regain some control of the time and experiences that are offered to their youngsters. A longer school day has also afforded kindergarten teachers new opportunities to extend children's learnings and provided the time for more relaxed, child-centered inquiry. A need for fresh sources of open-ended experiences for youngsters has emerged, ones that will provide stimulation for both children and teachers. *Learning Center Activities for the Full-Day Kindergarten* is a collection of activities and suggestions designed to help you incorporate some new ideas into your program, while keeping in mind that children's experiences should be integrated and interrelated.

Learning Center Activities for the Full-Day Kindergarten was developed with the underlying assumption that you will pick and choose from the array of activities to supplement and enrich your existing program. Activities are not given skill or subject designations, such as visual discrimination, handwriting, number concepts, and so on. Instead, this book is organized according to the physical set-up of most kindergarten classrooms, that is, according to the activity areas—or learning centers. You know where in your program you would like to insert some new learning experiences. The teaching suggestions offered in this book are easy to accomplish with readily available materials.

What's Different About This Book?

Kindergarten activity books generally include activities parceled out to specific subject disciplines. We know, though, that when children are engaged in doing something, they do not stop to think "Is this science, math, or reading readiness?" Instead, they seek to find meaning in their world. They connect current actions to prior experiences to interpret and mediate what they are doing and learning. Children are holistic in their approach; their world is filled with a multitude of stimuli, impressions, and images. In order to understand, they strive to organize and interrelate what they learn.

The intention of *Learning Center Activities for the Full-Day Kindergarten* is to present activities that are consistent with the way children learn, not to isolate specific skills. All new learning takes place along a continuum of prior experience. And every time a child encounters or experiences something new the basis is formed upon which to pin new learnings. For example, when youngsters first see the word *tree* in a book or activity, they do not just see the letters *t-r-e-e*, but they instantly make associations with their own prior experiences, sensations, and emotions.

The activities in this book are organized according to the physical areas of the kindergarten classroom. Most teachers of young children designate spaces for specific types of activities—block building, housekeeping, science and listening, for example.

The importance of dividing children's spaces into activity centers brings to mind an anecdote from my early years as a kindergarten teacher. As a fledgling in an urban school system, the "veteran" teachers had forewarned me to make certain that my bulletin boards were changed monthly so that I would pass the inspection of the grade-level supervisor during her visits to my room. A few weeks into the school year, my bulletin boards sparkled and met the enthusiastic approval of the supervisor. One day, though, she declared that the housekeeping area in my room was not defined well enough. Quite frankly, I was taken aback. The wooden sink, refrigerator, and stove formed natural barriers and prevented the children from being distracted by others who were playing in the adjacent block center. Whatever did she mean by "not well defined?" Only after several months' experience and a lot of discussion with colleagues did I come to realize that areas are not defined by space and furniture, but rather by the complementary objects and accessories that help children to explore and learn. So, I filled the housekeeping area with empty boxes of cereal and other food products and provided a bin full of funny hats and old clothing. I acquired a collection of toy cars and rubber animals for the block corner—all designed to provide richer experiences for the children's encounters.

Activities and spaces should "invite" children to enter. It can be a display on a table or an exhibit on the wall, a pocket chart or a file folder, but the criterion for inclusion in the program should be the degree of involvement an activity or material will promote. And that is how this book is different. Activities are not simply listed and outlined, but the notions of involvement, multiple opportunities, and extending children's encounters are prime considerations. Connections with other experiences are suggested to provide additional meaning through the integration of the young child's learning experiences.

More About Learning Centers

Learning Centers can help to individualize the curriculum because activities planned can be accomplished on a variety of levels depending upon a particular youngster's interest and skill. For example, in a writing or art activity, each child will bring whatever skill, imagination, or interest he or she may possess to the experience. Activity centers can be designed to supplement or reinforce experiences that the whole class has enjoyed, or they can comprise the central activity in which the children engage. A well-designed learning center should include a few basic components:

1. Clear instructions for self-directed activity must be provided. Directions may be posted in rebus (pictorial) format or provided orally by the teacher or classmates.
2. A variety of interesting materials for exploration should be included.
3. Learning center activities should have a built-in element of success. There should also be a way for children to evaluate their involvement. (They might be able to compare their work to a model or to gain satisfaction from manipulating objects.)
4. The activities at a learning center should be somewhat open-ended, permitting a variety of possible solutions or results so that all youngsters can have meaningful encounters.

Kindergarten learning centers can provide endless enjoyment and involvement for children, while fostering independence and meeting individual needs. An activity in this book will often require initial teacher demonstration or explanation, and then children may complete, follow up, or extend the activity in a learning center. (See the sample math center activity in the illustration.)

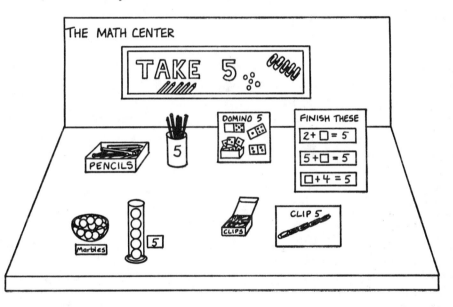

How Are the Activities Organized?

Although diverse, the activities in this book follow a similar organizational pattern. Each chapter has a general introduction that provides a context for the activities that follow. Teaching strategies are suggested and the importance of developing the particular area is discussed.

1. **The Title:** The title of the activity suggests something of what is to follow. Often, you will have to read beyond the title to find out about the nature of the activity.
2. **Why Do This?:** In this section, some possible outcomes of the activity are discussed. The benefits to the children are considered as well as some of the specific

skills that will be developed through their involvement. How the activity fits into the child's world is discussed, and curricular tie-ins are mentioned.

3. **What Will I Need?:** A detailed list of the materials required for the activity is provided. Most of the objects required are readily available in a kindergarten classroom or easily obtained from a local hardware or grocery store.

4. **How to Get Started:** This part provides suggestions for involving children and describes the procedure for the activity. The implementation may be for a large group of children, a small group, or an individual. Sometimes, it is best to introduce an activity to the whole class and then allow the children to participate on their own or in small groups during free-choice time. Some activities require teacher leadership and supervision; others do not. This is apparent from the nature of the activity described.

5. **How to Go Further:** Each activity can be extended and enriched. Here is an opportunity for gifted, motivated, or interested youngsters to dig deeper and make new discoveries and explore additional possibilities beyond the basic experience.

How to Use This Book

Look at your classroom. How is it defined? Look at the table of contents. You may notice a close match between the chapter titles and the organization of your own classroom. If so, you're ready to go. If not, you're still in business. These activities can be adapted to any classroom and any physical space scheme. Just pick up the book, open to a page, glance at the activity, think of where it belongs in *your* program, and "plug it in." Browse through the book. Start with the section that appeals to you the most. Try an activity. This book is intended to be used just that casually. Certainly there is no sequence of instruction implied by the organization of chapters.

If, on the other hand, you prefer a more structured approach, that's also fine. Look at your instructional plans for the week. Then glance at the section of the book that seems to best fit what you intend to teach. Pick an activity. If it involves a new approach or a novel twist on what you had planned, try it. You might want to look ahead and think of what you would like to incorporate into your own program. This is an informal book, yet it is also a handy resource guide. Since the materials required will probably be easily obtained, you could think of this book as a "read tonight, teach tomorrow" manual.

Reproducible worksheets accompany many of the activities. Feel free to use them at will. Some of the children will be able to complete them on their own; others will require teacher directions or explanation. In any case, these worksheets can be duplicated as often as you like.

Most teachers will find that they wish to adapt, amend, or transform the activities to their particular situations. That's great! If the ideas in *Learning Center Activities for the Full-Day Kindergarten* provide springboards for individual creation, so much the better. One thing that you might want to do is to involve your children in an assessment of how they enjoyed a particular activity. You'll probably find that if they liked an activity, you did too. Join in with your kindergarteners and have fun!

Abby Barry Bergman

THE REASONS FOR A FULL-DAY KINDERGARTEN

Full-day kindergarten programs are becoming more and more common. If a school district has not implemented an extended kindergarten day, it probably has at least considered doing so. As full-day programs are instituted, an important question is: What happens to the curriculum? Most teachers with whom I have spoken felt that their instructional programs were unusually "crowded" just prior to the inception of a longer school day for five-year-olds. It is probably no coincidence that several forces have come to bear when a school considers extending the kindergarten experience. Among these factors are:

- an increase in the number of children from homes where both parents work or children from homes in which the single parent works
- an increase in the number of children attending full-day preschool programs
- a growing realization that five-year-olds can endure a longer school day as long as ample periods of rest are provided
- an overburdened kindergarten curriculum
- underutilized school buildings

Many teachers have remarked that as school districts develop subject area curriculums, recommended components, workbooks, or both have been placed at the kindergarten level. Teachers found that with all of these curriculum mandates, little time remained in the kindergarten day to do many of the more exciting and enriching activities that attracted them to the kindergarten level in the first place. The advent of full-day kindergarten or extended-day programs has permitted teachers to let the children's experience expand, unfold, and allow time for exploring their interests once a topic or activity was introduced. Some teachers have worked hard to ensure that as the kindergarten day expanded, no new formalized instructional programs would be added, but the day would be allowed to become a bit more relaxed. The extra time would benefit those children who *need* time to play, explore, talk, practice language, socialize, and construct meaning by their actions within their environment. Many teachers say the longer day has brought some of the fun back into kindergarten.

As teachers find that they have time to expand children's encounters with the physical environment, *Learning Center Activities for the Full-Day Kindergarten* may be just what is needed. Here is a hefty set of activities that can be incorporated into any program and at any time. As children become interested, they may want to dig deeper, to go further. When this happens, they are setting the stage for lifelong habits of learning. This interest will help them to see how their current activity fits into other things they know and have done. The provision of a longer school day for five-year-olds may have a broader and more significant impact in terms of children's *involvement* in their learning than anyone might have expected.

WORKING WITH
THE KINDERGARTEN CHILD

All children are different. Among five-year-olds in particular, the range of attention span as well as readiness to profit from direct instruction is highy variable. Full-day programs allow the pace of instruction to meet a broad range of maturity levels and learning styles. Children can have the time to "smell the flowers along their way," to enrich their experiences with enhanced language development, to allow for more varied encounters with concrete objects, and to permit unhurried interactions with peers. Teachers in full-day kindergarten programs find that they are able to accomplish activities that are in line with their own instincts about children's needs and that are also more fun.

To attach meaning to a concept, children benefit from encountering a new idea in a variety of situations. For example, if a teacher wants to engage children in a study of the characteristics of light, multiple opportunities can be arranged for children to explore phenomena. Books about light can be featured in the classroom library, a flashlight and shadow box can be placed on the science table, drawings with sunny or gloomy moods can be executed, a lamp can be brought into the housekeeping area, children can produce a book about their investigations with light, and so on. By ensuring that children experience phenomena in a variety of situations and contexts, their development of concepts will take on more meaning and become better generalized.

Teachers of full-day kindergarten seek to establish balance or rhythm in the school day. Active times and quiet times are deliberately alternated. Experiences are varied to maintain pupil interest and enthusiasm, and a varitey of learning modalities can be exercised. Pacing and timing are important. Instruction is provided to the whole class, to small groups, and to individual youngsters as needed. If an assignment is given to the entire class, some children will undoubtedly finish before others. In these situations, teachers often provide a variety of self-directed activities so that the children do not become impatient and restless if they have to wait too long for their next involvement.

Teachers find that transitions are often problem spots during the day. For example, when children are asked to clean up after their work/play period, some will undoubtedly be finished before others. Having a clear procedure for what may be done will be helpful. Certainly, the activities selected at this time would not be ones that require additional clean-up. But, looking at a book from the classroom is ready to begin a new activity. A healthy snack, rest period, and outdoor time, inserted at appropriate intervals, are important parts of the day's rhythm and balance.

Children are curious and eager learners. They learn best when they are active and involved. Teachers use concrete objects, environmental stimuli, and many opportunities for manipulative experiences to engage the youngsters' interest and enthusiasm. Children also learn from one another. A healthy sharing of ideas, emotions, and discoveries should occur as teachers observe the children's interactions. Young children need time to form effective working relationships. Teacher mediation may be necessary, but time, maturity, and a rich environment are important, too, if youngsters are to develop a true sense of cooperation in the classroom.

Physical spaces are also subject to balance. A barren, sterile environment is no place for children to learn and grow; yet, too much clutter can be confusing and overstimulating for some. As teachers define areas that invite children to become active learners, a sense of purpose is established. Organization of materials and easy access provide a framework for inquiry. Many teachers rotate their storehouse of materials, not putting out too many things at the same time, changing materials after a week or two, and returning some to storage. Then, when appropriate, the stored material is reintroduced for the children to rediscover and use in new ways.

The Daily Schedule

Setting a daily schedule is a matter of balancing the needs of youngsters, curriculum requirements, and activities and events within a particular school. The daily schedule in September will be different from the schedule in May, because as the school year goes on, children can sustain activities for longer periods of time. Also, the schedule will vary from day to day within a given week, depending upon schoolwide events, programs provided by special teachers, and particular activities in which teachers and children are involved.

Outlined here are two sample schedules from full-day kindergarten programs. Notice that in Sample Schedule A, considerable time is allowed for youngsters to explore activities in learning centers. Sample Schedule B is based upon a greater degree of teacher-initiated instruction. Either schedule will work well—it's simply a matter of the teacher's emphasis. Note that in both situations, active and quiet times are alternated, and children are provided with a wide variety of experiences. Also, the schedules might be different on different days of the week. On Mondays, in many classrooms, children's "jobs" for the week may change. Plans for the week ahead may also be discussed. Some schools have assemblies each week, and so the schedule will be adjusted on these days. These samples are provided as guides to help you think about scheduling and to serve as a basis for discussion and consideration of the flow of a typical day.

SAMPLE SCHEDULE A	
8:45– 9:15	Opening Exercises, Jobs, Plans for the Day
9:15–10:30	Learning Center Activities
10:30–10:45	Clean-up
10:45–11:00	Snacktime
11:00–11:30	Outdoor Play, Physical Education, or Nature Study
11:30–12:00	Whole Language Activities: Writing, Drawing, Reading, Dramatizing
12:00–12:45	Lunch and Recess
12:45– 1:05	Story Time
1:05– 1:25	Rest and Listening to Music
1:25– 2:00	Math Activities
2:00– 2:40	Art, Science, or Social Studies
2:40– 3:00	Fingerplays, Songs, Review of Day, Distribution of Flyers, Preparation for Dismissal

SAMPLE SCHEDULE B	
8:45– 9:00	Opening Exercises: Pledge, Attendance, Calendar, Weather, Jobs
9:00–10:00	Small Group Work/Playtime: Reading Readiness, Writing.
10:00–10:30	Music and Rhythms
10:30–10:45	Snack and Show & Tell
10:45–11:15	Outdoor Play or Physical Education
11:15–11:45	Math
11:45–12:30	Lunch
12:30– 1:00	Rest and Quiet Time
1:00– 1:45	Art Projects
1:45– 2:15	Science, Social Studies, or Outdoor Nature Study
2:15– 2:30	Recess: Indoor or Outdoor
2:30– 2:55	Library or Story Time
2:55– 3:00	Dismissal

Integrating the Curriculum

The classroom is the scene of much activity. Brian is painting an ocean background in several shades of blue and green on a large sheet of brown paper; Joan is cutting out her fanciful drawings of fish that she will paste onto the background. In another corner of the room, the teacher is writing an ocean poem, taking down the funny phrases dictated by Valerie and Lloyd. In the block corner, Alex and Cynthia are building their version of the New York Aquarium replete with pictures of large tanks filled with plant and animal life and labels and signs. Nearby, in the housekeeping area, John and Wendy have just returned from a "fishing trip" and are about to prepare a meal from their day's catch. In the writing center, Adam and Meryl are writing the names of fish they have read about on index cards, later to be incorporated into a mural that the class will be making.

This teacher is integrating and relating the children's learning and is helping the youngsters see connections in their work. So great is the children's involvement that their school experiences spill over into their homes. One boy's father will come into the classroom to demonstrate the preparation of a fishing rod. He will also show pictures from his last fishing trip. One child has been working on making a fish-shaped pillow with her grandmother. The children's learnings are divergent, yet each new experience provides additional meaning. They are discovering that school is not a disconnected hodgepodge of compartmentalized episodes. The use of letters and words is not isolated from what they do in art or in music. The teacher relates present involvement to things the children have done in the past as the children are asked to recall former activities and impressions to see how they fit into the business at hand. Wherever possible, teachers can find ways to integrate learning, relate events, and help children to see connections. Occasionally, teachers will feel that an inordinate amount of time is required to work with children in this way, but if the depth of the youngsters' understanding is monitored by observing their involvement and by asking questions, then the importance of integrated learning will undoubtedly become apparent.

No single book or list of kindergarten activities can ever be complete. New experiences occur every day. The purpose of *Learning Center Activities for the Full-Day Kindergarten* is to suggest how to involve children in a variety of activities and how to extend their learning. The active kindergarten is spontaneous and alive. New experiences and approaches unfold each day. The only limit is the imagination of the teacher and the children. As you use this book, you may want to keep notes on what has emerged, and what new activities have come out of the children's involvement.

Five-year-olds work and play hard. Kindergarten is a wonderful time in their lives. Their days are filled with questions and curiosity. For most youngsters, kindergarten is usually the beginning of their formal school careers. Your role as teacher should be to provide a rich and stimulating learning environment, one that invites them to probe and to find out. You must let the children be five years old; after all, it only happens once in a lifetime. Each year is always a new beginning, full of wonder and fun and unique experiences for the children *and* their teachers. Above all, enjoy your explorations with the children and keep the joy of learning and discovery alive!

chapter 1

IN THE MEETING CENTER— THE CLASS GATHERING

Each day in the kindergarten usually starts with a class meeting. Opening routines are followed for attendance taking, the pledge to the flag, perhaps the singing of a song, reviewing the calendar and weather, the assignment of classroom jobs, and discussion of plans for the day. Not only are these important details accomplished, but the class meeting also helps to build a sense of group and community. Children share experiences, benefit from hearing one another's ideas, and *react* to each other's thoughts. This is also an important opportunity for teachers to set up the ground rules for group discussion: listening to each other attentively, waiting until one child is finished speaking before offering other comments, waiting a turn, stating ideas clearly. This class gathering is a time that can be used to foster group living skills and help youngsters to know how the day will be organized. It can be a "cozy" time as each youngster knows that he or she is a part of a group. The following activities are ones which can be readily accomplished at meeting time.

VARYING OPENING ROUTINES

WHY DO THIS?

It is particularly important in the kindergarten to establish routines for classroom activities. Routines help children to develop a sense of order; they know what to expect, what comes next in a sequence, and what their responsibilities are. Within any established routine, though, there should be flexibility for some variation to maintain interest and enthusiasm on the part of the children *and* the teacher. The following suggestions can help lead the way towards a greater variety of activities at the classroom gathering.

WHAT WILL I NEED?

- Large chart paper, markers
- A book of kindergarten songs
- A list or book of fingerplays

HOW TO GET STARTED.

Kindergarten teachers generally take attendance at meeting time. This routine can be varied in a variety of ways. Early in the year, the teacher can take attendance by showing the youngsters cards with a name on it. The child whose name appears calls out that she or he is here. This is a good way to build early name recognition. Another way is to list the children's names on a sheet of large chart paper. Children can take turns reading each child's name and having the youngster respond if present. (This also helps each child to recognize the names of all of the other children in the class—a handy piece of knowledge.) Some teachers even list the names next to a grid with a column of boxes for each day, sort of like an enlarged roll book, and the children check attendance in the appropriate box.

Children can take turns being the class leader and conducting the class meeting including, leading the pledge and a patriotic song, attendance taking, calendar and weather discussion, classroom jobs, and so on. This leadership position builds responsibility and enhances self-esteem. It is an opportunity that should be rotated among the children. Think of the proud child whose turn it is to be the class leader!

The class meeting is also a good time to learn or practice a new song or fingerplay. It sets a positive tone for the day and gets everyone off to a happy start.

HOW TO GO FURTHER.

The activities that can be incorporated into the class meeting are endless. Ask the children which group experiences they would like to share at the gathering. Once the children are familiar with the daily routine, they can be asked to predict the day's activities—what will come first, second, and so on.

WHO'S HERE TODAY?

WHY DO THIS?

Attendance taking routines can have many variations. Some teachers simply call the names on the class roll and the children respond. Other teachers try to make this daily necessity a little more interesting by helping children to recognize each other's names in printed form. (See previous activity.) There are many "games" that can be developed which would cause children to look forward to this daily routine.

WHAT WILL I NEED?

- Oaktag
- Markers

HOW TO GET STARTED.

Some teachers use attendance time as an opportunity to have children speak in full sentences. The teacher says, "William, are you here?" The children might respond, "Yes, I am." To make this simple activity a bit more interesting the children's names can be called in a chant or song, "I'm looking for Sara, I'm looking for Sara. Are you there?" Sara might respond singing back, "I'm right here, I'm right here." Children can be taught to respond to their names in another language. For example, "here" would be *ici* in French, or *aqui* in Spanish. How about some others?

At the beginning of the year, attendance can be taken by distributing name tags to each child. The tags left over are the absentees. Later on, attendance can be taken by showing name cards to the class. When the child recognizes his or her name, the card is taken. The remaining cards are the absentees. As the year progresses, an attendance monitor can record the names of the absent children on a chalkboard or chart.

The whole class can become involved in attendance taking by having each child look around the room and think of (or write the names of) those children who are absent.

Children usually know the number of youngsters in their class. One child can be assigned to count all of those present and from this figure, work out how many children are absent. (A little help will be required with the higher mathematics, but it's surprising how quickly the children will be able to subtract.)

HOW TO GO FURTHER.

An additional idea, for later on in the year, is to have each child draw a self-portrait. Then they put their names on the back. A display of the portraits will enable all of the children to see each other's likenesses. These pictures can be used to take attendance. As each portrait is shown, the children call out the name of the boy or girl they think it is. After all portraits of children present have been identified, those remaining are the absentees. The teacher can check the results and in the meantime, the children have enjoyed this game.

CALENDAR FUN

WHY DO THIS?

Working with a calendar on a daily basis helps children understand the sequence of time. With regular experience, youngsters come to realize what a calendar *is*. Using a monthly calendar allows children to visualize upcoming and past events. Most teachers mark holidays, the birthdays of children in the class, and important school events on a large calendar which is reviewed each day during the class meeting. As predictable events occur, for example, art on Mondays, music on Tuesdays, and so on, the children begin to develop a sense of the rhythm of activities and special classes within each week.

WHAT WILL I NEED?

- Large chart paper for a calendar
- Individual calendars for children to write or draw on

HOW TO GET STARTED.

Prepare a large calendar for the month on a sheet of easel paper or oaktag. During the class meeting, one child can state the day of the week, the month, the date and the year. Some teachers write special subjects the children will have in the calendar, for example, "Music-A.M." or "Library-P.M." Also, cut-outs of weather symbols can be tacked onto the calendar as the "weather report" is given. A sun would, of course, represent a sunny day. There could be clouds for an overcast day, an umbrella for rain, and a snowman for snow. Cut-outs to represent important holidays can also be tacked onto the calendar in the appropriate box. Children love having the responsibility for filling in the calendar, and this should be a job assigned to youngsters on a rotating basis each week. Discussions of the predictability of the calendar should take place at meeting time. Children can talk about what days their favorite TV shows are broadcast.

Children will learn a lot from studying a calendar. They should come to know the number of days in a week, that calendars are generally organized beginning with a Sunday and ending with Saturday, and that each day of the week appears below itself on the calendar. (As adults, we take all of this for granted, but these are important concepts for young children to learn through their experiences with a calendar.) Of

April 1991

Sunday	Monday	Tuesday	Wednesday	Thursday	Friday	Saturday
	1	2	3	4	5	6
7	8	9	10	11	12	13
14	15	16	17	18	19	20
21	22	23	24	25	26	27
28	29	30	31			

course, there are many songs and poems familiar to teachers which help the children to know the number of days in each month. For example:

> Thirty days have September,
> April, June, and November.
> All the rest have thirty-one,
> Except February, which has twenty-eight,
> And on leap-year, twenty-nine!

Don't even *try* to explain why we have leap-years to kindergartners. It's far too abstract a concept.

HOW TO GO FURTHER.

Duplicate individual calendars for each child in the class. Then, the youngsters can either fill in their own calendars at their work tables or copy the large calendar which was discussed at the class meeting. Some teachers ask children to maintain their own calendars and fill them in with the appropriate weather symbol at the beginning of each day.

THE HOLIDAY CENTER

WHY DO THIS?

Celebrating holidays helps children to understand and appreciate their national and cultural heritage. Discussions about holidays and celebrations are especially appropriate at meeting time, when all of the children gather together. Important days should be noted on the class calendar. This also helps to build excitement as children anticipate the arrival of holidays. The seasons during which holidays occur can also be discussed. Learning about the cultural and religious customs of the various nationalities represented in a class can go a long way towards promoting pride in the children's various backgrounds.

The study of holidays is an opportunity to integrate learnings. For example, at Halloween, children can really learn the meaning of the color "orange." Pumpkins can be compared on a balance, weighed, put in size order, and described in great detail. Jack-o'-lanterns can be designed to express a variety of moods and emotions. Blank jack-o'-lanterns can be duplicated and the children asked to make happy faces, sad faces, scary faces, mean faces, and so on. Creativity can be fostered by putting together costumes. There are many stories about Halloween in the school library. Opening a pumpkin, studying its structure, drying the seeds, and cooking it make for a very rich exploration. Children can also produce their own skits about Halloween and role play some of the safety situations discussed with the teacher. Art, science, math, drama, and social studies blend into a meaningful whole.

WHAT WILL I NEED?

- Materials vary with the holiday.
- A table, bulletin board, or chartstand would be an ideal location for a holiday center.

HOW TO GET STARTED.

It's always a good idea to ask the children what they already know about the holiday. This helps to find out where to begin discussions and can also provide a chance to clear up misconceptions. Once the children have contributed a few ideas, they can be recorded on an experience chart. Many new games, or variations of familiar games, can be adapted to holiday themes. At Thanksgiving time, an interesting game is "Pin the Tail on the Turkey." Tail feathers can be cut from a variety of colors, and after identifying the color, a child pins the feather on a drawn turkey. At the end, the feathers can be counted. A Thanksgiving feast can be planned specifying the foods to be eaten. Children can demonstrate their learnings about the first Thanksgiving by making up an impromptu play.

Teachers can move beyond the typical cherry trees and hatchets for Washington's Birthday and figures of the Nina, Pinta, and Santa Maria for Columbus Day, by helping children to learn more about the significance of these historic figures. What did they do? Why do we celebrate their birthdays? How did their special dreams set them apart from others? And talking about "dreams," as children learn about Martin Luther King, Jr. and his dream, they might "stretch" and think about some dreams they have for the world. These can be written, dictated, or tape-recorded, and a book or tape about the dreams of the children in the class can be compiled and duplicated. For Flag Day, the youngsters can learn about the history of our flag as well as how it should be displayed and honored.

HOW TO GO FURTHER.

Towards the end of the year, and as children become more aware of the months of the year, teachers can conduct a review of the various holidays celebrated and the months in which they fall. (See "The Holidays We Celebrate" worksheet.) A book about holidays around the world and how they are celebrated can be developed and shared with other classes or sent home, as a library book, for parents to enjoy. Parents of youngsters from various backgrounds can be invited to school to give a presentation of their special holidays.

Name _____

THE HOLIDAYS WE CELEBRATE

Draw a line from the picture of a holiday to the name of the month in which it falls.

December

May

October

February

November

June

Mom

THE WEATHER REPORT

WHY DO THIS?

Weather affects children's activities in so many ways. Will we be able to go outdoors today? Was it difficult getting to school this morning? Did we have to dress differently than we did yesterday? These are all questions which can be discussed to broaden children's awareness of how the weather influences their daily lives. Talking about the weather during the class meeting can provide many opportunities for youngsters to observe, predict, and draw inferences. Patterns can be observed, thermometers can be read, and those youngsters eager to give the "official report" will enjoy the assignment of tuning in to the morning weather report on the radio or television before they come to school. Many activities exist for varying the way to deal with the daily weather report.

WHAT WILL I NEED?

- Oaktag or cardboard
- Glue or paste
- Markers, scissors, paper fasteners
- A thermometer mounted outside of a window

HOW TO GET STARTED.

During a class meeting, begin a discussion of the day's weather. Is it sunny, cloudy, rainy, snowy, windy, foggy? How did we first find out about the weather this morning? Did mother tell us; did we listen to the radio report; look out of a window; step outdoors? How does the weather affect the way we dressed for school today? How has the weather been lately? Are we in the middle of a rainy, hot, windy week? How does today's weather compare to yesterday's? The thermometer can be read by some children. Record the outdoor temperature on a chart or graph. Analyze trends. Is it getting warmer or colder? How does this reading in our classroom compare with the weather report heard on the morning news?

Children can make a weather wheel for individual use. (See the "My Weather Wheel" worksheet.) Paste or glue the worksheet onto a sheet of oaktag or cardboard. Cut off the section of the worksheet below the dotted line. Cut out the pointer. Attach it to the center of the wheel with a paper fastener. As the weather is discussed, the children point the arrow on their weather wheels to the appropriate space. Some teachers prefer to make one large weather wheel for the class to share. One child can come up to place the arrow.

Instead of, or in addition to, making weather wheels, a large calendar with ample blank space for each day can be used to record the daily weather. Children can draw the weather symbol for each day, or predrawn figures can be placed into the right space. In any event, this activity should be rich in discussion about observations, trends, predictions, effects on our clothing and activities, and so on.

HOW TO GO FURTHER.

At the end of the month, weather records can be analyzed. How many days this month was it sunny, rainy, cloudy, windy? One way to show this information is to cut up the large calendar for the month, group the weather symbols used, count them, and then paste them so as to form a bar graph. (See the sample shown in the illustration.) This will provide a visual representation of the month's weather. If temperature readings were recorded, the children can find the warmest day and the coolest day of the month. How do these readings compare with those of previous months? Is it getting hotter or colder? How does this information relate to the seasons?

What Was Our Weather Like This Month?

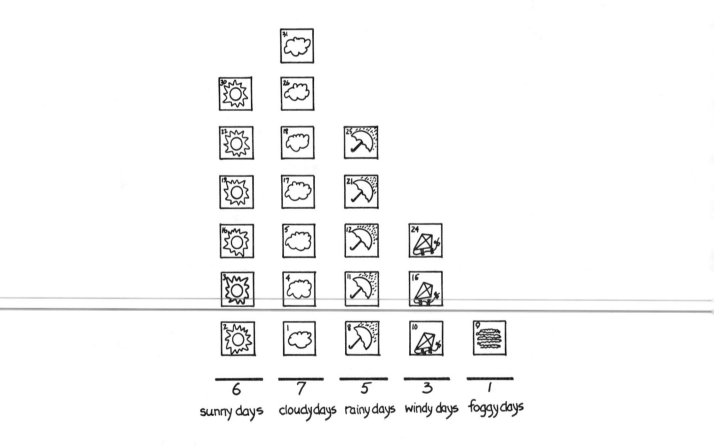

Children may wish to write or dictate stories, poems, or songs about the weather. A rainy day is an ideal time to share poems and pictures about the rain.

Name _____

MY WEATHER WHEEL

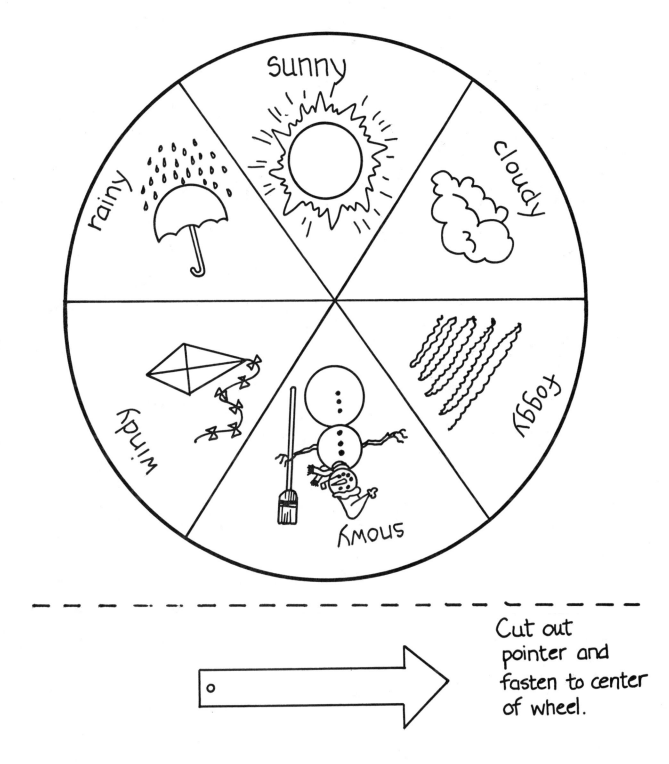

Cut out pointer and fasten to center of wheel.

SHARING PERSONAL NEWS

WHY DO THIS?

Young children love to share exciting events in their lives—family gatherings, a new pair of sneakers, a visiting pet, an upcoming trip, and so on. The class meeting is a fine time to share these important happenings. It builds a sense of community and provides opportunities for the teacher to promote caring, concern, and respect for one another's ideas. Many activities can spring from the discussion of individual or group news. One child can demonstrate and teach the others a magic trick, a new way to make something, a poem or a song. Recording classroom news also provides a meaningful shared language experience.

WHAT WILL I NEED?

- Chart paper
- Markers

HOW TO GET STARTED.

As a part of the morning routine, call upon individual youngsters to share a piece of news about themselves or their families. Rather than call upon the same verbal children, some teachers devise a sign-up chart, or post a class list, and then have only a few children contribute each day, thereby promoting the importance of events in the lives of all of the children. The youngsters may be asked to prepare something to demonstrate during the sharing session, a new song learned, a poem, or something they made or received. The sharing may be summarized in several ways. The names of the children can be listed on a chart and next to each, a sentence or phrase dictated to indicate what was shared. The chart can be left for examination throughout the day. It may be appropriate to summarize, in story form, an item shared by just one youngster. Children can offer sentences and the teacher can use this as an opportunity to review the use of capitals and periods, rich vocabulary, and expression. Once completed, the story can be read in unison.

HOW TO GO FURTHER.

If classroom news is recorded on a chart, these summaries can be kept on a chart frame or some other device for periodic rereading and review. Children like to find the sentences or parts they contributed. Others may just wish to browse through the batch of reports. Teachers can demonstrate to the children, at various points in the school year, their growing skill in dictation, expression, and vocabulary.

Some teachers like to send home a form indicating the "ground rules" for sharing personal news and specifying the date when the child is scheduled to share. This may also serve to involve the parent in the child's news. Perhaps the parent can visit, demonstrate a skill, or talk about a career as a part of the child's sharing time.

THE NEWS REPORT

WHY DO THIS?

As the school year progresses, children can "expand their horizons" and begin to report on interesting news in their city, town, or the nation and world. This can be considered as an extension or broadening of the personal news previously discussed. Children are naturally interested in the world around them, and there is much in newspapers or the evening news reports that young children can comprehend. Rotating through the class, each child should have a chance to offer a report giving his or her own interpretation of a news item. Not only do such experiences help to enhance verbal skills, but they also broaden and deepen the children's understanding of their community and the world.

WHAT WILL I NEED?

- Letter to parents (see next page)
- No special materials

HOW TO GET STARTED.

Begin with a discussion of how we find out about news in our community and the world. What is the purpose of news? How is it reported to us? Next, explain that each child will be responsible for reporting on one news item over the next few weeks. This item can be obtained verbally, through discussions with people, by having someone read and explain a newspaper or magazine article, or by listening to or watching a news program on radio or television. This is a wonderful opportunity to have children work along with their parents, so notice should be given informing parents of the assignment and that their help would be appreciated. (See the sample letter.) If a newspaper picture or a child's own drawing accompanies the news item, this should be brought to school. The child is to be asked to talk about the news item, show a picture, and discuss where the item appeared or how he or she learned about it. The teacher can ask leading questions for those youngsters who find it difficult to give an oral report. After the explanation, questions from the other members of the group can be entertained.

HOW TO GO FURTHER.

The news items can be summarized in a story chart with the "reporter" offering some of the sentences as well as members of the news audience. All of the items can be kept together for the children to browse through. The large sheets of paper can be bound into a large book called, *News Reports*. For added interest and appeal, the cover can be fashioned to look like a large newspaper. A compilation of the news items can be sent home and the children asked to review the stories with their parents.

Dear Parents,

Your child has become more and more comfortable at our sharing time. Some very interesting personal news has been discussed, and the class has enjoyed learning some new songs, games, and hearing about our youngsters' experiences.

Now it is time for them to "expand their horizons" and report on news items from the community, newspapers, television, and so forth. We have found that children are interested in what is going on in the world around them and that they are capable of comprehending a few simple items from newspapers and television or radio reports.

Your child is scheduled to give a news report on _____ . Please help him or her in this special "homework" assignment. You may wish to have your child speak with a friend or neighbor who can report about community news, or go through a newspaper to find an appropriate item which can be understood and reported to the class. (Children love items about animals, forms of transportation, special visitors, inventions, and so on.) Of course, you may wish to exercise your own discretion about what you would like your child to see on television news or look at in newspapers.

As a guide in helping your child to prepare for the report, you may wish to consider the following questions:

What is the news item about?
Who is affected by the news?
When did the news take place?
Where did it happen?
How does it affect me or my family?

If a picture accompanies the news item, or if your child would like to draw a picture about it, that would be great! I appreciate your assistance in what will surely be an exciting and enriching experience for the children.

Sincerely,

CLASSROOM JOBS

WHY DO THIS?

Children love to perform classroom jobs. The accomplishment of chores or responsibilities helps to enhance the youngsters' feelings of importance and at the same time assists the teacher in basic classroom functions. Performing classroom jobs also builds a sense of community and a shared feeling of importance for accomplishment for the day-to-day operation of the class. Teachers generally develop a system of rotation, on a weekly or monthly basis, which allows each child to assume several responsibilities throughout the course of the year. The construction of a job chart serves to remind children of the various jobs and the names of those who are responsible for their fulfillment.

WHAT WILL I NEED?

- A large piece of oaktag
- Construction paper
- String
- Paste
- Markers

HOW TO GET STARTED.

Discuss the importance of sharing classroom responsibilities. Tell the children that they will be expected to help with basic classroom jobs and how much you will depend upon their assistance. Explain the various jobs or assignments and what is entailed for each of the duties. Some of the most common jobs are: line leader, plant waterer, paper monitor, waste basket monitor, scissors helper, and class librarian. Teachers usually announce the various job responsibilities at the beginning of each week or each month and develop an attractive chart with pockets for the insertion of the names of youngsters who are assigned to each job (see next page).

After a few months, the children who held the positions can explain the requirements of the job to those newly assigned. It may be necessary to keep a record of which children fulfilled each of the classroom responsibilities so as to avoid duplication and give each child a chance at each job throughout the year.

HOW TO GO FURTHER.

Additional motivation may be provided by having the child who performed a certain job choose his or her successor. Then the child can explain the task to the new assignee. The large job charts can be changed from time to time to add additional interest and motivation.

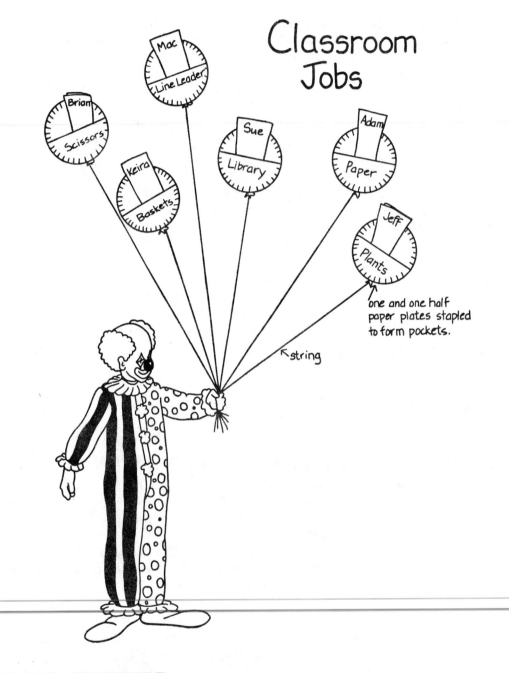

Classroom Jobs

Mac — Line Leader
Brian — Scissors
Keira — Baskets
Sue — Library
Adam — Paper
Jeff — Plants

one and one half paper plates stapled to form pockets.

string

TODAY'S SCHEDULE

WHY DO THIS?

Reviewing the day's schedule at the end of the class meeting helps the children to understand the rhythm and flow of the day. Often, teachers post a daily schedule listing times for involvement in activity centers, special classes such as music, **art, or** physical education, lunch, and outdoor recess. Through such discussion, the children know what to anticipate in the day and can prepare themselves for the events and experiences which follow.

In classrooms which are organized according to learning centers, the number of participants may have to be limited and this planning time will permit teachers to decide which children can start in each of the activity centers. The planning session also permits the teacher to demonstrate a new manipulative or object which will be placed in a specified area.

WHAT WILL I NEED?

- Chart paper
- Markers

HOW TO GET STARTED.

Discuss the schedule for the day in sequence. The children may well be acquainted with what will lie ahead. Develop a chart listing each of the various activities. As the year progresses and the children are more aware of time blocks, the times can be written before each activity. In time, the youngsters will recognize the names of the activities and special classes. This is an aid for promoting word identification for those who are ready.

Today's Schedule	
	April 4
8:45 – 9:15	Class Meeting
9:15 – 10:15	Center Activities
10:15 – 10:30	Clean Up
10:30 – 10:45	Snack
10:45 – 11:15	Music (Mrs. Smith)
11:15 – 11:45	Storytime
11:45 – 12:30	Lunch and Recess
12:30 – 1:00	Rest and Listening
1:00 – 1:45	Letters, Numbers, or Writing
1:45 – 2:15	Outdoor Time
2:15 – 2:45	Science Discovery
2:45 – 3:00	Round Up Meeting and Prepare for Dismissal

HOW TO GO FURTHER.

If it is necessary to limit the number of youngsters at the learning centers in the classroom, it is helpful to acquire a pegboard on which the name (and a picture) of each of the centers appears and then a few hooks below it. (The exact number of hooks should be determined by the number of youngsters who can comfortably work in the center at any given time.) Then, the name of each child in the class should be written on an individual round keytag. The names of the youngsters allowed in each center are placed on the hook. In this way it is possible to keep track of which children have participated in each center, and certain children can be encouraged to broaden their interests and involvement.

Our Classroom Centers

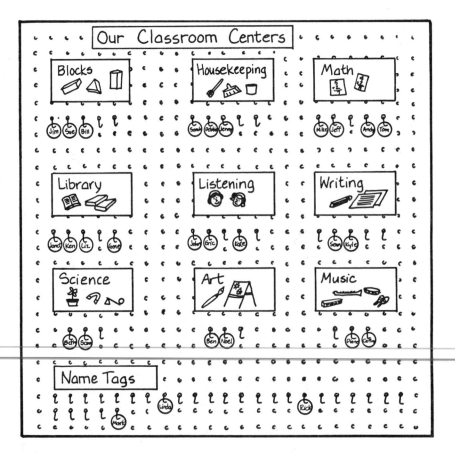

Some teachers allow children to "sign out" of a center by removing his or her name from a hook under the center name. This would then allow another child to enter a new center by filling the place vacated.

THE FINAL ROUNDUP: REVIEWING THE DAY

WHY DO THIS?

A meeting at the end of the day allows the group to gather together and review the various activities accomplished. This provides the teacher with the time needed to reinforce important learnings and attitudes. For example, "Bill, I was happy to see that you built a garage with a new friend today. It's great to find new playmates and to include others in what you do!" We know that the beginning and end of the day are considered "prime time" for learning, review, and reinforcement. The end-of-day meeting is also an opportunity for youngsters to practice time sequences. What happened first, second, third, or before and after lunch today? Beyond this, the final roundup sets a calm tone for dismissal and allows the children to look ahead at important events scheduled for the next day. Teachers often use this time to distribute notices or review any assignments that may have been given.

WHAT WILL I NEED?

- No special materials

HOW TO GET STARTED.

About fifteen or twenty minutes before dismissal, call the children together in the meeting area for an end-of-day class gathering. Review, in sequence, the various activities in which the children were engaged. Reinforce the vocabulary words that indicate sequence, for example, first, second, last, before, and after. Discuss important concepts which may have been introduced during the day and promote positive attitudes such as sharing, cooperation, broadening friendships, or whatever behaviors seem to be priorities for the class. Review a song or fingerplay and dismissal procedures. This is also a fine time to distribute notices, flyers, or other material which must go home.

HOW TO GO FURTHER.

Teachers often use this meeting time to play a sequence game dealing with events that occurred during the day. For example, "What did we do *after* music? What happened just *before* lunch? Who can mention ten different things that we did today?" Ask children to evaluate the day. What did they like best? What were some of the new things they learned?

chapter *2*

IN THE BLOCK CENTER

Block building is a natural activity for five-year-olds. With blocks children reconstruct, on a small scale, aspects of their environment. They gain firsthand experience with size and shape relationships and grow in their understanding of community life. When left to their own devices, children will create wonderful structures, but adult assistance and stimulation can make for enriched block building experiences. Block play can become a major learning tool. Teachers often listen to what the children are saying as they work with blocks and then find props and accessories which help children to realize a more vivid production. For example, if the children are making a highway, the alert teacher will ask the children if they would like road signs. Through discussion, the need may emerge for stop signs, street signs, one-way signs, railroad crossings, and so on. What a natural way to promote reading—the children will see the signs within the context they have created and the signs will extend their experiences.

The active, listening, circulating teacher can encourage more satisfying and complex structures by asking questions as children are building, prompting them to clarify their intentions and to realize new possibilities. Few kindergarten activities are as rich and full of meaning for understanding and imagining as block play.

A few organizational hints can facilitate block experiences and help the children to practice classification skills. Most often blocks are stored within shelves, in book cases, or cabinets. Where possible, it is best to have a storage section for each kind of block. Each type of block can be traced onto self-stick vinyl paper. After the shape is cut out, it is placed at the front of the shelf which is to house this particular block shape. Not only does this arrangement help children as they are looking for a block, but it also assists in cleaning up as the children will know just where to place the blocks. Additionally, as the children put the blocks away, they will be matching them to the stick-on form, thus sorting them into their proper categories of size and shape.

Many teachers find that a carpet placed at the center of the block area provides a pleasant, sound absorbing floor covering. (Low nap carpets are best.) Sufficient floor space should be allowed for block play as young children, in particular, tend to spread out their structures horizontally.

Unit building blocks lend themselves to the discovery of mathematical concepts. Their uniform size allows for direct comparison of fractional relationships when building. For example, two quarter units equal a half unit; two half units equal a large, full-size block. Blocks can be counted, arranged into a variety of geometric shapes, and used to study areas.

ENRICHING CHILDREN'S OPPORTUNITIES IN THE BLOCK AREA

WHY DO THIS?

When props and accessories are placed in the block area, opportunities increase for enriched block building experiences. A helmet, a toy car, or other object may be just what is needed for a youngster's imagination to soar. Labels for buildings and structures help children to realize that signs are a part of their environment and that words have meaning for their work and play. Children benefit from a stimulus to build. A story about a princess in a castle can become the springboard for building a castle or a medieval village; a trip to the firehouse could inspire the construction of one in the classroom. Introducing the right material at the right moment can make the difference between ordinary block play and enriched, imaginative, extended experiences in this important classroom area.

WHAT WILL I NEED?

The list of materials here is endless. A few basic materials to include in the block area are:

- toy cars, trucks, boats, and trains
- rubber, wooden, or stuffed animals
- street signs (see "Street Sign Cutouts" sheet)
- twigs in clay bases (for trees)
- free-form fabric cut-outs (for lakes)
- miniature people

HOW TO GET STARTED.

It would not be fruitful to place all of the above–mentioned items in the block area at one time, but start with one of them. See what children do on their own. If they do not use the objects right away, discuss some possibilities. Ask the children if they have ever seen road signs before. What do they say? Where do they occur within a street or road? Ask them to build a road and use the signs. Show them a free form fabric cutout shaped like a lake or a strip of fabric for a river. Discuss it with the children. Ask the children what kinds of buildings might be near a lake or a river.

HOW TO GO FURTHER.

Listen to the children's talk as they build with blocks. Where appropriate, ask them what objects they would like to add to their structures. Ask if they would like anything labeled. Once children realize that their block experiences can be enriched, they are more likely to seek objects or props to incorporate into their constructions.

If street signs have been used, the "Street Sign Match-Up" worksheet can be duplicated to check if children can match the words with the standard shapes of common street signs.

STREET SIGN CUTOUTS

Cut out the street signs below, paste them onto cardboard, and introduce them in the block area.

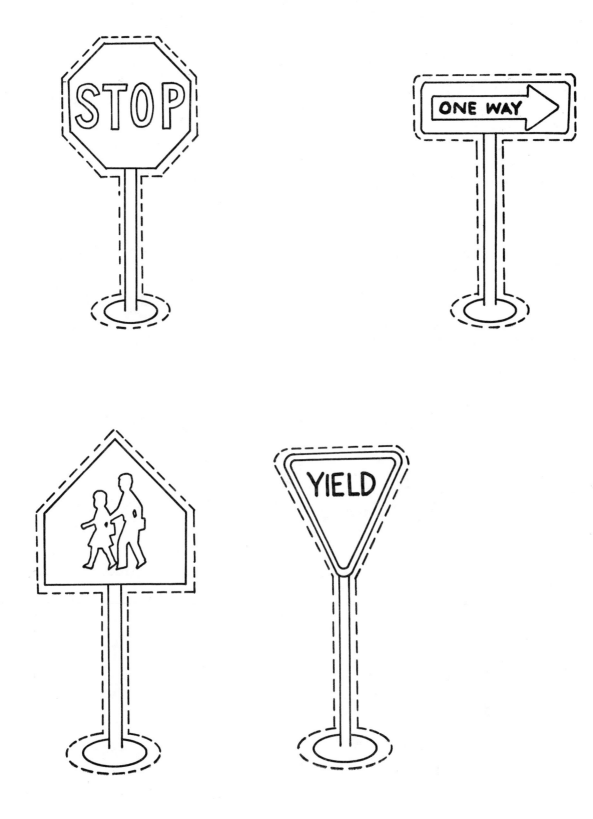

Name _____

STREET SIGN MATCH-UP

Draw a line from each word to the matching sign shape.

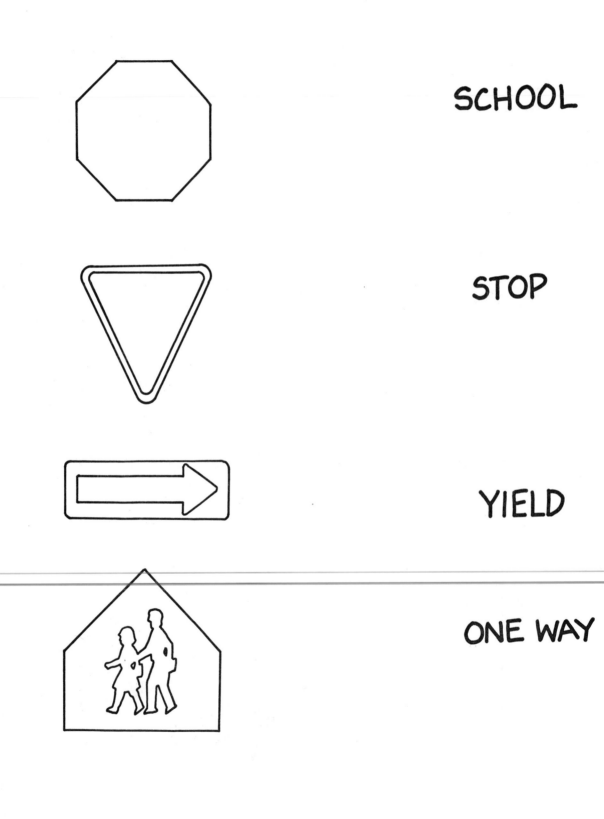

SCHOOL

STOP

YIELD

ONE WAY

TAKING PHOTOGRAPHS OF BLOCK STRUCTURES

WHY DO THIS?

Taking photographs of children's block structures provides a lasting memory of the results of a creative and energetic effort. After the building phase is completed, the children can write stories about their structures. Their building experiences provide meaning for their written work. The children will realize that one activity can provide the stimulus for another, thus integrating their learning. The ideas in the original construction are recalled and recorded establishing the link between thinking, imagining, and writing.

WHAT WILL I NEED?

- Set of building blocks
- Camera and film (preferably an instant camera)

HOW TO GET STARTED.

When the children have completed a block structure, photograph it. Try different angles to gain the total perspective. It is often desirable to take photographs of a block building in several stages of completion. After the pictures are ready, they may be displayed on a ledge, on a chart stand, or on a bulletin board. Children use the photographs to recall their intentions and the details of their constructions. A story can be dictated to the teacher and the photographs can be pasted into appropriate spaces on chart paper or on the pages of the book being created. (See the next activity, "Writing About Constructions".)

HOW TO GO FURTHER.

Some children may be able to draw the structure. These drawings can serve as illustrations for stories written. Other children may be able to write their own stories about their buildings. If pictures were taken at various stages of construction, the story can be sequential, starting with the idea for the building, what was done first, second, and so on.

If the structure was designed to represent a real building or area in the school neighborhood, that site can be visited and photographed. The children's building and the real one can be compared for similar and dissimilar elements.

If a video camera is available in the school, set it up on a tripod and record the building activity. When the tape is shown, the building process can be discussed and analyzed.

WRITING ABOUT CONSTRUCTIONS

WHY DO THIS?

When children dictate stories (or write) about block structures they are recreating, in another medium, an experience they have had. This brings relevance to their writing and allows them to see the connection between their efforts in two distinct activities. They will write because they have something to write about. Then, of course, they can read what they have written. As children dictate or write, they expand their vocabularies and find words to describe the building process.

WHAT WILL I NEED?

- Chart paper or paper to fold into a book
- Markers
- Photographs of block structures (optional)

HOW TO GET STARTED.

There are several ways to approach this activity. After a group of children completes a block structure, the children should discuss their creation. What is it? What purposes does it serve? Who can use it? Is it like anything in the neighborhood? How do people or cars get in and out of the structure? What motivated the construction of this particular building? How can it be expanded? These questions can serve as departure points for the stories that the children write or dictate. If photographs or drawings of the structure are available they can be incorporated into the text.

Another approach is to have one or two children "interview" the builders as they work on the structure. They can brainstorm ideas for the questions they will ask before the interview. If a teacher (or other adult) is not available to record the responses, a tape recorder can be used during the interview—children love talking into a microphone. The information gathered can then be the source of the writing activity. The interview can be written up in question and answer format, demonstrating to the children a form of writing that often appears in newspaper or magazine articles. The "builders" can then react to the story which results from the interview.

HOW TO GO FURTHER.

Some children may be able to write a poem about a structure. If the building can be easily represented in a two-dimensional cutout, the story or poem can be written within the outline of a cutout which resembles the structure, as shown in the illustration.

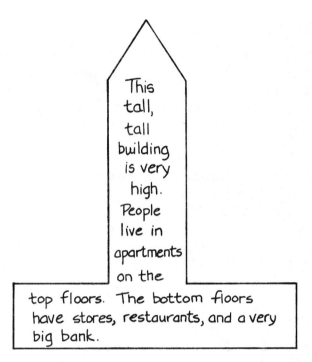

This
tall,
tall
building
is very
high.
People
live in
apartments
on the
top floors. The bottom floors
have stores, restaurants, and a very
big bank.

An easel can be set up near the block area and a child can make a painting of the structure (or draw it with markers or crayons) while it is being built. This introduces and integrates yet another medium into the total experience.

THE DESIGNER'S REPORT

WHY DO THIS?

In this activity, one or more children who have completed a block structure offer a "designer's report" in which they tell others in the class what inspired them to build their piece, how it was built, what it is used for, what parts were played by some of the builders, and other relevant aspects. The children who give the report are enriching their language experiences as they find the words to define the various kinds of blocks, parts of the structure, and the division of labor. Since this becomes a special event, it is no surprise that this activity can help to raise the self-esteem of the reporter.

WHAT WILL I NEED?

- Completed (or nearly completed) block structure
- Hard hat and a clipboard (optional)

HOW TO GET STARTED.

Ask the youngsters in the class to assemble on the floor in the block area. Tell them that they are going to hear a "designer's report" about the building they see before them. If available, give the designer a hard hat and clipboard to heighten the drama. The designer may include the following elements in the report:

Why was the structure built?
What materials were used?
Who was involved in the construction?
What part did each member of the construction team play?
What is the building used for?

The teacher may have to ask the reporter the questions, in which case this may be considered an "interview."

HOW TO GO FURTHER.

As the report is presented, the teacher can be developing a chart listing the essential elements discussed. Children can be asked to issue "reports" on a variety of classroom experiences. The more they do it, the more adept they will become with the process.

If a video camera is available, the "designer's report" can be taped. Generally, youngsters love to see themselves on television.

DEVELOPING COUNTING SKILLS WITH BLOCKS

WHY DO THIS?

A basic mathematics skill in kindergarten is counting. Children come to realize that as they add one item at a time, they say a higher number. Most five-year-olds can count, verbally, to twenty and beyond. However, the test of whether they understand the operation of counting is whether they increase one number with each object they count. Blocks provide a natural, stimulating material for practicing counting skills.

WHAT WILL I NEED?

- Unit blocks
- Large index cards
- A marker

HOW TO GET STARTED.

Ask two or three children to count out twenty blocks and place them in the center of the block building area. They should agree that they have obtained exactly twenty blocks by counting together or checking each other's work. Ask them to build a structure using only these blocks. After the building is complete, write "This building was made with 20 blocks" on a large index card and place the card up against the building.

Ask another group to do the same thing. Probably different blocks will be chosen. Follow the procedure as above. After the two structures are completed and labeled, gather the rest of the children in the block area. Discuss the fact that both structures were built using just twenty blocks. If they appear different in size, what might have accounted for this? What would happen if one group used twenty of the smallest blocks while the other group used twenty of the largest blocks? As the children put the blocks away, they can count them again.

HOW TO GO FURTHER.

Children enjoy the feeling of accomplishment in counting large numbers. After a relatively big structure is built, some children may want to count the number of blocks that were used. Some children may want to write a story about the large number of blocks used. Others may wish to make a big number chart on the floor in which the correct number of blocks are placed next to large printed numerals.

USING BLOCKS TO TEACH ADDITION

WHY DO THIS.

When teachers help children begin to explore the addition of numbers, it is best to use concrete objects. Buttons, ice cream sticks, checkers, or other counters are commonly used. When introducing the operation of addition to a large group, blocks can help to provide a vivid demonstration. These large, concrete objects will aid in concept development.

WHAT WILL I NEED?

- Several building blocks of the same size
- Paper
- Markers

HOW TO GET STARTED.

Assemble the group in the block area. Get about ten or fifteen blocks of the same size. Ask one child to take two blocks from the pile; ask another to take three blocks. Ask the others how many blocks the two children have all together. Demonstrate that two and three are five. Write the equation, or "number sentence", on a piece of paper and repeat the operation using blocks again. Introduce the addition sign and the equals sign. Have the children recite the number sentence. Continue the procedure with larger numbers of blocks. Before long the children will be able to make up their own problems and combine the numbers of blocks. As a check, use the "Block Addition" worksheet.

HOW TO GO FURTHER.

Some children may be ready to add three numbers; others may want to try subtraction. The number sentences can be written vertically and horizontally, thereby showing the children two ways of writing the same equation.

"Addition Books" can be made in which each page shows a different number sentence with pictures to illustrate the quantities specified, for example, two carrots plus three carrots equal five carrots. (See the sample page from an addition book in the illustration.)

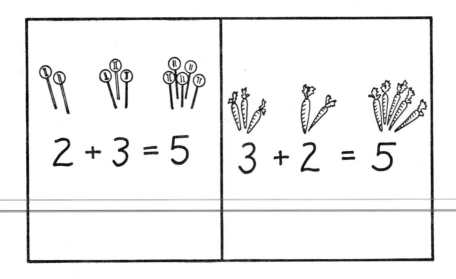

BLOCK ADDITION

Write the number underneath each set of blocks. The first one is started for you.

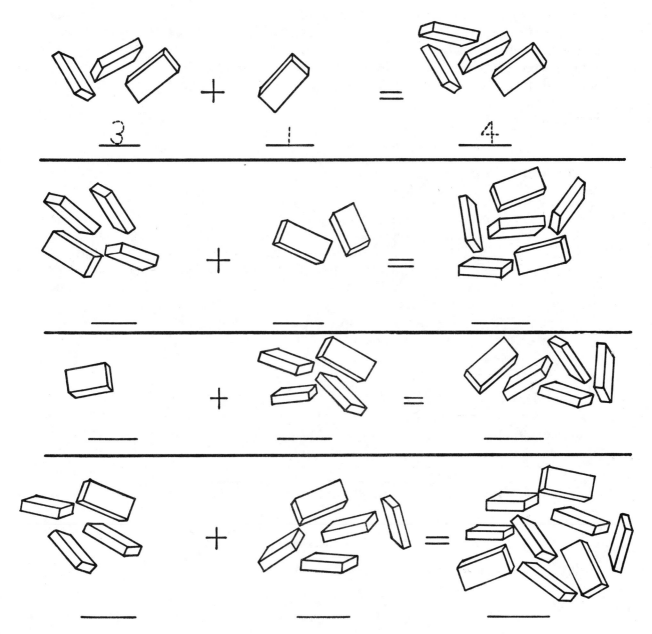

3   +   1   =   4

FORMING GEOMETRIC SHAPES

WHY DO THIS?

As children explore size and shape with blocks, they come to realize that blocks may be used to form new shapes. For example, four rectangular blocks can be used to make a new rectangle; two square blocks can be joined to form a rectangle; four squares can form a new, larger square. Through such manipulations, children discover basic geometric forms and size relationships.

WHAT WILL I NEED?

- Set of unit blocks

HOW TO GET STARTED.

Discuss the characteristics of basic shapes. Squares have four equal sides; rectangles have four sides with two of them longer than the others. Begin with a few simple relationships, for example, two of the same size square blocks when joined, form a rectangle; two rectangles can form another rectangle or a square depending upon the size of the original rectangles. Have the children perform a few of these operations. Then move on to more complex designs. Eight or ten blocks can be used to form one huge rectangle. If a sufficient number of curved blocks is available, they can be formed into a circle. Triangular blocks can be used to make diamonds or larger triangles. Have the children pose shape problems to one another.

HOW TO GO FURTHER.

The teacher can fit together several blocks to make a larger shape on a large sheet of paper. Then the outline of the large shape can be drawn with a marker. Remove all of the blocks and give the paper with the outline on it to a group of children. (See illustration.)

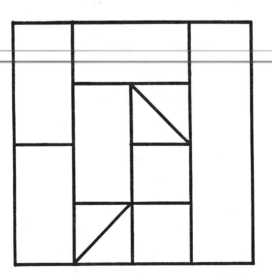

Ask them to fill in the outline using blocks. Different shapes and different sizes can be used. Various levels of complexity will stimulate children with different abilities in this area. For a real challenge, show a group of children the outline of the building like the one shown in the illustration. You may wish to mount it on a task card. Ask them to make the building by looking at the drawing.

Make a Building Just Like this One

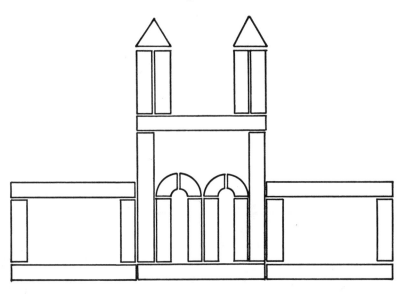

STUDYING FRACTIONS WITH BLOCKS

WHY DO THIS?

Since most kindergarten block sets are unit blocks, fractional parts are easily studied. The relationships of quarters, halves, and wholes are naturally discovered. Once these fractions are identified, they may be applied to other materials and situations. When dealing with young children (and even older ones), the use of concrete objects in the study of fractions is very important if the youngsters are to see and experience the relationships.

WHAT WILL I NEED?

- Unit block set
- Chart paper
- Marker

HOW TO GET STARTED.

Demonstrate that if two of the same size blocks fit on top of (and just cover the entire area of) one larger block, then each of the smaller blocks is equal to one half of the larger one. Relationships can likewise be established for quarters. Using large chart paper, the outlines of the smaller and the larger blocks can be traced and the fractional parts labeled. (See the illustrations below.)

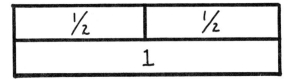

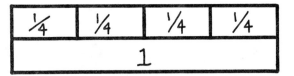

Fractional parts of the smaller parts may also be available, in which case these may be related as halves of the smaller ones. For example, in most unit block sets the "unit" is the smallest rectangle. Each small square block is half of the rectangle. Then there are generally small triangles, each of which is a half of the small square. What part of the unit block is one of the small triangles? Use the appropriate terminology freely, and ask lots of questions. How do we use halves during the day? Find books that deal with fractional parts.

HOW TO GO FURTHER.

Children can take a sheet of paper, fold it in half, and then by cutting out from the crease (and then back through it), a shape is created. The crease becomes the midline and the parts on either side of the crease are halves of the whole. Cutting along the crease creates two halves.

Some youngsters may want to make "Fraction Books" in which the fractional parts are cut out, pasted on pages and labeled. Use a variety of different shapes, including circles, ovals, and triangles. (See the sample pages in the illustration.)

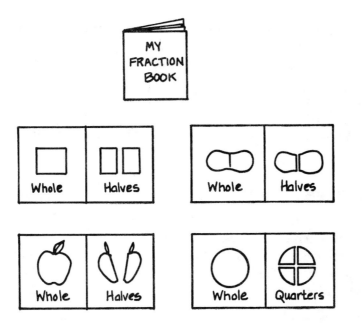

MAKING YOUR OWN BLOCKS

WHY DO THIS?

Most kindergarten classrooms come equipped with a set of hardwood unit blocks. Although several sizes and shapes are included, block constructions can be extended by securing some oversized blocks or odd-shaped blocks. Large blocks can be made from corrugated boxes; wood scraps can be sanded and finished and used along with the standard set. Additional blocks help children discover new possibilities in building.

WHAT WILL I NEED?

- Corrugated boxes with all flaps intact (no larger than a liquor box)
- Wood scraps
- Coarse sandpaper
- Clear varnish or polyurethane
- Package sealing tape

HOW TO GET STARTED.

Acquire a few clean boxes with all flaps intact. Close up the boxes evenly and firmly. Seal along the flaps with package sealing tape. The boxes (if not too large) can be used to support building blocks, make foundations for buildings, or other purposes as devised by the youngsters.

Obtain wood scraps from a lumber yard or mill. (Usually employees or owners of such establishments will be happy to save scraps for teachers.) Select the best scraps with a minimum of rough edges. The children can cut the blocks (if tools are available) to make desired shapes. In any event, sand all surfaces and edges. With guidance, the children can do this. To finish the blocks, apply clear varnish or polyurethane. Note the new and varied ways in which the children use these additional building blocks.

HOW TO GO FURTHER.

Have the children dictate or write thank you notes to the lumber company or mill. Some children and teachers may wish to paint the blocks or boxes (or paint pictures on them) before varnishing. Boxes can be painted red, and when completely dry, white lines are painted to make the boxes look like brickwork. What other objects can be used as building materials in the block area?

BUILDING A CITY

WHY DO THIS?

An extension of block building is the development of a city or village. This involves the youngsters' analysis of the various elements and structures within a city or village and the representation of these places with blocks and other objects. Not only do the children learn about communities, but they gain a sense of scale, perspective, and layout. There are many learning opportunities in such a project. Aside from the research and planning that the children will have to do, some children will assist in the building of the structures, others will make street signs and labels, still others can make parks, playgrounds, tree-lined streets, and so on. All in all, this is a very involved, stimulating project.

WHAT WILL I NEED?

- Large, stiff paper for the street outlines
- Building blocks
- Markers and paint
- Variety of other materials such as clay, egg cartons, milk containers, paper towel tubes, ice cream sticks, fabric, wood scraps, miniature people, cars, trucks, and other objects as defined by the teacher and the children

HOW TO GET STARTED.

Take the youngsters on a walk through the area surrounding the school. Note street names and the general layout of streets, roads, and other landmarks. Try to visit an area where there is a variety of aspects of community life, for example, shops, parks, factories, a library, police station, firehouse, and the like. Back in the classroom, attach several sheets of poster board or stiff paper together and begin to map out the streets and a general plan for the area to be constructed. Ask for volunteers, or make assignments, for children to complete various aspects of building the community. Some children will paint in the road outlines and surfaces, others will build the school, a few will design the park area, and some will construct the shops, and so on. Ask the children to plan their part and decide upon the materials they think they will need. (This may take a few days.) Small milk containers from the school cafeteria make nice houses or stores, egg cartons can be used to make a factory, a swatch of blue fabric can be a lake or pond, the school or other large building can be constructed from building blocks. An effective looking tree can be made from a small twig placed into a lump of clay, or from a pine cone. As aspects of the city are completed, ask the children to place appropriate signs on buildings and streets. Painting the various buildings and other structures will add a finished look. (See the sample in the illustration.)

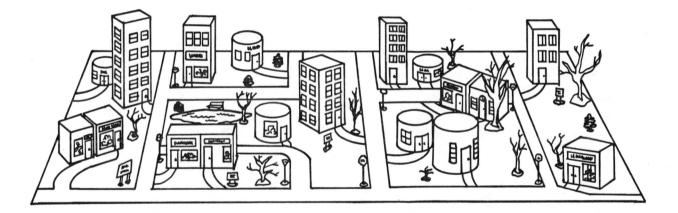

HOW TO GO FURTHER.

Other classes in the school will want to see the finished product. The kindergarteners can be tour guides and show their city. Don't forget to take photographs of this project while in progress and after it's completed. The youngsters can explain the phases of planning and construction. A book with photographs can be made explaining the stages of the project.

Some children may wish to focus on a single area and build a park, a shopping center, or a hospital complex in detail.

As a vocabulary check, duplicate the "City Street Match-up" worksheet and see if the children can recognize the names of the stores by matching them with the items they might find in each.

Name _____

CITY STREET MATCH-UP

Draw a line from each item to the name of the store that sells it.

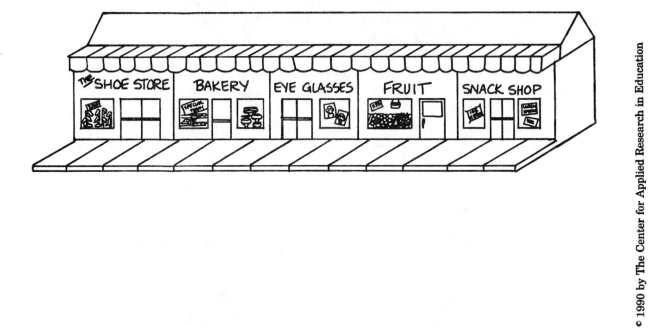

BUILDING MAZES WITH BLOCKS

WHY DO THIS?

Children can explore basic behavioral concepts by teaching a classroom pet to run a maze. Through such activity, the youngsters may come to appreciate principles of learning and apply them to how humans learn. When using classroom pets for such activities, teachers also have an opportunity to model humane treatment and respect for animals while allowing them to help us study behavioral concepts.

WHAT WILL I NEED?

- Building blocks
- A classroom mammal, such as a gerbil, hamster, or rat

HOW TO GET STARTED.

Demonstrate the construction of a basic maze using long blocks for the walls of the passages. The walls should be high enough so that the animal cannot jump over its sides. After demonstrating a basic design, allow the youngsters to construct their own maze including turns, blind passages, and dead ends, but finally leading to an end point. (See the sample maze in the illustration.)

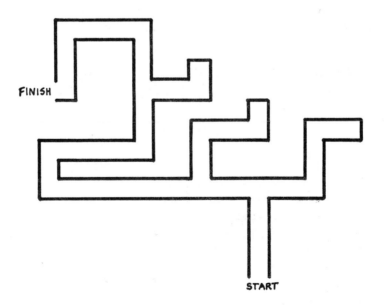

Ask the children to predict what things the animal might want that would provide motivation to run the maze. Most often food or "toys" are used as reinforcers. Have one child open the maze for the animal while another times (with a stopwatch or analog watch with a second hand) how long it takes for the animal to reach the reward area. (Many kindergarten teachers find that they will have a youngster or two capable of performing this operation; if not, the teacher should be the "timer.") Allow the animal to spend some time in the reward area. Keep timing the trials. Does the animal learn to run the maze in less time? What can the children generalize from this? What is the purpose of the reinforcers?

The children may wish to rearrange the maze to see if another learning cycle is established. They may also wish to discuss changing the reinforcers. Are some more effective than others?

HOW TO GO FURTHER.

A basic maze design is a "T-maze." Have the children build a simple "T-maze" like the one depicted in the illustration.

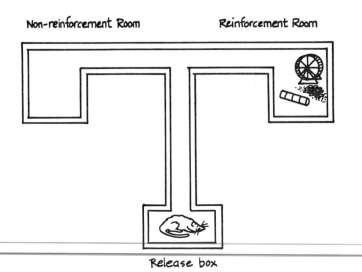

Non-reinforcement Room   Reinforcement Room

Release box

One of the end rooms is considered the reinforcement area and should contain food, "toys" and other objects which might motivate the animal to go to this side immediately upon entry into the maze. The other side of the "T" is the nonreinforcement area. Does the animal learn to go to the reinforcement area only? What happens if the areas are switched? Children who become involved in conditioning activities soon make up their own variables and experimental designs.

SORTING AND CLASSIFICATION USING BLOCKS

WHY DO THIS?

Building blocks lend themselves to a variety of sorting activities. Classification and sorting are important cognitive skills as they help youngsters to see relationships and order their world. Generally, teachers start with binary classification, or "yes-no" sorting. Later children can arrange objects by taking stock of specific attributes and properties and then arranging them into groups based upon similarity of property.

WHAT WILL I NEED?

- Building blocks
- Pieces of rope or clothesline

HOW TO GET STARTED.

Call a group of children to the block area. Tell them to form two groups of blocks based upon whether or not each one exhibits a particular property. Make two circles on the floor with large pieces of rope. Select more than ten blocks, some of which are square. Ask the children to place all of the square blocks inside one of the ropes and all of the "not-square" blocks inside of the other. Vary the property for sorting, for example, blocks with a curve and blocks with only straight sides, blocks that are "thin" (slats) and blocks that are "not thin." Have children make up rules for sorting.

Next, gather about twenty blocks that are of three or four distinct shapes. Place several ropes formed into circles on the floor. Ask the children to place the blocks that are alike into the circles. As children put blocks away, they are sorting them by similarity of property.

HOW TO GO FURTHER.

Arrange blocks into two distinct piles, based upon a "yes-no" criterion. Ask the children to examine the piles and play the game, "Guess My Rule." The children have to verbalize the rule that was used to separate the objects.

Another extension is to place the blocks in a sequence so as to form a repeating pattern, for example, triangle, rectangle, square; triangle, rectangle, . . . The children examine the sequence, state the rule, and then place the block that comes next in the sequence. Children can make up repeating patterns for their classmates to follow and identify. This skill can be reinforced using the "Which Block Comes Next?" worksheet. An additional challenge is provided by a worksheet in which children cut out diagrams of a block structure at different stages of development and then arrange the pictures in the sequence in which the structure was built. (See the "Which Came First?" worksheet.)

Name _____

WHICH BLOCK COMES NEXT?

Finish each line by drawing the correct block in the box. The first one has been started for you.

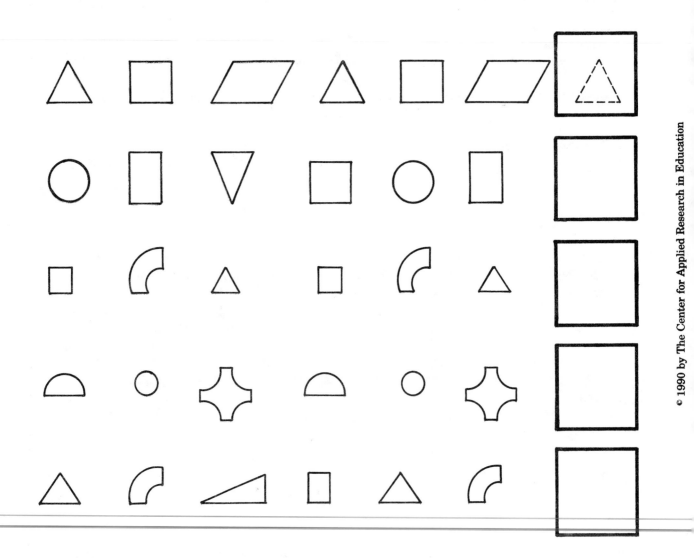

Name _____

WHICH CAME FIRST?

Cut out the four pictures on the dotted lines. Arrange them in order. Which came first, second, third, and fourth as children built with blocks?

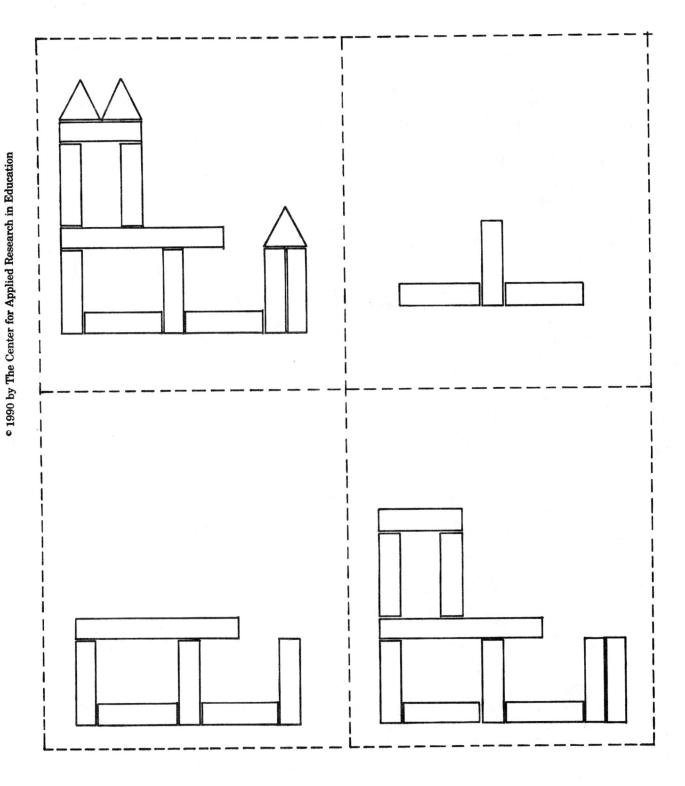

THE MARBLE RALLY

WHY DO THIS?

A marble rally is just plain fun! However, children learn about the importance of gravity while constructing the apparatus. Basically, the marble rally is a walled track that provides a pathway for a marble (or other small sphere) to travel from a high point to a lower point. Children delight in building twists, turns, and tunnels. This activity tends to bring out the "Rube Goldberg" in children.

WHAT WILL I NEED?

- Building blocks
- A marble or other small sphere

HOW TO GET STARTED.

Talk to the children about building a track for a marble. A few basic techniques may have to be demonstrated. For example, place a unit block on its side so that the narrowest dimension is up. Use blocks to raise one end so that it is higher than the other. Then use the blocks to make sides so that a marble is in a track. Demonstrate that a marble, when released from the higher part of the block, will roll downhill. Allow the children to build a track. (See the illustration.)

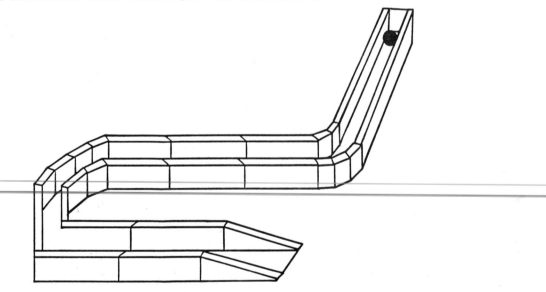

They will soon discover that they have to start at a relatively high point to allow for turns and other variations. (A large number of blocks will be required for an interesting, involved track.) The children may need help in the beginning, but undoubtedly, a few youngsters will catch on and provide some leadership in the construction. When the track is finished, call the entire class to witness the "marble rally." The children love seeing the marble on its journey. You may also wish to put two marbles in the track and see which one finishes first.

HOW TO GO FURTHER.

Ask the children to invent other types of machines or devices that are interconnected. Materials other than blocks can be used. What makes for the most interesting inventions? What physical principles are demonstrated? Can children demonstrate the effects of gravity in other ways?

Look through children's books which depict zany inventions and contraptions. Ask them to analyze what they do. Can any of these inventions be built in the classroom?

USING BLOCKS TO ENRICH VOCABULARY

WHY DO THIS?

There are countless opportunities for teachers to foster the development of conceptual vocabulary through the use of blocks. Positional concepts such as under, over, in front of, behind, next to, to the right of, to the left of, inside, and outside may be demonstrated and reinforced with blocks. Use the terms naturally in conversations as children are playing with blocks. "Which block is in front of the tower? Which one is the tallest? Which block is a triangle?"

As teachers and children use conceptual words, they are best demonstrated with concrete objects. This is clearly a more appropriate way for young children to learn the meanings of these terms, compared to the use of paper and pencil, two-dimensional diagrams.

WHAT WILL I NEED?

- A set of building blocks

HOW TO GET STARTED.

Sit down with the youngsters in the block area. Talk with them about their latest construction. Ask them questions in which they have to identify blocks which are on top of, under, inside, behind, and in front of other blocks. If necessary, demonstrate these positional concepts. Use size words such as: thin, thinner, thinnest; tall, taller, tallest; short, shorter, shortest. In each instance, have the youngsters demonstrate the concepts using blocks. The children may want to "quiz" each other using these terms.

HOW TO GO FURTHER.

Once the children are able to demonstrate these concepts, some may wish to make a book in which they draw pictures showing big, bigger, biggest; small, smaller, smallest; on top of; in front of, and so on. These books can be shared and become a part of the classroom library.

BLOCKS AND FOLLOWING DIRECTIONS

WHY DO THIS?

In hundreds of ways, kindergarten teachers help children to follow directions. This is usually done within the daily routines of the program. Blocks also provide the children with opportunities to practice following directions. For example, the teacher may ask one child to take three blocks, place them on the windowsill, get a box of crayons, and sit down. Another direction might be to take nine blocks and give three of them to each of three children. Carrying out commands of increasing complexity helps youngsters to practice their skill in following directions. Most kindergarteners can follow a two-stage command. It is interesting to check the varying level of complexity that different youngsters can handle.

WHAT WILL I NEED?

- Building blocks and a variety of other common classroom objects.

HOW TO GET STARTED?

Make this activity into a game. Tell the children that they must listen carefully to the instructions and carry them out as you send them on the various missions. Start with relatively simple directions, for example, "Bring me one long and one short block," or "Take two blocks and put them on the library table." As children become more adept at this activity, increase the level of complexity, for example, "Gather six blocks. Put two of them on top of my desk, two of them on top of the paper tray, and two of them in the refrigerator." Children often delight in being asked to do "funny" things like placing blocks inside of a hat, or taking a block and putting it into a coat sleeve. Such situations, because they are unusual, let the teacher know if the child is really comprehending the task. Also, if children see the comedy (or even outrageousness) in such actions, they are growing in their sense of humor.

HOW TO GO FURTHER.

The activity outlined above involved the following of verbal directions. To see how well children can follow *visual* directions, ask one child to build a simple structure with eight blocks. Then using eight of the same blocks, ask another child to duplicate the structure. Onlookers may wish to evaluate whether or not the task was completed properly. In this way, children are sharpening their visual skills.

Teachers may also provide a simple block diagram (as seen from the top or side) and ask children to make a structure according to the diagram.

chapter 3

IN THE HOUSEKEEPING CENTER

Work in the housekeeping area helps children to make sense of their world. Through the exploration of family and community helper roles, children develop their concepts of group membership and mutual support. The need for cooperation in a family becomes quickly apparent to the child who is pretending to be a mother, father, baby, or grandparent. Indeed, cooperative behaviors can be encouraged and supported as they are noticed by teachers while the children are playing in the housekeeping area.

Through role playing, children find a convenient means for expressing emotions, fears, and anxieties in an acceptable, nonthreatening form. Such involvement can help children to deal with feelings that might be uncomfortable or frightening for them. Leadership opportunities are always available in the housekeeping area for some children; this may be one of the few times where assertiveness may emerge.

Some kindergarten teachers feel that they should not interfere with or mediate any of the activities which take place in the housekeeping area. There are many other teachers, though, who feel that they *should* offer suggestions and ideas to engage children. A suggestion to act out a scene from a class trip, experience, or venture may be just what is needed to get things rolling. Gathering material, props, old clothing, and other objects for placement in the housekeeping area are extremely important for enhancing children's involvement in this area and for helping children to attach meaning to their play. There are countless opportunities for integrating learnings which may begin, continue, or culminate in this essential section of the kindergarten classroom.

LEARNING ABOUT FAMILIES

WHY DO THIS?

Through dramatic play in the housekeeping area, children can explore family roles. Aside from the pure fun of pretending to be one family member or another, such activity allows children to view situations from another point of view, thereby promoting intellectual and social development. Flexibility should be encouraged as boys and girls assume a variety of roles. Children can play the part of parents, older siblings, babies, grandparents, and neighbors. Through their play, they come to realize that families and family structures are not all the same. As children imagine and act out situations, teachers will hear them taking on the part (sometimes with great flamboyance and exaggeration) of a variety of individuals and their perceived functions within the family unit.

WHAT WILL I NEED?

- A variety of old clothing that can be easily put on and taken off: skirts with elastic waists, large blouses, shoes, sport jackets, hats, ties, and so on. Scarves can be used for many purposes.
- A telephone
- Empty cereal and food boxes, pots and pans
- Dolls and doll beds, baby toys, baby clothes
- If wooden housekeeping furniture is not available, a refrigerator, sink, and stove can be made from large cardboard boxes. Simply draw or paint the parts of these appliances and cut out spaces as appropriate.

HOW TO GET STARTED.

Along with the children, plan out the placement of props in the housekeeping area. Discuss how some of the clothing can be used. Imagine situations that can be acted out, for example, parents readying a toddler to go to the babysitter in the morning as they leave for work, a dinner meal at which time the parents talk about what happened at work, preparation for the visit of grandparents, and so on. The youngsters will have suggestions for situations they want to dramatize. Once the children have gotten off to a good start, they should have no trouble taking off into the world of dramatic play.

HOW TO GO FURTHER.

Take informal photographs of the children playing in the housekeeping area. If these are instant pictures, the teacher may show them to the children and ask them to dictate a story about what was happening when the picture was taken. The picture can be imbedded in the text on large lined paper, or if a series of pictures was taken, a book can be made with the photos placed appropriately within the story. This will help to promote language skills, sequencing, and memory. If the photographs arrive a few days or weeks later, the challenge to recall the action and the situation is even greater. A story can be developed around these pictures even if they are delayed. If the children do not recall what was happening in the pictures, imaginary incidents can be created and written to go along with the photos.

GOING TO MARKET

WHY DO THIS?

Shopping for food and other items is a wonderful activity for children to perform in the housekeeping area. Undoubtedly, the youngsters have accompanied their parents on trips to the market. Indeed, many parents claim that their young toddlers can "read" when they recognize the names on cereal boxes, cans, and other food products. And indeed this *is* reading since the children are associating words and pictures with familiar items. Through the "purchase" of items, children are learning the roles of storekeeper or checker and consumer. They exchange play money and can practice counting and making change. Playing store is an activity rich in learnings and opportunities for expression and dramatic play.

WHAT WILL I NEED?

- A toy cash register or money box
- Paper money (See "Cut-out Coins and Bills" blackline master) or pennies
- Empty food packaging, for example, cereal boxes, spaghetti boxes, empty pop bottles, egg cartons
- Paper or plastic bags for carrying parcels
- Pocketbooks or wallets
- Masking tape or pressure sensitive labels
- Markers

HOW TO GET STARTED.

With the children, plan how to set up a store or market. Discuss the various items which can be purchased and how they can be displayed. Use the blackline master to duplicate paper money and cut out the bills and coins. Using masking tape or labels, place a price on each item. (This is a fine opportunity to review the product names and reasonableness of prices.) Review the parts to be played—storekeeper or clerk, bagger, consumer, child. Encourage children to take turns with each role.

HOW TO GO FURTHER.

Children may wish to create a large store with separate departments. What are some of the sections to be included? Why is this called a "department store?" Make a sign for each department. Other youngsters may wish to make up trading games with play money. Some may wish to make their own money. A chart of equivalent values can also be a project—five pennies equal a nickel; two nickels equal a dime; four quarters equal a dollar, and so on. You may be surprised at how much today's children know about money before they begin kindergarten.

CUT-OUT COINS AND BILLS

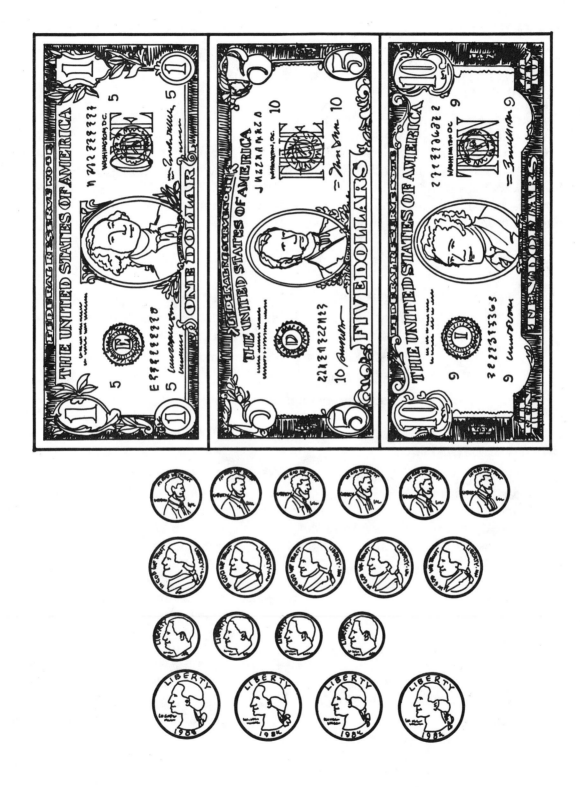

WATER PLAY

WHY DO THIS?

Few activities for kindergarteners are as joyful and as rich with opportunities for concept development as water play. Children love pouring liquids from container to container, and while they are playing, they are discovering important ideas about volume, the relationship between shape and capacity of a container, as well as the basic properties of water. Assorted objects to play with in water, including funnels, containers of all shapes and sizes, wide-diameter tubing, measuring cups, and the like, all enhance the experience.

WHAT WILL I NEED?

- A water table or a large plastic basin or baby bathtub
- Containers of various sizes: margarine tubs, yogurt cups, plastic ice-cream containers, drink pitchers
- Plastic measuring cups and spoons
- Funnels, plastic tubing
- Plastic aprons (optional)

HOW TO GET STARTED.

In the housekeeping area a basin can be provided as a sink in which to wash dishes. Going further with this experience, though, the children can do a great deal more as they work with water. Discuss a few ground rules for water play: no splashing outside of the basin, no carrying items from the water play area to other parts of the room. (Some teachers find it useful to place a large sheet of linoleum under the water play area.) Ask the children to discuss a few of the things they may wish to do in this area. The youngsters should be encouraged to build upon the ideas of one another. The children will soon find that water will flow easily from widemouthed containers, but bubble, plop, and gurgle out of narrow-necked containers. Once children are actively engaged in this area, the teacher may ask casual questions which will lead to enriched concept development. For example, "What does water feel like? What happens to the water when you pour it from one container to another? Which container do you think can hold the most water? How can you make sure? How many of these small containers does it take to fill this large container? How many cups of water does it take to fill this large container? Does this container which is tall and narrow hold more water than this one which is short, but wide?" As children play with water, they are likely to suggest other materials to incorporate into their activity. Water play can be ongoing all year, or introduced periodically.

HOW TO GO FURTHER.

A few drops of dishwashing liquid can be added to the water to make it soapy. Then, with hand beaters, the children can whip up a suds and foam. Pouring this sudsy liquid from container to container will be quite different from pouring water.

Children can also be given a variety of objects to drop into a basin of water and then predict whether each one will sink or float. What makes some objects float on the top and some sink to the bottom? Some youngsters will enjoy filling a container and then, one by one, submerging different porous objects (for example, a piece of sponge, a rock, a piece of brick, wood, a paper towel, a piece of cardboard) to see which ones soak up the most water.

As a related activity, children can cut out and rearrange the pitchers on the "Pitchers of Water" worksheet and place them in order from the least to the most water, just by looking at the water level indicated in the pictures. After doing this, some teachers may wish to duplicate their own drawings of an empty container and then ask children to draw their own line indicating a water level and then arrange the pictures from least to greatest amount of water.

PITCHERS OF WATER

Look at the pitchers of water below. Cut them out along the dotted lines and arrange them in order from the least amount of water to the greatest amount of water. Then paste them in order on another sheet of paper.

WATER AND SAND

WHY DO THIS?

Combining water with sand can provide many new possibilities for children to explore pliable, moldable materials. The tactile differences will be immediately evident to children who have previously worked with water and sand. Important learnings about consistency occur as children work with different mixtures of sand and water. If an outdoor sand box is available, it would be an ideal place to work. If not, sand play can occur in the classroom in a large basin or sand table. Indoors, sand play can present problems, but if done once in a while, the benefits of the learning far outweigh the difficulties. The youngsters should work with dry sand, before any water is added. As more and more water is combined with the sand, they discover that it becomes increasingly harder to mold and to retain shape and form. Ideas about consistency will develop. On a smaller scale, some teachers may want to introduce a bin of salt, instead of sand. Children can pour dry salt from container to container. The vessels will of course be smaller than those used with water or sand.

WHAT WILL I NEED?

- A sand box, sand table, or sturdy tub
- Dry sand
- Aluminum pie tins, scoops, cookie cutters
- Plastic refrigerator containers
- Sand pails, spoons, and shovels

HOW TO GET STARTED.

Give the children time to explore the properties of dry sand, pouring it from container to container, trying to mold it. Ask them to compare how it feels to pour sand as compared to water. What is similar and what is different about the two materials? Differences in weight, color, and texture will be evident, but both materials can be poured.

Let the children add water to the sand, little by little, making sure that they mix the water into the sand with spoons or other implements. (Try to control the amount of water added so that children can experience a variety of consistencies.) When just a little bit of water is added, the children can draw pictures in the sand with a stick or pencil. Have them try to fill pails or buckets and shape the sand with cookie cutters or scoops. Can they make structures, roads, bridges, and tunnels? As more sand is added, ask the youngsters to talk about the consistency. Is sand that is more watery easier to mold and form than sand that is less watery? What happens when a bucket of dry sand is turned over? What happens when a bucket full of slightly wet sand is turned over? What happens when a bucket full of very watery sand is turned over? Which is the best consistency for molding?

HOW TO GO FURTHER.

Children will undoubtedly devise many extension activities to enhance their learnings with sand and water. Some of their discoveries can be summarized in a chart called, "What Did We Learn About Water and Sand?" Some children may wish to dictate stories about the princess who lived in the sand castle.

If salt was used for this activity, it can be tinted with food coloring. Color combinations can be mixed and explored. Another popular activity with salt or sand is to have children write their names on construction paper with white glue or a gluestick. Then sprinkle salt or sand onto the paper and shake off the excess. The effect is very attractive.

For the sheer enjoyment of it, many youngsters will love to play with trucks, cars, and other vehicles in a large sand box. Especially early in the year this is a wonderful activity.

ACTING OUT FAVORITE STORIES

WHY DO THIS?

The availability of clothing for "dressing-up" in the housekeeping area can enhance children's acting out of favorite stories. As children become more and more aware of the dialogue of familiar stories, they will enjoy acting them out. For example, after hearing "The Three Little Pigs" a few times, the youngsters will be ready to perform the story for their own enjoyment, or for an audience. This is a rich language experience as children improvise words and actions. Some may remember exact expressions (for example, "Then I'll huff, and I'll puff, and I'll blow your house down!"); at other points in the story, children will make up their own dialogue. Scenery can be made and props constructed to enrich the experience.

WHAT WILL I NEED?

- Lots of dress-up clothing
- Props as appropriate to particular stories
- Large rolls of paper for scenery (optional)

HOW TO GET STARTED.

In discussing possibilities for involvement in the housekeeping area, ask the children if they would like to act out a favorite story. Help them to review the sequence of the story in their own words. Ask them for suggestions for clothing, props, and scenery which might be needed. "What should the wolf wear? What can you use to make yourself look like a little pig?" (Simple construction paper masks or hats can be very suggestive of the characters.) The children may volunteer to bring some of the materials from home.

If at least one of the youngsters involved is very familiar with the story, they should be able to get started on their own. But, some planning will be necessary, and that's where the teacher comes in. "Where should the first house be? The second house? How can we create a simple house that looks like it's made from bricks?" (Sometimes a piece of drawing paper with a brickwork design will suffice.) A narrator will be needed who reads the story to the group. (This can be the teacher or a child.) The narrator should also cue the children to the actions, for example, "Now the wolf moves along to the next house." As dialogue unfolds, the children may be asked if they remember the words. If they do not, a whispered reminder, with the child repeating the words will move things along.

HOW TO GO FURTHER.

Children will want to perform these familiar stories over and over again with continued delight. They may wish to perform their play for another class in the school. Some children may wish to make invitations, tickets, or programs. Others may wish to serve as ushers.

As an added dimension, the children might want to create a surprise ending, unexpected to the audience which may be anticipating the familiar conclusion. The new ending can be discussed with the visiting group and even more variations can be suggested.

For some familiar stories, teachers can draw five or six scenes on index cards and then jumble them up. Then the children can place the drawings in order as they occur in the story. If the sequence is changed, can a new story be created to follow the altered order of the pictures?

PEOPLE IN THE COMMUNITY

WHY DO THIS?

Learning about and pretending to be community workers is an exciting activity for kindergarteners. In the housekeeping area, children will often play "fire fighter" or "police" on their own, but with a little planning and gathering of props, the youngsters' dramatic play can be greatly enhanced. Children enjoy learning about the roles of community workers. They come to realize that many different individuals are helpful and share in the well-being of people, homes, and the community at large. Through discussions, field trips, guest speakers, and dramatic play, the youngsters appreciate the roles played by community workers. It's an ideal topic for the kindergarten.

WHAT WILL I NEED?

The list of materials which can be gathered for dramatic play about community workers can stretch as far as the imagination, but here are suggestions for a few basic props for some jobs.

- *Police officer:* cutout police hats, whistle, walkie-talkie, aluminum foil badge, toy gun (optional)
- *Firefighter:* cutout fire hat (see "Cut-out Design for a Fire fighter's Hat" worksheet), rain slicker, a piece of garden hose, walkie-talkie, a large box for a fire truck
- *Postal worker:* mailboxes made from shoe boxes with construction paper arched over them, rubber stamps, stamp pad, envelopes, mail bag
- *Doctor or nurse:* tongue depressors, gauze bandage, stethoscope, penlight
- *Farmer:* rake, overalls, straw hat, plastic fruit and vegetables
- Optional: Large cardboard cutouts of community workers for youngsters to stick their heads and hands through. (See the sample illustrations.)

HOW TO GET STARTED.

Children will begin their play about community workers spontaneously, but it's always helpful to discuss the various roles. How do police officers help us? What do they do most while they are working? What equipment do they use? Invite community workers into the classroom to discuss their jobs and demonstrate their equipment. Arrange for a visit to a fire station, police station, post office, or supermarket. (Fire Prevention Week generally occurs in October.) After the youngsters have had such experiences, their dramatic play about community workers will become more realistic.

Vehicles used by community workers can be constructed from large boxes. For example, for a fire truck, obtain a large, sturdy box, paint it red, cut out doors and a windshield, hang a paper or cardboard ladder on its side, and place paper plates on the sides for wheels. This can become a class project with each child adding an appropriate part or piece of equipment. A bell and a pull string can even be rigged up on the truck.

HOW TO GO FURTHER.

After children have played the various roles of community workers, they can make a booklet about each helper. The booklet should contain dictated stories about the worker, perhaps a summary of a visit, drawings, puzzles, and the like. These little books can be shared and "rediscovered" months after they were produced. Children can draw pictures of their visits to the fire house or police station and send them along with a thank you letter to the chief.

As a reinforcement activity of the various roles explored, the children can complete the "Community Helpers" worksheet (see page 65).

CUT-OUT DESIGN FOR A FIRE FIGHTER'S HAT

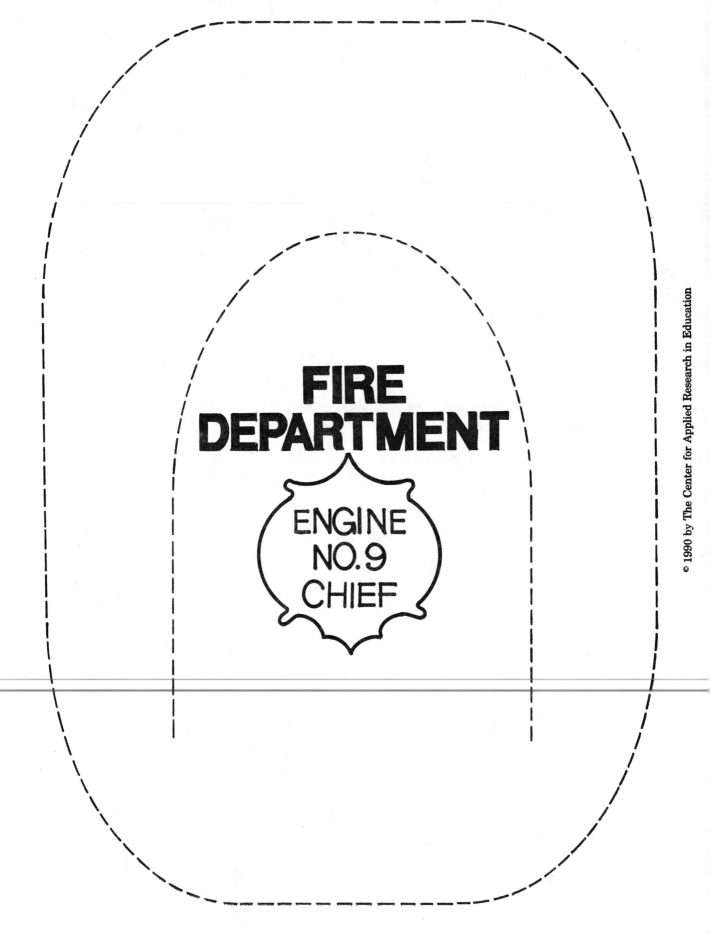

FIRE
DEPARTMENT

ENGINE
NO. 9
CHIEF

Name _____

COMMUNITY HELPERS

Draw a line from each community helper to the type of work he or she does.

DRESSING UP AND STEPPING OUT

WHY DO THIS?

Give children some fancy clothing to play with in the housekeeping area and let the magic happen! Children love to dress up and act out situations to go along. Such activity appeals to the more fanciful side of childhood and provides for endless episodes of imaginary play. A few extra articles of clothing can go a long way towards extending children's play when they are "dressing up and stepping out!"

WHAT WILL I NEED?

- Loose skirts with elastic waists
- Men's sport jackets and neckties
- Lots of hats—the more outrageous the better
- Long beads and other jewelry
- Scarves and shawls

HOW TO GET STARTED.

Ask the children to think of occasions for which people get really dressed up. What kinds of clothing do they wear? Why do people dress specially for different situations? Discuss what kinds of clothing they would like in the housekeeping area for dressing up. Perhaps the children can bring some things from home.

To create a situation, you can ask the children to make up a story called "Aunt Elvira's Visit."—just the sound of it should evoke a sense of formality. After the children have provided some details for the story, they should dress up and act it out.

HOW TO GO FURTHER.

Once the children have actually dramatized a story, they can dictate it and a book can be produced. Photographs of the various players all dressed up can be included as illustrations or some youngsters may be able to draw the costumes.

As another extension, it might be fun to declare a "dress-up day" in which children come to school dressed as storybook characters. Each child can give clues as everyone else tries to guess his or her identity.

PLAYING "SCHOOL"

WHY DO THIS?

Children like to imitate aspects from their daily lives. Why should their time in school be an exception? Many teachers have had a hearty laugh as they have heard their own words and expressions so adeptly parroted by children playing "school." There is much that children learn from this activity. Not only do they try to play the role of the teacher, but at the same time, they begin to see situations from a vantage point different from their own. The child playing the "teacher" will undoubtedly be a stricter disciplinarian than most teachers would ever be! If youngsters are playing "school," they can be prompted to teach a real lesson to others. How often have we heard that children learn a great deal from teaching things they already know to their peers. If correct information and positive attitudes are imparted, there are few activities which can be as important for strengthening skills than having to teach them to others.

WHAT WILL I NEED?

- Chalk and a small chalkboard
- Crayons, paper, pencils
- Books
- An alphabet or number chart

HOW TO GET STARTED.

Discuss the materials that the children would like to use in order to play "school" in the housekeeping corner. After children have dramatized classroom situations a few times, ask one or two individuals to teach a specific "lesson." Go over some of the things that the children might want to teach and provide materials as needed. Unobtrusive observation should yield important information about how well the children have internalized some of the concepts covered.

HOW TO GO FURTHER.

With the children, plan a lesson or activity which they would like to demonstrate to another class in the school. Invite the other class into the kindergarten. The youngsters can share books they've made or some pictures they've drawn, or they can act out an episode of playing "school" for the other children.

MOVING INTO THE BLOCK CENTER

WHY DO THIS?

Just as teachers look for opportunities to integrate various subjects in the youngsters' day, so too can activities in designated areas of the classroom be combined. Building block and housekeeping areas are often in close proximity to one another. Once in a while, the shelf, cabinet, or other barrier that divides these two areas can be removed to provide for movement from area to area and integration of children's play and investigation. Through the use of blocks in housekeeping play situations, the children can build structures in which they not only play, but can also explore new possibilities for extended learnings.

WHAT WILL I NEED?

● The normal complement of materials that are usually found in the block and housekeeping areas

HOW TO GET STARTED.

With the children discuss possibilities for building a structure that can be used as a part of their play in the housekeeping area. Some examples are a fort, a doghouse, or a shopping center. The outlines of rooms of a house can be made on the floor with building blocks. Then the children can act out scenes in the kitchen or the living room and actually move from room to room. Signs for the various rooms can be made. A puppet theater can be built, or a large square tower with an opening for a window becomes the turret where the prince and princess live to help add realism to dramatic play about kings, queens, and castles. The youngsters in the housekeeping area may have wanted a specific piece of furniture which can be constructed with blocks.

HOW TO GO FURTHER.

Once children have seen connections between activities in the housekeeping and block areas, they are likely to dream up new ways of joining these spaces. As children continue to work in this way, they can begin to devise special jobs—one can be an architect who designs the structure, while others are the construction workers who actually do the building. Also needed are sign makers, script writers, suppliers, shopkeepers, and so on.

CLEANING UP—THE TRUE HOUSEKEEPING

WHY DO THIS?

As children play and learn in the housekeeping area, they imitate a variety of housekeeping functions. One of the activities in which all families eventually engage is housecleaning. Children may have helped their parents dust, sweep floors, tidy their rooms, or clean up after spills. There are important learnings in analyzing how specific parts of a house are cleaned. For example, would you wax a wall or a floor? Which surfaces are best cleaned by sweeping? Performing such functions in the housekeeping area also helps to reinforce the need to put materials in their proper places in the classroom and to assume a part in maintaining classroom appearance and order. If children derive enjoyment from cleaning in their play, they will be able to see the connections between pretend cleanup and the real thing!

WHAT WILL I NEED?

- Small mops and brooms
- A dustpan
- Sponges, toweling, a plastic spray bottle, a plastic basin, clothesline, clothespins
- Doll clothes to wash

HOW TO GET STARTED.

Discuss the various tasks involved in cleaning house. Have the children ever helped their parents? What have they done? What are some of the cleaning functions children can act out in the housekeeping area? What materials will be needed? How are floors, walls, tables, or windows usually cleaned? What kinds of supplies are used? What is a thorough spring cleaning? Children may wish to act out such an event in the housekeeping corner. They may move out to other parts of the classroom and provide assistance as needed. Blackboards and tables can be washed. (Be sure to teach children how to wring out a rag or sponge, or the surfaces are likely to be wet for days.) If a spill occurs in the classroom, children can be taught to clean it up without humiliation. As children realize the sense of satisfaction for having performed needed tasks in the classroom, they are likely to develop a sense of pride in their school environment.

HOW TO GO FURTHER.

Organize a cleanup of a school yard or playground. Give groups of children a paper bag and ask them to canvass the play areas and pick up litter. (Of course, children should be instructed not to touch any glass.) Perhaps the children can do this with buddies from an upper grade. A list can be kept of the items found and a report made to another class or at a school assembly program. In many schools a rotation chart is developed for cleanup duty on the school grounds. How great the kindergarteners would feel if they knew that they were the ones to initiate such a project!

In the classroom, a cleanup chart can be developed with pictures of the various jobs to be done (blackboard washing, eraser banging, floor scrap cleaning, windowsill dusting, and so on) and the names of the children whose turn it is to perform these duties.

To check youngsters' familiarity with cleaning implements and tools, have them complete the "Housekeeping" worksheet.

Name _____

HOUSEKEEPING

Look at the items below. Circle five items you can use to clean a room.

chapter 4

IN THE CLASSROOM LIBRARY

Children associate letters and words with meanings long before they ever enter school. Street signs, product labels in the supermarket, and words in familiar advertisements all represent something specific to the preschooler. Indeed, the youngster reads these symbols. Throughout the classroom and the school, children are surrounded with printed material, some of which is clearly understood. The classroom library, though, can be a place reserved for words within the context of meaningful stories, not isolated letters or words.

Books open up the world for children. They help them to stimulate fantasy and learn about reality. They deepen the youngsters' understanding of life situations and emotions. They form the basis for literacy and a lifelong way of finding out. Beyond this, for most people reading is a pleasurable pastime which affords endless hours of enrichment and enjoyment. In kindergarten, one of the primary purposes of children's encounters with books should be to develop a love of reading. Finding the right space for such an important part of the classroom requires some advance planning.

The kindergarten library should be an inviting place. It is often located in a quiet (but not silent) corner of the classroom. A carpet on the floor, large pillows, and stuffed animals can help to make the area more comfortable and conducive to curling up with a book. Picture books, story books, homemade books, tapes, tape recorders, and headphones should all be available. Most teachers like to have the entire cover of the books in view, rather than just the spines. An open-faced book rack is good for this purpose, but the number of books on display is then somewhat limited. A common practice is to keep a few old favorites on hand and rotate other books so that some are highlighted and others are stored on bookshelves, but also accessible to the children. The reintroduction of books periodically throughout the year will have interesting results. Children delight in rediscovering a book they once read and enjoying it again, usually with new insights. If possible, the classroom library should be close to the writing center. Children read and develop a background for writing. Children write and develop something to read. The two processes are always intertwined, and the close proximity of these important areas will reinforce the connection. Indeed, one could argue that the two areas should be combined. In the classroom library, wall space should be reserved for some of the book activities described in this chapter.

We are often concerned about the acquisition of books for the classroom library. Several convenient sources come to mind. The first stop might be the school library. In most communities, public libraries allow teachers to borrow books on a long-term basis. Parents are a wonderful source for books. Just send out a flyer asking for any books at home that they might want to donate. Books that are made by the children or others in the school will have special meaning because of their origin. In searching for titles and subject matter, variety is the key. Stories with rhythm, repetition, rhyme, predictability, and attractive art work are particularly appropriate for kindergarteners. Tactile books and pop-up books are also popular. Books should be in all sizes and shapes, hardcover and softcover, realistic and fanciful, simply illustrated and busy. Selections should vary in length, but content should reasonably be within the grasp of a five-year-old. Occasionally a few more mature books will be of interest. Books should portray a range of human emotions; they should be genuine with real messages and stories as opposed to contrivances. Nature books are popular as are books about toys, dolls, trucks, and cars. Books for special purposes, such as a new baby, a hospital stay, or death of an animal or friend can all be used as needed depending upon circumstances. The benefit of this is that children can share emotional experiences and this can reduce feelings of isolation. Books will be produced about unimagined topics, and in the end, the best judge of a book's impact and suitability will be the interest of the children.

The classroom library is a place where children and teacher talk about books, discuss impressions and thoughts, and develop the special closeness that comes with sharing good literature. It is a comfortable, cozy spot that will be for many children the place where they build a lifelong interest in reading.

SHARING BOOKS WITH CHILDREN

WHY DO THIS?

Reading aloud to children has taken on new significance and importance as a result of recent educational research and practice, particularly in the area of the whole language. This is not a method or a program, but rather an outlook on how children use language and make connections as they derive meaning from reading, writing, listening, and speaking. It is language as it is used, language for a purpose. The goal of reading a book is not merely to identify words and phrases, but to derive a total sense of the book, its story, characters, rhythmic patterns, illustrations, and to relate and integrate children's own experiences to the book. Sharing literature becomes an extremely rich activity and forms a basis for children's use and appreciation of language. Children will associate printed words with actions or dialogue, interpret pictures, make predictions, repeat familiar passages, and enjoy the intimacy and warmth from the shared experience of listening, reading, and responding.

WHAT WILL I NEED?

- A storybook with large print
- If a big book is used, a ruler (for pointing to words) and an easel or chalk ledge to prop up the book are helpful.

HOW TO GET STARTED.

Select a good storybook to read to the class. At first, the book should not have too many words and the print should be large enough for the children to see. If a big book is not available, it might be best to start with a small group of youngsters who can come up close and see the words and pictures. Begin with a discussion of the book's cover. What is the title? What do the pictures show? Can we get any clues about the story from the title and cover picture? Who is the author? Which word helps us to know? What is an author? Is the name of the illustrator written on the cover?

While reading, point to each word. The children will naturally follow along. If the book has a repetitive phrase, it won't be long before the youngsters join in with the reader. The sweep of the ruler reinforces the left to right direction of the words and the downward progression of the lines. In this way, children become familiar with the structure of words in a story.

Discuss pictures and the clues they provide for finding out about the story. As pages are turned, children will often gain a sense of what is to come by looking at the pictures. Ask for predictions of what will happen next. What gives that impression? What are some of the possible endings for the story? Are some more likely than others? What makes them so? A few children can be asked to act out a part of the story, choosing to be a favorite character.

Read the story over again. Did the children make different comments or interpretations the second time around? What did they like best about the book? Is there anything they would like to change—a character, the ending, the sequence of events? Ask the children to retell the story in their own words, or if they like, they can read it with the teacher. Extending beyond simply reading a story to make it a richer, more meaningful experience will develop in the youngsters a greater appreciation for reading and literature and help them to understand the function and joys of language.

HOW TO GO FURTHER.

After the children are familiar with the book, they can be asked to find specific words in the story, copy them, make lists of familiar words, and make pictures to go along with the story. Some children may be able to write about the story. Try a "turn-around day" and ask the children to read a familiar book to the teacher. Invite schoolmates from other grades to come into the kindergarten and read to the children. If the story is a familiar one, the kindergarteners may be able to read to the older students. Won't that make them feel proud!

TAPE-RECORDING BOOKS

WHY DO THIS?

In any kindergarten group the children will display a wide range of reading abilities. Some children will begin the year as rather accomplished readers; others will have difficulty deciphering letters. Yet, all children can develop a love for literature. Indeed, one of the primary goals of any kindergarten program should be to develop in children an enjoyment of books, whether they can read alone, or delight in hearing stories read by another. We *can* teach children to read in the kindergarten, but this instruction does not necessarily mean having youngsters sit down and identify isolated letter sounds. We teach reading by encouraging children to draw stories, interpret their scribblings, record their dictations, and ask them to interpret what they have heard. One way to promote reading skills is to record familiar stories on a tape recorder and make the recording as well as the book available so youngsters can listen to them during activity or rest time. In this way, children can follow along, look at the words as they hear them, and develop, individually and informally, a sight vocabulary, not to mention the pleasures of hearing stories.

WHAT WILL I NEED?

- A few good books that children have enjoyed
- A tape recorder and blank tape

- A headphone or multiple headphones with connectors (often referred to as a listening center)
- A bell or other audible signal to remind children who are listening to the recorded book to turn a page

HOW TO GET STARTED.

Ask the children to identify a few of their favorite stories. Select two or three to begin with and obtain one blank tape for each book. Most cassette recorders have built in microphones, but if not, obtain a microphone. At your "leisure" (a decidedly precious commodity), record the story into the tape recorder as if you were reading it to the class. Indicate where the children should begin listening to the tape by giving a cue, for example, "Find the page near the beginning of the book that shows a picture of the girl and the dog and the big words that tell you the title of the story. Now each time you hear the bell, make sure you turn the page." As each page is turned, ring a bell, press a buzzer, or make some other sound to signal that the page must be turned. For the first few pages, provide a reminder of what the bell means as it is sounded. During the story, you may wish to ask the children to make predictions of what they think may happen next in the story. At the end of the tape, ask a few questions about the story which will help the children to remember a few of the important details. You may also ask them to let you know if they liked the story. Finally, make a label for the tape which is reminiscent of the story; the label can include a picture from the story, a color coding with a colored dot to match one placed on the accompanying book, or some other identification device that works for you.

Decide on a good spot for the tape recorder and headphones. (A desk or table with a chair will suffice.) Before leaving the tape, tape recorder, and book in the classroom

library, you will want to review the procedures for using the apparatus with the children—how to turn on the tape recorder, how to insert the tape, how to press *play,* how to find the first page asked for in the tape, how to rewind, and where to store the tape and book when finished. Most kindergarteners can follow this procedure with little difficulty. Before long, you will probably find that the children are following the words in the book as they hear them read on the tape.

HOW TO GO FURTHER.

Suggestions can be given at the end of each tape for the children to perform a related activity: draw a picture of something that happened in the story, tell the story to a classmate, or bring it home to share with parents. In some schools, children from upper grades can record the books for you. This kind of involvement can help to bring children from other grades into the kindergarten to serve as positive role models. It will also enhance the self-esteem of the older child who may feel quite important in having been selected to be a teaching assistant.

DRAWING SCENES FROM A BOOK

WHY DO THIS?

There are many ways that children can extend their appreciation of books enjoyed in the classroom. Dramatizing a story will undoubtedly be a popular activity. Drawing scenes from a story is another way that children deepen their appreciation for a story. Pictures drawn about a book not only convey a scene from a story, but also reveal the child's impressions, interpretations, and feelings. The amount of detail, use of color, and appearance of specific objects all provide a glimpse of the meaning the book represents for the child.

WHAT WILL I NEED?

- Drawing paper
- Crayons or markers
- A bulletin board or other spot to display pictures in the classroom library

HOW TO GET STARTED.

After a few books have been enjoyed in the classroom library, suggest that the children draw a scene, character, house, or some other object from the book. Discuss some of the most memorable parts of the story as well as ideas for related drawings. The books should be available so that the children can look at pictures or recall a favorite part. Children may dictate a caption to go along with their pictures. As pictures are completed, ask the children to talk about their work and how it shows something that happened in the book. Children can try to guess the name of the book that inspired the picture. A bulletin board can be made with the title and author of a book and a display of the pictures children have drawn. As a class activity, the youngsters can talk about the pictures on the bulletin board, read the captions, talk about characters, moods and impressions, and read the story again.

HOW TO GO FURTHER.

If sufficient interest and enthusiasm is apparent, a few youngsters may wish to join together for a group project about a particular book. One child can make cutout characters from a book, another can draw a background, still others can paint or color a scene on the background, one child may wish to print the title and author. Some teacher assistance and planning will probably be necessary for this group endeavor, but aside from enjoying the book activity, the children will derive the benefits of working together on a cooperative project and develop and exercise the social skills that are a part of such involvement.

THE READER'S CHAIR

WHY DO THIS?

As children begin to develop their ability to read or to tell stories, we can celebrate this emerging skill by designating a "reader's chair." This special seat can be a donated living room chair or simply a classroom chair with a painted or taped-on label. The youngster who sits in this chair is the one to read or tell a story to the others. Many appropriate activities can occur in the reader's chair. Just ask the children for suggestions!

WHAT WILL I NEED?

- A comfortable chair donated by a parent or friend of the school, or a classroom chair with a sign on it indicating that this is the "reader's chair." (Many teachers have been successful in securing donated chairs by writing a note home to parents or asking the school principal to mention this need in the regular school newspaper or school office communication.)

HOW TO GET STARTED.

As the teacher, you may wish to be the first one to read in the "reader's chair." Discuss its purpose. Model reading behavior by showing pictures as you read, talking about the action at appropriate intervals, interpreting pictures, and predicting outcomes.

Then, ask a youngster who can read to select a book and share it with others from the "reader's chair." The ability to read does not have to be a prerequisite for occupying this space. Some children will be able to take a book and tell the story in their own words as they show the pictures. Still others will be able to tell (or create) a story from memory. This variety of activity will enable each child in the class to participate.

If a particular character from a story is a favorite among the children, a special storybook character chairback can be made. Take an old pillowcase—a solid color is best. Decorate the pillowcase so that it resembles or suggests a character from the book. Felt can be pasted on for facial features. Yarn can be used for hair. Slip the pillowcase over the back of the classroom chair. As one youngster tells the story from the "reader's chair," another child plays the part of the character with the chair turned around.

HOW TO GO FURTHER.

A progressive story can be told from the "reader's chair." Ask one child to sit in the chair and begin to make up a story. The others should listen very carefully. Then, the child in the "reader's chair" selects a classmate to sit in the chair and continue the story until it is ready for an ending. Such an activity helps children to develop a story line and to sequence events.

BOOK TRADING DAY

WHY DO THIS?

Many kindergarteners will have a collection of books at home. Some will be lifetime treasures. Others, they may wish to trade with classmates. Arrange a Book Trading Day for the class. A few ground rules have to be established and outlined for parents. Through such an exchange, children will enjoy a wide variety of literature and hopefully encourage their parents to read to them.

WHAT WILL I NEED.

- A special table designated for the exchanges.
- A few extra books for children who may not have any books to exchange.

HOW TO GET STARTED.

Discuss Book Trading Day with the children. Think about ideas for how to organize such an event. You may wish to limit the trading to softcover books, picture books, or books about animals. Decide on the number of books (usually two or three) that each child can bring to school for exchanging. Send a note home explaining the program to the parents. Assign special workers. One child can "admit" youngsters one at a time to the trading table, giving each child a ticket indicating the number of books he or she puts into the exchange. (Have a few extra books on hand for those youngsters who may not have had any books at home.) Another youngster can arrange the books on the table so that all of them can be seen. Then, after all the books are in place, a system should be devised for how children will be readmitted to the exchange area to select new books. Usually four or five children at a time works best. You may wish to admit children by alphabetical order or reverse alphabetical order. Children select the number of books they donated. After the books have been exchanged, children should have some time to acquaint themselves with their new acquisitions.

HOW TO GO FURTHER.

As an activity to extend the book exchange, children can tell one another what they think their new books are about. Children can read some of the books to others. Perhaps the youngster who previously owned a book can read it, or tell something about it, to its new owner.

As an end of the year activity, you may wish to arrange for a toy exchange. Again, some limits and ground rules need to be set, but if the youngster's parents are informed, such trading can provide new stimulation and enjoyment for the children over the summer.

LIBRARIAN FOR THE WEEK

WHY DO THIS?

A classroom responsibility that some kindergarten children can assume is the job of librarian. This will require some explanation on the part of the teacher and practice on the part of the youngsters. The results, though, are quite rewarding. Not only will the children enjoy acting as classroom librarian, but at the same time they will be performing an important service. Arranging, managing, and checking classroom books in and out also permit the children to understand the way in which a library operates. A sense of responsibility for this vital classroom area is instilled.

WHAT WILL I NEED?

- Small letter-size envelopes
- 3-by-5-inch index cards (one for each book)
- Box to hold index cards

- Rubber cement
- Pen or pencil
- Date stamp and stamp pad (optional)

HOW TO GET STARTED.

Discuss the job of a librarian. Invite a school or community librarian to the classroom to talk about the various functions that must be performed to maintain a collection of books. Have one or two youngsters count the number of books in the classroom library. Suggest some reasons why managing this collection would be helpful. Discuss some of the procedures that might be followed. Select a classroom librarian. The first job is to arrange the books neatly within an area of the room. Those books highlighted should be placed on a table or book rack. Those on shelves have their spines showing with the titles all appearing in the same direction. You might want to establish sections for different kinds of books, for example, picture books, storybooks, books about animals, but this may be too difficult for most children to maintain.

In the back inside cover of each book, glue a small letter-size envelope just large enough to hold a 3-by-5-inch index card. Place the name of each book in the classroom library on a separate index card. Put the index card in the envelope glued to the back inside cover. When a child wants to borrow a book, the librarian removes the index card, asks the borrower to write his or her name on the next available line, and then places the index card in the card box or file. If a date stamp is available, it can be set for the due date (usually one week from the current date), and the index card and the envelope can be stamped as the book is checked out. The classroom librarian can check the cards in the box at the beginning of the week to see which books are out, discuss any "overdues" with the teacher, and train the next librarian. An ongoing responsibility is to straighten up the collection at the end of each day.

HOW TO GO FURTHER.

Take a class trip to the local public library. Ask the librarian to discuss the procedures followed for maintaining the collection. The children can compare the role performed by the librarian in the community library with the one performed by the classroom librarian. If possible, have all of the youngsters apply for a local library card.

POSTING POEMS

WHY DO THIS?

Young children love poetry. A variety of good selections are available for use in the kindergarten. The classroom library is an ideal place to post an enlarged copy of one or two poems that are favorites of the class members. Children are likely to go over to the poems displayed, read them spontaneously, provide their own versions of the poem, or read them together in small groups. The rhythm, meter, repetition, and rhyme of poems all serve to aid children in reading or memorizing them. Some youngsters who are not true readers may find that they can memorize a poem, follow the words, and read them to others in the class.

WHAT WILL I NEED?

- Chart paper (preferably lined)
- Markers
- Some good poems

HOW TO GET STARTED.

Obtain a few poems appropriate for kindergarteners. Good sources can be secured through the school or local public librarian. Read them with the children emphasizing the meter, rhyme, or repetitive phrases or words. If the poem has a clearly deliberate rhyme, you may wish to pause at the time the rhyming word would be said and prompt the children to supply the word. It's fun. After a while, the children will be able to recite the poems with just a few cues. Discuss different types of poems and the moods they create. Funny poems, eerie poems, poems which rhyme and others which do not should all be explored. Children should come to appreciate the diversity of poetic forms.

Once the children have decided upon a favorite poem or two, write out the poems on a sheet of large chart paper. Make sure to include the title and author of each poem. (It's not too early to help children learn that all work should be credited with the author's name.) If appropriate, a few youngsters can draw pictures to accompany the poem. Post the poem on a wall or bulletin board in the classroom library. Encourage children to read it from time to time, either by themselves, to one another, or in small groups. After a few days or weeks, you might even wish to let a child take the poem home to share with family members.

HOW TO GO FURTHER.

A few youngsters who are particularly sensitive to poetry, may be able to capture a poet's style and make up their own poems "in the style of . . ." Not too many children will be able to do this, but it's worth a try. It's an enriching literary activity.

With the assistance of the children, you may wish to make up shape poems, for example, a poem that is written in the shape of a circle, a square, or triangle. The verse, of course, should suggest something of the shape. The words of poems can be written in the form of other familiar objects, such as a tall building, a house, a winding road, or a tree with each branch containing a different phrase or verse.

A PUPPET SHOW

WHY DO THIS?

The classroom library is the perfect spot for a puppet show. As children read or are read to, they develop favorite stories. Children may wish to dramatize these stories; others may wish to put on a puppet show. When children reenact scenes from a story, they expand their literacy by realizing that stories can be conveyed in several forms: by reading, listening, illustrating, or dramatizing.

Kindergarten teachers are familiar with the benefits of puppet shows. They permit children to express a variety of emotions in an acceptable fashion and also provide the opportunity for them to extend their enjoyment of literature. The construction of puppets and a puppet theater can be very simple or quite elaborate, depending upon the interests of the children and the teacher.

WHAT WILL I NEED?

- A large refrigerator carton for a puppet theater, or a regular desk with a large box on top of it. (Appliance stores will make refrigerator boxes available to teachers and some, as a public service, will even deliver them.)
- Sharp scissors or other cutting tool
- Markers and paint
- Assorted materials for making puppets: fabric, styrofoam cups, tongue depressors, egg cartons, paper plates, clothespins, socks, and so forth.

HOW TO GET STARTED.

First make a puppet theater. Cut out an opening for a stage in a large refrigerator box. Another large cutout in the back will be the door for the puppeteers. It should be at the right height so that the children inside are hidden from view. Paint or decorate the box. Scenery can be placed inside of the box if desired. If a refrigerator box is not available, a large carton placed on top of a desk will suffice.

A variety of simple puppets can be made. After a story has been selected for production in the puppet theater, the most appropriate kinds of puppets should be selected. (Some simple kinds of puppets are shown in the illustration.) Perhaps the easiest puppet to make is a stick puppet. Simply draw a face on a large tongue depressor. Another easy puppet is made from a paper bag, and when the bottom is folded over, it forms a place for the child's hand to operate the puppet's mouth. The face can then be decorated. Other puppets can be made by attaching a paper plate with a face drawn on it to a stick. Socks can be formed into puppets and decorated. A single section of an egg carton can be decorated and held on a finger for another kind of puppet. Using a paper fastener, two styrofoam cups can be attached to one another

with the side of one attached to the base of the other to form yet another kind of puppet.

Once the theater and puppets have been made, it's show time! At first children will need some assistance with selecting roles and dramatizing the story, but with practice and experience, these shows will occur spontaneously.

HOW TO GO FURTHER.

There are many opportunities for children to extend the puppet show experience. Inviting another class in the school to view the performance always adds importance to the event. Then some children can write invitations, make tickets, programs, set up seats, serve as ushers, make and distribute popcorn, and so on. Everyone in the class can assume a different role.

BOOK OF THE MONTH

WHY DO THIS?

In the classroom library, in a corner or on a bulletin board, feature a special book as "Book of the Month." This can be a book which the children have particularly enjoyed or one which has seasonal significance. An attractive display with a book jacket, children's drawings inspired by the book, puppets of some of the characters, and so on will all add to the general appeal of this exhibit. By creating such a display, children learn how to appreciate and celebrate literature.

WHAT WILL I NEED?

- A bulletin board or display corner
- A book jacket from the featured book (or one made by the teacher)
- Drawings of scenes from the book made by the children
- Puppets or other projects inspired by the book

HOW TO GET STARTED.

With the children, conduct a poll to select the "Book of the Month." This can be a book which the children have particularly enjoyed listening to, a seasonal favorite, or one about an upcoming holiday. Why is this book special to the children? What do they like about it? What makes it different from other books they have enjoyed? Tell the children that they will create a display to highlight the book. What would they like to see included? Usually, a book jacket, drawings of scenes from the book, puppets of characters, and other items can be included in the exhibit. (See the sample in the illustration.) Ask the children to explain how the display helps them to enjoy the book. The featured book should be available in the classroom library for children to enjoy over and over again.

HOW TO GO FURTHER.

As an additional part of a display featuring a particular book, kindergarten children (with some adult assistance) can make a diorama or a scene from the book. Starting with a shoebox, ask youngsters to create scenery from a part of the book. Then, make cutout figures of characters from the book (you, the teacher, may have to do this) and place them appropriately in the diorama. Ask the youngsters to dictate what is happening in the scene and write it out on an index card. Attach the card to the shoebox and include it in the "Book of the Month" display.

THE ORAL BOOK REPORT

WHY DO THIS?

Book reports are often thought of as appropriate activities for upper elementary grade students. Yet kindergarteners are capable of delivering "oral book reports." Recounting a story and talking about characters they liked or particularly funny episodes are perfectly appropriate for five-year-olds. The children who are listening to the reports come to realize that there is a great array of stories which their classmates have enjoyed. Thinking skills are promoted as children are asked to select and talk about favorite characters or parts of a book and the reasons for their choices. In time, the youngsters will also be able to identify authors and their style. (Many kindergarten children can identify a Richard Scarry or Ezra Jack Keats book just by looking at covers or illustrations.) Through such activities we build children's literacy.

WHAT WILL I NEED?

- Picture books or familiar stories

HOW TO GET STARTED.

First, model the "delivery" of an oral book report by displaying the book that you will discuss. State the title, author, and illustrator of the book and give a very brief synopsis. Then, focus on a particular character. Tell why you liked (or did not like) the character. What did the character do that was humorous, mischievous, hurtful, or just like someone you know. Talk about the mood of the book. Is it scary or funny? Does it convey a special message or moral? What about the illustrations? How do they make you feel? What do they show? Are they busy, simple, colorful, and so on? Once you have given a report, ask a youngster to tell about a book. In the beginning, you may have to do some prompting with questions. Before long, the children will be able to give oral book reports on their own and not only enhance their literacy, but also instill a love for books.

HOW TO GO FURTHER.

A literary discussion may seem like a rather sophisticated, if not far-fetched, activity for young children. But, it can occur quite successfully in kindergarten classrooms. Not every youngster will be able to enter into such a discussion in the first place, but it's worthwhile for the others in the class to observe the action. Select two children who have read (or have heard) the same book. Pick a book which can have multiple interpretations of plot or character. For example, in "Goldilocks and the Three Bears," should Goldilocks have eaten the bears' porridge in the first place? Was this the right thing to do? Children can also argue about whether they liked or did not like a particular character or a book's ending.

THE BOOKWORM

WHY DO THIS?

A familiar way to boast about the increasing number of books enjoyed by the members of a class is to create a classroom "bookworm." Essentially this is an ongoing visual display of the titles and authors of books read by the children. It is a concrete demonstration of the breadth and scope of the books borrowed. As they gaze at the bookworm, the children can remember a book they may have enjoyed earlier in the year and be motivated to read it again, this time with increased skill and enhanced meaning. This project also helps to promote a norm for a literate environment.

WHAT WILL I NEED?

- Construction paper
- Markers
- Scissors
- A picture of an earthworm from a science book

HOW TO GET STARTED.

Show a picture of an earthworm and point out the segments. Discuss the great number of segments and how they all look pretty much like one another. Introduce the bookworm project to the children. Explain that you will be creating an ongoing bookworm around the walls of the classroom. Make a "head" for the worm and a supply of round segments on which to record the books read. Each time a child reads a book from the classroom, school, or public library, and can tell you or the class something about it, a new segment of the worm is developed and attached to the growing worm. On each segment, write the name and author of the book and have the youngster who read it write his or her name on the bottom of the segment. If space permits, a small drawing can be included on the segment. In most classrooms the worm is posted high along the classroom wall, above the bulletin boards or chalkboards, so that new segments can be added without obstacle. (See the illustration.) Children can count the number of segments periodically and recall books that they enjoyed earlier in the school year.

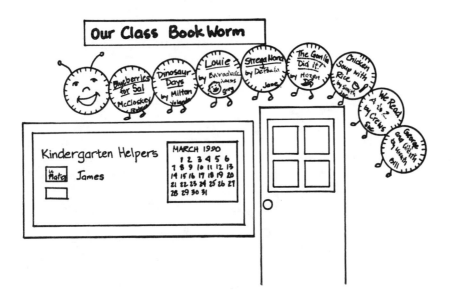

HOW TO GO FURTHER.

Bookworms can be made to depict any collection of similar objects. Individual youngsters may wish to construct a worm of words that begin with the letter *m* and call it an "M-worm." If the segments are attached with paper fasteners, the worm can be folded up and taken home or stretched out for display. Each child can be asked to create a worm using a different set of items, which are alike in some way. Some possibilities include food worms, color worms, number worms, or worms including the names of children in the class, names of songs, and so on. Young children love to make collections!

chapter 5

IN THE WRITING CENTER

It was not too many years ago that kindergarten teachers were admonished not to ask five-year-olds to do any writing. From a developmental point of view, it was considered inappropriate. But by May or June of their kindergarten year, many children were able to inscribe a Mother's or Father's Day card with "Dear Mom (or Dad), I love you. Jimmy."

Now we realize that many forms of writing are entirely appropriate in the kindergarten. At first, children will engage in "pretend writing" or scribbling. This is a legitimate form of writing, and many children can read back what no one else could possibly decipher. This is because the child attaches meaning to the scribbling. Dictating captions for pictures is a next step, and soon youngsters will be able to create their own labels. Signs in the classroom, the block corner, or wherever they serve a purpose are all a part of young children's writing.

The writing center should have a table or two and abundant supplies to promote successful attempts at writing. Paper of all shapes, sizes, and textures should be available in bins or on shelves. Markers, crayons, and colored pencils should be readily accessible as well as magazines, scissors, and paste. A typewriter on a desk will provide hours of meaningful occupation.

If youngsters write every day, using their "invented" or "kindergarten spelling," they will understand the purposes and joys of writing. Once they write, they then have something to read. They will use letters and words within a meaningful context, to convey a message, express a thought, or create a sign for a specific use elsewhere in the classroom. The more children write, the more their skill and enjoyment will emerge. As children ask for words to be written for them, word cards or lists can be developed and displayed or kept in a box in the writing center. Then, as children need or wish to use them, they will be readily available. Soon children will want to make lists of words for special purposes, for example, a list of words that are used in traffic signs. If an accepting attitude pervades this enterprise, without concern for spelling, grammar, or capitalization at this early level, children will write naturally to suit their own needs.

MAKING PICTURE CAPTIONS

WHY DO THIS?

Making captions for pictures is a great activity for ushering children into the world of writing. Pictures tell stories, but children often like to label their drawings with a phrase which captures the intended meaning. At first, most captions will be dictated by the children and written by the teacher. Later on, the youngsters may be able to write their own captions using "pretend writing" or "invented spelling." By so doing, they are using letters, sounds, and words within a context of their own creation. Writing captions for pictures helps children to realize that words convey messages and attach additional meaning to the picture. After the pictures are displayed, the captions provide a basis for reading, thus linking these two essential processes in childhood literacy.

WHAT WILL I NEED?

- Drawing paper
- Markers, paints, crayons, or colored pencils
- Lined paper (optional)
- "Happy and Sad" worksheet

HOW TO GET STARTED.

Begin with the "Happy and Sad" worksheet. Ask the children to draw something (a game, activity, place, or person) that makes them happy. Then, on the other side of the paper, they draw something that makes them sad. As each child finishes, complete the caption at the bottom of the page using the child's dictated words. Display the completed pictures, ask the children to read their own captions and then ask them to read each others' captions. Of course, each word will not be read just as it was written, but if the ideas come across, a big step towards reading is made.

As children create drawings for different purposes, conduct individual conferences to talk with them about what is happening in their pictures. Offer to write something at the bottom which will help others to understand their pictures. Some children may wish to scribble a caption; others may be able to write a few words which will remind them of their intended meanings. If the caption is involved and tells a story, it is useful to cut out a section of lined paper which will fit onto the bottom of (or elsewhere in) the drawing and print the dictated sentences. For a particularly attractive effect, cut out the essential part of a child's painting, mount it onto a larger sheet of paper, and write the caption.

The drawings should be posted in the writing center or elsewhere in the classroom. Ask each child to tell about the picture and read the caption. Before long, children will be able to read one another's pictures and captions.

HOW TO GO FURTHER.

Cut out action pictures from magazines, catalogues, and posters. Mount the pictures on construction paper or oaktag. Draw lines for words or sentences at the bottom. Give one picture to each child. Have them think about what is happening in the picture. Then ask them to dictate or write a caption for the picture. Some children may wish to relate two or three pictures into a sequence or a story.

Name _____

HAPPY AND SAD

Happy   Sad

I am happy when   I am sad when

MAKING A BIG BOOK

WHY DO THIS?

The use of big (or enlarged) books allows a group of children to enjoy a story simultaneously. They can hear and benefit from one another's reactions, and share impressions and interpretations. Making a big book is a very rich experience for kindergarteners. All of the children can become involved. They can dictate the sequence of the story or dialogue, some can draw pictures, others can help with printing, still others can assist in assembling pages and binding. Making a big book provides opportunities to model writing behaviors, and helps children to see print developed within the context of the meaning of a story.

WHAT WILL I NEED?

- Large construction paper (about 18 x 24 inches)
- Cardboard or posterboard for the front and back covers
- Markers, crayons, or colored pencils
- Glue or paste
- Hole puncher
- Rings or string for binding
- Easel or chalk ledge

HOW TO GET STARTED.

Discuss the project with the children. Talk about the advantages of using a big book rather than one that is difficult for children to see and share when reading to a group. (What are some of the advantages of all of the children being able to see the printed words?) You may wish to recreate a story already known to the children, or brainstorm ideas to make up a new one. (For a first attempt, it is best to select a story with a deliberate rhythm and rhyme.) Once the story is selected, involve the children in identifying the sequences of the book. What pictures should be included? What should the captions say?

Have children draw pictures for the various pages of the book. This can either be done by having the youngsters draw directly on the page to be used (leaving space for the text at the bottom), or drawing (or painting) pictures separately and then pasting them onto the large sheets of paper. The illustrations should be attractive, using vivid colors. The text should be large and bold enough to be seen when the entire group reads the book together. Make a cover and back page out of cardboard or posterboard so they will be stiff. If the pages are laminated, the book's life will be extended. Binding the pages and cover can be done in one of several ways. One of the simplest methods is to punch holes and insert rings or string. Another more complicated, but more "booklike," method is to use wide masking tape (or cloth tape) to attach each page to the next one so that they are all fastened together.

When ready to share the book, place it on an easel or chalk ledge. Gather the children around and read it while pointing to the words with a finger or ruler. Emphasize the rhythm or rhyme of the text. Discuss the pictures. (The "artists" may wish to talk about how they made the illustrations.) Ask the children to predict what will happen in the following pages. Leave the book out for the children to enjoy on their own. When reading the book again and again, you may wish to have the children supply missing words, phrases or even read the words in unison.

HOW TO GO FURTHER.

Once the children are familiar with the book, they can take it to other classes in the school and read it to other children. They may also want to dramatize the story.

It may be possible to have upper grade children interview kindergarteners about what they like best in books, their interests, and activities. Then the older children, in groups, can make big books for the younger ones. This involvement will be enriching for both the older and the younger children.

MAKING AN ACCORDION BOOK

WHY DO THIS?

An accordion book is simply a story with the pages attached together so that they unfold to form one continuous sequence of pages. Because of the way the book may be spread out, it can stand alone on a table or the floor and be seen, from beginning to end, in one continuous sweep of the eye. The construction of such a book helps children to realize that books come in many shapes and sizes. Aside from this, making an accordion book is just plain fun!

WHAT WILL I NEED?

- Cardboard or oaktag (9-by-12-inch)
- Paper and paints
- Markers and crayons
- Masking tape or cloth tape

HOW TO GET STARTED.

Explain to the children that they are going to make an accordion book. Can anyone guess what it is? Select a story to reproduce, either one that is familiar to the children or one that you make up together. Make each page of the book on a separate sheet of cardboard. (If oaktag is used, it is best to double it so that the pages will be sturdier.) Make a picture and print the text at the bottom of the page. Children's paintings can be cut out, mounted on a page, and used for the illustrations, or drawings can be made directly on the cardboard or oaktag.

Once all of the pages are ready, assemble the book by taping the pages together in sequence with masking tape or cloth tape. Tape both the front and the back surfaces of each page even though only one side may be printed. (Leave a little bit of space between each page so the book can be folded.) When the book is ready, fold it up "accordion-style" and show how it unfolds to reveal the entire story from beginning to end. Stand it up on a tabletop or on the floor in the writing center. Read the book together or have the children read it to one another.

HOW TO GO FURTHER.

A very sturdy "master book" can be developed, with the pages made from cardboard and clear plastic facings all bound together with tape. Then the individual pages of the book can be attached to the "master" with transparent tape rolled over or double-sided tape. When you want to make a new accordion book, simply remove the old pages and put the ones for the new story in their place. The "master" can be used over and over again.

Another variation is to make the book "wrap around" so that when finished reading one side, the story continues on the back, also reading the pages from left to right.

THE TYPIST'S STATION

WHY DO THIS?

The use of computers and word processors has left many offices and families with old typewriters they no longer need. A donated typewriter will make a welcome addition to the writing center of the kindergarten classroom. Children should be free to experiment with the typewriter and explore the various letters and symbols it can produce. They are likely to discover on their own how to make lowercase and capital letters. Eventually, the youngsters may even wish to write words or compose little stories, but this should not necessarily be an expectation. Using a typewriter can add the dimension of fun that will motivate some children to want to play with words and sentences. Beyond this, typing provides an additional play activity in which children can pretend to be secretaries, computer operators, or writers. They come to realize the importance of the written word in many occupations.

WHAT WILL I NEED?

- A typewriter
- Paper of different sizes and colors
- Index cards with words written on them

HOW TO GET STARTED.

The first thing to do is to acquire an old typewriter. (Manual typewriters are safer than electric ones for children.) A note of solicitation to parents, an item in the school newsletter, or appeals to local businesses are likely to yield results. Set the typewriter on a desk or table and allow the children to experiment. You may need to demonstrate how to insert paper. Before long the children will come to realize that the letter or symbol shown on a key results in printing that symbol when the key is depressed. Children may enjoy simply playing with the typewriter; at the same time they will be seeing letters in different forms, numbers, and other symbols.

After a while, some children may wish to type messages to one another. A "word bank" can be provided by printing words on index cards with a marker which are kept near the typewriter. Children can be shown how to copy these words and how to make spaces between words. If a youngster asks for phrases to copy, these too should be provided.

HOW TO GO FURTHER.

Greeting cards or letters that children compose can be enhanced by decorating them with rubber stamps. The combination of typed messages and different colored stamps will be most appealing. Children can make cards for different purposes or send notes to another class, the principal, school secretary, or custodian. Some letters can be dictated by the children and typed by the teacher. By creating typed messages and letters, children are experiencing a common form of communication in our world.

Another extension activity is to make a large drawing of a keyboard (with the same arrangement of keys as the classroom typewriter) on a sheet of construction paper or oaktag. Leave the squares or circles that represent the keys blank. A child, or group of children, can fill in the letters, numbers, and symbols on the drawn keyboard to match the arrangement on the classroom typewriter.

REBUS STORIES

WHY DO THIS?

A rebus is a picture, letter, or combination of symbols that suggest a specific word. Children enjoy figuring out rebus messages; it's like solving a puzzle. This is also a legitimate form of reading. Given an assortment of rebus cards, youngsters can arrange them from left to right to make phrases or sentences. The availability of rebus cards in an index card box can provide meaningful occupation in the writing center. After they form rebus messages, the children can call friends over to read them. After this, the cards, in sequence, can be copied onto a sheet of paper. Rebus stories represent one of many approaches that can be employed to promote early childhood literacy.

WHAT WILL I NEED?

- Index cards
- Markers

HOW TO GET STARTED.

Make a few common rebus cards. (See the samples given at the end of this activity.) Introduce the concept that pictures (or letters) can represent whole words. Ask the youngsters to suggest additional rebus words. Place the rebus cards on a chalk ledge and show how they can be combined to form a sentence or message (like the one shown in the illustration). Reinforce the left-to-right progression.

After a bank of rebus cards has been developed, place them in the writing center and encourage children to make messages for one another. Once a sentence is complete, some children may wish to copy the message onto a sheet of paper.

HOW TO GO FURTHER.

Children can make up rebus stories and try to stump other children in school, teachers, or parents. Collections of rebus sentences can be made and bound into a simple book to be shared. Who can form the longest rebus sentence that still makes sense? Some children will be able to make rebus cards that combine two or more pictures, symbols, or letters.

SOME REBUS WORD CARDS

THE VERTICAL STORY

WHY DO THIS?

Young children enjoy writing or seeing their dictations in different forms. One interesting format is the vertical story in which the text appears as a single long sheet of paper as printed on fan-fold or roll computer paper, or on sheets of paper attached to one another with the top of one page taped to the bottom of the preceding page. In this way, children may be motivated to dictate longer stories and then see the written version from beginning to end without turning pages. As children work towards making longer and longer stories, the sense and sequence of their writing will likely become more logical.

WHAT WILL I NEED?

- Markers
- Fan-fold or roll computer paper, or sheets of lined paper
- Tape

HOW TO GET STARTED.

Explain that the children are going to make a long story, one that will go on for a few pages. Brainstorm a few ideas for a long story. Once a general theme is chosen (such as "Our Trip to the Firehouse" as shown in the illustration), have the children dictate sentences and record them on the paper. Encourage use of detail and description to lengthen the story. Reread the story in sections and revise as warranted. (Modeling editing and revision practices provides youngsters with an understanding that their writing can be changed and improved as they work with it.) If individual sheets of paper were used, tape the top of each page to the bottom of the preceding page so that the story is displayed vertically from beginning to end.

When the long story is complete, read it all the way through and post it in the writing center or on a bulletin board elsewhere inside or outside the classroom.

HOW TO GO FURTHER.

As sentences are dictated, use a different colored marking pen for each child's contribution, then when the story is complete, ask each child to read his or her sentence. You'll be surprised by how many youngsters will be able to do this.

As time goes on, some children will want to write their own vertical stories using invented spelling or other word cues.

Our Trip to the Firehouse

On Thursday we went to the North Street Fire Station. Darren's mother and Lisa's mother went along with us.

We had to cross many streets. Each time Mrs. Kelly got into the middle of the street so we could all cross safely. On the way we saw a really big maple tree. Everyone picked up one of the "helicopters" that fell from the tree.

When we arrived at the fire station, Firefighter Olsten said, "Come on in!" We saw a big firetruck with ladders on the side and one that can be cranked up very high. We also saw an engine that can pump alot of water.

We also went upstairs and saw where the firefighters sleep. Firefighter Burns showed us the special clothing that he wears and the tools that he uses. Mrs. Kelly said that when she was a little girl, everything was pretty much the same, except that firefighters did not have walkie-talkies.

We walked back to school and saw the same big maple tree. We told our principal about our trip.   The End.

MAKING LETTERBOOKS

WHY DO THIS?

During the kindergarten year, children encounter letters in their work each day. They may have made signs for the block area or looked through books in the classroom library. At some point, children will be able to isolate letters and provide words that begin with each one. That's the time to introduce the idea of making letterbooks. These are simply sheets of paper, one page for each letter, with an appropriate picture for each page. Most of the time we want children to discover letters within the context of words or sentences, but after many such experiences, kindergarteners will more than likely be able to identify several words that begin with each letter sound.

WHAT WILL I NEED?

- Paper
- Markers or crayons
- Stapler
- Scissors

HOW TO GET STARTED.

Divide a sheet of blank paper into six boxes and make one box for each letter of the alphabet. Write each letter in capital and lower case. Duplicate the pages so that each child will have a complete set. Have the children draw a picture or write a word, or both, that begins with the letter indicated by each page. This project will probably take several days to complete. Perhaps it can be a long-term homework assignment. When all of the pages are finished, the children make the pages by cutting along the thick lines on the sheets of paper. Then, they place the pages in alphabetical order, decorate the cover page, and staple the pages together to form a book. The book can be enjoyed over and over again.

HOW TO GO FURTHER.

Some children may wish to make more than one letterbook. A variation is to cut pictures out of magazines and paste them on the appropriate pages to show objects that begin with each letter. Some particularly motivated youngsters may want to make word series that all start with the same letter for each page, for example, funny frozen fishcakes, lovely lemon lollypops, bright big books, tremendous tulip trees.

THE AUTHOR'S CHAIR

WHY DO THIS?

Children's attempts to write and read their writing should be celebrated as important events! A special chair should be designated as the "author's chair" and placed prominently in the writing center. (If not enough room is available for all of the children to gather together in this area, some teachers place the chair at the edge of the writing center and then turn it towards the center of the classroom when it is being used.) It is here that children can read their stories or scribblings to one another, interpret picture captions, or "read" a drawing. Young children ought to know the term "author" and come to realize that they are all authors. Using a special chair for this purpose lends a sense of importance to the act of writing and also serves as a motivational factor for attentive listening.

WHAT WILL I NEED?

- If possible, get an easy chair as a donation from a home or a used furniture store. A classroom chair can be decorated with a fabric seat or cushion and easily transformed into an "author's chair." Whatever you do, this spot should be made special in some way.

HOW TO GET STARTED.

As the teacher, you can model how to use the "author's chair." Read something that you have written for the children. Set ground rules for good listening habits at the very first session. Establish an air of importance for reading from this special chair. In the beginning, children can interpret a picture in the "author's chair" or read something that they have scribbled. As children use invented spelling and use letters to suggest whole words or phrases, you may be surprised to find how well they can read their own scrawl. Sitting in the "author's chair" may provide the extra motivation some children need to begin a written piece.

HOW TO GO FURTHER.

Invite guests to come into the classroom to read something that they have written, and ask the children where the guest should sit. Older youngsters in the school, the principal, parents, or others may come in and take the seat of honor. Such events promote the importance of writing and also help the youngsters to understand that anyone can be an author.

MAKING GREETING CARDS

WHY DO THIS?

Making greeting cards provides a *purpose* for children to write. There are many holidays celebrated in kindergarten for which greeting cards are appropriate. Among them are Valentine's Day, Christmas, Chanukkah, Mother's Day, Father's Day, or the first day of spring. If a parent or brother or sister has a birthday coming up, young children may not have the ways and means to go to a store to purchase a gift. But, if they do have an opportunity at school to make an original greeting card, this will surely be appreciated. Children can make cards for classmates, teachers, or friends of the school who are sick. Sending greeting cards lets others know that we care, and at the same time the children who prepare these cards find that writing is a vehicle for expressing their emotions and wishes to others.

WHAT WILL I NEED?

- Construction paper
- Markers, crayons, or paints
- Stickers
- Writing paper
- Paste or glue
- Scissors

HOW TO GET STARTED.

Discuss the purposes of greeting cards and the times of the year and situations in which they might be sent. Explain that if a parent or other relative has a birthday coming up or is ill, the children can make a greeting card in the writing center. Talk about times when everyone will be making cards, that is for certain holidays.

Demonstrate a few basic designs for greeting cards: the kind that are folded in four, those in which the message is printed on paper which is pasted onto folded construction paper, and those that are made a special shape. Undoubtedly, the youngsters will come up with other designs. Discuss messages that can be printed in cards, pictures that can be drawn, stickers or stamps that can be included, and so on. Children can dictate the message they wish to convey and then rewrite it in their own handwriting. For children who are not ready to do their own writing, a few handy phrases, such as "Happy Birthday," "Get Well Soon," and "I Miss You," can be preprinted and kept at hand in the writing center for children to use in making cards.

Sometimes special occasions for greeting cards will develop spontaneously. What about making cards for Groundhog Day, a new baby brother or sister, an anniversary, a "mid-winter card," or a "just to say hello card."

HOW TO GO FURTHER.

Children can make individual mailboxes to receive messages or cards from one another. A mailbox can be made easily from a large juice can or coffee can. The cans can be decorated with name, address, stickers, or picture of a favorite animal. Set up on a shelf or other surface, a game or activity can be developed for recognizing one another's mailboxes. These individual mailboxes will be especially valuable for Valentine's Day, when all of the children will more than likely make cards for one another.

THE "ALL ABOUT ME" BOOK

WHY DO THIS?

Just as professional writers are often advised to write about what they know best, kindergarteners can begin their first books by writing about themselves. An "All About Me" book can contain a self-portrait, pictures of favorite foods, toys, activities, family members, and even a wish for the future. If an instant camera is available, including a photo of each child is a real plus. Self-esteem is enhanced since each child becomes a central character. This book can be developed over a period of time and expanded throughout the year. What a wonderful thing to bring home to family and friends on the last day of school in June!

WHAT WILL I NEED?

- Drawing paper
- Markers, crayons
- Magazines
- An instant camera (optional)

HOW TO GET STARTED.

Introduce the project by explaining that the children are going to make books about themselves. The title page, "All About Me," with a space for each child to write his or her name, should be prepared in advance. Talk about the possible items that might be included in subsequent pages. A logical sequence would be to follow the title page with a picture (either a self-portrait or a photograph) of the child, then another picture of the child's family, a page for the child's house or apartment, a pet, favorite food, favorite color, favorite toy, an activity in which the child likes to participate, and so on. The caption for each page can be duplicated and then the children would fill in the blanks. For example, "My favorite food is _____." Pictures can be cut out of magazines and pasted on pages. Some children will want to bring in photographs from home to include in the book, especially ones showing how they looked as babies, family members, pets, favorite activities, and the like. One of the last pages should be reserved for some aspect of the future, such as a career choice, a wish for the future, or a picture of what the child will be doing in twenty years or so.

HOW TO GO FURTHER.

Have the children gather vital statistics about themselves. Height, weight, hair color, and eye color can all be included. Each feature can be recorded on pages designed for this purpose.

Parent volunteers can be asked to come into the classroom to assist the children with this project. Parents can "interview" the children about some of their favorite things and help them to locate pictures for their books. They can also act as scribes as the kindergarteners dictate some of the information they would like included on the pages. In some schools older children perform these functions and the book becomes a focus for the involvement of older and younger children. Both benefit from the interaction!

MAKING SHAPE POEMS

WHY DO THIS?

Poetry is an important part of any literacy program. Young children enjoy learning a few favorite poems, particularly humorous ones and those with definite rhythm and rhyme. After introducing new poems, returning to them weeks or months later will bring renewed delight and joy.

Kindergarten children can write poems as long as a few aids and suggestions are provided. Children can begin by dictating poems to be written on familiar shapes cut out of construction paper or oaktag. Rhyme need not be a requirement for young children's poetry, although some children will enjoy finding rhyming words to use in their poems. Through writing poems children will be exploring an important form of literature.

WHAT WILL I NEED?

- Construction paper or oaktag
- Markers

HOW TO GET STARTED.

Find a poetry book in the school library. With the children develop an appreciation for poetry by reading selections a few times each week. Demonstrate that poems do not necessarily have to rhyme. Discuss the poems with the children and find their favorites. What are there reasons for their choices?

Cut out a few basic shapes: triangle, circle, square, and diamond. Make up a few simple poems to fit into the shapes. Then try some shapes of familiar objects like a shoe, a fish, a suitcase, a leaf, or a garbage can. Develop poems that suggest the shapes and fit into them. Place some shapes in the writing center. As children wish, they can dictate poems to be written on the shapes. (See the samples in the illustration.)

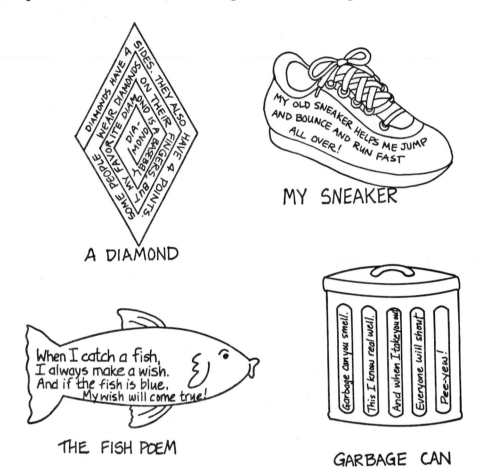

A DIAMOND

MY SNEAKER

THE FISH POEM

GARBAGE CAN

HOW TO GO FURTHER.

Once children have had a few experiences with poetry, they may wish to experiment with "formula poems," that is, poems with designated lines and contents. For example, try this formula for a poem about an animal:

Title: Name of animal	*LIONS*
Line 1: size of the animal	Lions are big.
Line 2: color of the animal	Most are light brown.
Line 3: a sound it makes	They let out a ROAR!
Line 4: where the animal lives	As they prowl in Africa.
Line 5: name of babies	Their babies are cubs.
Line 6: how you feel about it	I'd like to make friends with a lion!

chapter 6

IN THE LISTENING CENTER

We live in an environment filled with sounds. As we help children to learn about the world around them, we can provide activities designed to help children focus on the wealth of information they receive by hearing. There is much discussion among teachers about the need to improve youngsters' listening skills. Work in the listening center promotes these skills and helps children to become more aware of the great variety of sounds around them. Discriminating among sounds in the environment requires careful attention and can be a great deal of fun. Most children learn to "tune out" the sounds around them; but if we ask them to really focus, they are likely to hear sounds and identify the sources of sounds that had previously been just a part of the "background noise."

In the kindergarten classroom, the listening center need not be more than a table with a tape recorder, headsets, and the simple materials for other activities as described in this chapter. Children enjoy playing guessing games with sounds and producing different kinds of sounds themselves. The listening center can be the site for activities of this nature. Aside from the sheer fun of these experiences, children will develop the skills to become more attentive listeners and learners.

SOUNDS AROUND

WHY DO THIS?

Sounds are everywhere in our environment. Most often we see what is making a particular sound and we associate the visual and auditory clues to identify what we have seen and heard. Given the sounds alone, how well can children guess the source of commonly heard sounds such as running water, children at play, or a pencil dropped? Trying to do this with sounds heard on a tape recorder can be a real challenge and great fun. By tuning in to the sounds made by familiar objects, children construct meaning from auditory clues alone.

WHAT WILL I NEED?

- A cassette recorder with a microphone
- A worksheet with pictures of the sounds recorded on the tape

HOW TO GET STARTED.

Ask the children to close their eyes, keep very quiet, and think of the sounds they hear as they sit in the classroom. This will develop an initial awareness that there are many sounds around that we don't always pay attention to. Take a walk through the school and the immediate neighborhood. With a portable tape recorder, make a tape of some of the sounds heard during this walk. Once back in the classroom, play the tape back and have the children identify the sounds recorded.

Make another tape of familiar sounds heard at school and at home. Some common examples include: water running, a door bell, a piano, a bouncing ball, a vacuum cleaner, children playing, a pencil dropped, and someone typing, cutting with a scissors, and stapling. Explain to the youngsters that they will be identifying sounds that have been previously recorded on a tape recorder. Play the tape and stop after each sound is heard. Ask the children to think about and then identify the object making the sound.

Next, make a tape recording of the following specific sounds: a ball bouncing, water running from a faucet, a pencil dropped on a table, a stapler working, and a door being opened and closed. Use the "Sounds We Hear" worksheet for the children. As they listen to the tape recording, ask the children to draw a circle around the picture of the objects which make the sounds they hear. When the tape is finished and the children have marked their papers, rewind the tape and play it again. Talk about the various sounds heard. How many of the children identified the sounds?

HOW TO GO FURTHER.

Show a few children how to operate a portable cassette recorder. Give two children the tape recorder and let them go around the school to record some of the sounds they hear. (It may be necessary to ask an older child or school aide to accompany the children on this independent walk.) When the children return to the classroom, let them play the tape for the others. Can they guess the sounds that were recorded?

Name _____

SOUNDS WE HEAR

Each time you hear a sound on the tape recorder, draw a circle around the object you hear.

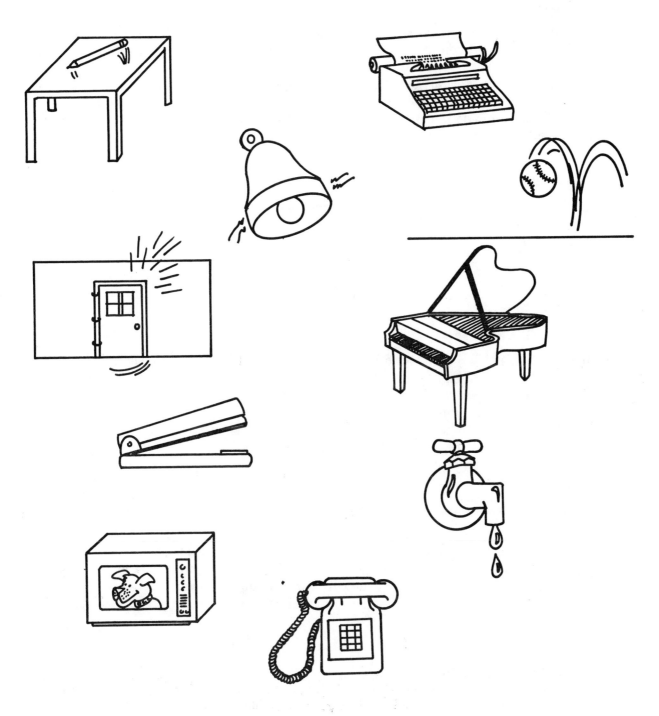

SOUNDS COMMUNICATE

WHY DO THIS?

As children begin to listen carefully to sounds in their environment, they come to understand that sounds communicate important information. The bell that rings in a school to announce a fire drill, the chiming of a clock, the ringing of a telephone, all signal a different, specific message. Through a growing awareness of what sounds tell us, and the activities at school which reinforce this information, children will become more attentive to the importance of sounds for not only communicating danger and alarm, but also for evoking a spectrum of emotions.

WHAT WILL I NEED?

- Magazines with pictures
- Construction paper
- Glue or paste
- Markers
- Scissors

HOW TO GET STARTED.

Discuss the importance of sound in terms of communicating information. What does a siren tell us? What signals do we hear at school that let us know an activity is about to begin or end? What sounds tell us that an ice cream vendor is near? Does your community have a siren blast at twelve noon?

Give each child a large sheet of construction paper. With a marker write "Sounds We Hear" on top of the paper. Allow the children time to thumb through magazines looking for pictures of objects that make definite sounds. Have them cut out the pictures and paste them onto the sheet of paper. Some children will find objects that others may have missed. Typewriters make sounds, cameras make sounds, as do cars, animals, and vacuum cleaners. Who can find ten pictures of objects that make sounds? Discuss the pictures the children selected. In some cases you may want to talk about whether or not the object makes a sound continuously or makes a sound only when it is switched on, as a radio. Ask the children to imitate the sounds made by the objects they put on their papers. Language development should be encouraged as children are asked to describe the objects they found and identify the part or parts that generate sound.

HOW TO GO FURTHER.

Sounds make us feel a certain way. What are some of the sounds that the children like? Do they like the sound of rain on a window, a tea kettle whistling, birds singing, or music on a radio? What sounds are unpleasant? Some children like the sound of wind rustling through trees; others do not. What sounds are associated with danger? Ask the children to dictate a list of the ways in which sounds affect their lives each day.

RECOGNIZING VOICES

WHY DO THIS?

As children become more skillful at identifying sounds in the environment, they can begin to make more careful discriminations by recognizing specific voices. Matching the names of classmates with the sound of their voices can help to build a sense of community among the members of a class. Children will have to focus their attention to identify their friends by the sound of their voices alone. Aside from this, the activity is just plain fun!

WHAT WILL I NEED?

- A portable cassette recorder with a microphone

HOW TO GET STARTED.

Gather a group of children in a cluster on the floor. Ask one child to stand up next to you. The child should then shut his or her eyes while you point to another child in the group who then recites a brief, specified phrase, for example, "The cow jumped over the moon." Ask the child standing at your side to guess the name the child who was speaking. What clues do we use to identify voices?

When all of the children are busily engaged at activity centers, call the youngsters in the class over, one by one and have them repeat a simple phrase into a tape recorder. A few days later, play back the tape. Ask the children to identify the name of the person whose voice is heard after each segment is played.

Once this activity is completed with the children in the class, take the tape recorder to other school personnel with whom the children have contact—the principal, school secretary, nurse, custodian, music teacher, librarian, and so forth. Record their voices. Play the tape back in the classroom and have the children name the people whose voices they hear.

HOW TO GO FURTHER.

To combine recognizing children's art work and the sound of their voices, first have each child draw a self portrait. The children should print their names at the bottom of their portraits. Have the children look at each other's portraits and try to identify one another's pictures. (Children will recognize their classmates' portraits not so much by the actual likeness, but rather by the style of drawing and the printed names.) Spread out the self-portraits on the floor so they are all within view. Then using a tape on which each class member states his or her favorite food, call upon individual children to point to the appropriate portrait as they hear the child's voice on the tape recorder. Try other variations of this game. Ask the children to make up their own activities and games using tape recorded voices.

TAPE-RECORDED STORIES

WHY DO THIS?

In building children's literacy we should provide many opportunities for them to enjoy good literature. Sharing stories as a whole class is an invaluable way to promote literacy. But, there are also times when youngsters want to hear a story and the teacher or other children may not be available to read to them. Tape recording a few storybooks will allow an individual child to enjoy a book during activity time without the necessity of waiting for someone to read to him or her. As children hear stories read on a tape and follow along in a copy of the book, they will recognize words and phrases, interpret pictures, and build some of the essential skills and attitudes that form the basis for beginning reading.

WHAT WILL I NEED?

- A few good storybooks
- A tape recorder with microphone
- Blank tapes
- A small bell or other sound device
- Headphones

HOW TO GET STARTED.

Conduct a poll, or in some other way, obtain children's opinions about the two or three favorite books they like to hear over and over again. Read the story into a tape recorder indicating first the page on which the child listening to the story should begin. (The title page can usually be identified by a picture, a large colored dot sticker placed on the page, or some other technique.) Ring a bell or make some other appropriate sound each time you turn a page. You may want to ask thought-provoking questions about what the listener thinks might follow in the story or questions about a picture in the story. Make one tape for each story that you record and label each tape with the title and, if possible, a picture identifying the book.

Make sure that the children know how to operate the tape recorder. Show them where the tape recorder, the tapes, and books are kept and the proper procedure for listening to tapes, following along in the books, and rewinding tapes. Explain the signal for turning pages. Show how to match books and tapes to make sure the children get the corresponding tape and book. Perhaps the school librarian would be willing to record a few stories for the classroom listening center.

HOW TO GO FURTHER.

Some children may wish to tell their own stories into the tape recorder for others to hear. Using the tape recorder might be a motivating factor for youngsters to become involved in this activity.

If recording a new book for the children, you might be able to stop reading at a particular point in the story, ask the child to close the book, and think about how it will end. For children who are quite adept at operating the tape recorder, they can even record their own ending, then as others listen to the tape, they will hear the proposed endings of their classmates. Then, as a group activity, the various conclusions can be discussed and compared with the author's ending.

LISTENING TO AND FOLLOWING DIRECTIONS

WHY DO THIS?

Five-year-olds can begin to follow fairly complex commands. In the preschool years, children are usually able to follow a simple verbal direction, for example, "Stand up and sit down." As children mature, such commands and instructions can become increasingly involved and children can make a game of seeing how well they can follow verbal directions. With a defined set of materials and tape recorded instructions, children can practice or play a following directions game in the listening center. Such activity can help to sharpen listening skills, stretch the youngsters' ability to focus, and foster vocabulary development.

WHAT WILL I NEED?

- Blocks of different colors and shapes
- A cassette tape recorder with a microphone
- Headphones
- Other simple objects as required

HOW TO GET STARTED.

Assemble a set of simple materials. Begin with a dozen or so small blocks of different shapes, sizes, and colors. Plan out a few multi-stage commands to be recorded on tape. For example, "Take the small red square block. Put it on top of the book. Place the orange triangle block on top of the small red square. Put a pencil behind the book." Use other such simple commands. Identify each tape recorded sequence with a preliminary statement such as, "This is Level One." After preparing a few such sets of commands, put the materials for each level in a separate box or bin labeled appropriately. Make sure the children know how to operate the tape recorder. Introduce the activity as a game. In order to check task completion, ask the child performing the operations to call you over, or ask another youngster to listen to the tape and see if the arrangement of objects is correct. If the children do not agree, they should talk about what they think is different. Usually, through such discussion they will arrive at the solution.

HOW TO GO FURTHER.

The directions on the tape recorder do not have to involve materials at a table. Particularly if using a battery-operated tape recorder and a headset, instructions can require movement about the room, for example, "Go over to classroom door, open it, close it, walk over to the window, wait until you see three cars pass, write your name on a sheet of paper and then give the tape recorder back to your teacher."

As children become more involved in such activities, they may record instructions for each other to follow. They may need some help to do this, but the actions and directions they create are likely to be quite interesting.

MYSTERY BOXES

WHY DO THIS?

Mystery boxes are sealed containers with an object (or objects) placed inside. In order to guess what is inside of the container, the children have to focus on the sound made by the object as they shake the container. This activity is perceived as a game by the children, and they will undoubtedly enjoy their involvement. At the same time, though, perceptual skills will be sharpened and listening skills are promoted.

WHAT WILL I NEED?

- Cardboard boxes of different sizes and shapes
- Assorted objects to place inside of the boxes
- Adhesive or package sealing tape

HOW TO GET STARTED.

Obtain a few boxes no larger than a shoebox. (The boxes that bank checks come in are ideal.) Place a common object in each of the boxes. Some examples are a pencil, a rubber ball, lima beans, rice, pennies, a small bell, a wooden block, and a marble. Seal the box with tape. You may wish to cover the box with giftwrap or paper with question marks drawn all over it. Make a variety of boxes each with a different kind of item, for example, metallic, rubbery, wooden, and plastic. Put the boxes out in the listening center. First allow the children to shake the boxes and guess the contents. After a while, demonstrate specific strategies. For example, gentle movements will tell more about an object than rough shaking. Let the object slide one way and then another way inside the box. A pencil, which is basically cylindrical, will slide in one direction, but roll as the box is moved in the other direction. (You might explain that blind people identify objects this way. Also, we sometimes have to figure out the identity of an object without actually seeing it.) After all, scientists described the structure of an atom, but no one has ever actually seen one!

HOW TO GO FURTHER.

As a real challenge, cut a section of an egg carton to fit into the bottom of a mystery box and glue it in. Put a ping-pong ball into the box. Seal it. As children explore this mystery box, they will find that the sounds are not the same on all sides. What might account for this? After a few days, open the box and ask the children if seeing the contents of the box can account for their observations.

Place a steel object in a box and provide a magnet for children to use as they explore. Does this give them any hints as to what is inside of the box?

LISTENING TO EACH OTHER

WHY DO THIS?

Children can play a listening game by duplicating actions dictated by one another. If one child gives instructions to a friend for making a design or completing a certain sequence and then the two compare their productions, they gain a sense of how well they listened. This activity promotes listening skills by making a game of following verbal directions.

WHAT WILL I NEED?

- A set of small building blocks
- Paper
- Markers

HOW TO GET STARTED.

Explain to the children that they are going to play a listening game. Ask two youngsters to demonstrate. The two children sit back-to-back at adjoining tables so one cannot see what the other is doing. Both children have identical sets of small building blocks. (Ten blocks each is enough.) One child goes first and tells the other what he or she is doing with the blocks. For example, "I put the red block down on my table. Then I put the smallest blue block on top of the red block. I put a yellow triangle block on top of the red block." The child who is listening to the instructions should try to duplicate each of the actions described by the first child. After a while, the two children should turn around, compare their structures, and talk about how well the directions were followed. Then the children change roles, and the one who was listening to the instructions should now give them.

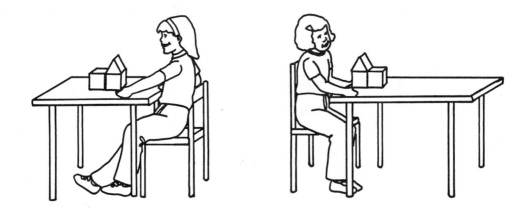

HOW TO GO FURTHER.

There are many variations of the game described above. Two children can each be given a piece of paper with a red circle drawn on it. Then one child can tell ways to mark the paper. "Draw a blue line under the bottom of the circle. Make a green square in the middle of the circle." Since drawing shapes and lines will be somewhat subjective, the children can talk about how similar or different their drawings are as compared to how much they are alike when they use a set of identical materials like building blocks.

THE OLD GAME OF "TELEPHONE"

WHY DO THIS?

The game of "telephone" has been enjoyed by schoolchildren for years. As youngsters sit in a circle, one child initiates a message which is whispered from child to child.

After the message reaches the last child, it is repeated out loud and compared with the phrase that started the game. Through involvement in this game, children realize that speaking in a clear, but very soft, voice is the best way to pass the message.

WHAT WILL I NEED?

No special materials for the basic activity

HOW TO GET STARTED.

Have the children sit in a circle. Explain the basic rules of the game of "telephone." Impress upon the children that they should whisper so that the others cannot hear the message. Begin with a simple phrase or a familiar rhyme. After the youngsters have played the game a few times, work up to more involved messages. Discuss with the children how messages are heard best. What happens if only five children play? What happens if twenty-five children play? What accounts for the difference?

Discuss telephone manners when using a real telephone. How do children answer the phone at home? Some parents let five-year-olds answer the phone; others do not. Some children answer by asking, "Hello, who's speaking please?" Why is this a good idea? Role-play how to take telephone messages from callers.

HOW TO GO FURTHER.

Make a string telephone using two small frozen orange juice cans. Remove one end of each can. Punch a hole (with a nail or an awl) into the center of the intact end. Obtain a piece of string about 8 feet long. Make a few knots in one end of the string. Pull the free end of the string through the open part of a can (from the inside to the outside) and through the hole. Then pull the free end through the outside of the hole in the other can. Pull the string through a little more. Knot the other end. The telephone should look like the one shown in the illustration.

Two children can play with this telephone. One child puts one end of the phone to his or her ear. The other child talks into the open end of the other can. The string must be pulled taut in order for this telephone to work.

LISTENING AND MOVING

WHY DO THIS?

One way to promote good listening skills is to make a game of children attending to statements that require certain responses—"Raise your hand if you're wearing blue today. If you walked to school today, please stand up now." By focusing on the teacher's statements, and then responding with a specific movement, the children have a *purpose* for listening.

WHAT WILL I NEED?

No specific materials are required for this activity.

HOW TO GET STARTED.

Have the children sit in a circle. Explain that they will be playing a listening game. Prepare a variety of questions which require that children attend and then respond in a specific way. Some examples include:

> If you're wearing anything with red in it, please stand.
> If you have brown hair, clap your hands.
> If you have more than one sister, tap your shoulders.
> If you are wearing a sweater, slap your knees.
> If your socks are white, blink your eyes.
> If you are wearing a sweatshirt today, touch your ankles.

The youngsters' listening skills can be checked by simply looking around the room and seeing how they respond. By involving body parts in the game, children can also broaden their vocabulary at the same time.

Appoint a leader to ask questions and give the commands. Aim for a wide variety of questions and interesting actions to perform.

HOW TO GO FURTHER.

As children become skillful at playing this game, give more involved instructions. For example, "If you're wearing something of a color that rhymes with screen (green), tap your head. If you brought something to school today that rhymes with punch (lunch), raise your hand." It's fun to see how involved the actions can become. Make the activity more and more of a challenge to see how complex the questions and commands can get.

"I WENT TO THE STORE AND I BOUGHT . . ."

WHY DO THIS?

A game that has been enjoyed by countless youngsters called, for lack of a better name, "I Went to the Store and I Bought . . ." requires careful listening and a good memory. This is a cumulative game, since when each child has her turn, she must remember items which were mentioned by those who came before. The more children involved in the game, the harder the task becomes for the children who have to remember a long string of items mentioned by others.

WHAT WILL I NEED?

No special material are required for this activity; however, some teachers like to incorporate pictures of various foods mounted on construction paper or oaktag.

HOW TO GET STARTED.

Have the children sit in a circle. Select one child to begin the game. This individual starts by saying, "I went to the store and I bought . . . carrots." (Any item that can be purchased in a store may be used.) The next child in the circle says, "I went to the store and I bought carrots and macaroni." Each child, in turn, tries to remember the items (in order) mentioned by those who came before and then adds his own item. The accuracy of the child who is trying to recall the list of items can be checked by the others in the group. Of course, the greater the number of children involved in the game, the harder it becomes. For this reason, you may wish to break the class into a few small groups so that the children can practice the basic rules and experience success.

An easier version of the game can be developed by supplying each child with a mounted picture of a food item (or anything else which can be purchased in a store). Then as each youngster has his turn, he mentions the item on his card and then turns the card face down on the floor. The next child tries to remember the items mentioned before, but if she cannot, she can ask to see a card held up previously. A limit on the number of cards requested can be set. In this way, more children will have successful experiences and at the same time, the children will have practice in naming foods.

HOW TO GO FURTHER.

Discuss strategies with children that can help them to remember more easily. Pictures certainly help. Another way is to ask children to relate their items to one another. For example, if the first child says "spaghetti," the next one can say "meatballs." See how many associations the children can make. Why does this make remembering easier?

LISTENING FOR A PURPOSE

WHY DO THIS?

In the listening center a radio can be used for many individual and small group activities. Children can be asked to listen for a specific purpose, for example, the time, the weather, or a commercial for a bank. When given a special assignment, children are likely to listen carefully and respond when their mission is complete.

WHAT WILL I NEED?

- A radio — one with a headphone is especially helpful

HOW TO GET STARTED.

Ask the children to talk about when they listen to a radio. Most will probably refer to a car radio, a kitchen radio, a stereo or rack system in a living room or den, or a personal-type radio. Discuss the source of radio sound. (Children may never have thought of the fact that the broadcast comes from a studio in a nearby city.) Ask the children to talk about what they listen to on a radio. Have they ever heard music programs, news, or talk shows?

Introduce a radio into the listening center. One with a headset is best, since listening children will not disturb others. (Radios should be very easy to obtain; many households have extra ones which can be borrowed.) Explain to the children that they will be asked to listen for a specific purpose. Begin with the whole class. Tune in to an all-day news show. Tell the children they will listen until they hear the time announced. As soon as someone hears the announcer give the time, he or she should raise a hand and when called upon, repeat what was heard. When listening for a specific purpose, children are likely to attend carefully.

Make up a few task cards each with a different thing to listen for (see next page). Read the cards to the children. A pictorial symbol on each card can aid the children in remembering what is asked for. Tune in an appropriate station so that the youngsters will have a good chance of hearing what is requested on the task cards. Children may want to do this in pairs.

HOW TO GO FURTHER.

One child can listen to a radio and then tell another what he or she has just heard. Youngsters may want to pretend to be a disk jockey and play records or tapes providing their own introductions. Children can ask each other to listen for a specific purpose and then discuss what they have heard.

One day, for homework, ask the children to listen to a news show and report on something that they understood. When given a specific purpose for listening, children are likely to "tune in" to what may have simply been considered background noise.

RADIO LISTENING CARD

Listen for a song you know. ♫♪ ♫♪

RADIO LISTENING CARD

Listen for the temperature. Write the number you hear. _____

RADIO LISTENING CARD

Listen for a weather report. What will it be like tomorrow?

RADIO LISTENING CARD

Listen for a commercial. What was it for? _____

RADIO LISTENING CARD

Listen for a woman's voice.

RADIO LISTENING CARD

Listen for the sound of a drum

RADIO LISTENING CARD

Listen for the time of day.

chapter 7

IN THE MATHEMATICS CENTER

The mathematics center is the place where children will have many opportunities to explore size, shape, number, and position of objects. In this very important area of classroom activity, youngsters discover, through exploration with real objects, relationships that form the basis for number sense and other mathematical learnings. When infants first realize that certain objects in the environment reoccur and are permanent, they begin to make order out of their world. Later, through daily activities preschoolers see that multiple objects can be represented by a number. As they go shopping with parents in a supermarket, they observe the exchange of money for objects. Long before they enter school, children have had a great deal of experience with numerical relationships and mathematics. They see numbers all around them. In the kindergarten classroom children can build upon this knowledge in a way that is just as natural for them as their everyday preschool encounters.

Through the manipulation of concrete objects, children will naturally count, group, and otherwise make order out of the materials they work with. Much of the mathematics learning in kindergarten will be spontaneous and stem from children's need to solve problems as they play. For example, if a child uses six blocks for the height of one wall of a house being built and an adjacent wall is added, it too will have to be six blocks high. If all of the available blocks of the largest size are used up, how many smaller ones are needed to cover the same area as the larger block? Certainly there are also concepts that teachers will want to convey in a somewhat formal, directed manner. Some of the major areas usually included in a kindergarten math program include understanding the value of numbers (or number concepts); comparing sizes, shapes and areas; forming and combining sets of objects; practicing one-to-one correspondence; using a balance to compare the weight of objects; and using clocks, calendars, and money. All of these important aspects of the math program can be conveyed with objects children encounter in their everyday lives. In mathematics activities, the goal is not to have children memorize mechanical computations, but rather to explore relationships, look for patterns, form generalizations, and attach meaning to symbols.

The mathematics center should be a table, or tables, with a great variety of materials readily accessible for children's exploration. Included among the objects in a math center should be containers of all sizes, sticks, buttons, counters, a balance, rulers, a measuring tape, and self-correcting games. As children have more and more opportunities to manipulate these objects, they will more than likely move from the concrete to the more abstract as they discover mathematical relationships on their own.

This chapter is divided into four separate sections to represent major themes in kindergarten mathematics: "Discovering Number Concepts," "Comparing and Measuring," "Shapes and Geometry," and "Sequence and Position." These distinctions are used to organize the activities that follow, but no sequence of instruction is implied. In reality, children will be working in several of these areas simultaneously. With a wealth of materials and multiple opportunities for children to explore materials in the math center, they will discover many fundamental relationships on their own and relate their learnings to other areas of the classroom.

Discovering Number Concepts

Children begin to understand number concepts when they count. As they count objects, they learn that each additional object represents a higher number. Before this concept is established, children may count out of sequence, or skip objects or numbers as they count. Once children recognize that each object is a unit and has a single identity, they can begin to form sets of objects and later, combine sets.

BOUNCE AND COUNT

WHY DO THIS?

Early in kindergarten children need to understand the concept of counting, that is, one object for each successive number. A good way to begin counting is with a large playground ball, counting numbers in succession for each bounce of the ball. Also, children need to know that the last number counted is the total number of bounces. Once this skill is firm, other math activities become possible; but simple counting is a fundamental operation.

WHAT WILL I NEED?

- A large playground ball

HOW TO GET STARTED.

Ask the children to sit in a circle. Count the number of children in the class. Then, begin by bouncing a ball and counting each time the ball hits the floor. Count up to twenty. Then have children count in unison as you bounce the ball. Stop at a certain number and ask the children how many bounces were made. (Knowing that the last number counted is the total number of bounces is not an easy concept for young children.)

Give the ball to a child. Ask him or her to bounce the ball six times while counting. Give all of the children an opportunity to practice, changing the number of bounces. If children have trouble bouncing the ball, stand next to them, bounce for them, and have them count the bounces. With each turn, ask the children to say the number of times the ball was bounced. Reinforce that the last number counted is the total number of bounces.

HOW TO GO FURTHER.

Have the children count other actions and objects. Distribute a set of buttons to each child. The buttons should be counted. If the children work in pairs, have them count each others' buttons as a check. Ask each child to find something to count in the classroom and share the results. Some possible items to count are the numbers of chairs, tables, windows, and lockers.

THROW AND COUNT

WHY DO THIS?

When children begin to count, they often skip numbers. Many experiences have to be provided in which children count up one number for each object. In the previous activity, children counted one number for each bounce of a ball. In this activity, as a set of similar objects is thrown into a container, the children will count in succession for each object thrown. It is yet another reinforcement of the counting operation.

WHAT WILL I NEED?

- An aluminum pie tin
- Fifty or so pennies, washers, buttons, chips, or other convenient objects to count

HOW TO GET STARTED.

Begin with about eight or ten pennies. Throw them one by one into a pie tin at close range so that getting them into the tin does not present a challenge. Count in succession as each penny is thrown into the tin. Have the children count along with you. Then, providing a turn for each child, give a child a set of pennies and have him or her throw them into the tin while the others count out loud. The number of pennies can be increased as the children become more and more successful in counting one number for each penny thrown. At the end of each child's turn, ask how many pennies were thrown. (Again, this reinforces the concept that the last number counted is the

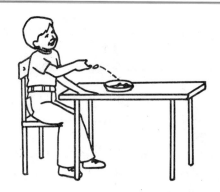

total number of objects.) Use different objects with the same game, like metal washers, buttons, chips, or paper clips.

HOW TO GO FURTHER.

Make the game a bit more challenging by placing the pie tin further away so that not all of the pennies (or other objects) are likely to land in the tin. (This will be like an amusement park game.) Then, as the game is played, ask the child to tell how many pennies landed in the tin and then count the number of pennies that fell outside of it. Some youngsters may be able to combine the total number of pennies, both within and without the pie tin, to tell how many pennies they started with in the beginning.

NUMBER PUZZLE PIECES

WHY DO THIS?

Many activities and devices can be used to help children associate a set of objects with the corresponding numeral. Children should encounter this matching process in a variety of experiences. One way to help children as they develop a number sense is to make simple, self-correcting materials. Such materials allow children to explore, try different possibilities, but by performing a simpler task (in this case fitting together two easy pieces of a puzzle) the concept is demonstrated. In this activity, children play with pairs of cards that can be joined in just one way. When the cards are placed together, the number/numeral match is shown.

WHAT WILL I NEED?

- Cardboard or oaktag
- Markers
- Scissors

HOW TO GET STARTED.

Cut out ten 5-by-8-inch pieces of cardboard or oaktag. (Index cards are not stiff enough.) Draw a squiggly line which approximately divides the card in half. (See the illustrations.) On the top half of each card draw a numeral. On the bottom half of the card, draw a set of dots, circles, or some other shape which corresponds to the number written above. Make cards from one to ten. Cut the cards along the wavy lines.

Show the children how to play the game. Mix up all the cards. Ask them first to place the cards together by matching the number of dots with the correct numeral. Then, they should check by seeing if the two pieces of the puzzle fit together. If they do, then the number match was right!

HOW TO GO FURTHER.

Give the children blank 5-by-8-inch cardboard cards and ask them to make their own set of puzzle pieces. Pictures cut from magazines can be pasted onto one part of the card and the numeral written on the other. The youngsters will enjoy making cards for each other and giving each other a challenge.

Letter cards can be similarly made, with a letter written on one half of the card and a picture of an object which starts with that letter on the other half.

FISHING FOR NUMBERS

WHY DO THIS?

In kindergarten a wide variety of activities can involve children in matching the number of objects to a written numeral. Practice in this skill can be provided through stimulating games. In the following activity, children try to "catch fish," each of which bears a set of dots. Then the child tries to match the fish with the corresponding numeral card. Even though the basic objective of this activity is repeated in other experiences outlined in this book, continual practice in this basic operation is important kindergarten work.

WHAT WILL I NEED?

- A "fishing pole" made from a thin wooden dowel or a twig about one yard in length
- A piece of string about one yard long
- A magnet
- Construction paper

- Ten index cards
- Paper clips
- Markers

HOW TO GET STARTED.

Make a "fishing pole" out of a twig or dowel. Attach one end of a string to the tip of the twig or stick, and a magnet to the other end of the string. Cut ten fish out of construction paper. With a marker, make a set of large dots on both sides of the body of each fish until the sets one through ten are represented. Place a paper clip near the mouth of each fish. On each index card, write a numeral from one to ten.

Show the children how to fish for numbers. Establish a sequence for taking turns. When a fish is caught, the child takes the fish and matches it up with one of the index cards on which the corresponding numeral is written. Children can check each other's matching or call the teacher over to check after all of the fish have been caught. To make the game a bit more fanciful, cut out a free-form "pond" from a few large sheets of blue paper taped together. The fish are then placed in the pond at the beginning of the game.

HOW TO GO FURTHER.

As children become more and more successful at matching the number of dots to the correct numeral, a more challenging version of the game can be played, in which a child must catch two fish and then match the *total* number of dots (on both fish) to a card which has the number which represents the sum of the two sets of dots. (Numbered cards up to 20 will have to be made for this variation.)

Using a "fishing pole" with a magnet attached and paper clips on items to fish for can be the basic structure for many kindergarten games. Ask the children to invent a game which uses a fishing pole and paper clips.

MAKING MATCHING SETS

WHY DO THIS?

As children develop a sense of a set of objects, they can match sets of dissimilar objects if the number of objects in each set is the same. This is best done with concrete materials before any such activities are done with worksheets. In this activity, children make their own sets of objects to match sets of a specified number. Through such experiences, youngsters will come to realize that the number of objects in a set of a specified size does not change depending upon the types or kinds of objects in the set. As adults we may take this for granted, but for five-year-olds, this is a fundamental learning.

WHAT WILL I NEED?

- Lumps of modeling clay
- Drinking straws, small wooden sticks, or golf tees
- Index cards
- Markers

HOW TO GET STARTED.

On each of ten index cards, write a different numeral (from one to ten) on one side. On the other side, draw the corresponding number of dots. Cut drinking straws into sections about two inches long. (If golf tees or small wooden sticks are available, use these instead.) Have the children form flat lumps of clay around three to four inches in diameter. Place one of the cards (numeral side up) in front of a child, and then have him or her place straws, sticks, or golf tees into a lump of clay to match the numeral on the card. As a check, the child turns the card over and matches each dot for each stick or straw.

HOW TO GO FURTHER.

Have the children make "number paintings." At an easel, write a numeral at the top of the paper. The child then paints the number of objects which corresponds with the numeral. After many paintings representing several numbers have been completed, post them around the classroom. "Number collages" can also be made. Ask the children to paste pictures cut from magazines or catalogs onto sheets of paper with a numeral drawn at the top. The number of objects pasted onto the paper should correspond with the numeral drawn at the top.

RING AROUND A SET

WHY DO THIS?

An activity which will help children to identify sets is to have them draw a ring around a specified number of objects. In this experience, the youngsters look at a numeral, count the number of objects that corresponds with it and then draw a ring around the appropriate number of objects. This experience provides practice in counting, numeral identification, set identification, and small motor coordination.

WHAT WILL I NEED?

- A collection of similar objects to count (pennies, chips, buttons, and so forth)
- Markers
- Yarn
- Chalkboard or chart paper
- "Ring Around A Set" Worksheet
- Pencils or crayons

HOW TO GET STARTED.

Ask the children to sit in a circle. Place a collection of similar objects (about ten) in the center of the circle. Draw a numeral on a sheet of paper. Ask for a volunteer to take the yarn and place it around the number of objects shown on the card. Try this with other numerals and call upon several children to have a turn. Next, moving from the concrete towards the abstract, draw a group of similar objects on a chalkboard or chart paper. Write a numeral next to the objects and ask a youngster to come up and draw a ring around the number of objects that corresponds to the numeral. Try a few different examples. Write the numeral that is exactly the same as the number of objects. Then write a numeral that is more than the number of objects available and check to see the children's response. Finally, have the children complete the "Ring Around a Set" worksheet. Ask the children to compare their papers and check each other's work.

HOW TO GO FURTHER.

Make collections of objects available for the children. Ask small groups of children to work together. One child sets up the objects in any arbitrary pattern on the floor or work table. Another child makes a numeral on a large index card. A third youngster takes the yarn and makes a ring around the number of objects indicated by the written numeral.

RING AROUND A SET

Draw a ring around the number of objects indicated by the numeral.

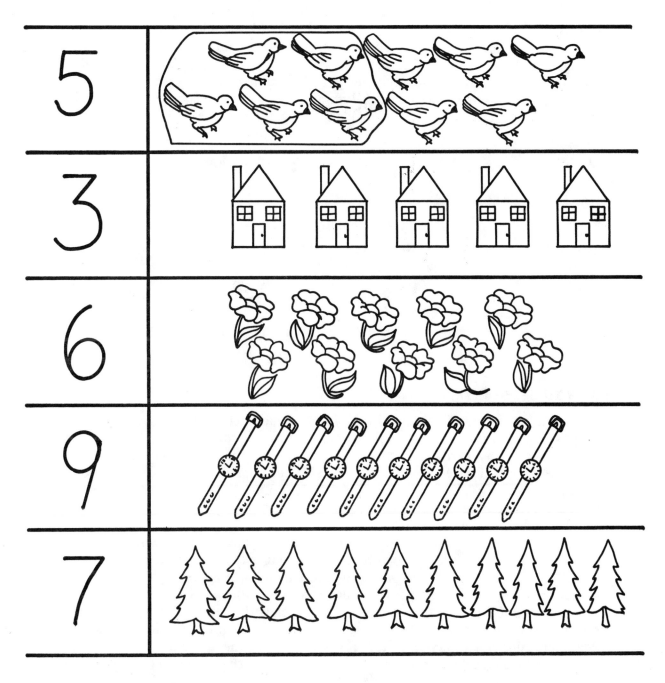

DELIVERING MAIL

WHY DO THIS?

Kindergarten teachers provide many activities for children to match numerals with sets of objects. A new twist to a familiar activity will add additional motivation and practice as children continue their explorations with numbers. In this experience youngsters pretend to deliver mail to houses which have a pattern of objects as their "addresses." Then they deliver envelopes with numerals on them to the houses according to the match of number and numeral. The work is checked by opening the envelopes and seeing if the "letter" inside matches the number of objects shown on the house.

WHAT WILL I NEED?

- Ten sheets of oaktag
- Markers
- Plain envelopes
- Index cards
- Paper bag
- A strip of brown construction paper

HOW TO GET STARTED.

Make ten houses out of oaktag. On the front of each house, draw a group of similar objects (dots, trees, birds, or cars, for example) from one to ten. Duplicate the patterns developed on index cards and put them aside. Staple the houses on a bulletin board within the reach of the children. Below each house, staple a folded-over piece of oaktag or paper to serve as the "mailbox." Next, write a numeral on the envelopes from one to ten. Place the index cards with the patterns inside of the envelopes which bear the number indicating the set of objects.

After the houses and mailboxes are displayed, place all of the envelopes into a paper bag. Staple a strip of brown construction paper to the sides of the bag to make a mailbag. Have the children gather around the bulletin board with the houses and explain that each letter carrier will reach into the mailbag, look through the letters, and deliver a letter with the numeral that matches the number of objects drawn on the house. When several children have had a turn and all of the letters have been delivered, open the letters and check if the pattern on the house matches the pattern on the card inside of the envelope. Children can count the number of objects out loud for further reinforcement.

HOW TO GO FURTHER.

Youngsters can make their own mailboxes by using a shoebox with construction paper arched over it. This results in a realistic effect. The children can place a number on their mailboxes as well as some distinctive design or pattern that will help to remind others in the class of who it belongs to. Set up all of the mailboxes on a ledge or counter. Then make a directory in which the mailbox number is listed with the name of the child it belongs to. Children can then draw pictures, send messages, or write letters to one another and deliver them to their mailboxes. Each day, the children check their boxes for mail and respond in kind.

WALK-ON NUMBER LINE

WHY DO THIS?

As children explore the relationships among numbers, they can actually see and experience the sequence of numbers by stepping on a large, walk-on number line. Using a number line, many activities can be devised to reinforce counting and sequencing and to develop concepts of the "distance" between numbers. Walking or moving as they count is an aid to learning for young children. This is a kinesthetic approach, that is, it incorporates bodily position, sensations, and movement into learning.

WHAT WILL I NEED?

- Eleven sheets of oaktag
- Masking tape, 1 or 2 inches wide

HOW TO GET STARTED.

Write a different numeral, from 0 to 10, on individual sheets of oaktag. On each sheet also place the number of dots corresponding to the numeral. Find an open floor area in the classroom. Place the number cards on the floor with an approximately 2-foot interval between each card. Next, tape all around each card to fix it to the floor, and make a line with tape between each number card. Now you are ready to begin. Start with a counting activity. Ask children to remove their shoes, and one by one count as they step on each card starting at 0 and finishing at 10. Vary the activity by asking a child to start at 4 and go on to 10. Ask a child to start at 10 and then go backwards down to 0. (Undoubtedly, the children will be familiar with a countdown.) Have some children "skip-count" by twos as they move on the number line and count out loud.

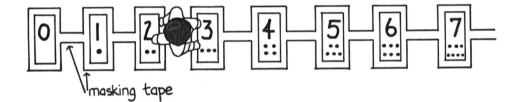

Once children are familiar with their movements along a number line, some simple addition and subtraction can be introduced. Have one child start at zero. Ask her to move up three steps on the number line and count as she goes. Then, ask her to move backwards one step. Where did she wind up? Give all of the children a turn to move up and down the number line by adding and subtracting numbers. Each time ask them how many steps they went forward and how many steps back.

HOW TO GO FURTHER.

Some children will be able to solve real addition and subtraction problems using the number line. Make a set of number cards. Also make separate cards, one with a plus sign (+), one with a minus sign (−), and one with an equal sign (=). Explain the names of the signs. Hold up a card with the numeral 4 on it. Tell a child to move forward four steps, that is from 0 to 4. Then, "add" two steps. Show the card with the plus sign and then a card with a 2 on it. Where did the child wind up? Ask a child to find a number card to match the position where the child is on the number line. With number cards show how the moves can be represented by a simple equation, 4 + 2 = 6. Then, ask another child to start on 0. Show the card with a 5 on it. Ask him to move up five steps. Then, show the minus sign. Explain that in this case it means "move back." Then, show the numeral 2. If a minus sign is shown before a number, the child moves back along the number line. Show how the cards can form a simple equation, 5 − 2 = 3. Children can show each other cards and ask their friends to move up and down the line depending on how the cards are combined.

NUMBER BOXES

WHY DO THIS?

Children reinforce number concepts by engaging in a variety of experiences with concrete objects. In this activity, youngsters place a specified number of objects into boxes labeled with a specific numeral. Once several sets of different objects have been put into the boxes, the quantities can be checked by one-to-one matching.

WHAT WILL I NEED?

- Ten shoeboxes or milk cartons
- Markers
- A wide variety of material objects, some of which are the same, for example, buttons, sea shells, pennies, paper clips, beads, blocks

HOW TO GET STARTED.

On each shoebox or milk carton, write a numeral from 1 to 10. (If milk cartons are used, cut off three sides of the top half, as shown in the illustration.)

Divide the children into groups of two or three and give each group a box (or carton). Gather a variety of objects, some of which are the same. Spread out the objects on a table or on the floor. Tell the children to make collections of different kinds of objects of the number which is shown on their box or carton. For example, if the box has a three on it, then the children collect three buttons, three shells, three pennies, three blocks, and so on. When the children are finished, have them take their objects out of the container and spread them on the floor. They can check for the correct quantities by lining up the objects, in a one-to-one matching. Having children work in groups of two or three enables them to check each other's work.

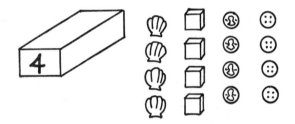

HOW TO GO FURTHER.

Take a "number walk!" Form groups of two or three children. Give each group a paper bag or a box each with a different number printed on it. As the children walk in an outdoor area, ask them to collect groups of similar objects (leaves, acorns, or small stones, for example) that match the number on the bag or box. Once back in the classroom, share the collections.

MAKING NUMBER BOOKS

WHY DO THIS?

As children become more and more comfortable in working with numbers, they can begin to apply their skills to the construction of number books. These are simply, blank pages, each devoted to a separate number on which youngsters glue pictures or draw objects corresponding to the numeral at the top of the page. As children identify pictures from magazines and catalogs, they are using language and learning new terms. As they cut and paste, they are exercising small motor skills, all the while reinforcing number recognition. The finished product will bring a sense of pride, and the children will surely want to share their own books with their classmates and families.

WHAT WILL I NEED?

- Ten sheets of plain paper for each child
- Two sheets of construction paper per child
- Magazines and catalogs
- Scissors and glue
- Markers, crayons, and a stapler

HOW TO GET STARTED.

Explain to the children that they will be making number books over the next few days or weeks. Give each child a piece of construction paper to make a cover. They can draw anything that reminds them of number work. Then provide ten pages for each child, numbered boldly at the top with a separate page for each number from one to ten. Put another sheet of construction paper at the back and staple all of the pages together along the left edge to form a book. In the math center, have catalogs, magazines, markers, crayons, scissors, and glue available for the children to work on their books. Beginning with the page marked with the numeral 1 the children should cut out a picture of one object and paste it on the page. (You may want to include a page for zero, with the numeral written at the top and *nothing* placed on the page.) For the page marked with the numeral 2, the children paste on two pictures of an object, and so on. At each working session, the children can complete another page or two. Once the number books are complete, time should be provided for children to share them in small groups or with the whole class. Then the books can be brought home and read to family members.

HOW TO GO FURTHER.

After the children are finished making their number books, they can review their counting and number identification skills by completing the "How Many?" worksheet.

© 1990 by The Center for Applied Research in Education

Name _____

HOW MANY?

Look at this city street.

Next to each picture write the number that tells how many you can find.

FINDING INCOMPLETE SETS

WHY DO THIS?

Many of the math worksheets that kindergarten children encounter require them to match like quantities, supply a numeral to match a set of objects, or circle a quantity of objects to correspond with a numeral shown. Rarely do children have to supply additional objects to complete a set. For example, if within a box the numeral 3 is written, but only two objects are shown, the child would then have to draw an additional object to make the set complete. This is another way to practice number skills, and the novelty of the activity will interest and challenge the children.

WHAT WILL I NEED?

- Index cards with a different numeral written on each
- A collection of objects: buttons, paper clips, chips, or other counters
- "Is Anything Missing?" worksheet
- Pencils

HOW TO GET STARTED.

Take any numeral card and place it on the floor. Gather a quantity of similar objects and place one or two *less than* the number written on the card on it. Leave a pile of identical objects within easy reach. Ask the children if the number of objects shown is the same, less than, or more than the numeral shown on the card. Invite children to complete the set shown by adding the required number of objects to match the numeral shown. Ask others in the group to check. Try this for a few different numbers. After several children have had a turn, distribute the "Is Anything Missing?" worksheet and ask the children to complete it.

HOW TO GO FURTHER.

Give the children collections of objects and number cards. Have them form incomplete sets for one another and ask them to practice the activity. Another variation is to show a quantity of objects that is *more than* the numeral shown. In this case, the children would take objects away to make the numeral match the number of objects. Worksheets can also be devised in which children have to cross out objects of which there are more than the numeral shown. By working with adding and taking away objects, the children come to realize that addition and subtraction are inverse operations.

Name _____

IS ANYTHING MISSING?

Make sure that the number of circles shown in each box is the same as the numeral shown. If not, draw new circles to make it correct.

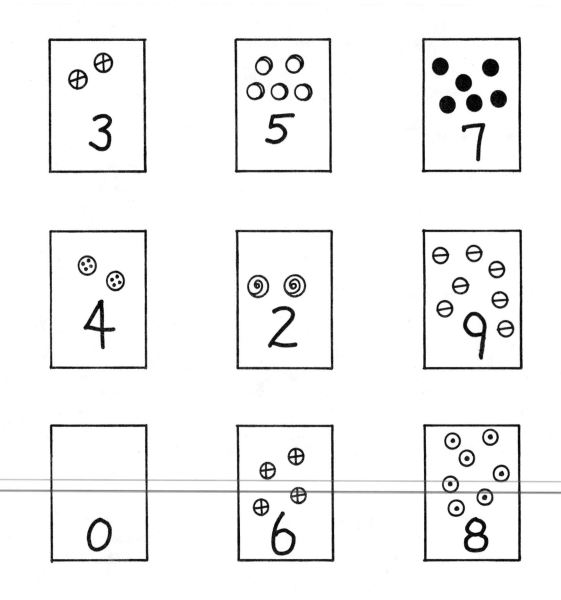

CAN AND STICK MATH

WHY DO THIS?

In the math center, an abundance of materials and simple, self-checking games should be available for children to work with during activity periods. "Can and Stick Math" is a simple number game in which children place sticks into a can which has a numeral on it. Children can check their work by matching the number of sticks in the can with dots printed on the bottom of the can. Not only does this activity provide practice with basic number concepts, but it promotes independence because children can accomplish this activity on their own.

WHAT WILL I NEED?

- Eleven small cans (the size of frozen orange juice cans)
- Self-stick vinyl adhesive paper (or construction paper)
- Markers
- "Ice cream sticks" or tongue depressors

HOW TO GET STARTED.

Obtain ten small cans, the size that frozen orange juice comes in. Select a light color of vinyl adhesive paper. Cover each of the cans with the vinyl adhesive paper. (Regular construction paper can be substituted, but it will not be as durable.) On each can, write a numeral from 0 to 10 with a thick black permanent marker. On the bottom of each can, draw large black dots corresponding to the number printed on the face of the can.

Demonstrate to a group of children how to play this game. Set the cans up in a row. Give a child a bundle of sticks. The child then places the number of sticks in each can indicated by the numeral printed on the front. After all the cans have been filled, the child can check her or his work by turning the can over and comparing the number of sticks with the number of dots printed on the bottom of the can.

HOW TO GO FURTHER.

As a challenge, make cans which show an addition or subtraction equation. For example, print "3 + 2", "6 − 4", or other such combinations on the face of the cans. Place the number of dots representing the solution on the bottom of the can. Then, the children place the correct number of sticks into the can using the plus or minus sign as a cue. If the equation was "3 + 2", the child would first place three sticks in the can, and then two. If the equation read "6 − 4", the child would first place six sticks in the can and then take four away. The solution is checked by turning the can over and comparing the number of sticks placed in the can with the number of dots drawn on the bottom.

WATERMELON SEEDS

WHY DO THIS?

This activity is yet another way to develop and reinforce number concepts. The novelty of placing "seeds" onto cutouts of watermelon slices provides additional motivation. As in most math activities, the children first work with concrete objects and then apply their skills to "paper and pencil" tasks.

WHAT WILL I NEED?

- Eleven sheets of red and light green construction paper
- Oaktag
- Scissors, glue, markers
- Watermelon seeds (optional)
- "Watermelon Seeds" worksheet

HOW TO GET STARTED.

Cut out eleven "watermelon slices." First, make the red "wedges" and then cut out the "rind" from light green paper a little larger than the red pieces. Paste the red paper onto the green so that the result looks like a watermelon slice. On the bottom of the rind, write a number from zero to ten. Next, collect a number of real watermelon seeds, if in season, or make "seeds" by first coloring oaktag black with a marker and then cutting out small seed-shaped pieces.

Introduce the activity by placing the watermelon slices on a table or the floor. Ask the children where the seeds are found in a real slice of watermelon. Have the children come up and put the correct number of seeds in the red part of the watermelon slice.

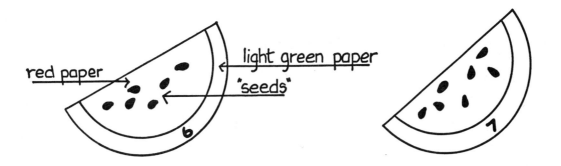

(As a check, the correct number of seeds can be drawn on the back of the watermelon slice and then after the children place the seeds on the melon, they can slide them off and compare the number with the seeds shown on the back.)

Place the watermelon slices and seeds in the math center for continued activity. After a few days have the children complete the "Watermelon Seeds" worksheet.

HOW TO GO FURTHER.

Using this activity as a model, ask the children to suggest a game in which the same type of skill can be practiced. Some possibilities include placing cut out leaves on "trees" which have a number on their trunks, pasting cut out windows on a "house" to match a number printed over the front door, and so on. Once the children are aware of some of the possibilities, they are likely to be able to come up with several activities on their own. In this way individual, creative thinking can be promoted.

WATERMELON SEEDS

Draw the right number of seeds on each slice of watermelon.

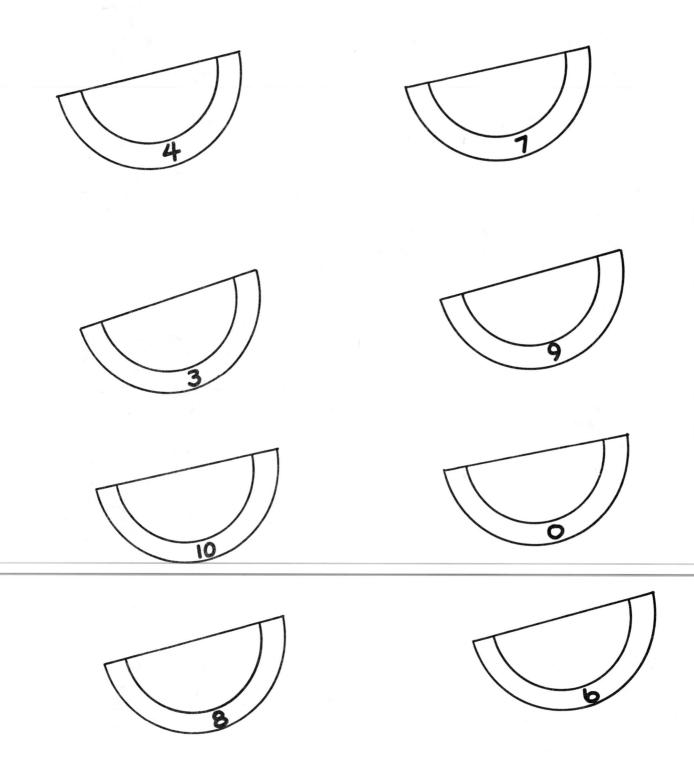

SNACK TIME CORRESPONDENCE AND ESTIMATION

WHY DO THIS?

In most kindergarten classrooms, children have a regularly scheduled snack time. Even if this is not the case, classroom birthday parties or holiday celebrations require that napkins, cups, paper plates, and other utensils be distributed. This is a perfect occasion to teach and reinforce the skills of estimation and one-to-one correspondence. It is always helpful to involve children in the distribution and collection of the necessary items for a class party. As a table is prepared, children learn readily that for each child, they will need one cup, one napkin, one plate, and so on. Also, as they take a sufficient quantity of plates, forks, and napkins from a pile for distribution to the children in the class, they are exercising their estimation skills. Simple, everyday routines can be loaded with important learnings for young children.

WHAT WILL I NEED?

- Paper plates
- Napkins
- Plastic spoons or forks
- Cups

HOW TO GET STARTED.

During snack time, or for a classroom party, have the children in the class sit in chairs around tables. Select a few children to distribute the necessary implements. (If the celebration is for a child's birthday, that youngster might choose other youngsters to help in the distribution.) Point out that for each child there will be one plate, one cup, one napkin, and so on. Talk about the one-to-one matching. Provide piles of each of the items to be distributed. Ask the children to pick up a quantity of each item needed without actually counting. Discuss that this is an estimation and that in the end they may need more, or they may have taken too many of the particular item. Have the children place one of each object in front of each child's place. (Make sure to provide a spot for the children who are giving out the items.) Discuss times when children have to estimate quantities in their daily lives and also times when they distribute items according to a one-to-one correspondence.

HOW TO GO FURTHER.

Using napkins, paper plates, plastic spoons, forks, and paper cups, show the children how to set a table. Put a large table in the housekeeping area or place a large sheet of kraft or butcher paper on the floor. Ask the children to set the table using the materials provided. Ask them to estimate quantities and then to tell whether they had taken too many or too few of the items needed. After they have practiced setting the table, the children can draw place settings on large kraft or butcher paper.

GUESS HOW MANY

WHY DO THIS?

Estimation is an important skill for youngsters to learn early on. When children take a pile of napkins for distribution to classmates, they are estimating a quantity that they will need. To improve youngsters' estimation skills, they should have some practice in looking at an array of objects, and then guessing the number in the group. Then, by counting, they can check the accuracy of their estimates. Many such experiences help to improve children's skill in estimation. Later on in school mathematics, estimation is a vital tool in checking the reasonableness of answers derived from simple computations.

WHAT WILL I NEED?

- A box of buttons
- A pile of paper clips, sticks, or some other counters
- The "Guess How Many" worksheet

HOW TO GET STARTED.

Define the term estimation. Basically, it is a guess. Discuss situations in everyday life in which estimation is used—taking a pile of paper plates for youngsters at a birthday party, picking up a pile of worksheets for distribution to a class, and so on. Ask the children if they can think of any situations in which they have had to estimate.

If the children are sitting at tables, ask one child from each table to come up to a box of buttons and take (without counting) a sufficient amount which would be enough to give one button to each child at the table. Try the same procedure with paper clips, sticks, or other counters.

Next, distribute the "Guess How Many" worksheet, review the procedure with the children, and have them complete it. (Other worksheets like this one can be produced and left in folders in the math center for children to complete on their own.) When the children have completed the worksheet, discuss the range of their guesses. How far off were their guesses from the actual number of objects counted? What helps to improve children's ability to estimate?

HOW TO GO FURTHER.

Place four rulers on a table so as to make a square. Put a handful of beans, counters, or pennies in the middle of the square. Ask the children to take turns at guessing how many objects are in the square. After several children have guessed, count the objects. What was the range of the estimates? With continued practice do the children's abilities to estimate improve? Are their guesses closer to or further away from the actual quantity when they are dealing with a relatively large number of objects? Would it be easier to estimate the number of children sitting at a table or sitting in an auditorium?

Another activity is to take a stack of an even number of index cards and then ask a child to take half of the stack without counting. Then count the number of cards taken and the number remaining. How close to half are the two piles?

GUESS HOW MANY

Guess how many there are in each group. Write your guess. Then count and write the answer.

My Guess ?   The Answer

_____   _____

_____   _____

_____   _____

_____   _____

JOINING SETS

WHO DO THIS?

Concrete demonstrations of mathematical operations help young children to form concepts. In this activity, children actually form sets of objects and then combine them to see the resulting set. In this way, they actually experience what happens when two sets of objects are combined (added). This, along with the activities that follow, will help youngsters to gain a concrete understanding of how our number system works. Of course, when working with young children, we always begin with the concrete before we expect them to be able to deal with written, paper and pencil tasks.

WHAT WILL I NEED?

- Thick string, shoelaces, or rope
- Objects to use for counting—pennies, chips, buttons
- Twenty-two index cards, markers
- "Joining Sets" worksheet

HOW TO GET STARTED.

With a thick marker, make two index cards for each numeral from 0 to 10. Gather the children around the floor or a table. Place a piece of string (or a shoelace) around four objects. Have a child find the index card with a 4 written on it and place it next to the four objects. Next, place a string around a set of three objects. Again, find the matching number card. Take a larger string and place it around both sets of numbers. Now there are seven objects within the larger loop. Have the children count them. Now remove the strings that were around the sets of three and four. Find the card that shows the result of the combination of the two sets.

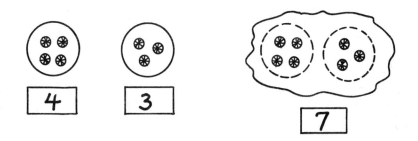

Ask a child to verbalize what happened and to repeat the procedure. Why do we consider this joining sets? Do the activity again using different sets. Each time, have the children use the numeral cards to show the numbers they are working with.

HOW TO GO FURTHER.

Once the children are comfortable combining sets with concrete objects, have them complete the "Joining Sets" worksheet. Make other, similar worksheets for practice.

Name _____

JOINING SETS

Write the number in the box that tells how many there are when the two sets are joined.

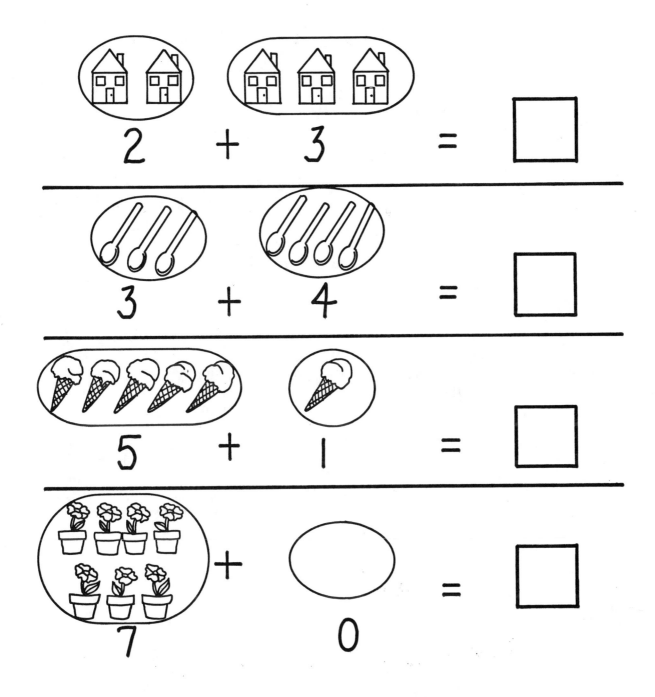

$$2 + 3 = \boxed{}$$

$$3 + 4 = \boxed{}$$

$$5 + 1 = \boxed{}$$

$$7 + 0 = \boxed{}$$

ADDING WITH CLOTHESPINS

WHY DO THIS?

Once children's number concepts are established, they can begin to combine numbers and determine their sums. As with learning number/numeral correspondence, becoming adept at combining numbers requires repeated practice with a variety of stimulating materials. In this activity, children combine clothespins which have numerals written on them and then find the sum of two or more numbers.

WHAT WILL I NEED?

- Two frozen orange juice cans with both ends open. (The cardboard centers from rolls of toilet paper may be substituted.)
- Twenty-five or thirty wooden clothespins
- Markers and construction paper

HOW TO GET STARTED.

Open both ends from two frozen juice cans. Make sure that there are no sharp edges protruding. Cover the cans with construction paper and draw an equal sign (=) in the middle of the can. Next, take the clothespins and on two of them draw a plus sign (+). On the remaining clothespins, write a numeral, from 1 to 20; as an aid to identification, make a corresponding number of dots next to the numeral.

Tell the children to place two clothespins each with a numeral and a clothespin with a plus sign on it between them on one side of a can. Then they can show the sum of the two numbers by placing the appropriate clothespin on the other side of the can. (See the illustration.) These materials can be kept in the math center for continued play and exploration. Children can make up problems for one another and check each other's work. If the clothespin on the "answer side" is 8 and there are two clothespins with 4 on each of them on the other side, what are the combinations of other numbers that can be used to make 8?

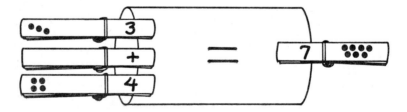

HOW TO GO FURTHER?

Make some clothespins which do not have dots next to the numerals and see if the children can continue to make successful additions. With paper and pencil children can record the equations which correspond to the combinations they made on the juice cans. Later, after children have made several combinations by adding the numerals on two clothespins, have them add the numerals on three clothespins.

SUBTRACTION "PULL-AWAY"

WHY DO THIS?

In most schools, addition and subtraction of numbers is often introduced in first grade. However, if kindergarten children understand basic number concepts, then simple combining (addition) of numbers is an appropriate activity. From the beginning children should work with "number families" (for example, the "six family" is made up of one and five, or two and four, or three and three), and then they will recognize (through their activities) that addition and subtraction are inverse operations. Not all children will be ready for work with number families, but if the activities are concrete, the experience will be both useful and demonstrative of how our number system works.

WHAT WILL I NEED?

- Modeling clay
- Small sticks, golf tees, sections of drinking straws, or other thin but rigid objects
- Twenty-two index cards
- Markers

HOW TO GET STARTED.

With a thick marker, make two index cards for each numeral from 0 to 10. Then form a flat lump of clay about 4 inches in diameter. Place six sticks (or golf tees, sections of drinking straws) into the clay. Ask a child to pull away a chunk of clay with two sticks in it. How many sticks are left behind? Review what just happened, "We started with six sticks. Katie pulled two away. We were left with four." Repeat this procedure several times. Use the index cards to show the numerals that correspond to the number of sticks used.

HOW TO GO FURTHER.

Have the children continue to play with the sticks and clay. They can make up problems for one another. Introduce the minus sign. A few children may be able to make equations to represent problems demonstrated, for example, $6 - 2 = 4$. Ask the children to use several combinations of numbers to pull away from six, including taking away zero.

Make "subtraction books." Begin with a book about birds sitting on a clothesline. Start with a picture of seven birds. The next page can show three birds flying away and four remaining on the line. Add captions to accompany the pictures, for example, "Seven birds were sitting on the line. Three flew away. How many are left?" Have the children suggest ideas for different kinds of situations.

DOMINO ADDITION

WHY DO THIS?

Dominoes are wonderful objects to help reinforce math skills. Since they use configurations of dots, children can count the quantities on each domino. Many activities for children can be created with dominoes. One such activity, about addition, is suggested below.

WHAT WILL I NEED?

- A set of dominoes
- Index cards and markers

HOW TO GET STARTED.

Make a set of addition cards by marking on index cards the number combinations shown in a set of dominoes, for example, $5 + 2 = 7$; $6 + 6 = 12$; $2 + 3 = 5$, and so on. First let the children play freely with the dominoes. Their first impulse will probably be to build with them. After a while, they may remark about the numerical quantities shown on the dominoes. Ask them to count both halves of a domino and tell how many dots there are all together on each. Show the addition cards and demonstrate how they can be matched up to a specific domino. (See the illustration.) Have the children work in pairs. Check to see if a correct match was made by counting the total number of dots on a domino and comparing this with the numerals on the addition card. Does the numeral to the right of the equals sign correspond with the total number of dots? Place the dominoes and addition cards in the math center for continued exploration.

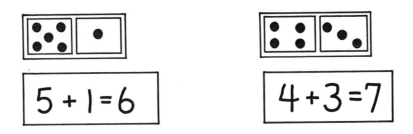

HOW TO GO FURTHER.

Children can make their own addition cards to match dominoes. Some children may wish to add the total number of dots on two dominoes. The "standard" game of dominoes can be played, in which children form a continuous line by matching identical sets of dots, edge to edge. Encourage children to invent games using the dominoes.

Comparing and Measuring

Children begin to understand the measurement of objects by first comparing them. Use of specific words in such activities is very important. For example: Which of two blocks is the *longer?* Which container can hold *more* water? Before children can use or understand the need for standard units of measurement, they should have a variety of experiences in comparing objects according to their length, width, capacity, mass, shades of color, and so on. Also, children enjoy placing objects in order from shortest to tallest, or according to other attributes. Young children should measure objects as the need arises during their work periods. For example, in cooking, they will need to measure quantities to follow a recipe. In deciding whether or not a table will fit in a particular spot in the classroom, the children should measure to gain the needed information. Whenever possible, measurement should be related to the need that it fulfills within our daily lives.

COMPARING BY SUPERPOSITION

WHY DO THIS?

The first step in learning to measure is to compare sizes. Is the classroom door wider than a desk? Do you think the large trash barrel in the lunchroom can hold more than the wastepaper basket? Children should be led to make direct comparisons by placing objects next to each other. For example, place two different-sized chairs side by side.

Which is the taller? Compare the length of strips of paper. Which is larger, your hand or your foot? Your ear or your nose? After a variety of such experiences, children will develop a readiness to compare the dimensions of an object to a standard unit of measurement.

WHAT WILL I NEED?

- Strips of construction paper of different lengths
- Tape
- Paper
- Markers or crayons
- Pieces of uncooked spaghetti
- Drinking straws
- "Longer or Shorter" worksheet

HOW TO GET STARTED.

Cut several strips of construction paper, each about 2 inches wide, but of different lengths. Tape them, one by one, onto a chalkboard or bulletin board. Make sure that the bottoms of the paper strips are on the same line. As each strip is placed, ask the children to decide whether it is longer or shorter than the strip just before it. Compare strips at different places along the line. For example, is the last strip placed on the board longer than the first one? Is it longer than the second one? You can even do this with considerable suspense and drama. "Here is the very tiniest one!" "This one is the very tallest of all the strips. Do you want to give it a name?" Keep reinforcing the appropriate vocabulary—longer, shorter, first, second, and so on.

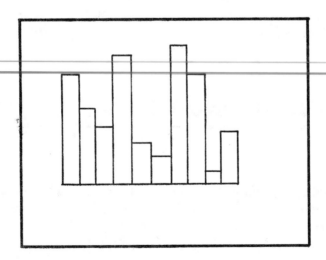

Next, break some pieces of uncooked spaghetti into lengths of various size. Give each child a few pieces. Ask them to compare the length of the pieces by placing them on a flat surface and discuss which ones are longer or shorter. Which is the *longest?* Which is the *shortest?* The same comparisons can be done with drinking straws which are cut to different lengths. Place the materials in the math center along with paper and markers or crayons. Children can trace the length of the various objects on paper and the result will look like a bar graph. They can also paste the spaghetti pieces, straws, or paper strips onto a large paper and label them with the words—shortest, longest.

As a reinforcement, have the youngsters complete the "Longer or Shorter" worksheet.

HOW TO GO FURTHER.

Some children may be able to arrange a variety of objects in order from shortest to longest. How did they accomplish this? They can then tape the objects in this order onto sheets of paper and dictate the procedure of how they made the arrangement.

LONGER OR SHORTER

Take a drinking straw and compare it to each of the objects pictured. If the object is longer than the straw, color the object red. If the object is shorter than the straw, color the object blue.

SERIAL ORDERING

WHY DO THIS?

An important part of comparing the sizes of objects is the ability to arrange them in order according to a specified attribute. Most commonly, children can put objects in order according to their length, as in arranging pencils in order from shortest to tallest. Beyond this, children can arrange objects on the basis of how much water they can hold, how light or dark a shade of color they are, or how they might rank along a continuum of smooth to rough. In order to do this, youngsters first have to compare an item with others in the series and then decide where it belongs. While developing an essential skill in learning how to measure, children often have a great deal of fun in accomplishing such activities.

WHAT WILL I NEED?

- Several cardboard tubes from paper towel rolls, toilet paper, or wrapping paper.
- Scissors

HOW TO GET STARTED.

Obtain a collection of cardboard tubes like the kinds that are at the center of paper towels, toilet paper, or wrapping paper. Cut the tubes into different lengths. Give a child six of the cardboard tubes and ask him or her to arrange them in order from shortest to tallest. Make sure that the bottoms of the tubes are on a flat surface so that the height of the tubes will be readily seen. Most children have to compare two objects at a time and then decide where in the order the next object should be placed. It is important to have children verbalize the procedure they follow as they arrange the tubes in order. Asking children to express the thoughts they have as they perform a task helps to model a procedure for others. Leave the tubes in the math center and provide opportunities for all of the children to arrange them in order.

What other objects can be arranged in a series? The possibilities are endless. For added variety try food container lids, grades of sandpaper (from smoothest to

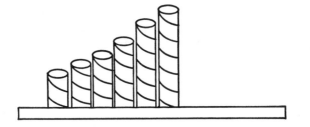

roughest), leaves (of the same kind), pieces of uncooked spaghetti, paper dolls, books, lumps of clay, and so on.

HOW TO GO FURTHER.

Cut eight circles of different colors and diameters. Give the children six of the circles and have them arrange the circles from smallest to largest. (A good way to check is to place one circle on top of another.) Then, give the children the remaining two circles. Have them find the place where each belongs. Devise other games in which objects are ordered according to a particular attribute.

A MEASURING TOOL TABLE

WHY DO THIS?

Each day children encounter many devices which are used for measurement. Rulers, watches, timers, tape measures, scales, and thermometers are all used to measure some quantity or another. While not necessarily needing to know how to use these measuring devices, youngsters should be helped to become aware of what they are used for. What does a thermometer measure? What does a clock measure? What does a scale or balance measure? In order to understand their functions, children should first have opportunities to explore these devices.

WHAT WILL I NEED?

- A variety of measuring devices, for example: sand timers, wind-up clocks, rulers of different size, tape measures, thermometers, measuring cups, measuring spoons, a scale or balance

HOW TO GET STARTED.

Demonstrate the operation of some of the devices mentioned above. Show the movement of the second hand on a clock, or the passing of sand in an egg timer. Dip a thermometer into cold water and then into hot water. Show how the mercury rises as the temperature rises. Demonstrate the use of a tape measure. In each case, discuss what the instrument measures. Leave the devices out on a table in the math center along with objects which can be used with them. Observe how the children use the instruments.

HOW TO GO FURTHER.

Children can make a "measuring book" in which they find pictures of measurement devices and then paste one onto each page of a book and write the name of the instrument. Catalogs will have pictures of such devices. Some children may be able to take measurements with the instruments, but this should not be a general expectation.

If an old, inoperable clock is available, it can be taken apart and the mechanism explored. What are the gears for? What turns the hands on the face of the clock? Where is the wind-up mechanism?

WATERPLAY AND EXPLORING VOLUME

WHY DO THIS?

Young children like to pour water from container to container, and this kind of activity is valuable in helping them to understand volumetric relationships. Through their play with measuring cups, plastic bowls, small vials, and measuring spoons, children begin to develop a notion of volume and capacity. After the youngsters have had time for free exploration with these materials, the need for the use of standard measures can be discussed and demonstrated.

WHAT WILL I NEED?

- A large plastic basin (a baby bath basin) or water table
- An assortment of measuring cups, vials, bowls, pitchers, measuring spoons, funnels, and food containers

HOW TO GET STARTED.

Set up an area where children can work with a large basin, water, and different sized vessels. Allow the children time to pour water from container to container and experiment freely with the materials. (You may wish to set a few ground rules about splashing.) After the children have had opportunities for free exploration, introduce some words commonly associated with volume. Children may have heard about quarts of milk, liters of soft drinks, pints of ice cream, and so on. Demonstrate how to fill a small vial to the brim and empty the water into a measuring cup. How many vials does it take to make one cup? Have several children repeat the procedure to confirm the results. Children can make many such comparisons with the various containers. Ask them which of two unmarked food containers can hold more water. Have them make a prediction and then check by using one vial to fill the containers and keep track of how many vials of water were required to fill each of the containers. How does this procedure test their predictions? Ask the children if they see any advantage to having markings of the side of a container, as in a measuring cup. How can such standards help us in our daily lives?

HOW TO GO FURTHER.

Children may be able to "calibrate" a large container. Obtain a clear plastic bottle from a soft drink. Find a vial or a small measuring cup with a marking for one ounce on it. With a grease pencil or permanent marker, draw a line for the exact quantity of one ounce on the vial. Then have the children pour a quantity of one ounce at a time into the large plastic bottle and as each ounce is poured, make a mark along the side of the large bottle to show the increments of one ounce. How many ounces does the large bottle hold? Instead of ounces you may wish to introduce and use metric measures, for example, one cubic centimeter (cc) or one milliliter (ml)—each of these measures holds the same amount of liquid.

DISCOVERING CAPACITY

WHY DO THIS?

Experiences in playing with containers will lead children to develop a concept of the relative capacity of different sized vessels. Most kindergarteners are unable to understand and recognize that a short, but wide container may hold more than a long tall one. (This is called the ability to conserve matter.) However, through many activities in which youngsters investigate how much various containers can hold, they build a background of experience for future understandings about the conservation of matter. As children explore the various amounts of material that these containers can hold, one of the things they can do is to arrange them in order of their capacity.

WHAT WILL I NEED?

- Cans or other containers of varying size, for example, soup cans, tuna fish cans, vegetable cans, margarine tubs
- Rice
- One small vial to use as a standard—this can be a small container that spice comes in, a very small jar from jelly, or a vial from pills

HOW TO GET STARTED.

Empty a bag of rice into a small pail, bin, or other container. Demonstrate how to fill a small vial of rice to the top. With the children, count how many vials of rice it requires to fill a few containers. (If the container being filled is a large one, you can show the children how to keep a tally with lines and slashes.) After filling a few of the containers with rice, ask the children which of them holds the most rice. Which holds the least amount of rice? Ask the children if there is another way they can tell if one container holds more than another. One youngster will more than likely be able to show that you can fill one container with rice, and then pour the rice into another container. If the rice spills over, the first container holds more than the one the rice was poured into; if the first container does not fill the second one, then the second container holds more. Place these materials in the math center and let the children explore. Listen to their comments and observe how they compare quantities. Ask questions to assist in their discoveries.

HOW TO GO FURTHER.

Once the children have explored the capacities of the various containers available, ask them to place them in order from the smallest to the greatest capacity. One way to place the containers in order is to use a standard (a small vial) and count how many vials of rice each container can hold. What is another way of telling which of two containers holds the most rice? How can this help to arrange them in order of capacity?

MAKING AND USING A BALANCE

WHY DO THIS?

Children should have many experiences lifting objects in each of their hands and guessing which hand is holding the heavier object. Later, these guesses (or hypotheses) can be checked using a balance. An equal-arms balance is a valuable device to have in the classroom. Children use it to determine the heavier of two objects. They learn that the side that "goes down" is the one which has more matter in it. (Actually a balance compares the amount of mass an object has; a scale, on the other hand, measures weight, which is the gravitational attraction of an object and the earth.) In this activity, children use an equal-arms balance to compare the masses of objects and later to standard weights.

WHAT WILL I NEED?

- An equal-arms balance.
- A collection of small objects to balance such as toy cars, crayons, blocks, and markers
- Large paper clips

HOW TO GET STARTED.

Obtain an equal-arms balance. If not readily available, you can make one rather easily by using a ruler, large spring clips, pie tins, and other common materials. (See illustration.) Make sure that the pans are level. This can be adjusted by sliding the ruler through the spring clip from which it is suspended.

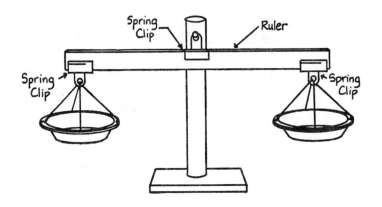

Give children small objects to lift in their hands. Have them guess which hand is holding the heavier object. Then check by placing the objects in the pans of the balance. Demonstrate that the pan that "goes down" is the one that is holding the heavier object. If the objects are in balance (have the same mass or weigh the same), the two pans will be level. Demonstrate two objects which are balanced. Provide a collection of small objects and ask the children to play a game with the balance. Tell one child to place an object on one side of the balance. Then ask another child to compare each of her objects to the first one, by placing them, one by one, in the other pan. As each object is compared, have her tell whether her object is heavier or lighter than the one placed in the other pan. How can the pans be brought to balance? What will be needed to do this? You may suggest adding a few large paper clips to an object which is not heavy enough to make an even balance. Make the balance and a variety of small objects available to the children in the math center.

HOW TO GO FURTHER.

Introduce a set of known weights such as large paper clips. Provide small objects and have children count out how many paper clips it takes to balance each of several objects. If a marker requires eight clips to balance and a toy car requires twelve clips to balance, which is the heavier? Simple worksheets can be made in which an object is pictured on one side, and then on a blank line opposite the picture the child writes the number of clips required to balance the object.

A few simple math activities can be accomplished with the balance. For example, if we have ten paper clips on one side, how many will we need on the other side to balance them? If we have twelve paper clips on one side and seven clips on the other side, how many paper clips will we need to add to the other side to balance them?

You may notice a broad disparity in children's ability to work with a balance. Some children may only be able to tell which of two objects placed on the balance is heavier. Others may be able to compare several objects and place them in order by weight.

WHAT TIME IS IT?

WHY DO THIS?

In this era of digital clocks we may wonder whether we should bother to teach children to read a clock face (an analog clock). Well, many have a suspicion that analog clocks will be with us for some time to come. Besides, many youngsters feel a sense of accomplishment and pride in knowing how "to tell time." Children see clock faces all around them—in the classroom, in offices, in stores, and at home. There are many activities that can be accomplished by helping children to tell time. For most kindergarteners, though, telling time on a clock face, beyond the hour and half hour, is not a realistic expectation.

WHAT WILL I NEED?

- A real clock or clock face from a broken clock or made of cardboard
- "Matching the Time" worksheet

HOW TO GET STARTED.

Discuss time with the children. What time do they get up in the morning? What time do they come to school? What time does school end? When do they eat dinner? When do they go to sleep? For each time discussed, show it on a clock face. Explain the functions of the hour hand and the minute hand. Ask the children what most people have with them to tell the time. How do we tell time in public places if we do not have a watch? Talk about the different kinds of clocks that children see in their environment—round clock faces, digital clocks, any others? Has anyone ever seen a sundial? Put a large clock (or clock face) in the math center for children to examine and play with. Cards can be made with times written in numbers. On the back of each card draw a clock face and show how that time appears on the clock. Then as children use the clock face in the math center to set the time written on the cards, they can check by comparing the time they set with that shown on the back of the card.

You may wish to make a small "desktop" clock face for all of the children and have them set the time according to when various events in their daily lives occur.

HOW TO GO FURTHER.

Show how time appears on a digital clock or watch. This time also has to be "read." Distribute the "Matching the Time" worksheet and have the children complete it.

Some children may wish to draw pictures of activities in their daily lives and then with a bold marker write the time of day in which they usually do that activity.

Name _____

MATCHING THE TIME

Draw a line from the time shown on the clock face to the time shown in numerals.

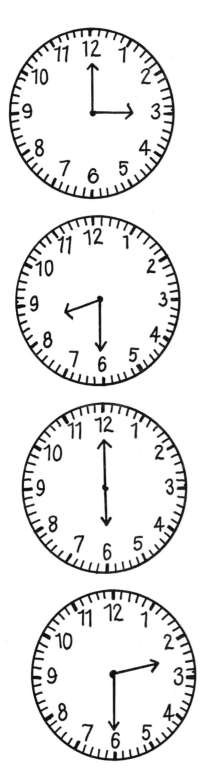

HOW WARM IS IT?

WHY DO THIS?

One of the basic measurements taken in our daily lives is temperature. Children may be familiar with different types of thermometers—those that measure body temperature, those that measure the temperature of the air, and those used in stoves. Children may not realize that thermometers *measure* something, namely, how hot or cold something is. Kindergarten children hear temperature stated in "degrees" in weather reports, when their body temperature is taken, or when finding out the temperature of a room. It may be difficult for young children to read a thermometer, but they should at least know about the uses of thermometers, what they measure, and how they operate, at least in a general sense.

WHAT WILL I NEED?

- An actual large thermometer, or a "ribbon thermometer" on which a rise temperature can be simulated.
- Smaller thermometers for pupil activity
- A bowl of hot and a bowl of cold water

HOW TO GET STARTED.

If a large, working thermometer is not available, make a "ribbon thermometer" out of cardboard. This is simply a model that looks like a thermometer with a red and white ribbon attached so that the rise and fall of the liquid can be demonstrated. Discuss the use of thermometers with the children. When have they seen and used thermometers? What are they used for? Explain that a thermometer is used to *measure* how hot or cold something is. How is it similar and different from other measuring devices such as rulers, scales, clocks, or speedometers?

Explain that the colored liquid in the tube of a thermometer rises as the temperature rises and drops as the temperature drops. Would the liquid be higher on a hot summer day or a cold winter day? Ask the children to predict whether the liquid will be relatively higher or lower as you cite certain conditions, for example, near a radiator or in a refrigerator. Take temperature readings at various locations in the classroom—on a sunny windowsill, near the door, high and low, etc. Some children may be able to read a large thermometer. All of the youngsters should be able to understand that the higher the number, the warmer the temperature. Also, they should begin to have some sense that 95 degrees is a very hot day and 25 degrees is a very cold day.

Take two bowls of water, one hot and one cold. Measure the temperature in each of the bowls. Have the children touch the water in the bowls and say whether it is hot or cold.

HOW TO GO FURTHER.

Use the thermometer outdoors. Take the temperature in the air, an inch into the soil, under a tree, in the bright sun, on a white car, on a black car, on a stone, and in other places. Have the children discuss their results and try to draw some conclusions about their observations.

Make an experience chart about explorations with a thermometer. What does it measure? What temperature readings were taken in the classroom and outdoors? When is it usually hot? When is it usually cold?

BOXES AND LIDS

WHY DO THIS?

One way that children can begin to develop a concept of the relative volume (or capacity) of objects is by seeing how objects can fit into one another. "Is it larger than a breadbox?" is an often heard phrase as we try to estimate size and volume. Just like the nesting dolls children love to play with, so too can we provide experiences in which children have to fit one thing into another. Through such activity children begin to gain a sense of volume.

WHAT WILL I NEED?

- A variety of gift boxes varying in size from very small to relatively large cardboard cartons
- A set of nesting dolls (optional)

HOW TO GET STARTED.

If a set of nesting dolls is available, ask the children to take them apart, assemble each doll, line them up in size order, and then nest them back together inside of each other. Children may talk about the origin of these dolls (usually from Russia) and when and where they have seen them.

Obtain a variety of boxes that can be nested into one another. Ask the children to talk about their size in relative terms. Which boxes are smaller than and larger than a telephone? Have the children place the lids on the boxes and then line them up in order from smallest to largest. Then, they can nest them inside of one another. The boxes can be taken apart and stacked, one on top of the other to form a tower. Take the boxes apart again and spread them out on the floor. Make a nest of just three boxes and then hold up the other boxes, one at a time, and ask the children whether each box would fit inside of the nested ones, or if the nested boxes would go inside of it. Test their inferences. Many other games like this can be devised to maintain interest. Leave the boxes in the math center for free exploration.

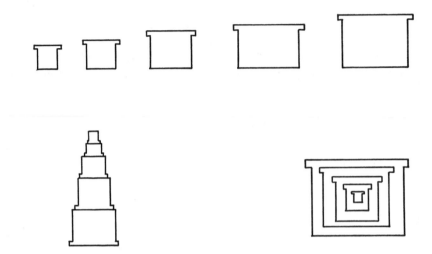

HOW TO GO FURTHER.

What other objects can the children find that can be nested? One possibility is a collection of plastic food storage containers. Yogurt cups, large and small margarine tubs, ice cream containers, and the like can be brought into school and nested to gain a sense of volume.

Some boxes, especially the kind that holiday gifts come in, have an embossed or patterned surface. Look for at least one of these boxes. Children may be interested in making a copy of the embossed pattern. One way is to place a sheet of paper over the pattern and rub the surface with a peeled crayon. Another way to get a print is to brush a thin layer of fingerpaint onto the surface of the box and then lightly pat a piece of paper onto the painted surface. A few tries may be necessary to get just the right amount of pressure, but the results will be fascinating!

MONEY BOXES

WHY DO THIS?

In this activity, children place an appropriate quantity of coins into clear plastic boxes. In order to do this they must compare the coins that they are placing in a box with those indicated on a reference card. Children find that there are a few ways to make the same amount of money. In a sense, they are "measuring" amounts of money. Working with money is an important life skill, and although some teachers feel that the use of real money presents a temptation for children, many feel that it can be used as an opportunity to build responsibility for classroom materials and a sense of community.

WHAT WILL I NEED?

- Self-stick labels or stickers
- Markers
- One dollar's worth of change in pennies, nickels, and dimes in a box
- Five or six clear plastic boxes about the size that would contain a deck of cards or an assortment of screws or bolts
- A piece of oaktag

HOW TO GET STARTED.

First, make a chart for equivalent coin values like the one shown in the illustration. Then, obtain the clear plastic boxes. On the front of each box, place a sticker or label and write an amount of money. Make boxes for 3 cents, 6 cents, 9 cents, 11 cents, and 17 cents. Place all of the change in another box. Discuss the names and values of the coins, penny, nickel, and dime. Beginning with one of the smaller amounts, ask the children to demonstrate how to fill each of the plastic boxes with the appropriate amount of coins. Can some of the amounts of money be made in more than one way? Place the money boxes in the math center for continued activity. Have the children check one another's work for accuracy.

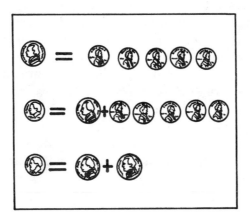

HOW TO GO FURTHER.

Have the children show each other the coin boxes they have filled. One child can show another child a completed money box and then ask if the box can be correctly filled using a different combination of coins. If so, then the other child does it. If not, the two youngsters should agree that this money box can be completed in only one way. Then they move to another money box.

GOING SHOPPING

WHY DO THIS?

Once children can make a specified quantity of change, they can extend their activity to go on a "shopping spree" and buy items in a pretend store. This activity goes beyond assembling the correct amount of change for a specified quantity of money because it requires children to make judgements about whether or not they have enough money to buy certain items and then offers the challenge for some youngsters to "make change." The activity is fun, promotes important life skills, and will provide enrichment for the most adept children in working with money.

WHAT WILL I NEED?

- Ten index cards
- One dollar's worth of change in a box
- Small pictures of common objects or foods
- Markers and tape or glue
- The "In the Fruit Market" worksheet

HOW TO GET STARTED.

Cut out pictures of foods or common objects and paste them onto index cards. (Catalogs, newspaper ads, and store flyers are a great source of pictures.) On the cards write an amount of money for the object. Label some of the cards with amounts that are more than and less than 50 cents. Show the cards to the children. Have them identify the items pictured and the amount of money that each of them costs. Provide 50 cents in change to "buy" the items on the cards. First show each of the cards and ask the children if they have enough to "buy" each of the items. Then have one child serve as the "storekeeper" and another as the "shopper." Give the shopper about one dollar's worth of change. Have him or her go shopping and buy some of the items. Which item costs the most? Which item costs the least? What is the greatest number of items that can be purchased? Have children take turns selecting and buying items. Have another child serve as the "storekeeper" who can make change as each item is purchased.

Distribute the "In the Fruit Market" worksheet. Explain the directions and have the children complete it.

HOW TO GO FURTHER.

Set up a "store" in the classroom. Have the storekeeper gather objects to sell and mark prices for them. Others can then go shopping at the store. A cash register is a necessary prop for this activity. This is a wonderful opportunity to incorporate a math activity into the housekeeping area of the classroom.

Name _____

IN THE FRUIT MARKET

You have 25¢ to buy a fruit. Color blue the ones that you have enough money to buy. Color red the ones that you do not have enough money to buy.

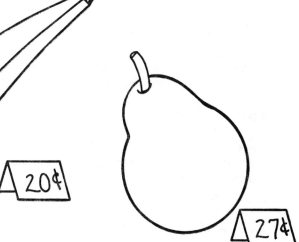

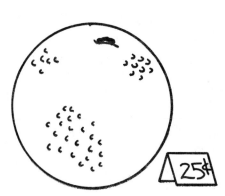

Shapes and Geometry

Most kindergarteners can identify and name circles and squares, but few of them are familiar with other shapes such as triangles, rectangles, and diamonds. The activities in this section introduce children to a variety of shapes that they can make, describe, and identify in their environment. As children gain more and more experience with shapes, they begin to realize how shapes and sizes are related and how they can fit together. Through such activities, youngsters develop important concepts about geometry and space.

MAKING AND USING GEOBOARDS

WHY DO THIS?

A geoboard is nothing more than a square piece of wood with nails spaced at regular intervals. Rubber bands can be stretched across its surface and hooked onto nails forming a variety of geometric shapes. With geoboards children can form large and small shapes, shapes within shapes, and generally explore sides, angles, and spaces within shapes. The vocabulary used to describe shapes can also be reinforced. This activity allows children to work with shape sizes and dimensions on their own and with ever-changing patterns.

WHAT WILL I NEED?

For each geoboard you want to make:

- A piece of wood, about one foot square
- Sandpaper
- Nails or brads (about 1-inch) with small heads
- Pencil
- Ruler
- Hammer
- Rubber bands
- Index cards

HOW TO GET STARTED.

To make a geoboard, obtain a square piece of wood and sand its edges. Make a grid on the surface of the board with intersecting lines, perpendicular to one another and about one inch apart. Decide how many nails you would like to have on the geoboard. A good size is five by five (twenty-five nails) or eight by eight (sixty-four nails).

Hammer the nails or brads where the lines intersect, leaving about 1½ inch of the nail exposed. (See the illustration.) Involve the children in the construction of the geoboard. Once the geoboard is finished, give it to a child with a batch of rubber bands and show how different shapes can be formed. Have the children experiment making squares (four equal sides), triangles, rectangles, and a few irregular shapes. Reinforce correct vocabulary as the children form shapes. Talk about the number of sides and points (angles) for each shape formed. Leave the geoboard in the math center and observe what the children do with it. You might suggest that they make large and small shapes, shapes within shapes, two triangles within a square, and two rectangles in a square. What would the children do if rubber bands of different colors are provided?

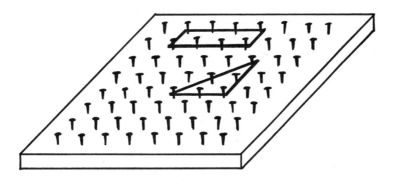

HOW TO GO FURTHER.

Make task cards for use with geoboards. On an index card, draw a particular shape as it would appear on a geoboard for the children to replicate. Make a variety of cards progressing from simple to more complex. (See the example in the illustration.)

Smaller geoboards can be made using a four by four pattern with a total of sixteen nails. A numeral can then be placed on a card at the bottom of the geoboard, and then the children can stretch a band around the number of nails which corresponds with the number on the card.

FINDING HALVES

WHY DO THIS?

Children often deal with fractions in their daily lives. They may share a cookie with a friend and each take a half, eat half of a candy bar, or take a slice of pizza. While the youngsters may understand the concepts involved, they may not always transfer their knowledge of fractions to other situations. In kindergarten, it is reasonable for children to understand that halves are two equal parts of a whole. They use the term frequently, but this activity can help them to find halves of a whole among a variety of objects.

WHAT WILL I NEED?

- Paper plates
- Oaktag or cardboard
- Magazines or catalogs
- Scissors and paste

HOW TO GET STARTED.

Take a few paper plates and cut them into two parts, some into two *equal* parts, others into two clearly *unequal* parts. First, show the paper plates cut into halves to the children. Discuss that each part of the plate is a half of the whole plate. Next, show the unequal parts of the plate. Can the children put them together to make a whole plate? Would we call these two parts halves? Discuss the concept that a half means one of two equal parts.

In a magazine or catalog, find some pictures of familiar objects and paste each one onto a sheet of oaktag or cardboard. Cut some of the pictures into two equal parts and others into two unequal parts. Ask the children to match up the parts and then sort the pictures into two different piles—ones that were cut in half and ones that were cut into two unequal parts. Put the pictures in the math center for continued exploration.

HOW TO GO FURTHER.

Paste pictures from magazines or catalogs onto pages in a notebook. Cut each page in half the short way, so that the left edges of the pages remain bound. Let the children leaf through the book, matching halves of the same picture.

In order to find halves of regular shapes (circle, square, triangle, rectangle), show children how to fold the shape in half along a line of symmetry, that is, a line that divides the object in half. What objects in the classroom can be divided into halves?

Some children may be able to find quarters or thirds of objects. They may be able to put together thirds of a pie, or quarters of a square. A square can be cut into quarters, each of which is also a square. How can you cut a square into quarters in which each quarter is a triangle?

GOING ON A SHAPE HUNT

WHY DO THIS?

An important property of objects is shape. Many objects in our environment have definite shapes which children can recognize and identify. By asking children to find shapes in familiar objects like a clock, a window pane, or a wastebasket, we are asking them to focus on an attribute of objects they see everyday and to begin to classify them according to a specific property. Children will undoubtedly delight in finding new aspects in things that are so very familiar to them.

WHAT WILL I NEED?

- An assortment of common shapes cut from construction paper
- The "Shape Hunt" worksheet

HOW TO GET STARTED.

Review the names of basic shapes. Ask the children to identify the shapes of common objects in the classroom. Some easy examples to point out are a clock (a circle), the top of a wastebasket (a circle), a windowpane (a rectangle), and a floor tile (a square).

Tell the children that they are going on a shape hunt to find objects which have specific shapes in the classroom. The shapes can be a part of an object—for example, a computer keyboard can be shaped like a rectangle, but one of its keys is shaped like a square. Extend this experience by taking a walk through the school and finding shapes.

HOW TO GO FURTHER.

Extend this activity by asking children to find objects which exhibit two attributes, for example, a blue circle, or a red square. (Try to look around in advance for objects that have these properties to be sure that the task is possible.) A game can be made from such an activity by saying something like, "I see an object in this room. It has the shape of a rectangle. It is green. It is larger than my desk. What is it?"

Go on a shape hunt outdoors. Take the children on the school grounds and ask them to work in teams of two or three to find a circle, a square, and a rectangle. (Many shapes can be found in a jungle gym.) Take a shape walk and have the children point out shapes they find around them. Shapes can be found in houses, buildings, in parks, on lawns, in trees, and even upon close examination in rocks and in the soil.

Once children can match and name basic shapes, and can find shapes within the context of real objects, they can identify shapes in two-dimensional pictures. Have the children complete the "Shape Hunt" worksheet. Youngsters can then draw or paint their own pictures in which they intentionally incorporate familiar shapes.

Name

SHAPE HUNT

How many shapes can you find in this picture? Color the outline of the circles red, the squares blue, the rectangles green, and the triangles yellow.

USING PARQUETRY BLOCKS

WHY DO THIS?

Parquetry blocks are a standard feature in most kindergarten classrooms. A great variety of activities can be devised for exploring these multicolored wooden blocks of different shapes. Most sets of parquetry blocks come with printed patterns on which children can match blocks of the same color, shape, and size. There are many additional experiences that can be provided for youngsters as they explore the nature of shapes and the relationships among them.

WHAT WILL I NEED?

- A set of parquetry blocks

HOW TO GET STARTED.

Before introducing any specific activities, allow children to play with a set of parquetry blocks placed in the math center and note their actions. In the beginning, most children will use the blocks to build structures or to create designs. Discuss the blocks in terms of their attributes, that is, shape, color, and size. Ask the children to sort the blocks by color, placing all of the blocks of the same color in a pile regardless of shape. Then ask the children to sort the blocks by shape, regardless of the color. Discuss the fact that the same block, for example a red square, can belong to two separate groups—the set of squares and the set of red blocks.

Pose a variety of problems to the children using the blocks. Some examples include: Make a square using two triangles. Use four squares to make a larger square. Use two squares to make a rectangle. Use three triangles to make a square. As an aid, these combinations can be traced onto paper and duplicated for children to use.

HOW TO GO FURTHER.

Make a worksheet on which shapes or patterns are outlined which can be formed by fitting different combinations of blocks into the outlines. How many different possible ways exist for filling in the outlines? If one youngster uses one combination of blocks, have another use a different combination of blocks to fill in the outline.

Ask the children to make up games or puzzles using parquetry blocks. What do they come up with? What other uses can children find for parquetry blocks in the classroom?

FRACTION PUZZLES

WHY DO THIS?

Young children deal with fractions each day. They may not use the customary terms like quarters, thirds, eighths, and so on, but they don't need to use this terminology in order to understand equal parts of a whole. Youngsters enjoy working with puzzles in which they have to fit pieces together. By making and using fraction puzzles, children will see and manipulate parts of a whole and in this way develop rudimentary concepts of fractions.

WHAT WILL I NEED?

- Sheets of heavy cardboard
- Construction paper
- Glue or rubber cement
- A good pair of scissors

HOW TO GET STARTED.

Glue a different colored piece of construction paper onto each piece of stiff cardboard. Cut out a large circle from each cardboard sheet. To make the "puzzles," cut each circle into different fractional parts—halves, thirds, quarters, sixths, eighths, and so on. Place the puzzles in the math center for free exploration. Observe what the children do with the materials.

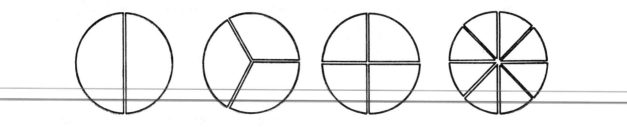

With a group of children, discuss the fraction puzzles. What is the same about each of the puzzles? What is different about them? Have children complete each of the puzzles and count the number of equal parts. Some children may be ready to call the fractional parts by name, but this should not be a general expectation. Ask the children to think of times when they deal with fractional parts like these. Certainly in cutting pies, pizzas, or large cookies they will have encountered fractional parts like those in the puzzles.

HOW TO GO FURTHER?

Find pictures of round objects in magazines. Mount the pictures onto cardboard and cut them into fractional parts. Put each "puzzle" into a separate manila envelope. Write or draw something on each envelope that will remind the children of the picture inside. Have the children use these puzzles in the math center.

Some children may wish to make a "fraction book" in which each page is devoted to a circle cut into a different number of parts. After being cut, the circles can be pasted onto the pages with enough space between each piece to show the parts. A few children may be ready to label each of the pages with the names of the fractional parts.

MAKING SHAPE PICTURES

WHY DO THIS?

As children work with shapes, they come to know their properties. Triangles have three sides and three points. Squares have four equal sides and four corners. Rectangles also have four sides and four corners, but all four sides are not equal in length. Children can discuss these attributes as they use shapes to make pictures. They will make discoveries through their play, which is, of course, the most natural kind of learning for young children.

WHAT WILL I NEED?

- A variety of regular shapes (squares, circles, triangles, rectangles, diamonds) of different size and color cut from construction paper
- Paste or glue
- "Shape Matching" worksheet

HOW TO GET STARTED.

Prepare a variety of shapes as described above. Some children may be able to help with tracing the shapes. If you cut through a few pieces of construction paper at the same time, more shapes will be produced.

Place the shapes on a tray in the math center and ask the children to make pictures of objects they know (houses, people, foods, animals) just by arranging the shapes provided. After they are satisfied with the picture, they should paste or glue the shapes onto a piece of paper. Perhaps they can write a word (or a story) telling about what is in the picture.

Can the children make objects by using only one kind of shape? Can they make a person using different sized squares? Can they make a house just using rectangles? Pose different challenges to the children. Let them suggest some interesting variations.

HOW TO GO FURTHER.

As an extension activity, have the children complete the "Shape Matching" worksheet. Have the children paint shape pictures. Make shape stencils by cutting large shapes out of sheets of cardboard. The children can then use these stencils to make shapes of their own.

Name _____

SHAPE MATCHING

Find the shape people who go with their special houses and pets.
Make all the ones that belong together the same color.

Sequence and Position

Among the important mathematical concepts that young children should be exposed to are sequence and position. Youngsters experience sequences in their daily lives. Who is first, second, and third in line? Which do you do first, put on socks or shoes? Also, important sequences are evident in the steps to follow in a recipe or in solving a problem.

Another concept which is commonly explored in kindergarten is position. The bowl is *on top of* the table. The wastebasket is *under* the desk. These terms, which describe relative position, are always appropriate to use in discussions and activities in kindergarten.

THE NUMBER WORM

WHY DO THIS?

Children enjoy putting things in order. They can arrange objects in order of size, shades of color, or numerical order. In this activity, children arrange numbered segments of a worm in order. The task is aided by the fact that the segments of the number worm can fit together in only one way. It is a self-correcting activity. Once children are somewhat adept at ordering objects, they begin to understand the notion of repeating patterns or number series.

WHAT WILL I NEED?

- 5-by-8-inch index cards
- A pair of scissors
- Markers
- A large manila envelope

HOW TO GET STARTED.

Write the numbers from one to ten on 5-by-8-inch index cards. Arrange them in order. Overlap about an inch or two of the left edge of one card onto the right edge of the next card. Cut a unique diagonal pattern on the overlapped edges. (See the illustration.) In this way, there is only one way in which to fit the cards together and the numerical sequence is reinforced by completing the puzzle. Make a "head" for the worm. Show the children how they can put the number worm together. Separate the cards and place them in a manila envelope. Draw a number worm on the envelope and place it in the math center.

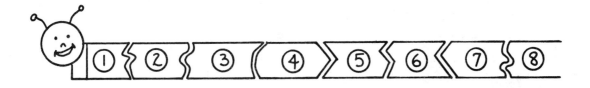

HOW TO GO FURTHER.

Use this idea to make other self-correcting games. A long worm can be made for the letters of the alphabet. Pairs of items which go together in some way (for example, shoes and socks) can be placed on a single card and then the space between the items can be cut along a zigzag line so that the resulting cards can only be put together in one way.

Observe a real earthworm and ask the children to look for something about the worm that is imitated in the Number Worm. (Children will notice the segmented arrangement of a worm.)

THE NUMBER TRAIN

WHY DO THIS?

As children practice putting things in order, they will want additional challenges. In this activity, the cars of a train are numbered from one to ten and the children place them in order behind the engine. This provides an ideal opportunity to introduce ordinal numbers—first, second, third, and so on. There are many opportunities during the kindergarten day for children to place objects in order. This activity can also help to strengthen left to right progression.

WHAT WILL I NEED?

- Construction paper of assorted colors
- Markers

HOW TO GET STARTED.

Cut out a train engine from a piece of black construction paper. Next, cut out ten train cars, using different colors of paper. Number the cars from one to ten. With the engine facing left, arrange the cars in any sequence following the engine. Ask the children to rearrange the cars so that they are in order from one to ten. After they have done this, introduce the words for the ordinal numbers, that is first, second, third, fourth, and so on.

One variation is to cut out pictures of automobiles and trucks and mount them onto oaktag or construction paper. Place a sticker with a number on the door of each car. Have the children arrange the cars in the "motorcade" from one to ten. If "matchbox" cars are available, they can be numbered on their hoods with opaque correction fluid and the children can put them in order.

HOW TO GO FURTHER.

What other things in the classroom can the children find which can be arranged in numerical order? For homework, ask the children to find a food or some other product package that has a large numeral on it. For example, A-1 Steak Sauce, 7-Up, Chlorox-2, vitamin B-6, Product 19, 4-C Tea Mix, 9-Lives Cat Food, and so on. Have the children arrange the packages, cans, and boxes in numerical order.

EGG CARTON NUMBER RODS

WHY DO THIS?

Number rods are used to provide a physical example of the relative sizes of numbers. By comparing the length of incremental rods, children can readily see, for example, that six is twice as large as three. They can compare number values in sequence. Many kindergarten classrooms have number rods as a part of their standard equipment, but if they are not available, they can be made from egg cartons. In this activity, children use number rods made from these everyday objects to explore the size and sequence of numerical quantities.

WHAT WILL I NEED?

- Several styrofoam or cardboard egg cartons
- A good pair of scissors
- Pennies, beans, paper clips, or other small counters which can fit into the small egg carton compartments

HOW TO GET STARTED.

With the children observing, cut several egg cartons down the center the long way so that the result is two strips of six compartments. Keep some of the "six strips" intact, but cut the others into ones, twos, threes, fours, and fives. Point out to the children that when you cut one compartment away from a "six strip," you are left with a one and a five. When you cut two away, you are left with a two and a four. Once the egg carton number rods are made, a variety of activities for the youngsters can be devised.

Have the children stack the number rods on top of each other, starting with six at the bottom, a five on top of that, a four on top of the five, and so on. In this way, a "staircase" is made. Review the numbers represented by the number strips. Line up the number rods, side by side, to form a sequence in another way. (See the illustration.)

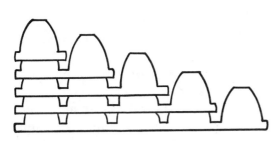

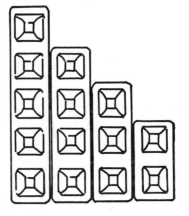

Youngsters can also practice basic number and matching concepts by placing one small object (a penny, bean, clip, or other small counter) into each compartment. They can count out loud as they place the object into the compartment. The egg carton number rods can also be used to perform a variety of other operations, for example, "Who can show me a rod which has one more than the rod I am holding up?" "Who can show me a rod that has two fewer compartments than the one I have?"

HOW TO GO FURTHER.

Make "number sentences" on index cards (for example, $3 + 2 = \square$). The children solve the number sentence by taking a three rod and a two rod and then counting the total number of units (compartments) in all.

FIND ME, I'M HIDING

WHY DO THIS?

This is a familiar game in which specific directions are given for finding a classroom object. By using terms to describe the location of objects in relation to other objects, children learn positional concepts. Youngsters have to focus on verbal cues and use them as they search for a specific object. Describing where something is in the classroom is not an easy task for young children. In this activity, children learn the meaning of words such as above, below, at the side of, behind, and so on. They also discover that the position of an object can be defined in relation to another object.

WHAT WILL I NEED?

- Any familiar classroom objects

HOW TO GET STARTED.

Begin by asking children to describe the location of objects in the classroom. For example, "Where is the clock?" Encourage the use of positional terms, "It is on the wall just *above* the easels." Ask a child to describe the location of an item to someone who has never been in the room before. Help with the appropriate terminology.

Next, have a youngster stand next to a chair. Have the youngster move *in front of* the chair, *behind* the chair, *to the side* of the chair, *on* the chair, and each time ask which words tell where the child is in relation to the chair.

Select a common object that the children are familiar with. Tell the children that you are going to describe where it is located. Use positional terms to provide the clues, such as, "The object is behind my desk. It is in front of the wall." Once the children are familiar with the rules of the game and have found a few items successfully, let them take turns describing the location of an object.

HOW TO GO FURTHER.

As youngsters become more aware of positional concepts and can tell right from left, introduce these terms as a variation in the game. "The object is to the right of the bookshelf. It is on the left side of the fish tank." If the walls of a classroom are labeled with the signs, "North," "South," "East," and "West," a few youngsters may be able to use these directions in locating objects. "It is just north of the refrigerator." This game can be made quite simple or rather complex depending upon the abilities of the youngsters.

Worksheets can be readily made in which children are asked to draw a red *X* under a picture of a table, a yellow circle on top of the table, a green square at the side of the table, and so on.

SETTING THE TABLE

WHY DO THIS?

A place setting for a table is a pattern. Once the pattern is established, children can copy it by placing each of the utensils in the same positions relative to one another as they appear in a diagram used as a guide. Not only does this activity help children to practice concepts of relative position, but it is also challenging and fun. Also, this activity promotes one-to-one matching and allows math activities to be incorporated in the housekeeping area.

WHAT WILL I NEED?

- A few sheets of 12-by-18-inch construction paper
- Markers
- Paper plates and cups
- Plastic spoons, forks, and knives
- Napkins

HOW TO GET STARTED.

Make a diagram of a place setting on a piece of construction paper. Teaching "table setting etiquette" may not be a legitimate kindergarten goal, but you can explain that this is one way to set a table. Provide the materials for the children to replicate the setting on a table several times. The sheets of construction paper can serve as place mats. It may be interesting to note how the children approach the task. Do they make one complete table setting and then move on the next one, or do they first put down all of the plates, then all of the forks, all of the napkins, and so on? Can the children think of any advantages or disadvantages to the various approaches?

After a while a game can be played with the place setting. Make one complete setting like the one shown. Ask the children to look at it carefully. Then ask them to

turn around. Take one of the utensils away. Ask the children to look at the place setting again. Can they guess which piece is missing?

HOW TO GO FURTHER.

Have a few children make a table setting any way they like. Ask them to study it carefully. Where is the spoon in relation to the fork, to the right of it, or to the left? Have them turn their backs. Then, have a child change the position of one of the items in the setting. Ask the others what has changed. Ask one of them to change it back to the original setting. Many games like this one can be devised to help children focus on the relative position of objects.

chapter *8*

IN THE SCIENCE CENTER

Science is a way of life. It is curiosity about the world around us. It is an inquisitive attitude in which we seek to find answers to puzzling questions. It is observing, exploring materials, drawing conclusions, and communicating findings. And the five-year-old is a natural scientist!

A stimulating environment will foster the investigative instincts that are evident in most kindergarteners. As they poke, pry, and otherwise investigate objects in the classroom, children are satisfying their quest to know. The observations of our youngest learners are fresh and clear and unencumbered by the misconception that "science is hard." Also, kindergarten is the ideal place to help eliminate the damaging gender stereotypes which have led many girls to believe that science is for boys. Science experiences promote cognitive growth and help children to learn about their natural and physical environments. A bird nest or large seashell prominently placed on a table will become the scene of active inquiry.

Kindergarten science experiences should also emerge as children ask questions: "Why does the water disappear after you wash the chalkboard?" "Where does the sun go at night?" "What makes the wind?" The questions children ask can launch an activity, a demonstration, or a visit to the school library to embark upon a "research project." As teachers, we cannot possibly know all of the answers to children's questions, but we *can* model an investigative attitude; we can show children how to find their own answers. After a while, as youngsters want to learn more about something that fascinates or interests them, we can help them to say "Let's try it!"

Young children should be encouraged to observe, to find similarities and differences in objects, to sort, classify, and otherwise group a wide variety of materials. They should grow plants and care for animals. They should be helped to describe what happens as they make observations.

The study of science offers countless opportunities to integrate learnings from several areas. As children need to communicate their observations and findings, they grow in their language skills. They can do wonderful artwork as they work with leaves and perform mathematical operations as they make a graph of the growth of a plant.

Science will have both planned and spontaneous dimensions. Certainly, activities and experiences should be provided, but spontaneous events should also be supported.

A pet brought to school, the first snowfall of the year, the first signs of spring are springboards for inquiry and involvement.

The science center need not be more than a table with an activity board and a few shelves. Objects can be displayed for independent investigation and activities can be devised in which children can follow a sequence shown in rebus form. Objects in the science center can be changed weekly to maintain interest and enthusiasm. Growing plants can be observed and measured over periods of time. The possibilities are endless. All that is required is a desire to help children find out about the world in which they live, a few common objects, and active, curious minds. Experiences in science can promote critical thinking and a sense of wonder. What follows is a mere sample of the abundant science experiences that are appropriate for children in the kindergarten.

OBSERVING A ROCK

WHY DO THIS?

In today's world of flashing lights, blaring sounds, and fast-paced video games, children do not often have the opportunity to focus on simple, natural objects such as leaves, seashells, snowflakes, or rocks. After a careful study of such items, children may be surprised at the number of intricate observations they can actually make. Indeed, it is an important goal in kindergarten to help children to improve and refine their abilities to pay close attention to a simple object, notice details, and communicate their impressions.

WHAT WILL I NEED?

- A rock for each child
- Construction paper
- Index cards and markers
- Tempera paints and small brushes

HOW TO GET STARTED.

If there is an area or field near the school where children can dig for rocks, have each one find a reasonably-sized specimen. (Of course, boulders and pebbles would be inappropriate.) Once back in the classroom, have the children examine their rocks carefully. Make a list of words that could be used to describe details of the rocks: rough, smooth, round, oval, jagged, sharp, sparkly, gray, brown, orange, pebbly, and so on. Encourage the children to make many observations of their rocks. Model a detailed description of your own rock if necessary. With each child, make a list of the observations made of his or her rock.

After the youngsters have studied their rocks, ask four or five children to place their rocks on a large sheet of construction paper. Have them turn their backs, while you mix up the rocks. Can they find their own rock? How well did they get to know it? Most children will be able to identify their own specimen. Try this same game with half of the class, and then the entire class. Were all of the children able to retrieve their own rocks? What does this tell them about their abilities to focus on simple objects and notice details?

HOW TO GO FURTHER.

Make a "rock garden" in the science center. Create a simple display area on a few sheets of construction paper. Have the children "name" their rocks and write the names on folded index cards so that they look like place cards.

With tempera paints and small brushes, the ciildren can paint faces, clothing, or anything else they like onto their rocks. The paint must be thick. (Some teachers like to use nail polish to decorate rocks.) Then the rocks truly become "pet rocks." Perhaps some children will want to write a story about their rocks. The rock and the accompanying story can be shown to other children in the school, the principal, and parents. Many youngsters will cherish their special rocks for years to come.

OBSERVING AN ANIMAL

WHY DO THIS?

Few events in the kindergarten are as filled with joy and enthusiasm as the arrival of a classroom pet. An animal can be a special visitor or a "permanent member" of the class. An animal in the classroom allows children to observe a living organism firsthand, to learn its habits, and to develop responsibility for its well-being. Common pets which can be easily cared for in kindergarten include fish, gerbils, mice, hamsters, guinea pigs, salamanders, lizards, chameleons, and earthworms. Children should not only be taught to care for classroom animals, but also to develop positive attitudes about handling animals and a general sense of compassion.

WHAT WILL I NEED?

- Any of the animals mentioned above and a proper cage or environment

HOW TO GET STARTED.

If you do not have a pet in the classroom, arrange to have one visit. The arrival of a classroom animal should be planned for by the entire class. What will the animal need? What is its normal habitat? Where does it come from? Can the animal be handled? If so, how? Ask the school librarian for books about the animal. Read them together. If the animal is going to stay in the classroom, make sure that you have all of the necessary requirements for its well-being—an appropriately-sized cage or tank, food, a water dispenser, and so forth. Children can take turns caring for the animal.

Once the pet is well established, children can begin their observations to learn more about the animal. Among the questions that may be considered are:

- How does the animal move? Are there times it moves faster or slower than at other times?
- How does the animal get its food? How is food brought to its mouth? What parts of its body move as it eats?

- Can you see the animal breathe? What parts of its body move when it breathes?
- Can you tell when the animal is sleeping? When during the day does it sleep?
- Describe the animal's skin covering. Does it change in any way during the year?
- How much does the animal weigh? Does its weight change throughout the year?
- Does the animal reproduce? How many young are born and how often? Does the mother care for its young? How?
- How does the animal react to environmental changes? What is its response to changes in heat or light? How can you set up experiments to check this?
- Can the animal be taught to do something like run a maze or respond to feeding time? (Many fish can be conditioned to swim to the top of a tank if the side of the tank is tapped each time just before feeding.)

HOW TO GO FURTHER.

Children should be encouraged to record or dictate their observations and draw pictures of the animal. They can write and illustrate stories about the animal. All of the children can contribute to the production of a "big book" about the animal which can be shared with others in the school.

SETTING UP AN AQUARIUM

WHY DO THIS?

Maintaining a simple aquarium in the classroom can help provide many opportunities for children to conduct observations of animals. An aquarium with goldfish is particularly easy to maintain since a heater, filter, and other such equipment are not required. Once it is set up, the aquarium can be used as a teaching and learning tool throughout the year.

WHAT WILL I NEED?

- A large glass container or fish tank
- Clean sand or gravel

- A few goldfish or other sturdy nontropical varieties
- Fish food
- A few aquarium snails
- Aquarium plants
- Bottled spring water

HOW TO GET STARTED.

If there is a pet shop near the school, make a field trip to acquire the necessary materials for a classroom aquarium. Wash the sand or gravel thoroughly a few times. Place about two inches of the sand or gravel on the bottom of the container or tank. Set a few hardy aquarium plants into the ground material. Let the water stand a day or two and then place the fish and snails in the tank. (Any aquarium will do better if an air pump and an airstone are used; however, these are not essential.)

Discuss the feeding of the fish with the children. Youngsters often overfeed fish. Generally, it is best to feed the fish every other day and to never give them more than they will consume in ten minutes.

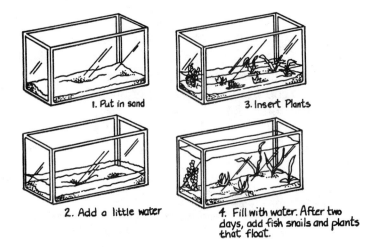

1. Put in sand

3. Insert Plants

2. Add a little water

4. Fill with water. After two days, add fish snails and plants that float.

Let children make their own observations and discuss them. The following questions may help to focus the youngsters' observations:

- What color are the fish? Describe their skin. Can you see through any parts of their bodies?
- How do the fish move? What parts of the body are involved? Observe the movements of the gill covers.
- Do air bubbles appear in the aquarium? How might they have formed? Do the fish ever come to the surface to gulp air? What could be the reason for this?

- Does the number of snails in the aquarium change? Keep track of how many are there from time to time.
- Study the movement of the snails across the aquarium glass. What are the steps involved in a snail's movement?
- Can fish learn? Tap the side of the aquarium just before the fish are fed. After a while see if the fish swim to the top of the tank if it is tapped before any food is given. What are some of the possible reasons for this?
- Do any deposits appear on the bottom of the aquarium? What might they be?

HOW TO GO FURTHER.

Children can conduct cooperative "research projects" about fish. First have them formulate a few questions, for example: "What are the biggest goldfish?" "How have goldfish been used in history?" "What other kinds of fish are related to goldfish?" "What are the different parts of the body of a goldfish?" "What does its skeleton look like?" Library books, visits to a pet shop, or calls to local experts may help children to answer some of their questions. The questions and answers can be listed on chartpaper or made into a book with illustrations. The whole notion of conducting research will be stimulating for the children and help to establish, early in their school careers, a love for learning and an understanding of how we can find answers to questions.

EXPLORING SEEDS

WHY DO THIS?

Seeds are abundant in our environment, yet youngsters are not always aware of them and their potential for growth. Seeds are found within fruit, in vegetables, on the ground, and blowing in the wind. Children can explore the many different kinds of seeds they may encounter in their daily lives, examine and describe them, and look for similarities and differences among them. They can understand the importance of seeds, sprout them, and identify a few basic structures.

WHAT WILL I NEED?

- A wide variety of seeds from apples, pears, oranges, peaches, plums, pumpkins, cucumbers, avocado, and so forth
- Lima beans

- A clear plastic tumbler
- Blotter paper
- Magnifiers

HOW TO GET STARTED.

Discuss seeds with the children. Explain that plants grow from seeds and that each seed contains a "baby plant." Where have they seen seeds? They are within many of the fruits and vegetables we eat. Can they name any? Take a walk outdoors and look for seeds. The common maple samaras (helicopters) contain seeds. Acorns are seeds from oak trees. The white cottony head of a dandelion contains thousands of seeds. Seeds are hidden within pine cones. (Cones will release their seeds if they are dried near a radiator or in an oven.) Cut open an apple and look at the seeds within. Remove the seeds from a variety of fruit and ask the children to compare their color, size, shape, and texture. Compare an apple seed and a peach (or plum) pit. Have the children examine seeds with a magnifier. How are they similar? How are they different? Which fruits have many seeds? Which fruits have only one?

Make a collection of a great variety of seeds. Ask the children to sort them according to type. Seeds can also be grouped according to color, size, shape, or other criteria.

HOW TO GO FURTHER.

Almost all seeds can be germinated and grown in the classroom. It is usually a good idea to soak the seeds for a few days before attempting to plant them. Most seeds can be grown in planting soil or vermiculite. Others, such as avocado seeds, are best started in a jar of water.

Lima beans are easy to germinate and they are large enough for children to see the various structures within them. Let the children examine and describe the dry beans. Then soak them in a jar or tumbler overnight. Help the children open a few of the soaked beans and examine them with a magnifier. Inside, they should see a tiny plant (embryo) and the main portion of the bean, which is stored food. Ask the children to compare the soaked beans and the dry beans.

Place some of the soaked beans between the inside walls of a plastic tumbler and blotter paper which is pressed up along the sides of the tumbler to hold the beans in place. Fill the tumbler with water. Place the tumbler in the science center along with magnifiers and a drawing of a sprouting seed like the one in the diagram. Have each child observe the seeds for several days. The stored food will eventually shrivel up as the embryo uses it for its "start" as a plant. As the plant grows, its main parts (roots, stem, leaves) will be easy to see. After a few weeks, the seeds can be put into a flower pot of soil, and it will grow and can be observed.

Children's experiences with seeds can be dictated and recorded on chart paper. Each child may wish to make a small booklet in which samples of various seeds are glued and then the type of seed is written. For example, one page can have apple seeds, another maple seeds, another orange seeds, and so on.

Dry seeds can be used in a variety of craft projects. Children can glue seeds onto pictures they make; they can also be used to fill the area of shapes and objects. Seed necklaces and other ornaments are interesting and fun to make.

STUDYING PLANT GROWTH

WHY DO THIS?

Children love to grow plants. They are also keen observers. Many youngsters will notice the small plants growing in the cracks of sidewalks or the changes in a tree seen from the classroom window. Observing a growing plant provides many opportunities for youngsters to explore and develop important concepts about the natural world. As they witness the growth of plants from seeds, they come to realize that bean seeds yield bean plants, avocado seeds grow into avocado plants. This is a part of the orderliness of nature. In this activity, children will observe plants in their environment, grow a few of their own, and learn about basic plant structures.

WHAT WILL I NEED?

- A variety of seeds for planting including seed packets, grass seed, pits from fruit
- Potting soil
- Plant containers or cups (cut-down milk cartons are fine)
- Markers

HOW TO GET STARTED.

Take a walk through the school neighborhood and ask the children to take note of all of the plants they notice—trees, grass, weeds, flowers. Once back in the classroom, discuss what the children saw.

Tell the children that they are going to grow plants. Ask them to bring milk cartons from home for planters. Show the children the variety of seeds. Ask them to find similarities and differences in their appearance. Have each child choose one kind of seed to plant. Mark the seed type on the container. (Use masking tape if you cannot write directly onto the container. Some children may wish to cover and decorate the container.) Fill the containers half full of soil. Have the children poke a finger into the soil and then place two or three of their seeds into the hole. The seeds should be covered with soil and then watered. (Seeds from grapefruit, oranges, apples, watermelon, and pears should be soaked overnight before planting.) Prepare a few extra plants for observation. Place the plants on trays in a convenient location for watering and observation.

Check the plants periodically. Which seem to be growing the most rapidly? What structures (leaves, stems, flowers) appear? What are the leaves like? How do the leaves compare from plant to plant? Which kind of plant is the tallest? Which is the shortest? Do they remain the tallest and shortest over a period of weeks? Gently take one of the extra plants out of its box. Show the children the roots. Discuss the purpose of the roots, stem, and leaves.

HOW TO GO FURTHER.

Place a ruler with inch markings into the cups of a few plants which seem to be growing well. Use this scale to make comparisons in the growth of the plants. Charts and graphs can be made in which the name of the plants and their heights are indicated. Children may also wish to maintain their own records in notebooks or folders.

New plants can also be grown from parts of plants. A sweet potato submerged in a jar of water and kept in a dark place will develop roots and begin to grow. The tops of carrots or turnips can be grown in a shallow dish. An onion, with its root end suspended in a jar of water with toothpicks, will grow rather quickly.

Read and write stories about plants, farms, and gardens.

ADOPT A TREE

WHY DO THIS?

Observing a nearby tree throughout the year provides children with the opportunity to focus on seasonal changes and how they affect one particular tree. By looking for signs of bud development, changes in bark, the appearance of leaves, and other characteristics, children can understand how trees and other living things change and grow. Adopting a tree can help children to *see* where they have only looked before.

WHAT WILL I NEED?

- A tree situated in a location convenient for year-round observation
- A camera and film
- The "A Tree in Four Seasons" worksheet

HOW TO GET STARTED.

Tell the children that they are going to select a tree to study throughout the year. (It is best to begin this project in the fall so that children can observe the tree selected throughout the school year.) First, look out of the classroom window. Is there a likely candidate within ready view? If not, walk around near the school to find a good specimen. On the first visit talk about the tree. Where is it located? What kind of tree is it? How tall is it? (Compare its height to buildings or other structures in its surroundings.) Talk about the bark, leaves, fruit, branching pattern, and the overall shape of the tree as seen from a distance. Discuss the environment in which the tree is found. Look for evidences of relationships with other forms of life—insects, birds, or plants. Take a photograph of the tree. Once back in the classroom, make an experience chart about what the children found out about the tree and have them draw pictures of the tree.

Visit the tree at regular intervals, preferably once each month. Ask the children if they see any changes in the tree. Note especially changes in leaves, bird visitors, twigs, fruit, and other structures. Are any effects of snow, rain, or ice apparent? Take pictures, if possible, each time you visit the tree. Display the pictures, with the months labeled, in the science center. Make an experience chart listing changes noted. Encourage children to draw pictures and write or dictate stories about the tree. Periodically, read through the experience charts to compare the observations made.

HOW TO GO FURTHER.

Give each child a copy of the "A Tree in Four Seasons" worksheet. Discuss what trees look like in each of the seasons and review the season words. Have them complete the worksheet.

Make bark rubbings on the tree. Peel a few crayons and have children place a sheet of paper onto the bark. Rub the sides of the crayons on the paper. The texture of the bark will show through. Children can also make rubbings of the vein patterns of leaves from the tree. Place leaves on a flat surface (vein side up), put a piece of thin paper over the leaves, and rub with the side of a peeled crayon. Compare the vein patterns of leaves from the adopted tree with other trees.

A TREE IN FOUR SEASONS

Cut out the names of the four seasons at the bottom of this page.
Paste each name on the picture that shows how the tree looks
during that time of year.

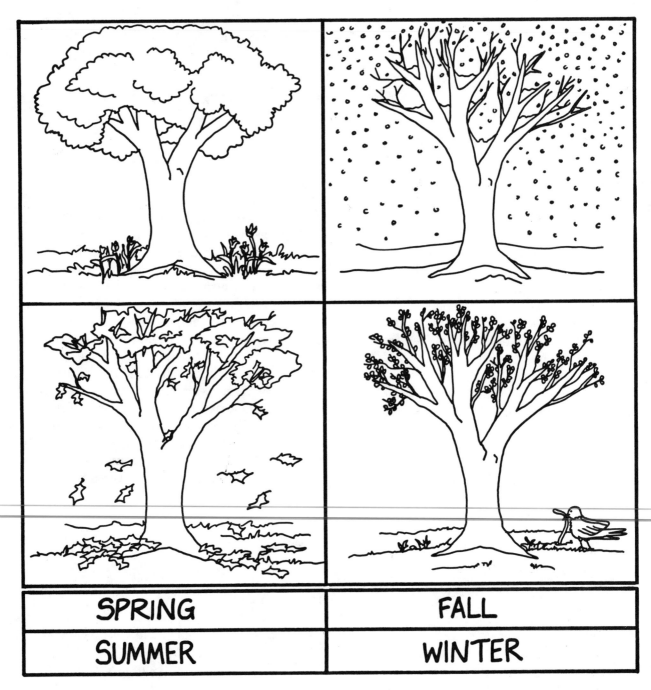

SPRING	FALL
SUMMER	WINTER

LIVING OR NONLIVING?

WHY DO THIS?

As children have experiences with plants, animals, and nonliving objects, they can begin to develop the ability to differentiate between living and nonliving things. Children can identify characteristics of living things and compare them with nonliving objects.

WHAT WILL I NEED?

- Small plant
- Paper
- Pencil
- A fish in a fishbowl
- Rock
- Grass

- A ball
- An insect or worm
- Scissors
- A glass of water
- "Living or Nonliving?" worksheet

HOW TO GET STARTED.

Prepare a display of the objects listed above. Ask the children to observe and describe each of the objects. Discuss the characteristics of living things. Most children will suggest that living things grow, eat, drink, move, and breathe. Have the children sort the objects shown into two piles, those that are living things, and those that are not. Ask children to name a living thing and explain why they think it is alive. Complete the "Living or Nonliving?" worksheet.

HOW TO GO FURTHER.

Gather several objects that are no longer alive, but once were, for example, fruit, an acorn, leaves, and so on. Ask the children if each of the objects is living or nonliving. Discuss the fact that these items were once a part of a living thing but are no longer alive. Have the children sort objects into three piles, those that are alive now, those that were alive once but are no longer living, and those that have never been alive. You can get into some very interesting discussions about this concept. For example, a piece of paper is considered a nonliving object, but it was once a part of a tree! Most teachers find it very rewarding to conduct such discussions with their youngsters.

Children can make books in which magazine pictures are pasted onto pages that are devoted to living and nonliving things. Youngsters can also make collections of objects on three trays according to whether they are living, nonliving, or once living but not now alive.

Name _____

LIVING OR NONLIVING?

Make a circle around the pictures of living things. Make an X on the pictures of nonliving things.

A TEXTURE-MATCHING GAME

WHY DO THIS?

Through a variety of activities in kindergarten children learn about the five senses. Youngsters can identify objects by feeling them and also come to realize that their skin (particularly on their hands) is the major sensory organ associated with the sense of touch. There are many opportunities for exploring the sense of touch, and making a game of it is great fun for the children. In this activity, children are asked to match texture samples using only their hands, without relying on any of their other senses.

WHAT WILL I NEED?

- A cardboard box (larger than a shoe box)
- A variety of texture sample pairs (two swatches of the same material), each about 4 inches square. Some interesting samples include corduroy, velvet, sandpaper, aluminum foil (mounted on cardboard), fur, and burlap.

HOW TO GET STARTED.

Discuss the sense of touch with the children and ask them how they receive information about the texture of objects. Cut a hole in the top of the cardboard box just large enough for a child's hand to pass through, but not so large as to permit the objects within it to be seen. Put one sample of each of the texture pairs in the box. Place the other texture samples in a child's hand, one at a time, and ask him or her to reach into the box with the other hand and try to find the same texture. The child should then pull the texture sample out of the box and check visually to see if a match was found. Continue until all of the textures have been matched. Place the box and the texture samples in the science center for continued exploration. Interest can be maintained by changing the materials from time to time.

HOW TO GO FURTHER.

There are many activities involving the sense of touch that can be created or improvised. One idea is to maintain a texture box in the science center at all times. Keep interesting texture samples around and ask children to take turns closing their eyes, reaching into the box, and describing the texture they feel. The use of descriptive words is particularly helpful in promoting language development.

SORTING BUTTONS

WHY DO THIS?

Classification is a basic skill in science, as it is in almost any subject area. Sorting objects into similar piles is an important cognitive skill for young children that involves determining what is the same about a set of objects. For example, in sorting pocket change, it is rather easy to put all of the pennies in one pile, the dimes in another, and so on. Another sorting approach would be to divide all of the change into two groups, silver-colored coins, and coins that do not have a silver color (pennies). This is called binary, or yes/no sorting. In more complex classification systems, however, more subtle distinctions have to be made. For example, if a youngster has a set of blocks of varying shape, size and color, the materials can be sorted by color, by shape, or by size, and thus the child has to decide upon criteria and then judge each of the items against the criteria established. In this activity, youngsters will find that there are various ways to sort familiar objects—buttons.

WHAT WILL I NEED?

- A large assortment of buttons

HOW TO GET STARTED.

Obtain a good number of buttons. (Many teachers are successful in asking children to bring in buttons from home.) Spread the buttons out on a table top, and working with a few youngsters, ask them to divide the buttons into two piles—ones that have two holes, and ones that do not. Explain that this operation is called yes/no sorting, the buttons either have two holes, or they do not. Ask the children to think of other ways to sort the buttons into two piles. Some possibilities include: brown/not brown, rimmed/not rimmed, four-holed/not four-holed, and so on.

Now ask the children to sort the buttons into more than two piles, grouping those in the same pile together in some way based upon a common feature. Children can sort buttons by color, size, number of holes, shape, and other attributes. After each child has had a chance to sort the buttons, ask him or her to tell the others the basis upon which the buttons were sorted. A good thinking skill is to ask children to break down and communicate the steps they went through during the sorting operation. For example, once the criteria for sorting were established, the children had to ask themselves how each button was similar to others in the piles and how it was different. Did they ask themselves if each button fit the rule for making the piles?

HOW TO GO FURTHER.

Demonstrate how to play the "What's My Rule?" game. First, sort the buttons into two piles on a yes/no basis. Ask the children to guess your rule for dividing the buttons into two piles. Then, sort the buttons into more than two piles based upon observable criteria. Again, ask the children to guess your rule. Have children work in pairs with one sorting buttons into categories and the other trying to guess the rule used for sorting.

Find other materials to sort. Some good possibilities are blocks, leaves, money, beads, pictures of animals, and crayons.

WHAT'S INSIDE?

WHY DO THIS?

Children will begin to understand how they receive information through their sense of hearing if they have to gather information just from sounds. Even if they do not see an ambulance, how do they know that one is in the vicinity? How can they tell if another class is playing outside on the school grounds? More subtle distinctions can be made by shaking a box to try and guess what is inside of it. Such an activity seems like a game for the youngsters, but they will exercise perceptual skills, become aware of their senses, and learn to focus.

WHAT WILL I NEED?

- A few small boxes (smaller than a shoebox)
- A variety of objects to place inside of the boxes

HOW TO GET STARTED.

Take a small box and place three or four pennies in it. Tape it shut. Ask the children to shake the box and try to guess what is inside. Discuss the clues they used to guess. What helped them to know that the contents were made of metal? What part of their bodies helped to give them this information? Place other kinds of objects into the box, made of different materials. Try a rubber ball, a wooden block, a plastic cup. Help the children to develop strategies for discovering the contents. For example, if they move the box slowly from side to side and hear something rolling, what does that tell about the shape of the object? If the object does not roll but slides from side to side, what does that indicate about its shape? Can a magnet be useful in finding out what is inside a box?

HOW TO GO FURTHER?

Have children conceal objects in small boxes and then have a classmate guess what was placed inside. Activity sheets can be made to accompany mystery boxes in the science center. Make five boxes and place a large number (from one to five) conspicuously on the lid of each box. Seal the boxes. Then, duplicate a set of activity sheets with spaces for children to write their names, a box number, and their guess about the contents. If they cannot write the name of the object they think is inside of a box, they can draw a picture of it on the sheet. Collect the sheets, read them at a class meeting, and then open the boxes to reveal the contents. Have the children discuss the strategies they used for guessing.

A SMELLING PARTY

WHY DO THIS?

As children explore the five senses, they should have many experiences working with stimulating materials and describing their sensations. Odors can evoke a range of human emotions—the smell of pancakes frying may fill a child's mind with anticipation of a great treat, the smell of something burning may cause alarm, the smell of perfume or after-shave lotion may signal that a parent is going out. Children can describe odors in their environment, increase their vocabulary, and also discuss how odors can communicate.

WHAT WILL I NEED?

- Orange peels
- Vanilla
- Perfume
- Bananas
- Cloves
- Mints
- Coffee
- Chewing gum
- Moth Balls
- Chocolate
- Small boxes, spice cans, jars with pierced tops or other containers into which the above objects can be placed and smelled but not seen.

HOW TO GET STARTED.

Discuss odors that children experience in their everyday lives. What are some pleasant odors? What are some unpleasant odors? Ask the children to go on an "odor hunt" around the room and describe the odors that they smell. It is difficult for most children to attach descriptive words to odors, and most often they will use an analogy: "It smells like a rose. It smells like the stuff you clean a bathroom with."

Place the odor objects listed previously into boxes or containers in which they can be smelled but not seen. Introduce one of the objects. Pass it from child to child. Ask them to smell it, but not say what they think it is until all children have had a chance. Then, discuss the odor. What does it remind the children of? Have they ever smelled this object before? Under what circumstances? Encourage the use of descriptive vocabulary. Pass around some of the other objects and discuss them.

Place the odor boxes in the science center so children can smell them individually. Caution children not to taste objects provided in this activity. Change the contents of the boxes to maintain interest and involvement.

HOW TO GO FURTHER.

Experiment with ways to prevent odors from being smelled. What happens if they are wrapped in paper, aluminum foil, or plastic wrap? Which is the most effective in terms of masking the odor? When might we want to mask the odor of an object?

Make several pairs of odor boxes. Tell the children that there are two boxes for each odor. Have them try to find the pairs.

Go on an outdoor odor hunt. Have the children find and describe objects that have distinctive odors. Record what was found in a notebook. Once back in the classroom make an experience chart describing the objects that the children found and where they were located.

SORTING LIQUIDS BY TASTE

WHY DO THIS?

One science activity that combines the process of classification with exploration of the sense of taste is to sort liquids by taste. This adds an additional dimension to what might otherwise be a purely sensory task. In this activity youngsters find pairs of unknown liquids by matching and grouping them by similarity of taste. Children ought to be cautioned that they should only taste materials provided by a teacher or parent.

WHAT WILL I NEED?

- Nine small paper cups filled accordingly: three with diluted lemon juice, three with orange juice, three with apple juice
- Nine index cards
- Nine drinking straws

HOW TO GET STARTED.

Prepare nine small cups of the liquids specified above. Punch a hole in the center of each of the index cards large enough for a straw to fit through. Place the cards with a straw in each on top of each cup so that the contents cannot be seen. Ask a child to take a sip of each of each of the liquids and describe the taste. Ask the youngster if he or she recognizes the taste of each of the liquids. Then have the child find pairs of liquids that have the same taste and make groups of the same liquids. Provide additional sets of liquids and have other children try the activity. Discuss the tastes in terms of sweetness. Ask the children if they can think of other ways to sort the liquids. Is the lemon juice more sour than the orange juice?

HOW TO GO FURTHER.

Have children make books about "My Favorite Drinks." With pictures cut from magazine advertisements or labels from familiar drinks, children can make books about drink products they enjoy. One picture can be pasted onto each page with a small caption about the drink below.

Have a "tasting party" and bring in a variety of different kinds of unfamiliar foods to encourage children to try new things. Ask them to describe the new foods that they try.

ME, MYSELF, AND I

WHY DO THIS?

Each child has a laboratory—his or her own body! In the kindergarten children can study human anatomy by identifying body parts, comparing the similarities and differences exhibited among the members of a class, and taking stock of their prominent features. As children look in a mirror and are asked to look for specific features, they will notice aspects of themselves that they may have overlooked in the past. Then, as they create a lifesize likeness of themselves, they will focus on features that make them unique.

WHAT WILL I NEED?

- A mirror
- Large butcher or roll paper
- Newspapers
- Crayons or markers
- A stapler
- The "Body Parts" worksheet

HOW TO GET STARTED.

Ask the children to look at themselves in a mirror. Hundreds of observations can be made. How many fingers do we have? Where do we have hair? How many eyes and ears do we have? Which body parts come in pairs? Discuss the notion of symmetry in the human body. If an imaginary line is drawn down the center of the body, which features are noticed on both sides of the body?

Discuss similarities and differences among the youngsters in the class. Almost all of the children will have two eyes, two ears, two arms, two legs, hair, and so on. What are the differences among them? Hair, eye, and skin color may be an obvious difference. Hair may be black and straight, blond and curly, brown and wavy. Make a list of the various kinds of hair types in the class. Which kind is the most common?

Children can learn more about their own features by tracing their own bodies. Obtain some butcher paper or large roll paper. Have the children lie down on the paper and trace around them with a crayon or marker. After the tracing is complete, the children should cut out their outlines and then draw, as accurately as possible, their prominent features. Let them use a mirror to check eye color, hair color and texture, clothing, and so forth. (If you want to make three-dimensional bodies, cut out a front and a back of the body, stuff it with crumpled newspaper, and then staple all around the outline.) When each child has completed his or her own likeness, all of the bodies may be discussed and compared. Height differences will be immediately noticeable. Discussions regarding the variety of individual types will naturally occur and positive values about the nature of human differences may be reinforced. Why should people consider differences in skin color any more important than differences in height, hair type, or clothing worn? (By the way, this is a wonderful project to exhibit on a parents' night or a back-to-school night.)

HOW TO GO FURTHER.

Discuss body proportions and measure them with the children. Are legs longer than arms? How do the head circumferences of children in the class vary? What other measurements would the children like to make? As a follow-up, have the youngsters complete the "Body Parts" worksheet.

Name _____

BODY PARTS

Cut out the parts of the body and paste them onto a sheet of paper so that the person is put together correctly.

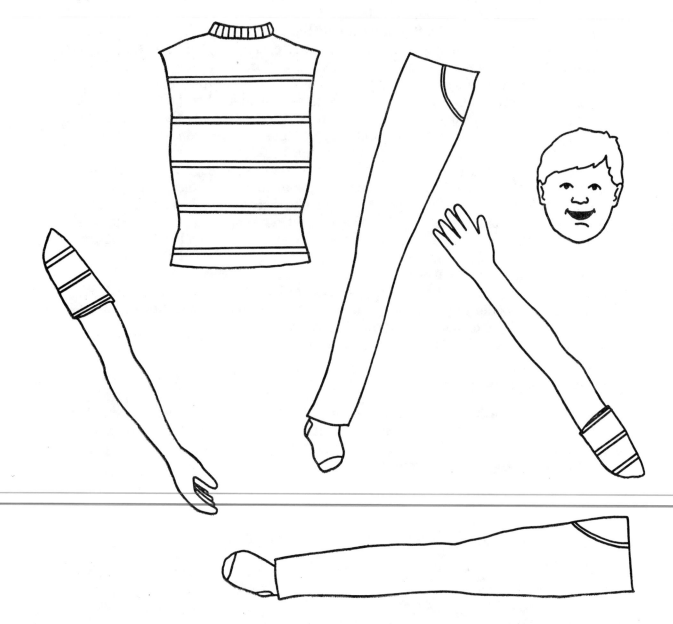

FLOAT AND SINK

WHY DO THIS?

Young children can explore physical phenomena without necessarily having to understand the underlying principles. Testing objects for whether they float or sink in water helps to improve youngsters' observational skills. After a few trials, they can also make predictions and then check if their predictions were accurate. The concept of density, which dictates whether an object will float or sink in water, is too complex for kindergarten children to deal with. But, they will certainly enjoy and profit from testing a wide variety of objects.

WHAT WILL I NEED?

- A large basin (baby bath tub) or large aquarium with water
- A paper bag for each child
- Various objects to test for floating: rocks, wood, sponges, marbles, pencils, plastic, crayons, blocks, nails, styrofoam

HOW TO GET STARTED.

Fill a large basin with water and ask children to note what happens each time an object is dropped into it. Define the words float and sink if necessary by explaining that something that floats stays on top of the water, while things that sink go down to the bottom. Remove each object after it is tested and put it into one of two piles labeled "floats" and "sinks."

Try some other objects, but this time, have the children make a prediction before each item is tested. Ask if they think the item will sink or float. Were the predictions accurate?

Take the children outdoors on the playground. Give each child a paper bag and ask them to find six objects—three that they think will float and three that they think will sink. Back in the classroom have them test their objects and evaluate their predictions. Discuss similarities among objects that float and similarities among objects that sink. Make a chart listing objects that float and objects that sink in water.

HOW TO GO FURTHER.

Have the children make little boats from clay, small aluminum pie tins, or by shaping aluminum foil. Check to see if the boats float in water. Have the youngsters experiment with differently shaped boats. Which seem to work the best? Collect a variety of objects from the classroom to place into the boats. Ask children to make predictions about what will happen when objects are placed into the boats. Will the boats keep floating or will they sink? Have the children determine how many nails, marbles, pebbles, or other small weights each boat can hold before it sinks. Which boat can hold the most weight? What do the children think accounts for this? Leave the basin of water, materials to test, and boats in the science center for continued exploration.

WEATHER OBSERVATIONS

WHY DO THIS?

Weather affects children's daily lives. The types of activity they can engage in is often controlled by weather. The clothing they wear is also affected by changes in weather. Young children can begin to make weather observations in and outside of the classroom. Understanding the operation of a thermometer, talking about wind, sky conditions, and precipitation all help youngsters to know more about how atmospheric conditions are observed and measured. With this background, they can discuss how weather predictions are made. Also, the study of weather will result in the development of a new set of vocabulary words.

WHAT WILL I NEED?

- A large thermometer
- A shallow dish or tray, preferably made of clear glass
- A newspaper or newsprint easel paper

HOW TO GET STARTED.

Discuss weather and how it affects children's daily lives. Together, listen to (or watch) a weather report and record the types of information given. Temperature, sky conditions, and barometric pressure will probably be mentioned and perhaps wind velocity. Then a prediction will probably be made about future conditions. Discuss each of the items reported. How is temperature measured? How is rainfall recorded? How is wind speed and direction determined?

Begin with a study of temperature. Discuss and demonstrate the operation of a thermometer. Place it near a radiator or in the sun and show how the liquid inside the tube rises. Explain that as the liquid rises, the temperature reading is higher. Help children read the scale on the thermometer. Mount the thermometer in the classroom (or better yet in a shady spot just outside of a classroom window) and maintain daily records, taking the readings at the same time each day. Ask the children to make predictions of the temperature for the next day. Were they accurate?

Discuss the importance of rain and why we need it for growing plants, for a water supply, for transportation, and recreation. On a rainy day, place a shallow glass pan in an accessible outdoor area. Bring in the pan after the rain has stopped and record the depth of the water with a ruler. Children may be surprised about how much it actually has to rain to accumulate an inch of water. Using a deeper container, the rainfall for a month can be collected and measured. Charts can be kept comparing the rainfall for each month. Was this a particularly wet or dry month when compared to others during the year?

Discuss the appearance of the sky. Compare sunny days, partly cloudy days, mostly cloudy days, rainy or snowy days, and so on. Explain that clouds are actually large masses of water droplets. Children can learn to identify the various types of clouds, for example, cumulus, cirrus, and nimbus. By studying clouds, children will begin to associate different cloud patterns with weather conditions.

Many studies of wind can be conducted with kindergarten children. On a breezy day, first have them observe the effects of wind. Can they see treetops swaying, flags waving, or smoke moving from chimneys? Ask the children if they have ever felt the wind and to describe how it feels. What do they think wind is? Wind is air in motion and the children can be helped to realize this by a few of their own experiments. Cut a piece of newspaper into 2-inch strips. On a windy day give each child a paper strip and go outdoors. What happens to the streamers in the wind? Attach some of the streamers to a jungle gym or other permanent structure. Observe what happens. What happens if a streamer is made longer or shorter? Note the direction that the streamers are blowing. What do the children think this tells us about the direction of the wind? Which way is it blowing? On another windy day, go outdoors again with streamers. Is the wind blowing in the same direction? How do wind and wind direction affect the weather?

HOW TO GO FURTHER.

Make books about the weather. Devote one page to temperature, one to clouds, one to wind, and so on. Children can draw pictures of a windy day. Read books about wind and weather. There are many appropriate titles in a school library. Use ideas in these books for writing stories, making experience charts, or conducting additional experiments.

IS AIR REAL?

WHY DO THIS?

Air is all around us, yet we are usually unaware of its presence. Often, children do not think that air is real. After all, they cannot see, smell, or taste it; yet it is vital for life, and the behavior of air is largely responsible for our weather. As children explore their environment, they have an opportunity to gain some understanding of air and its characteristics. First, though, children should be helped to develop the concept that air is real. One way, is to demonstrate that air takes up space. All substances occupy space. For air to be considered a substance, it too should occupy space. In the activity that follows, children will be involved in demonstrations that help to promote this important scientific understanding.

WHAT WILL I NEED?

- Plastic food storage bags with twist-ties
- A glass or plastic tumbler
- A clear basin or tank filled with water

HOW TO GET STARTED.

Ask the children what they know about air. Discuss how air is used, for example, to fill inflatable toys, balloons, and tires, to breathe, to move sailboats, and so on. Ask the children if air is real. If so, why? If not, why not?

Take a plastic food storage bag and wave it around, trapping air inside of it. Close the bag with a twist-tie and ask the children what is inside of the bag. Pass the bag around and let the children feel it. Ask the children to think of places within the classroom where they think there is no air. Take a plastic bag and try to trap air in these places. Slowly, develop the idea that air is all around them. Have each child take a plastic bag and go around the room to trap air. (You may need to demonstrate the technique of waving the bag to trap air.) Have them discuss their conclusions. Where did they find air? (Some children may think that air is only outside. Trapping air in several areas within the classroom may lead them to the understanding that air is all around them.)

As an additional demonstration, collect air in a plastic bag and tie the end with a twist-tie. Place the bag on a tabletop and balance a book on top of the bag. (See the illustration.) Ask the children to tell what is keeping the book up. What substance is between the table top and the book? How does this show that air is real? Place these materials in the science center and have the children perform the demonstration on their own. (Balancing the book will also be an interesting challenge for the children.)

HOW TO GO FURTHER.

There are many other demonstrations that can be performed to suggest that air is real. Try this one: Crumple a piece of paper and push it down into the bottom of a clear glass or plastic tumbler. Turn the tumbler upside down and push it straight down into a large basin or tank of water. (It is important that the tumbler be pushed down straight and not at an angle.) Pull the tumbler straight out and inspect the piece of paper. Did it become wet? How does this demonstrate that air takes ups space?

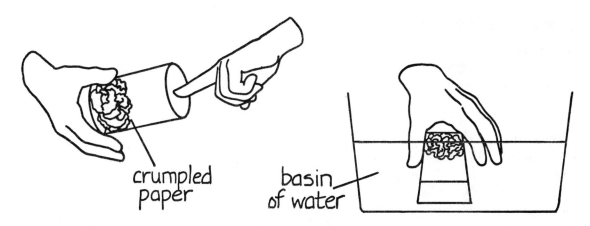

crumpled paper

basin of water

Children can observe one another as they inhale and exhale. Do they notice any changes in their bodies? Children can make folded fans and pinwheels to feel and see the effects of air in motion. Make a book about air and include pictures of things that use air or need air to operate. Ask children to pretend that they are the wind. What would they like to do if they were the wind?

USING MAGNETS

WHY DO THIS?

Young children are intrigued by magnets. They enjoy playing with them and testing objects in the classroom. Part of the fascination is the fact that the invisible force of magnetism attracts items at a distance, without making direct contact. Although kindergarten children cannot understand the theory underlying the operation of a magnet, they can nonetheless try to find magnetic and nonmagnetic objects and discuss the differences between them. They can also sort materials into two categories based upon whether or not they are attracted to a magnet.

WHAT WILL I NEED?

- A few different types of magnets—bar magnets, horseshoe magnets, U-magnets, circular and rectangular magnets
- A variety of objects to test for attraction to a magnet including, paper clips, a key, buttons, a plastic hair comb, crayons, scissors, a small book, a spool from thread, and other familiar materials.
- A few cardboard or plastic trays
- The "What Does a Magnet Pick Up?" worksheet

HOW TO GET STARTED.

Show the children a magnet. Ask them if they know what it is and what it can do. Test it out in the classroom by finding materials that are attracted to it. Show some other kinds of magnets, especially the rectangular or circular ones that are often found on refrigerator doors. Ask the children how they use magnets in their daily lives. (Some common examples are indeed the kinds found on refrigerator doors and on electric can openers to hold the lids.) Discuss differences in objects that are attracted to a magnet and objects that are not. What is the same about all of the objects that are attracted to a magnet? Ask the children to think of ways in which magnets can help us.

Place a magnet and a variety of objects on a tray in the science center. Have the children test each object to see if it is attracted to the magnet. (Define and use the term "attract.") Have them place each item tested into one of two trays that are labeled "yes" or "no" depending upon whether the object was attracted to a magnet. If a metal object was not picked up by the magnet ask the children to try to think of some explanation. (It may have been too heavy.) Show other objects to the children before they test them with a magnet and have them predict whether or not they think each object will be attracted to the magnet. Test each object. How accurate were the predictions? How could they tell? As an additional activity, have the children complete the "What Does a Magnet Pick Up?" worksheet.

Have children test the relative strength of different kinds of magnets by asking them to count the number of paper clips that each type can pick up. Which magnet is the strongest? Are all parts of the magnet equally strong? On bar magnets it is easy to show that the poles are the areas of greatest magnetic strength.

HOW TO GO FURTHER.

Have the children experiment to see which materials a magnet's strength can pass through. Cover a magnet with a piece of paper. Place some paper clips on top of the paper. Move the magnet around underneath. Does magnetism pass through the paper? What is the evidence? Try other such experiments. Can a magnet's strength pass through a glass jar, a plastic tumbler, a styrofoam tray, a piece of plastic, or aluminum foil? If paper clips are dropped into a glass of water, and a magnet is pushed into the water, will it pick up paper clips? Does magnetism work in water?

Ask the children to examine a bar magnet carefully. Do they notice any letters on the magnet. (Usually bar magnets will be marked with an *N* and an *S* for the north and south poles.) Ask the children if they know what these markings mean. Show how two bar magnets can attract one another and can also repel one another by trying to have the two like poles touch. The magnet which is free to move on a tabletop will seem to push away. If one of the bar magnets is suspended with string from a stand or bracket, the children will be able to explore this phenomenon.

Name _____

WHAT DOES A MAGNET PICK UP?

Draw a circle around the objects that a magnet can pick up.

PLAYING WITH SHADOWS

WHY DO THIS?

It is a wondrous moment when a child first discovers his or her shadow. Whether it is on a sunny sidewalk or a moonlit night, it is fascinating for the child to see the shadow move wherever he or she moves. Shadows are formed when light is blocked by opaque objects. In kindergarten children can learn how to make shadows, how to stretch them out or make them small, and also how to recognize objects from their shadows alone. Not only will the children discover some important properties of light (and how to block it), but they will also practice recognizing objects from different vantage points.

WHAT WILL I NEED?

- A strong light source, like the beam from a slide or filmstrip projector
- A flashlight
- Clay
- Construction paper
- Chalk
- A large cardboard box
- A piece of white cloth (as from a bed sheet)
- Tape
- A variety of common classroom objects: pencils, blocks, stapler, tape dispenser, a paper cup, and so forth

HOW TO GET STARTED.

Talk about shadows. Explain what they are. When have the children seen shadows? What do they already know about them? Shine the beam of a slide or filmstrip projector onto a wall or screen. Place your hand in the path of the beam. Use finger motions to form animal shadows. Have children try to make shadow pictures with their hands and fingers. Define a shadow as the outline of something that blocks a path of light.

Have the children sit in front of the projector beam facing the wall or screen. Place familiar objects in the path of the beam of light and ask the children to guess the objects by looking at their shadows. Children can play this game with each other in the science center using a flashlight.

On a sunny day, have the children go outside and find their shadows. If it will be sunny all day, go out in the morning and have a child stand in a specific spot. Trace around his or her shadow with chalk on the pavement or blacktop. Return to the same spot after a few hours. Trace around the same child again. The shadow will be smaller.

Ask the children to note the difference in size of the two shadows. What do they think accounts for the change? Explain that when the sun is higher in the sky the shadow will be smaller. (The smallest shadow will be around noon.) You can demonstrate this phenomenon in the classroom by placing a pencil in a wad of clay so that it stands upright. Put the pencil on a large sheet of paper on a sunny windowsill. Trace the shadow of the pencil at regular intervals throughout the day. Label each line with the time that it was traced. When is the shadow longest? When is it shortest? Show how this happens by directing the light from a flashlight onto the pencil at an angle. Then shine the flashlight from a point almost straight above the pencil. How is this situation similar to the shadow cast by the pencil and the sun?

A favorite project to make as a holiday gift for parents is a silhouette of their child. Using a projector beam, shine the light onto the side of each child's face. Project the image onto a sheet of black construction paper. Trace around the silhouette with chalk. Have the children cut out their profiles around the outline and mount them onto pieces of construction paper of a contrasting color. Display all of the silhouettes. Can the children identify their classmates by looking at the profiles?

HOW TO GO FURTHER.

A wonderful challenge is to have children view and identify objects, the shadows of which are seen from different vantage points. Obtain a cardboard box. Cut off one face of the box and cut out a large hole on the opposite side of the box. Stretch a piece of white cloth over the side of the box where the cardboard was removed and tape it so it remains in place. Put a tape dispenser into the box. Turn it so that the narrow side is facing the screen. Focus a flashlight through the hole so a shadow is cast onto the screen. Ask the children if they can guess what the object is. Now turn the tape dispenser so that the broad side is facing the screen. Shine the flashlight into the box. Now can the children guess the identity of the object? Try different objects in the shadow box, such as a block, a paper cup, a stapler, and so on. How does this activity help to promote children's thinking skills?

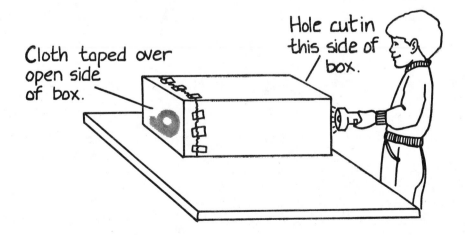

Cloth taped over open side of box.

Hole cut in this side of box.

chapter 9

IN THE MUSIC CENTER

Music is a part of our world; it is part of our rich cultural heritage. Music is also a form of personal expression and a shared experience. Music is everywhere around us. Children hear music on radios and television, on record players and tape recorders. Children make music spontaneously as they work or play. Children's chants are often heard on the playground or while youngsters draw, paint, or build. Singing in the kindergarten is a joyful time when children can all be a part of the large sound that comes from making music together.

Many kindergarten teachers also use music as an instructional technique for promoting conceptual development. A wide variety of songs exists to help youngsters learn colors, numbers, letters, and other concepts. Music can help children to mimic the movements of animals and pretend to be princes or princesses, or school bus drivers.

Through experiences in music children can explore, discover, and invent. Music can create moods and emotions and can cause children to respond with feeling. Music can be gleeful or sorrowful, and children can discuss the feelings and emotions evoked. Music makes us want to move, to respond naturally, and helps us to retain melodies and rhythms.

Music is also a social experience. As children sing together, they are a part of a group. No child alone could produce the strength of sound that comes from a large group singing together. Somehow the big sound makes each little voice sound better.

Children enjoy music as they play rhythm instruments and maintain beat and rhythm. They can learn to respond to auditory cues—when to begin, when to play, when to go fast or slowly, and when to stop.

Music is often integrated with children's language. They learn new words from songs, they make up their own songs, they identify rhymes, and they express feelings and moods.

Musical activities can occur anywhere in the classroom or the school—in a music room, an auditorium, or a corner of the classroom. A music center in the kindergarten room can contain a variety of materials for happy music making. Among the items to include on a table or corner are natural objects for making rhythm instruments, a record player or tape recorder, and electronic instruments. The increasing popularity and availability of electronic instruments allows for musical experimentation. Keyboards, synthesizers, small pianos, or other keyboard instruments are relatively inexpensive. A wide range of instruments with a bewildering array of options and possibilities is available. When working with young children, however, it is best to keep these devices simple.

CLAP-BACK

WHY DO THIS?

Most kindergarteners are able to repeat a rhythmic pattern established by a teacher. This is, however, quite a complex skill when you think about the various steps that the child must go through to accomplish this. The teacher establishes a rhythmic pattern and claps it out. The child must hear it, remember it, and then duplicate it exactly as heard. Such an activity not only helps children to appreciate rhythm and meter in songs, but also helps to promote listening skills.

WHAT WILL I NEED?

- Chalkboard and chalk or paper and marker

HOW TO GET STARTED.

Explain to the children that you will make up a clapping pattern that they should listen to carefully and then clap back. Establish a simple rhythmic pattern of about five claps. (In music methodology the syllable *tah* is often used to represent a long sound and *ti-ti* to represent two short sounds.) You may insert a deliberate pause within the pattern which you would want the children to hear and then duplicate. Start with a simple pattern such as *tah, tah, ti-ti, tah* in which each beat of *ti-ti* is twice as fast as the *tah*. Have the children listen to the pattern and then ask one youngster to clap it back. You may be surprised at how easily some of the children can do this. Make new patterns and give each child a chance to clap back an established pattern. You can also ask the whole class to clap back in unison. How accurate are the children as a group?

Once the youngsters have had some success with repeating simple patterns, try more and more complex patterns. Vary the sequence of short and long sounds, insert pauses and accents. Ask the children to make up patterns for one another.

HOW TO GO FURTHER.

Have the children establish any system of notation that makes sense to them for recording the sequence of long and short claps and pauses. Many children use long horizontal lines (or dashes) for long notes and two shorter lines (such as hyphens) for short notes. Blank spaces or boxes can be used for the pauses. Share and talk about the various notation systems which the children devised.

MAKING INSTRUMENTS

WHY DO THIS?

Simple rhythm instruments can be made from a variety of readily available materials. This is an area where the children's imagination can lead to new and interesting possibilities for producing sounds. As children explore materials and the kinds of sounds that can be made, they will also be learning important properties of materials. Sounds of differing quality can be produced by metals, cardboard, wood, natural objects, and the like.

WHAT WILL I NEED?

- A variety of materials for making simple rhythm instruments, including:

  —paper plates and beans
  —coffee cans and lids
  —cardboard boxes and rubber bands
  —metal cans, string, and sticks
  —wooden blocks and sandpaper
  —food containers and dry pasta
  —35mm film cans and pennies
  —plastic bottles and sticks

HOW TO GET STARTED.

Acquire a large assortment of materials for the children to use to make simple rhythm instruments. First let them explore the objects. Then ask them how they can use the materials to make rhythm instruments. Demonstrate a few possibilities: place dried beans between two paper plates and staple them together; tap on the lid of an empty coffee can; tack sandpaper onto wooden blocks and rub them together; hit plastic pop bottles with sticks or twigs; spin an empty food can on a stick or suspend it by a string and tap it like a bell; place rubber bands over open cardboard boxes and pluck the strings.

Once the children have made instruments, have them demonstrate them and tell how they were made. How is the sound produced? Discuss the quality of the sounds made by the instruments. Are the sounds soft or loud, hollow or full, tinny or booming? Try to encourage the use of new words as children try to describe and compare the sounds they can make with the various instruments.

Have a few children play their instruments together in small "ensembles." Which instruments sound the best together? Why? Can a melody be played on any of the instruments? Do any of the sounds produced remind the children of any instruments they know or have heard? Allow the children to experiment with one another's instruments. Working in pairs, have the children show their partner a different way to play their instruments.

HOW TO GO FURTHER.

Have the children paint or decorate their instruments. Clap out a rhythm and have the children try to duplicate it using their instruments. Make a tape recording of each child playing his or her instrument without identifying the child. Display all of the instruments and see if the children can identify which one is being played as they hear it on the tape.

THE RHYTHM BAND

WHY DO THIS?

Children enjoy maintaining the rhythm of a song by keeping beat with rhythm instruments. This skill, though, is somewhat variable among five-year-olds; some children will follow along naturally while others may need a little assistance in clapping or tapping in time with the music. Such activities promote listening skills and also help to develop small motor coordination. Playing rhythm instruments can be combined with movements such as stamping, walking, skipping, hopping, or sliding.

WHAT WILL I NEED?

- A variety of rhythm instruments from musical suppliers or made by children as in the previous activity
- Records or tapes of songs with distinct rhythms, for example, spirited marches or waltzes
- A record or tape player

HOW TO GET STARTED.

Begin by distributing a rhythm instrument to each child. Let the children experiment playing with their instruments. Then, demonstrate how to control the sound of the instruments by playing loudly, softly, fast, and slowly. Have the children play their instruments in a loud, soft, fast, and slow manner. Exchange instruments and give each child an opportunity to try a few different ones.

Play a record or tape of a march. Clap to the beat of the music and ask the children to join along with you. Then, have the children keep the beat with their instruments. Ask them to play softly and then loudly, all the time maintaining the beat. Have the children march around in a circle and play along with the music. Play different kinds of songs and ask the children first to clap along with the rhythm and then play their instruments. Ask the children to move to the music. They can slide to a waltz, stamp to a march, and hop or skip to a polka. Have some children invent new movements that are inspired by the music.

HOW TO GO FURTHER.

Play a song and have the children keep the beat with their instruments. Tell the children that you will stop the song abruptly and that this will be their cue to stop as well. Challenge the children to respond as quickly as possible.

USING THE BODY AS A RHYTHM INSTRUMENT

WHY DO THIS?

Some children naturally make interesting sounds using parts of their bodies. They can clap, tap, snap, slap, stamp, and so on. Children enjoy discovering the many different kinds of sounds they can produce and some youngsters can become very creative and inventive. Finally, children can put all of the sounds together to provide accompaniment to a song.

WHAT WILL I NEED?

- A record or tape player and a few records or tapes
- A large sheet of butcher or roll paper
- Markers
- Index cards

HOW TO GET STARTED.

Ask individual children to demonstrate how they can make sounds using parts of their bodies. Some examples include: clapping hands, slapping sides, snapping fingers, tapping a cheek with the mouth open, patting an open mouth with an opened hand, popping an index finger into the cheek, rubbing their hands together, and clicking their tongues. Ask children to invent new ways of making sounds with their bodies that have not been shown before. Discuss differences in the sounds made. Which ones are loud? Which ones are soft? Which make a popping sound? Have all of the children try to practice each of the sounds demonstrated. (Some will clearly be more successful than others. Snapping fingers is a rare ability among kindergarteners.) Have the children try to produce the sounds together as they keep the beat of a song. Then try to arrange for groups of children to make different sounds and ask them to come in on cue during a song at times that seem appropriate according to the music. Make up a song using the various sounds the children can produce.

HOW TO GO FURTHER.

Draw an outline of a child on a large sheet of butcher paper. Have the children color it in with markers. Place the drawing on a bulletin board. Then ask them to review the various parts of their bodies that they used to make sounds. For each one, write on an index card how the sound was made and then staple it next to the appropriate body part. For example, if a child suggests clapping, write "You can clap with your hands" on a card and place the card near a hand on the drawing. Make a title for the display—"Using Our Bodies as Rhythm Instruments."

MOVING TO MUSIC

WHY DO THIS?

In creative movement, youngsters can forget about rules of movement and let music carry their bodies away from prescribed sequences. Responding to music through creative movement is an experience filled with music, freedom, and joy. Imagination is valued and all efforts are successful. The experience may be enhanced with props for example, scarves, hoops, and hats. Creative movement provides rewarding interaction between muscular, listening, and emotional responses.

WHAT WILL I NEED?

- A record or tape player
- Records or tapes of various kinds of instrumental music
- A few props to incorporate into movement such as scarves, hats, hula hoops, and shawls.

HOW TO GET STARTED.

Explain to the children that they will be moving, in any way they like, to music which is played on a record or tape player. Play a song and ask a few children to move in any way they like in response to the music. Make it clear that any movement is all right. Some of the movements which emerge may involve clapping, slapping, stamping, walking, running, gliding, sliding, tiptoeing, twirling, spinning, swaying, marching, galloping, bending, crawling, and high stepping. Children should be encouraged to be original, but they may also copy one another's movements.

Play different kinds of music including spirited marches, scary music, pieces from ballets, and waltzes. Ask the children to listen to the music first, plan their actions, and then respond with movement. Then ask them to change their movements. Look for movements that are expressive and seem responsive to the mood of the music.

HOW TO GO FURTHER.

Provide "props" for the children to use with creative movement. Scarves, hula hoops, shawls, hats, brooms, and other such objects can be incorporated into children's dances and actions. Ask the children to identify objects that they would like to use with their movements. Be alert to different types of songs which will promote unusual responses in the children. Gather such music and save it for a "rainy day" when children cannot go out of doors.

ACTION SONGS

WHY DO THIS?

Action songs tell a story in words, actions, and movements. Some familiar action songs include "London Bridge," "The Farmer in the Dell," "Skip to My Lou," "In and Out the Window," "There Was a Lovely Princess," among many others. In each case, the children arranged in a circle or other formation portray a story with movements or actions and song. Many song books and music guides include the music for action songs as well as the associated movements. Such activities not only provide joy in music and movement, but also serve to increase the youngsters' literacy as they enjoy classic stories, poems, and chants.

WHAT WILL I NEED?

- Action song books
- A piano or a record or tape player and tapes or records

HOW TO GET STARTED.

Acquire a book or two of action songs appropriate for kindergarten. Some of the action songs mentioned above may be familiar to most of the children in the class. Start with a relatively easy song, such as "London Bridge." Select two children to form the bridge by joining their hands together high up over their heads. Have the rest of the children form a line, and as everyone sings the children in the line march through the "bridge." When the children sing the part "Take the key and lock him up, lock him up, lock him up," the two youngsters who form the bridge should drop their hands and trap the child who is passing through at that time. The child who was caught can then pick a classmate to form a new bridge, and the game proceeds.

There are dozens of familiar song plays that children will memorize quickly and add to their fund of known stories or poems. If a book suggesting the associated movements to action songs is not available, the actions can be readily improvised. In fact, some of the more creative actions are probably the ones that are invented by children and teachers.

HOW TO GO FURTHER.

Select an action song that the children have particularly enjoyed. Ask them to picture the scenery that might accompany the song. Have children paint a scene from an action song onto a large sheet of paper. Get some props to go along with the song and have the children perform the action song for another class. The children can make invitations, tickets, and a program (with a cast of characters) to distribute to others.

RESPONDING TO MUSICAL MOODS

WHY DO THIS?

Music is a language that conveys feelings and emotions. Children can discuss the way that a particular piece of music makes them feel. Spirited marches inspire confidence and bravado. A funeral dirge can make the child feel sad. (In fact, most songs in minor key will communicate a sad, sometimes mournful quality.) Children can be helped to feel free to respond to musical moods, to trust their instincts, and to express their feelings. Music can be a powerful tool for helping children to relate emotions and to verbalize their feelings.

WHAT WILL I NEED?

- An assortment of records or tapes which convey different moods. (School or public libraries can be a wonderful source of such records.) Happy songs are relatively easy to find. For a eerier mood, try to get Saint-Saëns's *Danse Macabre* and Mussorgsky's *Night on Bald Mountain*.

HOW TO GET STARTED.

Play recordings of music that represent distinct musical moods. After playing a section of each piece, discuss how the children feel about the music. What kind of scene can they imagine as they hear the selection? How would the children move to the different kinds of music? Have a few children demonstrate. Then give all of the youngsters a chance to respond to the music.

HOW TO GO FURTHER.

Make up stories that match the mood of the music and ask the children to relate the stories to the pieces of music. For example, if you play a spirited march, a corresponding story might be, "One fine day, all of the musicians from the high school decided to come out and march down the street. They were proud and played briskly as they marched one behind the other. There were trumpets and tubas, clarinets and trombones." Ask children to make up their own stories to match the mood of specific musical selections.

DRAWING TO MUSIC

WHY DO THIS?

After children are exposed to a variety of musical moods, they can try to express themselves in art as they hear different types of music. As children draw to music, they need to feel free to experiment without worrying about right or wrong responses. This is a true opportunity to integrate children's school experiences.

WHAT WILL I NEED?

- Records or tapes which convey various moods
- A record or tape player
- Drawing paper
- Crayons, markers, paints, or fingerpaints

HOW TO GET STARTED.

Acquire records or tapes in which a variety of moods are expressed. Sad songs, happy songs, marches, holiday songs, seasonal songs ("Winter Wonderland" is a great one), represent a good variety. Have the children listen to one of the songs. Then, give them some drawing paper and crayons, markers, paints, or fingerpaints. Play the song again and tell the children to draw or scribble on their papers to express a mood created by the music. Make it clear that there is no correct response to this activity and that it is a very individual matter. After playing three distinct kinds of music, each child should have three drawings. Play a portion of the first song. Can the children find the picture that was drawn to this music? Try this with the second song, and so on. Ask individual children to show their drawings as the matching song is played. Have children express what it was about the music that caused them to want to draw as they did. This may be very hard for some youngsters to verbalize.

Name each of the songs heard in some way, either by title or by kind (march, winter song, and so forth). Display some of the drawings on the floor or on a clothesline. Ask the children if they can associate the drawings of others with the song as the music is played again.

HOW TO GO FURTHER.

On the floor spread out a large sheet of butcher or roll paper. Give each child a few crayons or markers. Play a specific song on a record or tape player. Have all of the children work together on the paper drawing to the mood of the music. Place the title of the song or music at the top of the paper and display this "musical mood mural" on a large bulletin board or in the hallway. If possible create a few such murals and display them. Ask the children to interpret some of the differences they see in the murals and the possible reasons for these differences.

EXPLORING THE PIANO

WHY DO THIS?

Most kindergarten classrooms have a piano. If your room does not, there will undoubtedly be one somewhere in the school. Pianos may be used for exploration and discussion. There was a time when many school districts required kindergarten teachers to play the piano. This practice is no longer prevalent, but the pianos have remained. Even if you cannot play the piano, there are several activities that can be done with a piano to enhance children's understanding of musical concepts.

WHAT WILL I NEED?

- A piano, an upright, console, spinet, or baby grand
- Twine or string
- Scissors
- Flat washers to serve as a weight

HOW TO GET STARTED.

Locate a piano in the school which will be available a few days for pupil exploration. First, allow children to experiment with the sounds of the piano in a controlled manner. Which keys make the high-pitched sounds? Which ones make the low-pitched sounds? Have the children suggest a body movement for each; for example, they can put their hands way up high for the high sounds and down towards the floor for the low sounds. Play loudly and softly and ask the children what they think accounts for the difference in sound.

Then, open the piano. If it is a baby grand, prop up the top as high as possible and slide off the part of the piano that holds the music stand. If the piano is an upright or console, try to remove the bottom panel, above the pedals, and the top panel, above the music stand. Almost all pianos can be opened this way. You may need the assistance of a school custodian. Once open, ask the children to examine the inside of the piano. They will find some short strings and some long strings with coils around them.

Locate the pegs that hold the strings in place. Push a key on the piano. Ask the children to observe the way the hammer hits the string. Trace how the mechanism works from the piano key to the hammer. (This is a wonderful demonstration of simple machines.) Pluck a string with your finger. Have the children associate a string with a key depressed on the piano. Compare the length of the strings that make high-pitched sounds with the strings that make low-pitched sounds. Are there any other instruments that exhibit a similar situation? For example, on a xylophone, the long bars make the lower sounds while the short bars make the higher sounds. Engage the children in developing this analogy. Have the children feel the vibration of the string as a key is hit. Explain that sound is made by vibrating objects. Have them touch their throats as they sing. Can they feel a vibration?

HOW TO GO FURTHER.

Take a ball of twine and lay it across the length of a short piano string. Cut the twine so that it is as long as the piano string. Find the piano key which hits the string just measured. (If you are doing this on an upright piano, attach a washer or other flat weight to the end of the twine, so it can fall along the length of the piano string.) Next, find a long piano string and similarly lay a piece of twine along its length. Again, find the key that corresponds to this string. Cut the twine. Have the children compare the length of the two pieces of twine. Again, hit the two keys that are responsible for the vibration of the two piano strings measured. Have the children associate the sound produced by the piano with the length of the string.

Ask the children if there is anything else they would like to explore about the piano while it is opened.

MAKING AND EXPERIMENTING WITH A MONOCHORD

WHY DO THIS?

A monochord is simply a string stretched across the top of an open box. (A small wooden desk drawer is ideal to use as the box.) This device provides a wonderful laboratory for the investigation of sound. Children can manipulate the length of the vibrating string, and the tension on it, to produce changes in pitch. The use of a monochord can aid in the development of many concepts about sound and music. Then the children can apply their learnings as they observe other stringed instruments.

WHAT WILL I NEED?

- An open wooden box (a wooden desk drawer is ideal for this purpose)
- Guitar strings or nylon fishing line
- A spring scale

● A small strip of wood, longer than the width of the box (a triangular drafting ruler would be perfect)

HOW TO GET STARTED.

Empty a wooden desk drawer or a wooden box and attach a guitar string (or nylon fishing line) to the knob of the drawer and pull the free end over the top of the drawer. Stretch the string across the top of the box and have a child pull on the free end of the string. Have another child pluck the string several times and try to vary the loudness. Point out the obvious vibration of the string. How can the loudness of the string's sound be controlled?

Next, the children should investigate various ways of altering the pitch of the string. This is done by changing the length of the vibrating portion of the string. To do this, place a strip of wood across the top of the box and under the string, so that its effective vibrating length can be changed. (A triangular drafting ruler is perfect for this purpose because of its relatively sharp edge.) With one child holding the string at constant tension, another child can slide the strip of wood (or ruler) under the string to change the length of the vibrating portion. Does the pitch seem higher when the string is lengthened or shortened? How does a guitar player vary the length of a guitar string? How does a violin player do it?

Pitch may also be varied by changing the tension on the string. Pull the string across the top of the box and have one child vary the tension on the box while another child plucks it. Is the pitch of the string higher when more tension is applied? Changes in tension may be observed directly by attaching a spring or dial face scale to the free end of the string. (See the illustration.) As more tension is applied to the string, the number registered on the scale will increase. This will help demonstrate the direct relationship between pitch and tension.

HOW TO GO FURTHER.

Obtain guitar strings of different gauges. (Some of the lower-pitched strings will be coiled.) Given a string of the same length and tension (kept constant by using a spring scale), which string produces a higher sound, a thick one, or a thin one?

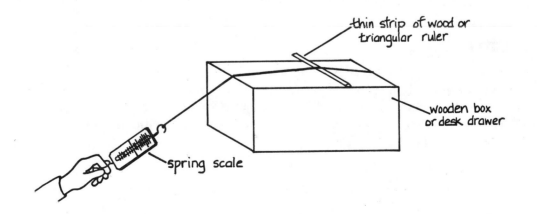

IDENTIFYING INSTRUMENTS

WHY DO THIS?

Even at age five, children can begin to identify the sounds produced by different instruments. As they hear records or tapes of orchestral music, especially pieces that feature instrumental solos, they can associate the sounds they hear with a specific musical instrument. Such an activity can bolster the children's sense of accomplishment and also help to sharpen listening skills and focus.

WHAT WILL I NEED?

- A record or tape player
- Records or tapes of music which feature specific instruments, for example, *Peter and the Wolf* by Prokofiev, *Young Person's Guide to the Orchestra* by Britten; *Carnival of Animals,* by Saint-Saëns
- Prepared or drawn pictures of familiar instruments

HOW TO GET STARTED.

Obtain records or tapes of music which features specific instruments. (Librarians can be very helpful in this regard.) Play the music for the children and have them listen for specific instruments. When an instrument is clearly identified, show the children a picture of it and discuss some of the qualities of its sound. For example, a piano may sound "tinkly," a trumpet sounds like a horn blowing, and so on. After the youngsters have had a variety of experiences in listening to and identifying instruments, give each of several children a picture of an instrument to hold. Play a selection of music which features several instrument solos. (Some teachers use a tape recorder to record instrumental solos, one after another, so that a variety of instruments can be heard within a relatively short period of time.) As each instrument is heard, have the child who has the picture of that instrument hold it up.

HOW TO GO FURTHER.

Have the children pretend to be conductors. As they listen to an orchestral selection, other children, holding pictures of instruments, can pretend to be the musicians as they hear their instruments played. Some particularly musical youngsters may be able to pretend to be conductors and point to or signal specific musicians as they hear those instruments played on a record or tape.

chapter *10*

IN THE ART CENTER

Art is a form of expression for the child, as it is for all humanity. Through art activities children can work out ideas about themselves and their world. They can create, explore, invent, and relate events in their lives. Through experiences in art, children have a natural vehicle for the expression of their imagination and fantasy. They can also imitate and reproduce reality by drawing objects or events. Art can help to strengthen a youngster's self-confidence and sense of worth.

In providing art activities for young children, it is important to withhold judgment. An atmosphere of freedom will encourage children to experiment, to explore media, and to develop unique ideas. On their own, children are likely to attain a sense of aesthetic awareness as they experience success and satisfaction with their products.

A kindergarten art program should have a balance of free, undirected activities and stimulating experiences of a more directed nature to help children develop a variety of techniques for using different media. Rich, satisfying art experiences can build upon the youngsters' experiences in other areas. Children can visit a pet store one day and then recreate an aspect of their visit, another day, through art. Writing and art will blend naturally to help children reconstruct an idea. Because pictures tell stories, ideas are expressed in art as well as in writing, and in combinations of the two.

Children's self-esteem can be enhanced through activities in art. Once pictures or other products have been finished, an "art show" or exhibit can be developed in which work can be displayed with pride. Children can talk about their creations, and just as young writers can read their work in "an author's chair," so too can children talk about their artwork in the "artist's chair."

Through art, children can become more attentive to their natural environment. Looking for changing colors in the sky, analyzing the texture of fabric, studying a rock, tree bark, or a seashell all serve to help children see art in their surroundings. Experiences in art are rich with opportunities to help children learn more about themselves, their environment, and how they can use art to convey ideas, feelings, and to attach additional meaning to other forms of expression.

In the kindergarten classroom the art area should be near a source of water. An easel or two should be available at all times, large work tables should be clear for projects, and a wide variety of paints, crayons, markers, scraps of all textures, yarn, and other materials should be stored in accessible containers. Children can and should be involved with the maintenance and cleaning of this area of the classroom.

TEXTURE RUBBINGS

WHY DO THIS?

Textures are everywhere around us. This activity helps children to find interesting textures and to "make a copy" of them by producing a texture rubbing. As children do this, they come to see the intricacies of various textures as well as differences among textured objects. As they capture the texture of natural objects, like leaves, bark, and pine needles, they will also learn more about the properties of objects in their environment.

WHAT WILL I NEED?

- Crayons
- Newsprint paper
- A variety of textured materials, for example, leaves, tree bark, corrugated cardboard, window screening, pine needles, wood, sandpaper, keys, paper clips, and string

HOW TO GET STARTED.

Peel some crayons. Without the children seeing, take a few paper clips and place them under a sheet of newsprint. Hold a peeled crayon on its side, and lightly rub it over the sheet of paper so that the paper clips make an impression on the paper. Show the texture rubbing to the children and ask them what they think was under the paper. Try a few more texture rubbings to demonstrate the technique and to generate enthusiasm for the activity. Then, give each child a peeled crayon and a few sheets of paper. Provide a box with an assortment of textures for the children to use. At first, the children may need some assistance with the technique of rubbing gently over the surface of the object. After they have had a few successful experiences, take the children outdoors to make rubbings of materials they find. Some children can collect objects to bring back into the classroom for continued use.

Ask each child to identify a rubbing that he or she is particularly proud of. Mount it on a sheet of construction paper which is larger than the rubbing so as to make an attractive border. Make sure the picture is labeled with the child's name and perhaps a word or two about the rubbing. Make a display of the children's texture rubbings.

HOW TO GO FURTHER.

Give the children an assortment of objects for texture rubbings, paper, and peeled crayons. Ask the youngsters to make a picture of a person (or an object they choose) by arranging a variety of textures into a definite pattern and then making a rubbing. (See the illustration.) Display the results.

My leaf and cardboard man.   by Scott

PAPER TEAR COLLAGE

WHY DO THIS?

Young children love to paste a variety of objects onto sheets of paper or cardboard to make collages. This activity will almost always be met with enthusiasm. Once in a while, it is interesting to define the task in some way so that children have to stretch their use of one particular material. By using only pieces of paper for children to tear and then paste, they can experiment and realize the broad possibilities of working in a single medium. Also, the children will see the endless variety of forms created just by how they tear paper. The products will be as varied as the children.

WHAT WILL I NEED?

- Construction paper of different colors
- Paste or glue

HOW TO GET STARTED.

Explain to the children that they will make a collage by tearing paper into any shapes they like, arranging the shapes into a pattern, and then pasting the shapes onto a sheet of background paper. Ask the children to think about what they want to do first. They can try to create something realistic or purely abstract. They can overlap pieces of paper or keep them separate. Tell them that the "planning phase" is an important part of the project.

Once the children have completed their pieces, let them tell about them. Was there anything in particular they had in mind as they made their collage? They may wish to give their works a title and sign them, like an artist.

HOW TO GO FURTHER.

Talk about the techniques the children used in making their paper tear collages. Did they overlap pieces? Did they go off of the boundary of the background paper? Were their creations realistic or abstract?

Now give the children a specific theme for making another paper tear collage. Some possibilities include: the ocean, a stormy day, the forest. Encourage the children to create something which relates to the theme. When all of the collages are complete, tack them onto a large sheet of roll paper. Ask the children to dictate captions or sentences which tell how their collages relate to the theme.

CRAYON RESIST

WHY DO THIS?

This is a familiar kindergarten art project in which children first draw a picture in crayon and then brush a dilute watercolor wash over the drawing. The watercolor tends to "resist" the crayon leaving an attractive background and making the original drawing stand out. Through this project children explore working with two types of media and notice the interaction between them. The results are satisfying, and it is easy to achieve a very attractive effect.

WHAT WILL I NEED?

- Crayons
- Drawing paper
- Tempera or watercolor paints
- Paint brushes
- Paint tins, plastic containers, or cans

HOW TO GET STARTED.

Acquire the necessary supplies for the project. Make a light watercolor wash by diluting tempera or watercolor paints. Place the diluted watercolors in paint tins, plastic containers, or cans. Demonstrate the technique of "crayon resist." Make a simple drawing with crayon, pressing very firmly. Then, brush the water color wash over the drawing. Ask the children to describe what happens. (The watercolor should bead up over the waxy crayon surface and make the original drawing stand out against the dilute background.) Use the term "resist" if it seems appropriate with the group.

Set up the materials for the project on tables or easels. Ask the children to share their pictures and tell something about them. They should print their names, pressing firmly with crayon, on their pictures.

HOW TO GO FURTHER.

Use other materials to create the resist effect. One way is to let the children create a simple drawing with white latex glue. Then, wash the surface with a dilute watercolor. The watercolor wash will resist the glued areas.

TOOTHBRUSH PAINTING

WHY DO THIS?

Children will see how the application of paint with a toothbrush yields a variety of interesting results. They can use the brush like a paint brush, sweep it across the paper, shake it onto paper, or they can use it to spatter the paint. Each technique has a different result, and this is a fine way of demonstrating the multiple uses of a single, simple tool.

WHAT WILL I NEED?

- Painting paper
- Tempera paint
- Toothbrushes

HOW TO GET STARTED.

Ask the children to bring an old toothbrush into school. Make it clear that they will no longer be able to use the brush for their teeth. Provide each child with a paper, a toothbrush, and some tempera paint. Ask them to use the toothbrush to paint in any way they like, but reinforce that they should not splash themselves or their classmates. Observe the different ways that children use the toothbrushes. Some of the children will use them like ordinary paintbrushes. Others will "scratch" paint onto the paper, shake paint onto the paper, or spatter it. Ask the children to notice the effects that result from the different ways that they used the toothbrush.

After the children's paintings are finished, have them talk about their work. What techniques did they use? What did they learn about how to apply paint? Did they like to paint this way?

HOW TO GO FURTHER.

To use a toothbrush to its fullest, have the children dip the tip of the handle into paint and then tap it rapidly onto a paper to fill in an area or create a picture. In a sense, this is like pointillistic technique. Encourage the children to experiment by trying to make the dots closer together or further apart.

PAINT A ROCK

WHY DO THIS?

Just as young children should learn to use different implements to apply paint, so too should they try to paint on a variety of surfaces. By "adopting" a rock, getting to know it, and then decorating it, the children will learn about painting on different textures, but they will also have a "special friend" of a rather permanent nature to take home.

WHAT WILL I NEED?

- A smooth, fist-sized rock for each child
- Paint and paintbrushes
- Vinegar
- A toothbrush
- Nail polish (optional)

HOW TO GET STARTED.

Go outdoors and have each child select an interesting rock. Although size is not very important, it is convenient for the children to select rocks about the size of their fists. (Explaining this relative way of estimating size is an activity in itself.) Once back in the classroom, have the children wash their rocks in a solution of water and vinegar and then brush the rocks clean with a toothbrush. Tell the children that this will be their special rock so they should get to know it. They should examine it carefully and talk about its color, texture, and shape.

Using tempera paint of thick consistency, have the children paint their rocks. They may wish to paint a face or some other design on the rocks. Nail polish will adhere well to a rock, but it should be used under careful supervision. Have the children display their rocks and perhaps write stories to go along with them.

HOW TO GO FURTHER.

The children may wish to make a base or pedestal for their rocks. Take a block of wood and a wad of clay. Put the wad of clay onto the center of the block and then press the rock into the clay. The resulting *objet d'art* can be used as a paperweight. This may make a nice gift for parents.

SPATTER PAINTING

WHY DO THIS?

One of the concepts young children can explore in art is the production of a negative impression of a familiar object. This means that instead of seeing a picture of an object, its outline or shape is seen. A stimulating way to create this effect is by spatter painting. Essentially, the children spatter paint over an object by scraping paint through a piece of screening. The result is a negative image of the object. The technique is interesting and enjoyable for children to use.

WHAT WILL I NEED?

- Wire screening
- Heavy vinyl tape or duct tape
- Paint
- Toothbrushes
- Paper
- An assortment of small, flat objects

HOW TO GET STARTED.

Cut a few pieces of wire screening about 8 inches square. Place heavy vinyl tape or duct tape over the edges of the pieces of screen. Acquire a few flat objects such as leaves or shapes cut from paper. Demonstrate the technique of spatter painting: scrape a toothbrush dipped in paint across the piece of screen held over a sheet of paper. Give each child a large piece of absorbent drawing paper. Have him or her select one of the flat objects and place it in the middle of the sheet of drawing paper. Then, holding the screen over the paper with one hand, the child scrapes the toothbrush (with paint on it) across the screen. Stop scraping when the area around the object is covered with spatters of paint. Let the paint dry. Then remove the object. The result is a negative image of the object. The paintings can be mounted onto larger pieces of construction paper and displayed.

HOW TO GO FURTHER.

What are other ways to make negative images? One easy way is to cut a shape (like a heart) out of a piece of construction paper. Keep the paper from which the shape was cut. Staple or glue it onto a larger sheet of paper of a contrasting color. Mount the shape that was cut out onto another sheet of paper. Explain that the shape mounted onto a piece of paper is the "positive" image, while the outline of the shape is the "negative" image. Display the two together.

STRING PAINTING

WHY DO THIS?

Another interesting art project involving different materials is to make a painting with string. The results are interesting and attractive. Because children will color string with paint and then place it onto a background piece of paper, they will have to make judgments about which colors provide a nice contrast.

WHAT WILL I NEED?

- Heavy string or yarn
- White glue
- Tempera paint
- Construction paper

HOW TO GET STARTED.

Make a mixture of white glue and tempera paint. (A good proportion is one part of glue to eight parts of paint.) Prepare these mixtures for a few colors of paint. Cut heavy string or yarn into lengths of about one yard. Demonstrate how to dip the string into the paint-glue mixture until it is submerged, remove it, and then lower it onto a piece of background paper letting it wiggle into a design or pattern. Discuss sets of contrasting colors (for paint and background paper) that children may wish to choose. For example, a mixture of white paint and glue may have a stark effect on a black background. How about yarn painted yellow on a dark blue background?

Have the children select a background paper, yarn, and a paint color. Then, let them create their string paintings. Each painting should be signed. If the backgrounds are dark, children can write their names with chalk.

HOW TO GO FURTHER.

Try to make string paintings using thin string. How are resulting pictures different from those made with thicker string or yarn? Try to make a picture using clothesline. How are these pictures different from the others?

ROLL ON!

WHY DO THIS?

Children enjoy applying paint in different ways. The most common device is a paintbrush, but children should be allowed to discover some of the effects of other ways to paint. One interesting device is to use a roll-on bottle for painting. After collecting a few empty roll-on deodorant containers, they can be filled with paint and then used to make pictures. This is a novel way to paint, and children can compare the results to pictures made with brushes.

WHAT WILL I NEED?

- A few empty roll-on deodorant bottles
- Tempera paint
- Corn starch
- Painting paper

HOW TO GET STARTED.

Collect a few empty roll-on deodorant bottles. Screw off or pry open the caps. Wash them out thoroughly and let them dry. Then, fill the bottles with paint that is somewhat thick in consistency. One way to thicken paint is to leave the paint jars opened a few days. Another way is to mix a little corn starch into the paint.

Leave the roll-on paint applicators and paper in the art center. As children make pictures, ask them to talk about the way the paint looks as it is applied by the roll-on. Compare roll-on paintings with those made with brushes. How are the strokes of paint similar? How are they different?

HOW TO GO FURTHER.

Think of other unique ways to apply paint to paper. Sponge painting is an old favorite. Cut a sponge into small shapes. Let the children dip the sponge into a tin of paint and press it lightly onto paper. Describe the effect. Can the children see the impression of the "holes" in the sponge? Can an empty spray bottle be used to apply paint? What happens when a thin consistency of paint is put into a spray bottle?

A COOPERATIVE MURAL

WHY DO THIS?

A cooperative mural is a large scene that several children, or all of the youngsters in a class, have worked on. Aside from the large, impressive size of such a picture, children can plan in groups and work together to make a single creation. Such a project extends beyond artistic expression and also helps children to develop a sense of community and cooperative effort.

WHAT WILL I NEED?

- Large roll or butcher paper
- Pencils
- Markers
- Index cards

HOW TO GET STARTED.

Get some large roll paper or a large piece of brown nonwaxy butcher paper. Discuss the production of a cooperative mural. Brainstorm some ideas with the children for the content of the mural. (It should be related to a unit the children are studying. It could be about folktales, winter scenes, or a favorite book the children have read.) Once an idea for the subject of mural is decided upon, discuss whether the mural will be a collection of separate pictures all dealing with the central theme or whether each child will contribute a piece to a total scene. For example, in a winter scene, a large mountain or ski hill can be outlined and then drawn by several children, then individuals can add skiers, skaters at the bottom, a ski house, and so on. Decide upon how the children will work on the mural—all at the same time, in small groups, or as parts of the scene are developed. Divide up jobs for the mural and then pencil in some of the large areas to be drawn. Provide markers and other materials that may be needed to complete the project.

After the mural is finished, display it on a bulletin board or in a hallway. Perhaps it can be hung in or outside of the school office! Discuss the cooperative nature of the project with the children. Could this have been made by one or two children alone? Have each child identify his or her contribution to the mural. Ask them to think of what behaviors or actions were necessary in order to complete a cooperative project.

HOW TO GO FURTHER.

On index cards write captions that children dictate relating to the mural. These captions can tell a story or just identify parts of the mural for those who see it. In this way, reading, writing, and art work can all be integrated into a meaningful whole.

WATERPAINTING

WHY DO THIS?

An activity that combines artistic expression with the observation of a scientific phenomenon is to paint with water. Children can use brushes of all sizes to draw any number of objects or designs with water. As they do this, they will see the varying effects of using brushes of different widths. Beyond this, they will note that it is not too long before their pictures disappear. This is a preliminary experience with evaporation. It is important for the children to understand the physical principles which explain evaporation, but they can have a direct experience with the phenomenon through this activity.

WHAT WILL I NEED?

- Paint brushes of assorted size (bristle or sponge brushes are readily available in hardware stores)
- Easel brushes
- Buckets or pails of water

HOW TO GET STARTED.

Begin by having children use easel brushes and water to paint on a chalkboard. They can write their names, draw designs or pictures. As the water evaporates, ask them which parts disappeared first—their beginning strokes or the ones made last? Ask the children if they know what is happening to the water. Introduce the term "evaporation." Ask them if they have experienced evaporation in any other situations.

On a nice warm day, provide a variety of paint and easel brushes and pails of water to take outdoors. On the playground allow the children to "paint" with water anywhere they like. They should try different surfaces, for example, the sidewalk, the wall of the building, a fence, parts of the jungle gym, etc. Ask the children where the water goes. Some children may think that the water goes into the material, that is, into the brick, concrete sidewalk, or wood. Encourage the children to make hypotheses and ask them thought-provoking questions. Just to provide accurate information, you may explain to the children that the water goes into the air.

HOW TO GO FURTHER.

Conduct a "study" of how well different substances can absorb water. Try to gather a variety of materials—brick, wood, metal, and concrete, for example. Make an even brush stroke with water on each of the surfaces. Which material seems to soak up the most water? Can the children think of any reasons to explain their observations.

ENRICHED FINGERPAINTING

WHY DO THIS?

Fingerpainting is a common kindergarten activity and children delight in it. This activity can be enriched, though, by having children make "prints" of the pictures they make on a smooth surface with finger paint. Many learnings emerge from such an activity. The children can experiment with different types of paper for making the print and then they may notice that the print is a "reverse picture" of the painting they made.

WHAT WILL I NEED?

- A smooth surface to paint on. A formica or plastic laminate tabletop is ideal. (A smooth lap board can also be used.)
- Fingerpaints
- Paper with different finishes: glossy shelf paper, absorbent paper, fingerpaint paper, for example
- Construction paper
- Index cards

HOW TO GET STARTED.

Show the children how to fingerpaint on a desktop or a lap board. Place a small portion of fingerpaint onto the surface and spread it out. With one finger draw a design or a picture. Demonstrate how to "erase" the picture by smoothing out the paint again. Using this technique, children can paint as many pictures as time will allow.

Now comes the "magic"! Make a small drawing with the fingerpaints on a smooth surface. Then, take a piece of glossy shelf paper or fingerpaint paper and lay it on top of the drawing. With your fingers gently press the paper onto the painted surface. Let it set for a minute or two. Then, carefully "peel off" the paper and you are left with a print of the finger painting. Young children will need some help in pressing the paper gently onto the painted surface and also in peeling it off. Try different kinds of paper for different effects. Demonstrate to the children that the print is actually a mirror image of the design painted on the table top.

HOW TO GO FURTHER.

Have children make fingerpaint prints of pictures relating to a story they have enjoyed. Mount the prints onto construction paper. Write appropriate captions onto index cards and attach them to the pictures. Staple or sew all the pictures together into a fingerpainted book. (Alternatively, they can be stapled or tacked onto a bulletin board.) The prints will make a very attractive storybook or display.

MAKING PLAY CLAY

WHY DO THIS?

Play clay is a modeling substance that can be used to make an endless variety of three-dimensional sculptures. Children love to squeeze and form plastic materials into new forms. Since this activity calls for the *making* of play clay, the children will have the added benefit of seeing how the substance is produced from everyday kitchen supplies. They can combine the ingredients to form a material that is clearly quite different than any of the ingredients that went into making it.

WHAT WILL I NEED?

- 3 cups flour
- ¼ cup salt
- Water
- Food coloring
- Cooking or salad oil
- Cookie cutters
- Sticks and tongue depressors
- Cylindrical building blocks or a rolling pin

HOW TO GET STARTED.

With the children, follow this basic recipe for making play clay: Combine 3 cups of flour with ¼ cup salt. Add 1 cup of water and a few drops of food coloring. Gradually add 1 tablespoon of cooking or salad oil. Knead the ingredients together until they have a claylike consistency. If the substance is too flaky, add more water. If it is too sticky, add more flour.

Once the clay is made, encourage the children to play with it. Provide sticks and tongue depressors to use as tools to carve shapes and objects. A cylindrical block or rolling pin can be used to make pancakes. Cookie cutters and inverted plastic cups are wonderful for stamping out shapes and forms. Show the youngsters how to roll out snakes and then coil them up to make cups or baskets. The clay, if left out to dry a few hours, will harden and then can be painted.

Some teachers like to work with salt dough. This is made by combining 4 cups of salt with 1 cup of corn starch and enough water to form a paste. The mixture must then be cooked and stirred over medium heat. If you choose to make salt dough, have the children compare the feel of salt dough and play clay.

HOW TO GO FURTHER.

Children can mold story figures from play clay, paint them, and them mount them onto cardboard. Captions can be written to tell a story about each of the figures.

Some children will enjoy forming the clay into numerals or letters. Have the children make snakes out of the clay and then form the snakes into letters which spell their names. This is a wonderful reinforcement for letter recognition.

AN ENVIRONMENTAL COLLAGE

WHY DO THIS?

Children can make a collage using only natural materials that they collect from the environment. At the same time, they can be helped to develop a respect for the environment by learning to distinguish between those materials which can be taken from and those which should be left in their natural surroundings. When children make their collages, they can form interesting arrangements of materials.

WHAT WILL I NEED?

- Leaves
- Acorns
- Pebbles
- Seeds
- Twigs
- Evergreen needles
- Plastic bags
- Heavy drawing paper
- White glue

HOW TO GET STARTED.

Explain to the children that they will be making a collage out of natural materials, that is, objects found in the natural environment. Give each youngster a bag and take them for a walk to a specific location outdoors. Tell them that they may take samples of leaves, pebbles, twigs, grass, acorns, seeds, and other such objects, but caution them against picking any flowers or breaking twigs or branches from a tree. It is best to collect items that have already fallen to the ground. Do the children know why they should not pick parts of growing plants? Once each child has collected at least ten items, return to the classroom.

Ask the children to discuss the items they collected. What do they think they are? Let other children identify some of the items. Distribute heavy paper and white glue to the children. Let them arrange their objects on the paper and then glue them on. You can have all of the children work at the same time or provide the materials needed in the art center and then, children can take turns making their collages. Display the collages.

HOW TO GO FURTHER.

Make an experience chart about the environmental collages. Have the children dictate sentences about where they collected their items, what they found, what kinds of things they would *not* take, and how they made their collages. Display this experience chart alongside of the collages.

JUNK ANIMALS

WHY DO THIS?

Throughout the year, many objects are thrown away which might be "recycled" and used in art projects. Maintain a scrap barrel into which children throw cloth swatches, styrofoam packing material, paper scraps, and the like. Periodically, children can put these materials to new uses by making a collage from them. In this activity, children take such "junk" to create animals. This is an interesting experience which conveys to children that materials they might think of as garbage can be put to good use.

WHAT WILL I NEED?

- Heavy drawing paper
- White glue
- Markers
- An assortment of scraps: swatches of cloth, cardboard, styrofoam packing material, scraps of felt, velvet, and other such fabric, buttons, and so forth

HOW TO GET STARTED.

Each child can make his or her own junk animal, or a group of three or four youngsters can work together to make a cooperative creation. Begin by explaining that the children will use materials that might have otherwise been discarded to make an animal. Have the children draw an outline of a real or imaginary animal on paper. (Some teachers may wish to ask the children to make a monster.) Then, the children should gather materials from the scrap barrel that they think can be used to fill in their outlines. Have them think first and then *plan* how they want to place the materials. Buttons are wonderful for eyes. What would make a good tail? Then have the children glue the scraps within the outline of the animal. If they wish, they can draw an appropriate background. Ask the children to name their animals and display their creations.

HOW TO GO FURTHER.

Ask the children to make amusing labels for parts of their animals' bodies. For example: "These are her floppy feet." "This is his tangled tail."

The children may also want to write stories about their animals, particularly the imaginary ones. Stories or captions can be dictated to the teacher and then displayed alongside of the animal.

WAX PICTURES

WHY DO THIS?

An interesting material for children to work with is waxed paper. After assembling an arrangement of materials onto a sheet of waxed paper and then covering it with another sheet, a "sandwich" can be made and then ironed. Some of the wax melts, and colors and textures may change. The result is a semipermanent collage which can be enjoyed for quite some time. Children can also experiment with different ways to display their creations. The pictures may be mounted on a sheet of construction paper for contrast, or taped to a window so that light can pass through the translucent areas of the picture.

WHAT WILL I NEED?

- A roll of waxed paper
- Colored tissue paper
- Leaves
- A plastic knife
- Crayon shavings
- Flat pieces of material
- Drawing paper
- Newspapers
- An iron (*CAUTION: to be used only by an adult*)

HOW TO GET STARTED.

Assemble a box or tray of leaves, colored tissue paper, and other flat materials such as fabric swatches. Peel a few crayons and with a plastic knife make a dish of crayon shavings. Give each child a piece of waxed paper and ask him or her to use pieces of tissue paper, leaves, fabric and crayon shavings to make an arrangement on the paper. Provide enough time for the children to play around with their arrangements until they achieve a satisfying result. When each child is ready, tear a sheet of similar size waxed paper to fit over the picture. Then, place a piece of drawing paper under and over the sheets of waxed paper to form a "sandwich" for ironing. Place the "sandwich" on a pad of newspapers. With a medium hot iron, press down on the "sandwich" for about thirty seconds to one minute. (*CAUTION: the iron should be used only by an adult.*) Remove the drawing paper and examine the results. What happened to the crayon shavings? Did any of the items change color?

HOW TO GO FURTHER.

Have children experiment with different ways to display their pictures. Some may wish to mount them onto a piece of construction paper. Tape one of the pictures onto a window. Observe how light passes through it. Which objects block the light? Which ones permit the light to shine through?

WOODEN SCULPTURES

WHY DO THIS?

In kindergarten children should have experiences working with many different kinds of materials. Art projects from three-dimensional objects will be especially stimulating for young children. Wood scraps and pieces can be assembled into forms or sculptures and then glued together. As children work to assemble scraps of wood, they will discover size relationships among the various pieces. This project gives particularly satisfying results since wood scraps are generally porous and will maintain a tight bond when glued with white glue. Children will be especially proud of the sculptures they create.

WHAT WILL I NEED?

- Pieces of cardboard for bases
- Wood scraps
- White glue
- Paint and brushes (optional)

HOW TO GET STARTED.

Call a local lumber yard and ask if they will save wood scraps for you. Most lumber companies are happy to oblige, and some will even let you visit with the children to collect the scraps. (This can be a wonderful community field trip if there is a lumber company near the school.)

In the art center of the classroom, provide the materials needed to make wooden sculptures: cardboard for bases, wood scraps, and white glue. Some children will want to make boats, cars, trucks, houses, or other realistic structures. Others will want to make objects without any recognizable form. Both are fine. Once an object is completed to the child's satisfaction, it can be painted. Then, the finished product can be glued onto a cardboard base. Some children may wish to make their sculptures over a period of days, but most kindergarteners will want to complete it in one sitting. Label the projects with the artist's name and display them.

HOW TO GO FURTHER.

Provide opportunities for the children to incorporate their wooden sculptures into the block area. Children can build around them or place their projects appropriately on a roadway, on a river, on a street, or as a decoration for the front of a building. Have the children ever seen an outdoor sculpture near a large building?

A PHOTO COLLAGE

WHY DO THIS?

Young children can begin to see humor in art. By arranging unwanted photographs in unusual ways, some very amusing results can occur. Many families may have envelopes full of photographs that never came out right. These can be put to good use by children as they create photo collages. Where photographs are not available, magazine pictures can also be used. The goal is to have children cut and paste the photographs in ways that will result in funny creations.

WHAT WILL I NEED?

- Drawing paper
- Glue
- Scissors
- Unwanted photographs from the children's homes or pictures from magazines

HOW TO GET STARTED.

Cut out pictures from magazines and arrange them in various ways on a sheet of drawing paper. Try to put a head from one picture onto the body of another or place a car on top of a bowl of cereal or any other such humorous combinations. Ask the children why the resulting pictures are funny.

Provide the children with unwanted photographs or magazine pictures, drawing paper, and glue. Ask them to cut out the pictures and place them in on the paper in interesting ways. Tell the children that they may wish to experiment with different arrangements before they glue their pictures onto the paper. Have the children discuss their collages and try to tell each other what is funny about their productions. Such activities also help to promote children's sense of humor.

HOW TO GO FURTHER.

Have children make greeting cards with photo collages. Provide folded paper in the proportions of a card and help the children with the written greeting. Then let them find pictures which appropriately relate to the purpose or holiday for which the card is written.

MAKING ANIMAL MASKS

WHY DO THIS?

Simple paper masks depicting familiar animals can enhance young children's play and story dramatization. Effective masks do not have to be elaborate at all, but they should exaggerate a particular feature in some way. For example, a bird mask can be no more than a paper head band with a triangular beak, a lion's mane can be a paper plate with yarn attached around the edges, rabbit ears are simply a head band and two long ears cut from paper. Using such masks will bring added enjoyment and a sense of drama to children's play.

WHAT WILL I NEED?

- Construction paper
- Scissors
- Paper plates
- Markers
- Yarn
- Glue and stapler
- Other assorted materials as needed

HOW TO GET STARTED.

Read a story about an animal to the children. Ask them to talk about some of the animal's prominent features. With construction paper make a face mask which suggests the animal in the story. Talk about other familiar animals which children know or have read about. Provide each child with materials to make a face mask depicting an animal. Show the children how to make a simple head band onto which a mask or facial feature can be attached. Fit the head band to a child's head. Demonstrate a few simple types of animal masks. After all of the children have made a mask, ask them to show their masks and ask the others in the class to guess which animal it represents.

A Rabbit Headband

A Yarn and Paper Plate Loin's Mane

A Bird's Beak

A Pig's Nose and Ears

HOW TO GO FURTHER.

Wearing their animal masks, ask the children to make up a play or a skit in which a few of the animals are characters. Are any of the masks of animals in some of the children's favorite stories? Have the children act out one or two of these stories.

EXPLORATIONS IN PRINTING

WHY DO THIS?

Making prints is yet another kind of art experience that kindergarten children will enjoy. Children will see that by dipping a particular object in paint and then pressing it onto a piece of paper, they can reproduce the same impression time after time. Special designs can be created and a combination of different printed shapes in various colors can be created. Simple everyday materials can be used for printing. For example, vegetables, bottle caps, toilet paper rolls, and blocks are among the wide variety of objects that can be used to make an impression.

WHAT WILL I NEED?

- Pie tins for paint
- Tempera paint
- Painting paper
- Plastic knives

- An assortment of objects to use for printing, for example, blocks, sponges, toilet paper rolls, potatoes, carrots, nuts and bolts, cork, styrofoam, and pencil erasers.

HOW TO GET STARTED.

Fill pie tins with tempera paint. Take a cork or the cardboard roll from toilet paper and dip an end into the paint. Press the cardboard roll or cork onto a sheet of painting paper to make an impression. Make several such prints on the paper, arranging them randomly or in a pattern. Show the results to the children.

Ask the children to think of objects which have interesting textures which can be used for printing. Bottle caps, wooden blocks, pieces of sponge, styrofoam shapes, sliced potatoes and carrots, and nuts and bolts are among the great variety of objects that can be used for printing. Have the children make prints using these familiar objects.

Cut a potato in half. With a plastic knife, carve a shape into the face of the potato. Start with something simple like a square, a circle, or a heart. Show how to use the potato to print the shape onto paper. Other hard vegetables can be used similarly

HOW TO GO FURTHER.

Many teachers collect rubber stamps. A wonderful variety of stamps is available from supply magazines or special catalogs. Allow children to use stamps and stamp pads to create their own interesting pictures. They can make greeting cards and write messages. Some stamps have printing on them and this is a wonderful opportunity for children to read. With the additional motivation of working with stamps, the youngsters are more than likely to learn to read the words they are printing.

EGG CARTON ART

WHY DO THIS?

Cardboard or styrofoam egg cartons can be put to many interesting uses in kindergarten art projects. Egg carton insects and caterpillars are favorite projects among kindergarten teachers. The caterpillars are easy to make and the effects are very appealing.

WHAT WILL I NEED?

- Egg cartons
- Scissors
- Paint and brushes or markers

- Books with pictures of caterpillars
- Pipe cleaners

HOW TO GET STARTED.

Let children use egg cartons, scissors, and pipe cleaners to make their own creations. Undoubtedly some interesting projects will emerge.

Then find some books in the school library that show pictures of caterpillars. Have the children study the shape and body parts of the caterpillar. Ask them if they can guess how to make a caterpillar with egg carton sections and pipe cleaners. Demonstrate one way to do this. Cut an egg carton in half lengthwise. Cut the six cup section in half so that you are left with two three cup sections. Insert a pipe cleaner into one of the end sections and curl the ends to look like antennae. Other cut pieces of pipe cleaners can be used as legs. The caterpillars can then be painted or colored with marker. (It may be difficult for paint to adhere to styrofoam.)

HOW TO GO FURTHER.

What other kinds of projects can the children make from egg cartons? How could a spider be made with an egg carton section and pipe cleaners? Incorporate egg carton sections into block building. Make a penny tossing game from an egg carton. The top part (lid) of an egg carton can serve as a tray for a variety of uses.

STUFFED ANIMALS

WHY DO THIS?

Making three dimensional objects is an interesting variation for young children. Stuffed animals can be readily made by drawing and then cutting out a form on folded over paper or fabric. Then, the animal can be partially stapled, stuffed with cotton or shredded newspaper, and closed up with more staples. The results are puffy creatures which can be hung in the classroom or at home.

WHAT WILL I NEED?

- Brown wrapping paper or paper grocery bags
- Fabric (optional)
- Paints and brushes or markers
- Pencils
- Shredded newspaper or cotton balls
- A stapler and staples

HOW TO GET STARTED.

Provide each child with a piece of brown wrapping paper or a paper grocery bag. Help the children to fold over the one side of their paper so that it is double thickness. (Fabric may be substituted for brown paper, but it will be harder for the children to cut.) With pencil or markers let them draw an animal shape that can be readily stuffed. A dog with thin legs will be problematic, so encourage large shapes without small appendages. Fish, worms, bears, seals, and similar animals will be most effective. (Provide pictures of animals to help the children get ideas.) After they have traced their animals, have them color them with paint or markers. On the back side of the doubled paper, the youngsters can draw the back of their animals. The children should then cut around the outline of their animal. The result should be two similar pieces, a front and a back. Help them to staple about three fourths of the animals around the edges of the paper. Then give the children shredded newspaper or cotton balls to stuff the animals. (Cotton balls, if available, are easier to work with than newspaper.) After the animal is stuffed, help the children to finish stapling the remaining open section. The resulting animals can be hung by a string or displayed on a counter.

HOW TO GO FURTHER.

Make a special project with stuffed animals. For example, cut out one side of a large cardboard carton. Tell the children that this will be a fish tank. The children can find books about fish that show several different kinds. Then each child can make a fish which can be hung with thread from the top of the box. The aquarium can be displayed and shared with other classes.

All I Have in This World

- -

A NOVEL

MICHAEL PARKER

ALGONQUIN BOOKS OF CHAPEL HILL   2014

Published by
ALGONQUIN BOOKS OF CHAPEL HILL
Post Office Box 2225
Chapel Hill, North Carolina 27515-2225

a division of
WORKMAN PUBLISHING
225 Varick Street
New York, New York 10014

This is a work of fiction. While, as in all fiction, the literary perceptions and insights are based on experience, all names, characters, places, and incidents either are products of the author's imagination or are used fictitiously.

LIBRARY OF CONGRESS CATALOGING-IN-PUBLICATION DATA
Parker, Michael, [date]
   All I have in this world : a novel / by Michael Parker.—1st ed.
      pages cm
   ISBN 978-1-61620-162-3
   1. Couples—Fiction.   2. Reconciliation—Fiction.
   3. Buick automobile—Fiction.   4. Texas, West—Fiction.
   I. Title.
PS3566.A683A45 2014
813'.54—dc23   2013038533

10 9 8 7 6 5 4 3 2 1
First Edition

Rose Ann Thompson
1946–2011

All I Have in This World

One

Pinto Canyon, Texas, March 1994

The town was small, and so was the boy. His name was Randy and he was Maria's size exactly. They fit together tongue and groove, which to Maria, who at seventeen had never had a boyfriend, meant that it was meant.

Because he was too wispy to play football, a near requirement of every boy with a pulse in their small West Texas high school, Randy devoted himself to auto mechanics. At sixteen, his fingernails were oil-blackened and his jeans smelled of exhaust. Maria had never given one second to the thought of a car. To her mind a car moved you from one place to the next, essential in the immense county where she lived, but hardly anything to get excited about. Still, when she and Randy hugged beneath the bleachers during the football game on Friday nights, she felt her body covered by his, exactly covered, and his interests were of no consequence. She made him pink ham and rat cheese sandwiches, which they ate in the Airstream parked behind her house. No one in Maria's family went inside the Airstream, and only in late fall and winter was it even possible to enter it, since her father had long ago disconnected the air-conditioning, and open windows were useless in the heat of day.

It bothered Randy that the Airstream sat unused, probably because it had wheels and therefore qualified as automotive.

"I'd take this sucker everywhere," he said one day after school. She had fixed him a ham and cheese. He liked extra mayonnaise. Maria preferred mustard, though she did not care for the squirt bottles her mother bought, which made a noise that quelled her appetite.

"Like where would you take this sucker?"

"Grand Canyon."

"We went once to Big Bend in it. And I think I remember going to the campground at Balmorhea."

"We could get in the car right now and be in either of those places before dark."

"Your point?" Maria said, though she knew what his point was. She said this to Randy all the time because it drove him crazy. He would pick her up for school in the morning and say, "We need to stop on the way to town to get gas," and she would say, "And your point is?"

"My point is get your butt over here." He pulled her up from the tiny booth, littered with his half-eaten sandwich and their half-empty glasses of Pepsi, and led her to the bed in the back of the Airstream. Even though the Airstream was shut tight against the wind, dust found its way inside. Dust on the mattress, dust on the blinds, dust coating the ceiling, which was bare and silver, her father having yanked out the upholstery years ago because it had started to sag.

It wasn't as if they were unaccustomed to dust. Sometimes

at night Randy drove her out to the end of Golf Course Road, where they parked the car at the turnaround and strolled out onto the pastureland of the Weil ranch. He liked to claim a plane had gone down just over a rise and was still filled with sacks of drug money. "You silly boy," she would say when he went on about downed planes and unclaimed treasure. He needn't have white-lied to recline next to her on the dry-rotted tarp they'd pulled from the floor of her garage. The tarp smelled of spilled oil, but the roughness of the sand her father had spread to soak up the oil beat the prick of cactus and cocklebur. Stars shot across the night sky so slowly she could nearly narrate their passage. From far down the valley came the faint whistle of the train to El Paso; nearby, a sudden rustling that both knew but neither admitted was a snake.

Inside the Airstream that never went anywhere, Maria and Randy made out for so long their lips were raw, their cheeks reddened. At first, out on the ranch under the night sky, their kisses had been tentative and clumsy, but once the newness had worn off they became aggressive, frenzied, as if force might make up for lack of experience. Maria had seen strangers in movies drawn together by lightning-quick chemistry and she tried to mimic the soft/loud lip brush and tongue plunge she saw on the screen, but to fully master such required the assistance of her partner, whose impatience with the softer verse she preferred to interpret as passion.

Soon they were sliding against each other on the vinyl in only their underwear. When Maria discarded her bra for the first time, Randy, not wanting to acknowledge it (she supposed because he feared she might put it back on if he even changed his expression), clamped his mouth on one nipple and then the other. To Maria's mind—not to mention her body—Randy overtended to her breasts, as if this step were crucial to perfect before moving on to the next. It made little sense to her, given his rushed kisses. Maria thought about stopping him to say, And your point is?

This made her smile, then laugh a little. Randy raised his head to look at her as she imagined a baby might when a nursing was interrupted.

"What?" he said, smiling in a way that barely hid his worry that she was about to tell him he was doing it wrong.

"It tickles a little," she said.

"Well, good, that's good," said Randy. "It's supposed to."

He went back to work. Maria ran her fingers through his hair, tucked a strand of it behind an ear. It occurred to her that they were two children playing in a camper behind a house after school let out but before their parents came home from work. Randy tasted like mayonnaise. But was it not also true that they could say to each other with their bodies, I want this part to be over, I want to move on to the next part? With their bodies there were ways to leave the Airstream, home, Texas. She pulled him up to her and she kissed him and she slid him off her so she could slip off her panties. She gave him two minutes to explore her with his fingers and then she told him to take his boxers off. She waved him forward. Dawdling grade-schooler at the crosswalk, weighted down with textbooks, your poor back bent, let me help you out of that backpack, I will lighten you, I will see you safely across.

"I don't have one," he said, hovering above her, his arms locked as if he was about to do a push-up.

"At least you didn't say that word. I hate that word."

"What word?"

"What y'all call them. Actually I hate every other word for them, too."

But they would use them after this first time except for a few occasions when someone's mother was in line at the drugstore, or when the men's room at the Fina station—where there was a machine—was occupied for what seemed like a century. She would not let him name or even comment on it as he tore open the wrapper with his teeth and took his time unrolling it.

"I trust you," she said, unlocking his arms at the elbows and pulling him onto her, and she did, mostly because they were equal in their inexperience. When would that ever happen again? When would she ever be with someone and not have the touch of past lovers to compare his with? When would the burst she'd heard about but never felt (though she knew, she'd heard, that it got better, longer, even more explosive) ever equal the unknown trajectory of her first?

The ceiling of the Airstream, so starkly silver, was not the night sky of the pasture, so slow with stars. It might not have been *where* but it was *when*. And when he finally pushed inside her and they both gasped at its fit, she felt they had stumbled upon something they both could learn from. As they pushed against, away from, and farther into each other, she hoped that soon—not now, but in a while—they would discover a new beauty, they would learn how friction, the slightest strife, could lead to a pleasure terrifying but also somehow containable. Not today, but soon, she and Randy might also arrive at some common understanding of what in this world might matter most, and together they would find in their hearts a special chamber where they could worship these most meaningful things.

For the next two months they did it in the Airstream, out on the Weil ranch on the oily tarp, twice at thrilling risk in the band room after school, even on a field trip to a water park near San Antonio. And then their story grew so familiar and ancient that it might have been written on crinkly parchment or charcoaled across the wall of a cave.

Only after years away from home did Maria accept the notion that her predicament was not original, that such things have happened to people across time continuous, and she no longer felt the sting of the word her mother used to describe it: "unthinking." It was not incorrect, her mother's word, for surely some other factor besides the intellect ruled her time with Randy until, after touching her forehead to the porcelain for the fourth day in a row, she admitted to herself that the only way they truly fit was anatomically.

Randy wanted to drop out of school and go to work at his uncle's body shop and learn to play bass so he could join this band Rockfish his buddy Johnny Rodriquez had put together. He spoke about a standing Saturday night gig at Railroad Blues down in Alpine as if it were surefire stardom. He was so excited by the life he described for himself that Maria, loath to disappoint anyone, nearly went along with it. But the night she took the test, they had driven sixty miles to Skyline Drive and below them the lights of Fort Davis blinked before the valley fell away to empty and desolate ranchland, and each twinkling light reminded her of all the people who hardly ever left this valley. "Unthinking" turned out to be the word that saved her, for she thought about what she would say, and yet no matter how much time she had devoted to saying it gently and no matter how much she knew that this was the kinder choice to all involved parties, she could not bear to look at his face when she told him she wanted to go away to college and get, eventually, her master's degree in deaf education.

Maria's father, Mexican and deeply Catholic even if during Mass he could often be found breakfasting with his buddies at Alicia's Café, knew nothing of her predicament, much less how she chose to deal with it. It was he who, a week after that night atop Skyline Drive, came home to find Randy's car in the drive and his body behind the Airstream. Maria and her mother were on their way back from the clinic in El Paso when it happened, and for years—even though she knew it did not matter—she wondered where they were in their journey when Randy pulled the trigger.

Junction, Texas, 2004

His third day on the road to Mexico, somewhere west of San Antonio on I-10, Marcus Banks noticed, for the first time since relinquishing his property to the Bank of America, the world outside the window of his truck. Or perhaps it was the landscape that noticed him and announced itself, arid and tawny, as the opposite of the farm he'd fled in the lush sea-level swamplands of southeastern North Carolina. Even though he had not yet crossed the border, looking out the window, he felt as if he'd escaped.

He passed through Sonora and Ozona, after which the towns dried up and the gnarled oaks were replaced by even more stunted scrub. Near Fort Stockton he decided to get off the interstate and take a back road toward Presidio, where he could cross over into Chihuahua instead of going all the way west to El Paso and entering the country through Juárez as planned. The sunset made the land appear slightly less parched. Miles of nothing much but tufts of some vegetation unknown to him, mountains so distantly shrouded he decided they belonged to Mexico. The only sign of settlement he saw was an abandoned homestead, its windmill rusted to a stop above a long-dry stock tank, cabin and outbuildings beaten by wind, dirt, time everlasting.

Would that nature take his farmhouse as quickly. After loading up his pickup two nights earlier, he'd sat for hours in the kitchen, drinking bourbon and listening to mice skitter behind the walls. Dusk inched closer across the side yard and he switched on a lamp and stared at the yellow cone it diced from the coming darkness. Dust swirled in the lamplight. Another galaxy to which he was blind. There had been a woman, named Rebecca, who left him because of his inability to recognize any universe other than his own.

Drinking bourbon in his farmhouse that last night, his pickup packed and ready, he had reminded himself that whatever happened inside his heart, the world continued apace. Nature was on its way. Just beyond the kitchen, Virginia creeper curled up the downspout. Kudzu sent its snaky tendrils almost perceptibly out of the dark-mouthed woods. He damn near prayed that as soon as his truck disappeared up the sandy two-track, the farmhouse would be wrestled to the ground by sapling and vine. Already it was giving way, for in the darkness either the mice grew in number or squirrels and possibly raccoons and possums joined them in the secret spaces of his farmhouse. Next the stray mongrels would come sniffing up from the swamp, black bears irascible and sluggish in early spring, ever-abundant deer, copperheads, corn snakes, diamondbacks, a few beautifully banded but deadly corals. Bored teenagers who had a nose for derelict structures would arrive with warm beer and aerosol cans of paint. May those teens be the last humans ever to set foot in his farmhouse, and may it instantly revert to what they called the elements. He owed those elements a sacrifice, the mighty fortress of his ruin.

Of course at dawn the next morning, when his head was free of sour mash, he accepted the fact that someone representing the bank would arrive in a few hours to assess the property it now owned. By that time he would be well on his way to Mexico. He had a long-standing offer to stay with an old friend from graduate school who had also failed to put to use his degree in history and joined the expat enclave of San Miguel de Allende. Thousands of miles behind him would be the farmhouse and those acres of swamp and scrub and pine forest to which he had retreated in his late thirties with a plan to profit from the sale of a plant native only to his property and a few thousand contiguous acres, not to mention realize his dream of building a museum to educate the world about the Venus flytrap.

Six years earlier, when he first started the flytrap enterprise, he had called his older sister, Annie, who lived three hundred miles west in Asheville. Though she co-owned the property with him, she rarely visited the farm. It was only right to consult her, though he suspected he would be annoyed by her reaction to his plan, which turned out to be true.

"Don't they grow wild?"

"Yes, but there's not nearly enough for us to make money off. I could harvest what's out there in a few day's time. I'm talking about an operation that would supply not only flytraps but all the other carnivorous plants to wholesalers all over the country."

"So, using greenhouses, you mean?"

"Sure," said Marcus, though in fact he had no plans to grow

his traps in greenhouses. He had no use for a greenhouse, hated its look, its design, most of all what it represented, which was cheating, an attempt to circumvent nature. Growing his traps in greenhouses seemed contradictory to the very purpose of his educational center, which was to celebrate the fact that the plant grew wild only in the very region where his ancestors had settled in the mid-eighteenth century.

"I don't know, Marcus," said Annie. "You think you can pull this off?"

"It's not like we're doing anything with the land but sitting on it until we die and our heirs parcel it off and sell it to developers."

"What heirs would those be? I'm gay and you're getting too old to have a child."

"Gay people have children now, Annie. So do old people."

"I realize that gay people have children, Marc. I think I know more gay people than you do. It's just that I don't want a child," she said. "If you want one, though, I would support you. You know that, right?"

"Of course," he said, though he had no idea what she meant by support. Offer moral guidance? Financial assistance? As far as he knew, his sister changed jobs as often as she did girlfriends. They did not talk much, but every time they did, a new name cropped up. She was living with June, she had to go because she and Lucia were having a party, Molly wrecked her car.

"Anyway, even if there were heirs, if it were up to me, I'd have sold it yesterday. The only thing worth anything is that shack you live in."

Actually, the logging rights were worth quite a bit of money, truck, a Ford F-150 4×4 with only 70K on it, and the contents of its bed: clothes, a few cooking implements, a bicycle, some couple of dozen books, and three boxes of sentimental junk—deeds, maps, love letters, a family Bible charting the lineage of those who had occupied the land he'd let the bank take away.

Shedding all the detritus of home did not bother him. He loved a certain type of movie in which a drifter turned up. The drifter was all about the present tense. If the actor was any good, you could see—in the way he lay across his cot smoking, wearing a wife beater, with his feet flat upside the pine-paneled walls of the trailer house behind the diner, horse farm, or sawmill where some gruff but kindly soul had given him gainful employment—the terminal crush of his yesterday.

The present-tense drifter might occasionally be sighted in some rainy city, but small towns and back roads were his territory. Here is Marcus Banks drifting right on up into right now. Good riddance to those years saddled by something chthonic and corrosive in the land he'd lost. Marcus here, Marcus now. He timed his steps down the street to the beat.

Pinto Canyon, Texas, came to life quickly of a morning. Three-quarters of the vehicles passing by on the street were pickups, and two-ton ones at that, which seemed to Marcus a good sign. Ranchers, maybe a few farmers. It felt like a fine place to break his trip, even though he knew he could stretch out his stash far longer across the border. The quicker he crossed over, the sooner he'd be able to live off something other than peanut butter and banana sandwiches. But he broke his fast on a bench by the train station, conjuring a new diet heavy given the demand for cypress of a certain age and size, but he did not share that because Annie had more than once voiced her opinion that primogeniture belonged to her even if she was female.

"Wait: Didn't you just say something about developers? Is someone interested in developing it?"

"Actually, no," he said. "I mean, no one besides me."

"Well, maybe you could put it out there that the land is available? I mean, if the flytrap thing doesn't work. Actually, I'm a little strapped, to be honest."

"What exactly is your occupation right now?"

"You go first."

"Entrepreneur," he said.

"There's a lot of that going around these days," said Annie. "Though I have never figured out what it means. Up here I think it means you're cooking meth in your trailer."

"I'm peddling plants," he said, "but they're fantastical, not medicinal."

"Well, as long as you can make money off it, and as long as any money you do lose, I mean if you happen to lose any, comes out of your half, I mean, what am I going to do? Come down there and plant some hydroponic lettuce?"

"So is that a yes?"

"You should call Mom, Marc," said Annie. "She told me the other day she hadn't heard from you in six months."

"I called her on her birthday. A matter of weeks, actually. She's not so good at math."

"Let's hope *you* are," said Annie.

Marcus did not feel bad lying to his sister about the greenhouses because she clearly had no interest in anything but collecting a check. He felt no compunction to share with her his plans to build the educational center, either, for that part of the plan he was sure she would have an opinion about—the word *nonprofit,* he suspected, would get her attention—but since he had not even broken ground for his museum at that point, it seemed premature to alarm her.

So he signed contracts to provide wholesalers with his traps and he planted not only flytraps but pitchers and butterworts and all the other varieties of carnivorous plants that thrived in the swamps on his property. His first crop, the yield was pitiful. Everything that might align against him did so swiftly and with no mercy. A killing frost late in the season took away all that he'd planted. Deer and feral pigs feasted on the seedlings. Most worrisome were the poachers who came in the night or for all Marcus knew in the broadness of the day, sneaking in while he was in town or having lunch on his porch, the sort of desperadoes who yanked copper wire from nearly finished houses to sell on the black market for money he assumed went into their arms or bellies.

Even had his business thrived, the not-for-profit center itself would have floundered. Though there were dozens of reasons for its failure, he still had a hard time believing that he had built a shrine and no one had come. He liked to remind himself that the location was remote, miles from any interstate, in a region of the country so besotted with swamp and river and sound that roads, based on old stagecoach routes, were circuitous, and routes to the center managed to elude even MapQuest. But it was for the center that Marcus had borrowed the brunt of the loans, and he'd been wasteful from the start, conducting research with a month-long road trip around the country to visit similar sites. Any nonprofit whose aim it was to provide information about nature to the public made his list, and there were a surprising number of them: museums devoted to rice, to corn, to kudzu, cacti, redwoods, wildflowers, even pine trees. Because this was business and he planned to write the entire excursion off on his taxes, he had been foolishly extravagant, forgoing campsites and the mom-and-pop motels for more luxurious accommodations with fitness centers, minibars, wireless access.

He never got around to telling Annie about the center even after the structure—a geodesic dome that was Marcus's only concession to the idea of a greenhouse, given that he needed the light for his exhibits and he had long been a fan of Buckminster Fuller—was completed. One day she would show up for a visit and discover it nestled among the pines just off the highway. What a surprise it would be for her, the dome glinting in the afternoon light, the buses parked in their own special lot.

But she did not come, and he did not worry about her because there were dozens of other things to consider even after the center was built. He certainly never figured that creating a museum called for the expertise of those whose sole job it was to design exhibits. Only when his plans proved both crude and without substance, the copy he wrote to accompany them formless, rambling, and short on actual fact, did he succumb to looking up such professionals on the Internet.

He settled on a woman from Washington, since the district

had not only the most museums, but the best. He did not like her from the moment he saw her. She was humorless and inappropriately shod. When he explained that they would be walking in the woods, she asked about snakes and said she was particularly sensitive to mosquitoes. Finally she asked to use his restroom and emerged dressed in a vest of many pockets that one might wear while trout fishing or on safari.

The rest of the day was miserable with questions Marcus not only could not answer but deemed maddeningly literal. They sat at his kitchen table, two floor fans trained on them, for she declared herself overly sensitive to humidity and could not believe he did not have air-conditioning. Air-conditioning to Marcus was like a greenhouse. He started to explain why but stopped himself from such a futile task.

"What do you want the public to know?" asked the woman, whose name was Carrie, though she introduced herself as Dr. Elwood. He did not ask what he wanted to ask: Doctor of what, exactly? Exhibit design? Having spent some time in the halls of academe, he knew better than to disparage the pursuit of a high degree in a subject obscure or obsolete. But he refused to call her, or anyone else who did not set bones or dispense drugs, Doctor.

"I want them to know all about the carnivorous plant," he said, as if this was understood.

"Right," she said, smirking at the screen of her laptop, which she claimed to have brought along to show him some of her work. "But you need to be more specific if we are to come up with specialized and targeted exhibits."

After a pause, he said he thought the word *leach* was crucial to his mission.

"Leech? As in what primitive medicine believed to be a panacea?"

Marcus laughed, mostly at her diction.

"No," he said. " L-e-a-c-h. As in the soil my plants grow in is so acidic that it leaches the earth of nutrients. Most plants can't survive in this habitat because they are deprived of ingredients essential to their health." ·

She was nodding now, Carrie Elwood. "Such as?"

"Nitrogen, phosphorus, magnesium, sulfur, calcium, potassium."

"Okay, good," she said, clacking away on her keyboard. "That's a start. But I'm not sure why you emphasize the term *leach*. Especially since it is hardly an attractive word, even if it is a homophone."

Marcus stifled a sigh at the word *homophone*.

"I emphasize it because the very elements we need to survive are taken away from us by life itself." I, too, can fill the room with pretentiousness and pedantry, Marcus realized, though it seemed silly to be playing this game, given the amount he was overpaying her.

She studied him over the top of her computer as if he was a student in one of her classes who had said something so off the mark that it was worth pursuing, though only to kill time until the bell rang.

"What elements are those?"

"Most crucial is the ability to connect with other people."

"Love?"

"Not even. The capacity to merge your reality with someone else's version of same."

"I'm not following you. What does this have to do with the Venus flytrap?"

Now Marcus was just irritated. But more than irritated, he was deeply amused.

"It's not that complicated a metaphor. Nature made us a kind of kingdom unto ourselves. The natural world plants us in our habitat but then it leaches the soil surrounding us of sustenance essential to our subsistence, if not survival. But the flytrap, in the harshest of circumstances, perseveres."

Carrie Elwood began to type again. Marcus wondered what she could possibly be writing. He decided she was making a list of homophones. Perhaps she was just feigning industry to legitimize her fee. But after a minute or two of furious typing she closed the laptop and began to talk. She spoke of objectives. She mentioned business models, as if he had not explained to her more than once his desire to make the education center not for profit. She spoke of the need for the center to have a "narrative," a term Marcus distrusted for its odor of linearity. She spoke of "flow," another term he disliked for its elasticity. She spoke to him of her previous designs, of their successes. Then she invited him to sit next to her and opened her screen and began a slide show of her accomplishments, replete with many fancy photographs, which went on for what seemed to Marcus six weeks. He did not listen or look at the photographs. He smelled the newness of her safari vest, the odor of fabric stiff and unwashed, and he wondered how anyone could wear something straight off the rack and not itch to death, and he rued the mix of insecurity and ambition that had led him to doubt his ability to tell the true story of the Venus flytrap in his own words, with his own visual aids.

The insanely large check he wrote to Dr. Carrie Elwood at the end of her endless visit was the second strike, after his stubborn refusal to use greenhouses, which he ought to have heeded and did not. There was a third strike—he could, if pressed, name any of a dozen—but Marcus, at some point, quit counting. The reasons for his failure were not worth contemplating, especially now that he had left all that behind.

Marcus had been off the interstate for close to an hour and had seen no sign of, nor even signs for, a town. He could pick up just enough of the wayside with his high beams to see that it was broken only by the most tenacious flora, stunted and sparse. A place forgotten by rain, foreign to creek, stream, pocosin, sound. No nearby ocean to court storms fierce enough to be named. Just the opposite of the land he'd lost, this place appeared inhospitable to any exotica on which he might squander what money he'd managed to hide from the bank. And, far more importantly, from his sister, who deserved the money far more than the bank did. Marcus cranked his window down and let the desert wind blow the thick drift of receipts and bills lining the dash onto the seat beside him, the floorboard. A few flew out the window, but he wasn't littering. Let this breeze wipe clean at least this dash. Who would come upon the remnants of his failure in this backcountry untrammeled by humans? But Marcus was not naive enough to think that the desolation into which he sped was nothingness. More the sweet beginning of something else.

Wentzville, Missouri, 1983

In the break room of the Buick plant, they called Brantley
"Preacher." Not just Brantley but everybody who worked on the
line in Marriage, fitting chassis to body. "How many you guys
marry this morning already?" they'd say to him, and he'd say,
"Like I'm counting," and they'd say, "Sounds like Preacher-man
has got tired of tying knots," and then someone would point
out that he alone out of his team of four wasn't married, and
someone who knew him from high school (for half his gradu-
ating class from Wentzville had ended up on the line at the
plant, wasn't anything else to do except make the hour drive to
Saint Louis and find some other manufacturing job that maybe
paid a little more, but you'd eat up any profit in gas) would say,
"When you and Carmen getting married?"

This question made Brantley do something with his face.
He would try to smile but he felt like what happened with
his mouth was fixed somewhere between smirk and wince.
Which was dangerous because Carmen's dad worked on the
line and so did two of her four brothers, and he never knew
who was in the break room because it was half the size of
his high school cafeteria. He kept his head down, didn't talk

much during lunch, sat most of the time with Arthur from his team, even though he knew some people made fun of him for eating lunch with a black dude. What the hell, it was 1983. Sometimes Brantley would say something to Arthur, and it was always about work, but Arthur didn't like to talk about work. He liked to eat when he ate and that made Brantley eat his sandwich and his chips and drink his Coke in, like, five minutes so he could wait in line for a pay phone in the hallway by the bathrooms and call Carmen if she had worked the night shift and was hanging out at home.

Carmen worked at Long John Silver's. The apartment she shared with Cindy Dakeris smelled like fried fish. Carmen's hair did, too. Her skin sometimes. Cindy was always complaining about it. "At least you could get work at Wendy's, I like the way their fries smell." Cindy was a big girl and so dumb that when she got high she got smart. Or smarter. Brantley and Carmen loved to get her high because she would watch a commercial for laundry detergent and say something really surprising about it. Other times she'd go on about stupid shit. Carmen and Brantley spent most of their time in Carmen's room, anyway, listening to music, turning it way up so Cindy couldn't hear them fooling around. Carmen always got furious when Cindy said she stunk up the apartment. She would go into her room and slam the door. She was just working there to save up money for community college. They were going to move to Saint Louis after Christmas. "It isn't like working at Long John's is my life's dream," Carmen would say. "No one wants to smell like this." She loved to complain about her job, but that didn't mean she wanted Cindy even to mention it.

One night she said, "You know what's like the grossest thing ever to me?"

"Me?" Brantley was stretched out on the bed, waiting for her to shed her uniform.

"Shut up," she said. "Tartar sauce."

"What is it, anyway?"

She was pulling off the T-shirt she always wore under her uniform. It, too, reeked. She threw it across the room at him. He batted it away lest it land on his head and cover his mouth.

"You know what it is. Tartar sauce!"

"No, I mean what's it made out of?" said Brantley.

"Mayonnaise mostly. I have no idea what those green specks are that are in it."

"Nor do you want to know."

"Exactly," she said. She had unhooked her bra and thrown it in the corner and was pulling on her Pretenders T-shirt. They'd seen them last year in Saint Louis and Chrissie Hynde talked shit about Ohio where she was from and on the ride home Carmen was all, like, in a British accent, "I live in London, England, and I have escaped the exasperating Midwest never to return except to play my songs for you poor unfortunates," even though Carmen hated Wentzville more than Brantley did even, she was always talking about moving to Arizona because she'd flown over it once on the way to her cousin's wedding in California and everybody on the street had a swimming pool in their backyard.

Brantley knew better than to raise himself up off the bed, where he was propped on pillows to rest his back, which hurt after his shift from all the bending over (even though this week all he had been doing was standing along the line and sig-naling Arthur, who was running the crane that lowered the chassis onto the body, to move a few inches left or right), and reach around and cup her breasts before she had had a chance to pull her T-shirt on. That was a good way to get slapped. Carmen had to be in the mood. After work for at least an hour was not a good time. She hadn't even showered yet. He'd rather wait until she got the smell out of her hair at least, but he was a boy, what could he do, even her bare back stirred him.

"I bet they're like chopped-up olives," he said.

"I said I didn't want to know."

"Mayonnaise is disgusting."

"You like it on hamburgers."

"No, I don't," said Brantley.

"You never tell them to hold it."

"I hate telling people stuff like that. People working for a liv-ing and you're going in there all picky about what they put on some slab of beef you're paying a buck fifty for. Special orders on a Big Mac?"

"Yeah, well, you're not like most people. Most people will stand there for five minutes telling you how to fry their chicken strips. Like the girl taking their order is going to go fry up chicken strips right then and there."

"Like that chicken has not *been* fried."

"Seriously. But I can't say a word because fucking Dorset is all about counting the 'Ring the bell if we did well' bell. If he doesn't hear the bell for five minutes, he'll flip out."

Brantley heard this every night. Complaints about Dorset,

the manager. "'Ring the bell if we did well' bell" was as common a phrase out of her mouth as "I love you." Way more common, in fact. She never asked him about his job, which kind of bothered him even though he didn't want to talk about it. She could at least ask. Maybe if she did, he'd want to marry her. But he wasn't going to marry Carmen. He knew he wasn't. She was the first girl he'd ever slept with and he wanted to sleep with more girls and she was sort of mean. Still, they talked about getting married and moving to Saint Louis, and she was going to get her associate in arts degree and go to work as an administrative assistant for a law firm like her girlfriend Melissa did. One time Brantley said, "So wait, you want to get your AA so you can become an AA," and she got seriously pissed and said, "Better than getting stuck in Wentzville." To which he had to agree. A kid by the time they were twenty. Go to work on the line, come home bone-tired, and have to deal with a screaming kid. She said, "I hate rubbers." He didn't say, I hate little babies. But he thought it. He thought, I hate mayonnaise but I'll eat it rather than make a big deal out of some poor asshole taking it off if they screw up and put it on. He thought, I hate that about myself because mayonnaise really is disgusting. I hate how I am sometimes. Hate that she never asks me about work and would hate it if she did.

Oddly enough, it was Cindy who asked him. Train tracks ran right behind the apartment they rented. They'd drag a bench from the picnic table someone had left behind one of the units and they'd get high and wait for the train. One night Cindy all of a sudden said, "So okay, Brant? When you're putting the cars together, do you ever wonder, like, where they will end up? Like, who's going to end up driving the one you're working on at that moment?"

Carmen was doing something to her fingernails. She was looking at them in the weak flood lamp some neighbor had turned on, probably to keep an eye on the kids in 9D. Carmen held her hand up close to her face, did something to her nails. Cindy was looking at him. Her question in the air was like the first faraway thrum of train in the night, coming closer. Brantley did not feel like her question would flash past and leave trails like the train always did when they got high and came outside to watch it. He felt like Carmen had pushed him on the tracks and instead of the train coming it was Cindy's question.

"No," he said.

Carmen stopped looking at her hands and reached one down to the grass and picked up her wine cooler and sipped it and put it back down in the grass.

"That's cool," said Cindy. "I guess you got to keep your mind on what you're doing."

But that wasn't it, really. He could not say why. The next day at work Cindy's question kept needling him. He even heard it. To hear anything in the plant was not possible over all the machines. The shift supervisor, when he wanted you to do something, came close in to your face and yelled in your ear. At home his ears rang for hours. Carmen loved to go see shows at the Checker Dome and he never did have the heart to tell her that was the last thing he wanted to do, go hear every band that came through town when his ears were already ringing. That day Cindy's question kept rising from the noise. It reached him as he worked on a light blue Electra. They'd been running Electras all week. He didn't want to think about her question because if he thought about it for this blue Electra he would have to think about every car on the line, and Brantley remembered this one time when high Cindy, all of a sudden not-so-dumb Cindy, said when they were watching something on TV, "Hey, do you guys think it's possible to, like, not think? Because I was just thinking that if you knew you wanted to clean your head empty, then that wouldn't really be like not thinking because you'd have to think, I'm not thinking, which isn't that like a thought?" Then she said "I'm not thinking" again and then again louder until she was sitting on the couch during a commercial for nasal spray screaming, "I'm not thinking, I'm not thinking," and Carmen was laughing so hard that later she claimed she wet her pants a little and then when they were in the bedroom with the door closed Carmen said, "I wanted to say to her, Yeah, girl, I think it is possible for you not to think."

Brantley remembered Cindy's question as the Electra, at his signal, directing Arthur from above — I now pronounce you chassis and body — became a car. Or the shell of one. Down the line it would become more of a car until finally it was a car, washed and detailed and gleaming among hundreds of others of various colors on the lot, where it would sit until a carrier came and loaded it up and took it to a dealer and someone would buy it. He did not want to know who. But who? Who would buy it? Who would drive it? Every time he thought about it he would say quickly, "I hate rubbers, too"; he would say it louder and louder to stop himself from thinking about where this car would end up, and then he saw it merging onto an interstate and at first he was above it like in one of those choppers that worked for the news and reported on the traffic and then he was inside the Electra, on the interstate, and Carmen was with him and then there was a UPS truck ahead of them and the truck swerved to miss someone stopped half in the lane to change a tire and then Brantley was standing by Carmen's grave and people were coming up to him and hugging him and saying the same things to him, and Cindy, who Carmen had made such fun of, was bawling under a canopy and it was raining. Brantley put his left hand up and signaled to Arthur a little to the right. What kind of sick shit was that, thinking his girlfriend was dead and everybody was, like, all thoughtful and sad for him and he was standing in the rain and it felt, I don't know, like, glorious somehow and then he felt so selfish and awful for allowing that thought into his head, a fantasy about his girlfriend's death by vehicle while he emerged without a scratch, and how people would come up to him and say stuff about doing things for him and he would nod and his tears would mix with rain. "You are at work, asshole," he said, "you're going to be here for another six hours and this car is just another car and I AM NOT THINKING I AM NOT THINKING I AM NOT!"

El Paso, Texas, 2004

Maria's mother was waiting in Baggage Claim.

"It's only this one," said Maria, holding up her carry-on. They embraced and Maria noted the stiffness in her mother's thin and sun-ravaged body, and the tightness of her lips, which she had almost forgotten. She watched her mother stare at the bag as if she were trying to decide whether to acknowledge what it represented.

"Well then, we better get on to the car," her mother said finally. "They charge you an arm to park and it's not even got a roof over it to shade."

Maria had not seen her mother, nor set foot in the state of Texas, for ten years. For five of those years she had had no contact with her family. One day she was peeling chilies in the restaurant where she worked and she thought of her father, who used to stuff chilies with string cheese and wrap them with bacon and grill them under the carport. All afternoon came pangs she had long accustomed herself to, but at some point she realized these were not the usual feelings of guilt she felt at the thought of Randy behind the Airstream. That night she sat down and wrote her parents a letter. It was short and perhaps curt; it said where she was and what she was doing and it said that she was fine and it was signed "With love." Daily she held her breath when she slid her key into the post office box, but there was nothing but flyers and bills and postcards from traveling friends.

Later when she got a computer and an e-mail account, she found a website for the Mountain View Motor Lodge, where her mother had worked for thirty years, and sent a message to the address listed under Contact Us. When she did not hear back, it was not hard to convince herself that her mother had no use for computers, that she still kept her books using a ten-key adding machine. Then one day there was a card. A photograph of a horse, backlit, nestling a colt. Inside, her mother had written the following lines in a hand so precise it bore the stamp of some strict small-town teacher who saw as her calling the teaching of proper letter form as well as expert penmanship to West Texas girls bound to marry ranch hands and promptly forget, by the time they returned from their honeymoon, the meaning of the word *salutation*.

Dear Maria Grace,

[For Grace was Maria's middle name and never had she heard her mother say or write her middle name and already she was choking with sobs at the sight of her mother's careful capitalization of the letter *G*, especially the slightly curled stem she added to give it a flourish.]

I hope this address is still good. Your dad and I are doing good. Manuel and his wife Alicia got a divorce. He has moved to New Braunfels and is driving a truck for H-E-B. They have two children, Inez (7) and Iris (4). I don't know that he's seeing someone else new, we never talk about all that on the phone. I am still at the motel. We do pretty good except you know how it slows down when the park gets too hot for the tourists. But I keep busy over there. Your grandmother Gloria died. They buried her up in Odessa with her husband's people. Your daddy did not like that but they claimed it was what she wanted. I wonder how you are doing. Well I must go it's nine at night here and I've got some accounts to go over, you be well now.

"With love,"

Your mother

The quotation marks did not annoy Maria as they might have had she seen them misplaced on a billboard, for although they might literally have called her mother's love into question, she knew her mother thought they added emphasis. And this is what turned, after so long, her blinking and swallowing into steady streaming tears.

Maria spent a week writing and rewriting her reply. In grave question was the tone. There was nothing forced or unnatural about her mother's tone, for what she wrote was exactly the sort of letter she'd have written had Maria not run away at seventeen and stayed gone for so many years. But Maria could tell her mother craved more information, and she knew, as well, that she owed her more than, Here I am, I have a steady job, doing fine, with love. In her letter she described her job and the ocean. (By that point she had settled in Newport, Oregon.) She said she was busy at the restaurant. She nearly had a breakdown trying to fashion a letter of facts—the sort of facts her mother would understand and appreciate. Only later, after she had been home for a while, did she begin to understand the arid, brittle way her mother expressed love, and only then did she realize that her mother desired everything she left out. Friends, boyfriends, and above all, Maria, honey, are you happy? And have you learned, my sweet girl, to forgive yourself for what happened? Have you moved on or is all this moving about some substitute? Some attempt to stop the revving inside you, some way to try and quiet it? Oh, how I wish there was something I could do or say to ease your suffering. If it could be me, if I might carry that burden for you, if I could take your place that night we pulled up in the drive to see that yellow tape strung along from the carport back to the juniper tree where your daddy hung a tire for you and Manny to swing on, your father talking to the sheriff and both of them not looking at the car pulling up into the drive carrying a girl who'd just had her life pulled right out from under her . . .

She did not hear from her father ever, for in the absence of Manny, her older brother, who had settled in San Antonio after a stint in the Coast Guard and never came home, her father had really taken to Randy. When her mother wrote to tell her that her father was in the hospital up in Midland, that the doctor had given him less than a week, Maria knew her father blamed her still for Randy's death. Her mother never responded to the card Maria sent telling her that she did not think she could make it home for the funeral.

Five years after her father died, her mother wrote with news of another death: the owner of the Mountain View. He had left her mother the motel. "I was there about as long as he was," her mother wrote. "I'm just way too tired to run it on my own. Come on back home, we'll make a little money, I'll not get in your way." The way her mother promised to keep her distance made Maria realize how deeply her mother must have assumed, for years, the worst about her life. Lap dancing, trick turning. GIRLS! GIRLS! GIRLS! blinked the neon in her mother's nightmares.

The plane she flew home on had circled the busy airport as if it was a car seeking prime parking at a shopping mall. Yet it was filled with people's lives and as it wasted time and fuel it flew right through clouds. Had the world changed? Was there suddenly time to kill hanging about in the heavens? Below, Maria studied the sprawl of El Paso and, across the river, smoggy Juárez. Technically they were the same town, but far more than water divided them. As they circled the city she thought of how she had never let herself separate the events of that September afternoon ten years earlier. The weight of both lives were her burden, but as long as she did not divide them into two distinct if obviously related incidents, she did not have to admit that had it just been the one—had Randy accepted her decision and held out a little longer to get past the crust of his hurt, had he found someone more suited to the life he desired—she might have known that airplanes sometimes orbited their destinations, which were not quite ready for their arrival.

In the car they talked of people she had forgotten.

"You know your first cousin Jan married a guy named Tony. He's—what do they call them—a bodybuilder?"

"I think that is what they call them," said Maria, as if playing dumb was the polite thing to do.

"Well, he spends a lot of time on his muscles," her mother said. "At a gymnasium somebody built behind the fairgrounds."

"You mean a gym?"

"Isn't it short for *gymnasium*?" her mother said. "It's got to be short for something."

Ten years away and here she was, talking to her mother about abbreviations.

"I've never thought about it," said Maria, which was certainly the truth, "but I guess you're right."

"Well, whatever you call it, he's up there more than he's home with Jan and those kids. If I were her I would tell him he had to choose between a gymnasium and her."

"Maybe she likes them muscle-bound," said Maria.

"Likes what like that?"

"Her men."

"Well, she's not got but the one," said her mother. A half mile of dark desert passed. Maria stared out the window toward the darker shadow of the Davis Mountains. "Least that I know about."

"What about Marcie? Isn't that her sister's name?"

"Marcie lives down near Sanderson somewhere," said her mother, and then she was off for a good half hour, ticking off cousins and classmates, their whereabouts and accomplishments and failures. Lives were narrated by her mother without inflection, as if having your child die in Iraq or getting filthy rich off mining rights and oil leases and building an four-thousand-square-foot mansion high up at the Fort Davis Resort was simply what lay ahead in this life. And yet perhaps her mother chronicled the things that happen to people so flatly to let her errant daughter know that all was forgiven. No surprise and no judgment. You are born and then this happens and then something else. Just like you, child.

"Just a visit," Maria had said on the phone. "I can't take too much time off work." She did not outright decline to run the motel, which she remembered as a string of brick sunbaked rooms with a humming ice machine in a dank closet and a pale blue pool with cracks in its concrete, but she certainly made clear her round-trip ticket.

Since Maria could remember, her mother, the daughter of a ranch hand from Valentine, had worked the front desk at the Mountain View Motor Lodge. Until Maria was in junior high, her mother worked only during daylight, but at some point she seemed to always be working the third shift, so that Maria saw her mother only on weekends, which her mother spent cooking, cleaning, and working in the garden.

Ahead on the highway the high beams caught the rippling away of a snake come to warm up on the blacktop. Maria rolled down her window and wished for more moon. Dear God, the smell of creosote and the brilliant starry sky between Van Horn and Valentine. Living for so long in cities forever cloudy or contaminated by streetlights had turned her from looking skyward. She had forsaken stars. Now one seemed to break loose from whatever held it and streak wildly away. She followed its progress even through the bug-crusted windshield of her mother's Jeep Cherokee. Wind from the open window thickened her hair and she opened her mouth wide enough to drown on the thin air of home.

"How's Manny?" Maria asked. Since Manny was six years

older and had joined the Coast Guard right out of high school, she'd not seen much of him even before she left home. She'd worshipped him once, even after he was old enough to shun her. When she was six and he was twelve, he used to let her come along with him through the fields behind the house to shoot birds with his air rifle, but as soon as his friends showed up, she was shooed away, often just this side of cruel, to impress his pals.

Manny had been stationed somewhere on the East Coast when Randy died. Maria had no idea how much he knew, how much her parents had told him. Oddly, it was Manny she grew to miss the most during her years away, though he was mostly ghost, the scent of sneaked cigarettes at the dinner table when she was young enough to equate smoking with sniffing glue or shooting heroin. She had trouble even remembering what he looked like, though she knew he favored her father, but only physically. In memory he'd inherited her mother's taciturn way, though she couldn't say whether this was true or she'd just made him this way, whether his terseness made her all the more eager to talk to him. Because she never had talked to him, not as an adult, and with her reserved, long-gone brother she could start over, clean slate. He would not judge her because he had not been there to witness the way her father shunned her after Randy died, the way her mother refused to talk about it. Plus the Manny she concocted had so few words to spare, and the ones he would choose when they at last talked would be soothing.

But she had no idea where he was. The Coast Guard never kept him long in one place. She couldn't call home and ask for his address, and so she spent years imagining their reunion, which always took place at the depot, her train pulling slowly into the station during the last dusty light of day, a time of incomprehensible beauty back home, pink-and-blue clouds hugging the mountains, and Manny leaning on the hood of his truck, his skin tinted by the last slat of sun.

"Manny's getting along all right," said her mother.

"How about his children?"

"Cute as can be."

Maria waited for more but her mother had nothing else to report, perhaps because they were almost home, and taking her daughter home after all these years made her mother nervous. When they pulled into the driveway, the headlights streaked across the Airstream, a silver flash like the backsides of cottonwood leaves ruffled by a breeze. That she thought of trees instead of what had happened behind the camper comforted her, for wasn't the reaction she'd feared at the sight of it what had kept her in foggy foothill towns for so many years?

Her mother followed Maria's eyes to the camper and killed the headlights before she even reached the carport. The carport had been her father's domain. His name was Luis, and she associated him with the oil-stained concrete and also with the edge of the yard, where he liked to burn trash at dusk. Most of her early memories of him were in silhouette, aglow against the endless flatness, the huge sky blue-black and primed to soon explode with planet and star. Somehow he managed to be sweet and distant at once. He could be kind to her, even doting, when he saw that she was pained about, say, the boring tribulations of high school, but all too often her real pain, the kind that had nothing to do with bitchy girls or getting the right part in *Grease,* the kind that was vague but persistent, could not penetrate his aloofness. He liked things she did not know how to talk about: rockabilly, cars, hunting, football. Like the rest of the men in their town, he was up and out of the house before the sun rose. Lying in bed, she would hear his boots on the kitchen floor, the screen door slam, the throaty stutter of his pickup before it finally turned over.

She remembered her father taking her along on his errands, the way he always cut off his truck and coasted into the mostly dirt parking lots of the local stores, tapping the brake with the toe of his boot, yanking the keys from the ignition, swinging open the door and hopping out of the cab in what seemed to her a single motion. It pleased her, this memory, for once she was inside, the house bore no trace of her father, not that it had when he was alive. As in all the houses of her childhood, any trace of masculinity was banished to garage or outbuilding. Men were not supposed to notice decor, but she could not imagine her father feeling at home in her parents' bedroom, with its fleur-de-lis wallpaper, ruffled curtains pulled tight against the intense summer sun, and cherry-red comforter and matching pillows plumped atop the white-framed queen-size bed. A lace doily covered the top of the dresser on which lay the tortoiseshell comb-and-mirror set handed down to her mother by her great-grandmother, a teacher from Lone Wolf, Oklahoma, from whom her mother had gained the name Harriet, which she hated.

"I've got some brisket in the fridge I can warm up for you," her mother said, and Maria thanked her and went to put her bag in her old room, which contained, aside from the single, sloping twin bed, an ironing board and a sewing machine covering the desk where she had once written term papers. As she sat down on the bed she heard faint music that she'd not listened to in years but that she had once been so proud of having "discovered," since it wasn't something her friends were listening to and they did not play it on the local radio. Jeff Buckley, the Breeders, Catherine Wheel. "Whatever happened to Mazzy Star?" the woman with the single suitcase said aloud to the girl who used to live in this bedroom.

EVEN THE SWEET DESERT air could not keep Marcus from feeling that he ought to call Annie and confess. Such guilt brought on a rare but familiar rise of what he had come over the years to call the black tide. Without warning was he subject to its waters. At least this time he was alone, for when he was swamped, words were useless; the effort to construct a sentence was like digging stumps set in concrete slab. Especially elusive were verbs, their implied action and motion so hopelessly out of range that he sometimes felt exhausted by the presumably passive to be. *I am, I was, we were:* the subtlest proclamation of existence sounded hyperbolic.

The coming tide drove him to turn on the radio in search of pedal steel, the lyric twang of which had been known to turn the tide from tsunami to seep. The local NPR affiliate was the only clear signal he could find. Marcus was surprised, then ashamed for thinking that no one within two hundred miles would care for public radio.

To the west the moon lit a sawtooth ridge as a raspy-voiced bluesman on the radio sang of walking down the street and seeing a lady so fine he described her as "a lump of Lord have mercy." Here was the heart talking if ever the heart did talk. He turned the radio off and concentrated on the blinking of lights in the distance. Then a town appeared, which a city-limit sign confirmed was about the size of Silt, nearest hamlet to the flytrap farm.

In the compact business district he found a faded three-story hotel.

"What brings you to Pinto Canyon, Texas?" asked the man behind the counter when Marcus handed over his North Carolina driver's license with his credit card. The clerk was tall and thin, with spotted skin and ears translucent in the overlit lobby. His was the first accent Marcus had heard since arriving in Texas, though he'd been in the state for only a day and the only words he had exchanged had to do with whether he would be paying with cash or credit and where the room was located. For this reason the man behind the desk came at him sideways with his question.

"Ran out of gas going east, north, south, or west."

The man studied Marcus for longer than Marcus was comfortable with.

"Well, there's a gas station right across the street," he said. "That's not the only one we got, either. I believe you might've passed two or three to get here off the highway."

Blood flooded the capillaries in Marcus's face.

"I was just kidding," he said. "I read that in an interview once. With the film director John Waters? Someone asked him why anyone would live in Baltimore and that was his answer: 'Run out of gas going east, north, south, or west.'"

"John Waters," said the man. He was no longer looking at Marcus but over his head. This did not make Marcus feel any less uncomfortable or keep his cheeks from reddening. The man said "John Waters" again, as if he was someone who had moved away from this town years back and he was trying to place him. Marcus swallowed. His first exchange with a human not routine or impersonal in days, and what was he supposed to say now? "You know, *Pink Flamingos*? That movie with the three-hundred-pound transvestite named Divine?"

"My favorite movie is *Cat Ballou*," said the man. "I don't know who directed it, though. I have no idea."

"Lee Marvin, right? And Jane Fonda?"

"Before she went all Hanoi on us."

"Is that the one where Lee Marvin tries to ride a drunk horse?"

"Yep. He's my favorite actor."

"Lee Marvin?"

"Naw, the horse."

The laugh they shared might have been at Marcus's expense, but he was so grateful to the man for not making him feel as if he had lost the ability to talk to another person that he put down sixty-five bucks on a two-room kitchenette overlooking the Fina station and a train yard. The furnishings befit a county drinking shack: A listing La-Z-Boy, the sort of couch found on the front porch of communal houses in college towns. On the wall above the bed, a horse's head made from dried macaroni, half the pieces of which appeared nibbled.

Later, when Marcus went down to his car for a bottle of wine, a couple in their seventies was performing in a restaurant to a half-dozen ranchers drinking bottles of Shiner and Bud. He stopped to listen. They played a Don Gibson tune and then some Freddy Fender and the lady plucked her bass mechanically and did not add much at all until suddenly she started a song in Spanish so high and lovely it was like river carving canyon from rock. "Lo siento" was the only phrase he could understand, and as he stood alone on the landing his eyes grew wet, touched off by the brittle Spanish of this woman who, to look at her, had long since come to terms with the world and her place in it. "It is what it is," he had heard people say, usually about some situation they lacked the energy to try and change. Marcus had always winced at the phrase, which struck him, improbably and simultaneously, as both obvious and incorrect. What else could it be besides what it is? he wanted to counter on the one hand, yet on the other—what he really believed, what he needed to believe—was that it was what it wasn't. In that sliver of discrepancy between *is* and *is not* lay the most succulent meat, the tender flesh upside the bone. He felt, without allowing himself to think, the presence of that flesh in this place of wind and rock and dust.

MARIA'S MOTHER STOOD AT the kitchen counter, her arms crossed, a dish towel slung over her shoulder as she watched Maria eat. She claimed she'd eaten on her way to El Paso but Maria did not believe her. Her mother had always been thin but now the only extra weight on her was the slightest sag of wrinkly skin around her elbows and beneath her chin.

"I've been working as a chef for the last five years," said

Maria, taking her seat at the table, a plate of brisket and warmed-up beans and a puddle of slaw in front of her.

"That's what you put in one of your letters. What kind of place is it where you work now?"

"It's called Beverly's Bistro. My friend Beverly owns it."

"Well, what sort of food do y'all cook?"

"It's pretty eclectic," said Maria, and she then immediately wanted to take the word back, since even if her mother knew what it meant she might take it as a slur, given her diet, which varied only in that some days it went from unhealthy to unhealthier.

"I mean, the menu changes every night," said Maria. "Depends on what's fresh."

"Sounds like too much work to me. Seems like most people would come back in looking for what they had the last time. That's the way I run my business, anyway. I have a lot of people come back because they know nothing's changed."

"Well, we do have some staples," said Maria. "Mostly appetizers. Anyway, I'd love to cook for you while I'm here. I know you probably don't care to spend what little time you have in the kitchen."

"Either I pick something up on the way home or I just open cans and pour them into pots," her mother said, "It's nothing to care about one way or the other. Something wrong with brisket?"

"Not at all," Maria lied. "I love the sauce."

Her mother stood at the counter still, watching her make her way through the slab of beef. Maria was used to eating alone and reading magazines while she ate. To eat without reading made her feel as if she was seated at the table topless.

"Did you ever think of moving?" said Maria, mostly to divert her mother's attention.

Her mother stared at her as if she were translating, with difficulty, her question into some language she could understand.

"After Dad died, I mean," said Maria.

"Move where? Why?"

Her mother and father had bought their turn-of-the-century adobe from her father's uncle in the late sixties. It was two miles from town, and the land surrounding it still belonged to her cousin, who ran a couple of dozen head of cattle in the pastures behind it. The walls were thick and pocked and Maria liked to lie on the floor and put her bare feet on them in the summer when no one was home. She would carry the chalky odor of stucco to bed with her, wake with it scenting her sheets.

Minutes of deep silence. She was used to it from years of living mostly alone, but here at home with her mother it made her fearful that something was not being said. And so she said, "Do you ever run into Randy's mother?"

"Some," her mother said after a pause.

Randy's mother had been born again before her son's death, and after learning why he took his life, she became not only more fervently devoted to her beliefs but vicious in her vilification of that slut who killed her son and grandchild. Randy's mother enlisted her entire church to help spread hate. God's Rodeo, the church was called; Randy loved to make fun of it. "Yippee-yi-yo, praise be, pardner," he used to half yodel whenever they drove past it. He hated going there, found it gimmicky and absurd with its jowly pastor—some claimed a former drug dealer from Wichita Falls who had come to Terlingua on the lam—delivering the word in tight Wranglers and pointy-toed, alligator-skin Luccheses.

"Does she speak to you?"

"She doesn't have anything to say to me that I care to hear come out of her mouth."

Maria forced herself to chew. She drank some water. "So she still blames me?"

"She's mourning still. Might seem like to us she's mourning the wrong way? But I guess there's just a way. No right or wrong to it. Whatever works until it don't, and then there's something else gets you along."

For two weeks after Randy's funeral, which her father did not allow Maria to attend, she had lain in bed and cried. Her mother tended to her wordlessly. She brought her soup and set it on a tray table by the bed and that was as close as she got. Maria could not ask anyone for anything, ever again, much less ask her mother to lie next to her and hold her and wipe wet bangs from her forehead. But it wasn't as if she expected her mother to say, Baby, it gets better. Never in her life had her mother said something so banal. She was not an educated woman but her sense of the world was as hewn as a fence post. It did not extend to comforting people, even her daughter, even, Maria suspected, Ray, who loved her enough to leave her a motel.

The guidance counselor from school had called finally and explained that if Maria missed any more days they could not by law allow her to continue with the class she had been with since kindergarten. Through the closed door, Maria heard her mother say, "So she'll just have to get held back, won't she? If that's what y'all are calling it instead of fail."

And now, hearing her mother talk of mourning, the lone way through it, no rightness or wrongness to it, she blinked and swallowed.

Her mother came and took her plate and scraped it and washed it and put it away.

"I just couldn't . . . ," Maria said. "I just could not ever . . ." But when her mother did not turn around from the sink, she said, "I'm pretty tired. I think I'll go to bed."

In the morning Maria found her mother drinking coffee, dressed in her work clothes, which were no different from anything else she wore: a sweatshirt and jeans.

"I figured you'd want to see the motel?"

"Just let me get ready."

"You look fine. This is Pinto Canyon. No need for makeup."

"I hardly ever wear makeup," said Maria.

"You used to."

"Can I brush my teeth, Mom?"

Her mother turned away, filled the teakettle, watered a plant. Maria realized that this was the first time she had called her mother "Mom." Or anything at all. But while she was brushing her teeth, she realized that this was the first time her mother had referred to Maria's past, to how she was before. Did she wish she'd caught herself? She couldn't imagine her mother feeling guilty about such a slip. What she could imagine was saying to her mother, It's okay, we can talk about stuff that happened before Randy died, and her mother saying to her, Well, I don't know about any of that, I was just saying you did used to put on makeup, I threw out nearly a whole box of stuff after you'd been gone for years and we never heard from you.

But on the way to the motel, her mother spoke only of the motel. On the tour, Maria recognized two of the girls hired to clean rooms—Consuela Navarette and Luisa Jaquez—from high school. Had she not been held back she'd have graduated with them. As she chatted awkwardly with them and her mother, her mind got stuck on the phrase *held back*. Was that how she'd lived her life since that day she left? While her mother was at work, Maria had packed a suitcase and called a friend she knew she could trust to drive her to the train station. She took Amtrak first to Las Cruces and then, after a few weeks' work at a Dairy Queen and truly terrifying nights at the Desert Treasure Inn, a Greyhound to San Luis Obispo, chosen for its name. She liked the familiarity of Spanish, though she spoke it badly because her father had been paddled in grade school for not speaking English and therefore was not inclined to speak it to his Anglo wife and children.

She had left a note of apology for her parents but she did not say where she was going because she had no idea. Her parents were better off with her gone, which was one reason she had not returned for so long, even for her father's funeral—not out of spite but in deference to the suffering she had caused him, which she believed to be so deep that attending his funeral would have gone beyond hypocritical into just plain mean.

"I need to run check on that clerk I hired last week," said Maria's mother. "If I don't stay on him, he'll keep somebody on hold for five minutes and lose a room."

The way Consuela and Luisa turned warmer and more relaxed in her mother's absence confirmed what Maria suspected: that her mother was a harsh and humorless boss.

"Girl, you are so thin," said Luisa, reaching out to touch her just above her hip in a way so guileless that Maria wanted to hug her.

"You take after your mother," said Consuela, which made Maria anxious until she realized they envied her mother's metabolism.

They talked a few minutes more, of things that happened so long ago they appeared to flicker in memory as if on a grainy newsreel. At the sight of her mother coming along carrying a stack of clean towels, the girls excused themselves and disappeared into the open room. Maria waited outside while her mother delivered instructions on which rooms needed cleaning.

"I didn't realize you knew them," her mother said on the way to her office.

"We were in the same class."

"I guess what I ought to say is I did not realize they knew you. They never mentioned you to me."

Why would they? Her mother's way with them did not encourage the sharing of personal information. Plus, everyone in this town knew what had happened, particularly those who were in the same class as she and Randy. Why would they risk bringing it up? Her mother's cluelessness was unlike her, but Maria held her tongue and accompanied her mother on the tour of the motel, which seemed cleaner than she remembered it, though no less worn. On the tour, her mother mentioned Ray only in the context of repairs or additions or the lack thereof. Maria tried to remember what he looked like. She'd met him only a few times over the years because usually when her mother was at work, Ray was at home, as he had worked the night shift before her mother switched over. Maria had been surprised to see that he was white, though she wasn't at all sure why; just because her father was Hispanic did not mean that her mother preferred only Hispanics. She'd suspected there was something between Ray and her mother before she'd left home, but only in that vague way in which a suspicion crosses your mind like a cloud over a mountain, temporarily darkening it. Ray was not only white but terribly white, the sort of white person whose skin takes on the glow of fluorescent lights from too much time under their flickering buzz. She had no idea where the man was from, but she suspected he was not from around here, or even Texas, and she wondered why, given his pallor, he would choose to live in a place so close to the sun.

They had come to the restaurant. In high school it had been called Johnny Garcia's. She had come here after games for burritos. Now it was empty, its doors padlocked. Her mother searched her key chain and unlocked the door and led them inside. Dust coated the counters. In the deep triple sink was a pile of broken dishes, and a few novena candles were still set out on the tabletops.

"Johnny Garcia died about seven years ago. His son wanted

to take over the business, but Ray said no. Funniest thing, toward the end of his life, Ray got this thing about Mexicans. All the years I knew him he never had an unkind word to say about any of them, but when he got sick it affected his brain, I guess, and overnight he was convinced he was being trailed by members of the cartel and that they were going to take him across to Ojinaga and assassinate him, which is how I knew he was sick in the first place."

"What did he die of?"

"What a mess," her mother said. "I haven't been in here in ages. I need to get the girls in here and clean this sty."

She turned to Maria as if she'd been talking to herself. "Alzheimer's."

Maria nodded, then swallowed. The math hit her without her even having to add: If Johnny Garcia died seven years ago, and Ray was already sick, that meant her father would have been in the last stages of cancer when Ray was diagnosed. How could her mother have endured all that and kept her house running, and a motel? No wonder she was too tired to run it.

"Did Ray have any family?"

"Somewhere. Ohio? Oklahoma? Starts with an O."

"But none came to help?"

"He never talked about any of that with me."

At least she'd had a few years with her lover, Maria had thought after her mother wrote to tell her of Ray's death and asked her to come home. But the whole time her mother had been reminding Ray to eat and trying to keep him from wandering out into the street, she'd also nursed her father, who had no insurance and hated hospitals and demanded to be taken home to die in the very bedroom where he had always seemed so out of place. For the first time ever she came close to asking her mother why she stayed with her father all those years, when he must have known about Ray. How had he lived with that? She knew him to be the kind of man who cared how others saw him, which is why Randy's death bothered him so deeply. But this was not the time to ask such a question, if indeed she was going to find a time, after not having laid eyes on her mother for ten years and neglecting her during that time of life when, though her mother would never have accepted help from her or anyone else, she might at least need someone to call her every day and ask her what she'd had to eat or whether it had rained, some small, mundane question that had nothing at all to do with whatever answer she supplied and everything to do with the sound of their voices traveling hundreds of miles to close the distance between them.

MARCUS SLEPT POORLY, DESPITE the fact that he'd driven over ten hours that day. All night he was awakened by train clank and warning beep. In the morning he walked across the street to the Fina station for gas-station coffee and a breakfast taco. This was a luxury, as he was accustomed to eating only one real meal a day, consisting of items bought on the cheap in a grocery store and kept fresh in an Igloo in the cab of the truck. Restaurants did not fit the budget. All he'd managed to hide from Annie and the bank was several thousand dollars — about twenty, give or take what it would require to get him down to San Miguel. Aside from the money, he had only his

on tortillas. Never again the tasteless squares of whole wheat Merita that passed for healthy from the Winn-Dixie in Silt. Everything swaddled in a layer of warm corn and flour. The chorizo in the burrito was so delicious that he walked back across the street and told the desk clerk he'd like to keep his room through the weekend.

Afterward he strolled the streets sipping coffee, checking out a hardware store, a thrift shop, and more than one gallery with questionable art more of the southwestern than border variety. Though what did he know? He'd never even given a thought to the notion of Texas. He'd only changed planes in Dallas once on his way to Mexico with Rebecca. It was one of the few places in the country that had somehow escaped his curiosity.

Small towns are the same anywhere, he'd been taught to believe, but this wasn't Silt, which allowed him, walking the streets, a comfortable anonymity. Though no one he encountered was unfriendly, they did not know him beyond his smile, his nod, if they even noticed him at all. They did not know his family, his failures. They did not know or care that the money he paid with belonged by rights legal and ethical to his sister.

For weeks he had looked forward to disappearing, and walking the streets that afternoon, it seemed small-town Texas was just as good a place to court invisibility as Mexico. At least here he sort of spoke the language.

But this was still town. Marcus had come to prefer the country. He'd been happiest living twelve miles of back roads from Silt, which could only generously be referred to as town. Rebecca was of a decidedly more urban stripe. Once a week or so, Marcus would give in and take her into Wilmington, where they would shop at Target and see a movie and eat overpriced pasta and drink a bottle of wine marked up enough to make Marcus wince. Then they would head home up Highway 17 and turn finally onto 431, and immediately the wayside would close in above them, canopy even in the wintry months, turning their journey shadowy and lush, as if they were driving straight into a secret.

Marcus would welcome what Rebecca would dread. As they drove home, she'd tense up against the passenger door, so far away he felt his voice rising when he tried to small-talk her out of her moodiness.

The day she left, she said for the first time what she'd known for months, and what he had known she had known, had felt in the way she held it in: "You say you can't move because of your business, but your business is about to get taken away from you."

"It's not as bad as all that," he said.

"You think I don't ever get the mail? You're always trying to beat me out to the box, but sometimes the mailman comes when you're up at the center. Jesus, Marc. Just say it."

"Say what?"

"You won't move for me. You'd rather stay here and lose everything than meet me halfway."

"Where is halfway?" he said, and it had turned out to be the last thing he'd said to Rebecca before she got in her Honda and drove away.

Remembering these words made Marcus crave back road. He needed to see the desert in daylight. According to the map,

Big Bend National Park was nearby. A short hike would feel good after all those days driving. He was headed back to the hotel to fetch his truck when he spotted a park ranger coming out of the TransPecos Bank.

Marcus's long-standing admiration of park rangers had peaked when he'd briefly been one himself. Well, sort of—he neither wore a khaki uniform nor drew a pension from state or government, but he was stationed there at the center to answer the questions, however idiotic, his visitors asked about the local flora. Who better to ask about a hike than a park ranger?

The man was halfway into his vehicle when Marcus hailed him from the middle of the street.

"Excuse me," said Marcus. "I'm assuming you work down in the park?" Marcus knew enough not to call it by its full, proper name, having visited enough parks on his fact-finding road trip to know that employees and locals always referred to Yellowstone or Great Smoky Mountains as "the park."

The man nodded. He looked to be about thirty. He had his keys in his hand, his other hand on the door of his truck. Marcus attributed his standoffishness to the fact that he'd just come out of a bank. Terrible places run by crooks. He was about to say so to the ranger but remembered his John Waters comment to the desk clerk and thought that, now that he was among people again, he best stick to business instead of trying to come across as funny or conspiratorial.

"I'm just here for a few days. You wouldn't happen to know of a day hike down in the park, or anywhere around here, that would not prove too strenuous for a man who has been living at sea level for the last decade?"

"Where you coming from?" asked the ranger. He relaxed a bit, put his keys in his pocket, but still seemed a little curt, as if it should have been obvious to Marcus that he was off the clock.

"North Carolina."

They small-talked for a few minutes about the Outer Banks and Asheville, which were the two places in the state people who had never been there wanted to visit.

"The park's over a hundred miles from here, just so you know. And you'd have to go pretty deep in to get to the good trails. I know a place about an hour from here. Nice little walk that will take you along the border by the river."

"Rio Grande?" said Marcus.

"Only river around, unless you want to drive four hours to the Pecos."

"I'd love to see the Rio Grande."

"I wouldn't get too excited," said the ranger. "Where I'm going to send you, it's more like a creek. You could wade across, though I don't have to tell you what a bad idea that'd be. The road's paved for the first forty miles or so, but then it gets a little rough. You're going to need some clearance. What are you driving?"

The ranger seemed suitably impressed by the F-150. Marcus did not tell him that it was filled with all he owned in the world and that he was not about to unload it. He'd left it packed both nights, in motel parking lots in Jackson, Tennessee, and Mesquite, Texas, and walked out the next morning to find the tarp as taut as he'd tied it back at the farm.

"Tell you the truth, it'd be best to wait till tomorrow. It's not that far from here but the hike in will take you at least an hour. You wouldn't want to get lost and be stumbling around in that terrain after dark."

Tomorrow he might have changed his mind and be well into Chihuahua. He nodded at the park ranger in a way that suggested he'd take his advice, and left armed with a back-of-a-napkin map. Only later, when he was on the road, did Marcus realize that, aside from the brief and awkward exchange with the desk clerk, this was the only real conversation he'd had with another person in weeks. But two miles outside town, as he crested a hill and spotted a herd of pronghorn antelope springing away from him through high grassland, Marcus had the strangest feeling that soon he would no longer need to cut himself off from everyone he had ever loved and those foolhardy enough to love him back.

Brazil, Indiana, 1983

Courtney could tell her mother was terrified of the double-decker truck carrying a load of cars on its back by the way she sat up in the driver's seat of the Astro—too straight, the same way she drove when it rained, or when she had to get on the interstate. Courtney's mother hated to drive and had learned how only a month ago, when Courtney's father made her. Mainly her mother had to get her license so she could drive Courtney to see the doctor in Indianapolis. Courtney had a hole in her heart. It wasn't a big deal, but usually such holes closed on their own and Courtney was eleven and still had her hole in her heart, so she had to go to the doctor every month for chest X-rays and sometimes EKGs, and her father could not take a day off work every month.

"Elaine, you've got to learn," he said, not one night at dinner but many nights, nightly, it seemed, for years.

But her mother said, "I will not do it. I am not a good driver."

"And you know this how?" her father said. Courtney pretended not to listen but in fact she thought her father's question pertinent if not obvious and she might have asked it herself, though she understood that her mother would probably not even acknowledge the question if put to her by an eleven-year-old girl. It was like her mother didn't have to acknowledge it, even if the question involved the welfare of her eleven-year-old girl.

Her mother put her fork down. "When I was in high school," she said, "everyone I knew claimed to have dreamt that they were driving. Before they got their learner's permit, I mean. And I would ask them about their dreams, which is not something I would have done in any other circumstances, because frankly, listening to people recount their dreams bores me to the bone. But I would always ask about their driving dreams because I never had one, never ever. And everyone else did."

"Sometimes you don't remember your dreams," said Courtney. "That doesn't mean you don't dream, though."

"So you're saying that because you never dreamed about driving, that's your excuse for never getting your license?" Courtney's dad said.

Courtney noticed how her father bit into the word "dreamed," as if to highlight how affected her mother's "dreamt" was.

"It's not an excuse," said her mother. "It's a reason. There is a difference."

"God Almighty," said Courtney's father. Sometimes when he was exasperated, he said, "Hell's bells." She loved it when he said, "Hell's bells."

"What did you dream about?" Courtney asked her mother, because suddenly her mother, who usually seemed far away and short and indifferently attired, as if a sheriff's car had, deep in the night, trolled the neighborhood and some deputy had shouted through a loudspeaker for everyone to evacuate now and her mother had sleepily pulled open dresser drawers and yanked on the first garment she touched, seemed interesting.

"Flip turns," said her mother.

Her father was chewing his chicken divan. He shook his head, chewing.

"You mean that thing where they somersault off the wall?"

"I was on the swim team," her mother said loudly, as if this meant she did not have to get her license. As if she swam everywhere.

But one day at school, Courtney felt so tired she did not even think she could raise her hand to tell the teacher how tired she felt. This girl Dawn Delgado, who sat across the aisle from her in math, asked her what was wrong with her face. It took everything Courtney had to say to Dawn Delgado, "What's wrong with yours?" Then Dawn Delgado raised her hand effortlessly and told the teacher that Courtney had said something, and the teacher, plainly annoyed, said, "Well, what something?" which even in Courtney's deep exhaustion (she felt faint by then and nauseated) she enjoyed, and Dawn, mysteriously, instead of ratting Courtney out, said, "There's something wrong with her, look at her," and then Courtney was in the office. Only later, at home, did Courtney learn that her father was out in the field, as he called it—he bought timber for a lumberyard and spent much of his time wandering around woods wearing work boots that left little clots of mud all over the kitchen floor, the wavy tread of his soles stenciled in the mud—and that they called her mother to come pick her up and her mother had said, "I'll be there in a minute," and called the one cab company in Brazil, Indiana, but since their town was so tiny, there were only two cabs, both driven by Africans, and both Africans were either busy carting someone else who did not have a driver's license around town, or, Courtney imagined, asleep in their cabs up under the pecan trees beside the auto parts store on the outskirts of town. Courtney imagined them dreaming of their home in Tanzania or Burkina Faso as her father said to her mother, "This is it. What if it had been more serious? You CANNOT NOT show up for an hour while you're depending on Blue Bird. For God's sake, you have to get your license."

And so her mother learned to drive. But she hated it. And she was correct when she claimed she was not good at it. She could handle driving around town, but driving in the rain scared her, and snow and ice, forget it. The interstate made her cry. Even Courtney knew not to stop at the end of the ramp like it was a stop sign; even Courtney knew to nose the car out into the stream like you had a right to, and you did, they were supposed to move over and welcome you into the lane, it was like a law or something.

So her mother took the back roads from Brazil to Indianapolis. Courtney couldn't say she minded. It took a little longer but that meant she did not have to go back to school if her appointment was in the morning. Slow and lovely back roads: barns and rippled fields, buzzards circling woods, old men in Windbreakers zipped to their Adam's apples peering into open mailboxes at the end of their long driveways.

That day, though, they got stuck behind the truck carrying cars. The cars rocked a little when the truck took a curve. One of them, bright blue, brand new, sat on the top layer, but the tier was sloped so the blue car looked like it was parked on a hill above them. Even though it was chained it shifted a little. Her mother, Courtney knew by the way she stayed as far back from the truck as she could, backing up traffic, was convinced the blue car was going to break loose and kill them.

"Why did he not take the highway?" her mother said of the driver of the car-carrying truck. "Highway" was what her mother called the interstate.

"Same reason you don't. Maybe?" said Courtney. The "maybe" she tacked on to her sentence because she worried that without it her mother might think she was sassing her.

"I highly doubt that. It's his job to drive. He is a professional. He was hired to drive all over the place, carrying all sorts of things like cars. It would be highly ironic if a man hired specifi-cally to drive were scared of driving on the highway."

"How do you know it's a man?" Courtney said to distract her mother, who was growing more terrified because the road was becoming more twisty. It wasn't the blue car's rocking that terrified Courtney but her mother's fear of the blue car. Maybe because she had a hole in her heart, the things that terrified other people, her friends—for instance, big, snarling dogs, spiders, movies where people did thoughtless things like going into a cellar during a power outage when a known serial killer was on the loose—had no effect at all on Courtney. Of course she understood that it was the brain and not the heart that produced, or in her case did not produce, fear. But since she was born with a hole in her heart and she did not fear the things others feared, she had to think that it was not only her brain at work in this matter.

The blue car was the blue of a sometimes sky. A sweet and peaceful blue. Were it not for the trees and the swirling buzzards, the car might become the sky. There were things that terrified Courtney. Once, she had been standing by the bookcase in the living room. In a book she saw a pink slip of paper. Curious as to where whoever was reading the book (certainly her mother, as her dad did not read much) had stopped, she had opened it to where the pink slip held place. But she did not even notice the words on the page, because it was the slip that both fascinated her and made her shudder.

It appeared to have come from an office. WHILE YOU WERE OUT was printed across the top of it in blocky bold type. Below, there were a series of options, arranged in two columns, each followed by a box to check. But none was checked. TELEPHONED, CAME TO SEE YOU, RETURNED YOUR CALL, PLEASE CALL, WILL CALL AGAIN, WANTS TO SEE YOU. All boxes unchecked, nothing written in the space that ought to have told who called. Why did this make her feel so lonely and fearful? Why did she slip it quickly back inside the book and put the book back on the shelf and go to her room and crawl under the covers and cry and, later that night, when her parents were asleep, sneak downstairs and find the book in the faint streetlight that fell across the room and yank the pink note from the book and crumple it and throw it away in the trash can in the kitchen and then, on her way upstairs, turn around and retrieve it from the garbage and run it under the tap and wad it up all wet and throw it away again?

Her mother had become a parody of a woman terrified that a blue car was going to break free from its mooring and crash into her Astro, crushing her and her daughter, who was on her way to Indianapolis to get the hole in her heart checked out by a doctor with comb marks in his hair. Her mother shook and grabbed the wheel so tightly it was as if she were acting rather than alive, in real time, behind the truck on a back road. Courtney did not particularly wish for the hole in her heart to close on its own. She looked up at the blue car. It was not going anywhere but to some car lot where someone would buy it and drive it around and merge it with other cars fearlessly on an interstate. Hell's bells, some blue car was not going to kill Courtney and her mother. Courtney, fascinated rather than terrified by the car, placed it in a sparkling pool, at the end of a lane, somersaulting, pushing off the wall, rising up from the water, blue car swimming.

Pinto Canyon, Texas, 2004

At dinner that night — takeout enchiladas so soggy it was difficult to distinguish tortilla from cheese — Maria discovered that
when conversation with her mother dead-ended into silences
that made her anxious and guilty for staying gone for so many
years, all she had to do was ask a question about the motel.

Her mother might well have been tired — how could she
not be, given all she'd endured in the past decade — but Maria
quickly came to doubt she was too tired to run the motel. Running that motel would save her mother's life. Men, love, romance,
sex, domesticity, definitely motherhood — her mother was done
with all that, at age fifty-three. She'd had enough of trying to accommodate the alternately selfish and helpless doings of men.
Maria could see it in the way her mother had dealt with the few
men they had come into contact with since she'd been home.
Her cousin Alberto, who ran cattle behind the house, came by
to check the water tanks and happened to spot Maria and her
mother pulling into the drive coming back from the grocery
store. He whipped in behind them and hopped out of his still-
running truck to give Maria a hug and say to her mother, "How
come you won't even tell somebody Maria's home?"

Maria's mother looked at Alberto as if he was still back in high school, hotdogging around town in the Nissan Sentra he'd been so proud of, a tight end for the Javelinas who had scored a lucky touchdown in a play-off game against Sierra Blanca and let it ruin the next five years of his life.

"How come somebody won't learn to keep his cows out of my yard?"

Her mother grabbed the groceries and went inside.

"She never did understand me," said Alberto. "She just don't get me."

Maria laughed instead of denying it, for though she had been gone for ten years, she knew it was true: her mother did not get why Alberto thought catching a ball could affect his life one way or the other beyond the time it took for the ball to be caught. Lorenzo the maintenance man at the motel provoked in her a similarly crusty demeanor, as did some poor electrician who stopped by the house to get paid for putting up a motion detector in the carport and made the mistake of attempting small talk. Her mother was over men. She would live alone for the next twenty-five or thirty years and she would not get lonely, having had to take care of two men at once and then watch them get sick and die within months of each other, and no one who knew her, who really knew her, would feel the least bit sorry for her or say aloud or even think, I wish Harriet would find someone to share the sunset with, it's a shame, she's not all that old, really. Maria herself knew some things about being alone but not lonely. But being back home, and around her mother, she understood them in a way that surprised and slightly worried her. Perhaps her independence, her need to have men enjoy their time with her without entitlement or jealousy or some claim on the next day, had less to do with what had happened with Randy than it did with her mother.

Was it inherited? Or something that arose out of the soil where both had been born? Theirs was, after all, land hospitable to only the least needy vegetation nature had to offer. Mesquite was a worthless plant but not a useless one, for though it was only good for flavoring grilled meat, it was useful as an example of the thick-skinned, thorny nature it took to survive here.

"What are you going to do with the restaurant?" Maria was hoping to draw attention away from her plate of enchiladas, from which she'd taken only a few bites.

"Let it sit. I don't know what else."

"Couldn't you use the money?"

"I always have uses for money, but the question is, do I want to put up with what I have to put up with in exchange for an extra five or six hundred a month? Some things cost more than they pay."

"But why? Wouldn't you just rent it out and sit back and collect the rent?"

Her mother took a bite of her enchilada, which she had only picked at, as if talk of money, or at least of her livelihood, brought back her appetite.

"Way more complicated, Maria. I don't get the four-star types in my place they get down at the Gage, but I keep it clean and my prices are fair. I have a responsibility to my guests. If I put a restaurant in there and the food is not worth hog slop, don't you think it's going to hurt my business?"

"What about Johnny Garcia's son? Didn't you say he was interested in taking over?"

"I got on pretty good with Johnny but it took some patience on my part. Ray and Johnny drank together and they'd get to playing cards and Ray'd get half-lit and lose his hand and Johnny'd come out good and he'd say to Ray, 'Tell you what, Ramon'—that's what he called him, Ramon, even though Ray's just Ray, he's not even a Raymond, I don't even think the man had a middle name, to hear him tell, his parents did good just to give him a name, because they didn't give him much else after—anyway, Johnny Garcia'd say, 'Tell you what, Ramon'—he'd be about half-tipsy himself except he could hold it way better than Ray—'Tell you what, Ramon,' he'd say—and he'd be rolling his *r*'s at Ray, I could hear them back in the office, that's where they went to do their drinking— 'Tell you what, Ramon, I need a new stove hood and how about you just apply what you owe me to a new stove hood?' and Ray would have gotten to that point in his fun times when he didn't want to talk about money, he'd say, 'Okay, Juan'—he'd try and pronounce it in the Spanish manner but it would come out sounding like a drunk man named Ray from some state that starts with an *O* would think Spanish sounded like, even though he had heard it spoke every day of his life for the past thirty years—'Okay, One,' he'd say—that's how he pronounced it, like number one—'Just deal them cards, One, I got some money to win back from your drunk ass.'"

Not only was this the longest speech Maria had ever heard out of her mother's mouth, but it was the funniest by far. And she knew not to reveal how utterly delighted she was by this side of her mother, since if she even slightly egged her on or registered her pleasure, her mother would deem her speech frivolous, and silence would surely and swiftly drape the table.

"What about his son?"

"Who's? Ray didn't have any kids."

"Johnny Garcia's son?"

"Ray said no to him."

Right, Maria wanted to say, but Ray is dead. But she would never say such a thing, and of course she understood perfectly that whatever bad financial decisions he had made while drinking with Johnny Garcia, Ray's word was law. If he said no to Johnny Garcia's son—even though it was his illness, his delusional state, that had turned him against Mexicans—then the last person on earth she would rent that restaurant to would be the son of Johnny Garcia.

Maria realized her mother was staring at her.

"Why are you so interested in what I do with that space?"

"I just think it's a waste to have it sit there empty," she said, realizing too late what idea she'd put in her mother's head, if—and Maria felt dumb then, and slow—her mother had not had it in her head already, when she unlocked the padlock to the restaurant, or even as far back as a few weeks ago, when she wrote to tell her daughter, I'm tired, come on home now, we'll make us some money.

Because Marcus did not know the names of things he saw along the route mapped out on a napkin, which ran first, as the ranger promised, miles down a paved road through open pasture and ranchland covered in blond grass and then a half hour on a dirt road that dropped, hairpinning, through low, denuded hills and finally into a series of gulches, and because yucca and agave were the only two plants he could identify, he took to reciting the flora native to his farm. Trees: red bay, sweet bay, bull bay, bayberry, swamp myrtle, red cedar, cypress, fetterbush, loblolly and longleaf pine. Then his blessed carnivores: pitchers, sundews, bladderworts, butterworts, and of course the grande dame *Dionaea muscipula.*

That the flytrap adapted to the lack of nutrients in the soil by trapping lunch surely made it a cousin to the cunning cactus whose survival in this harsh place depended similarly on all sorts of adaptive strategies. Adaptive strategies were on his mind as Marcus stripped off his T-shirt in the late afternoon heat, though the air was so dry that his sweat evaporated instantly. He had only a few hours of sunlight left, so he'd grabbed a flashlight from the glove compartment and a bottle of water. He wore his boots against snakebite. Years of scouring swamps for traps had made him respectful, rather than skittish, of reptiles. People made him far more nervous, though this place was so isolated that he'd not thought twice about leaving all his belongings (save the duffel bag and a bag of toiletries that also contained his money back at the hotel) in the bed of the truck, which he'd parked under a stand of cottonwoods at the trailhead.

The trail was rock and sand, almost lunar in its sparseness, and once again he was overwhelmed by the contrast between here and home. After a half-hour hike he came to a wide, dry riverbed in the middle of which was, true to the word of the ranger, a muddy trickle. The Rio Grande, great dividing line, boundary both literal and abstract. Its decidedly ungrand stream both comforted and encouraged him, for he realized he'd grown increasingly nervous about crossing over, so much so that far West Texas seemed the same thing as Mexico, only lawful, safe, tame. Maybe he'd already settled? But now this stream. It was shallow enough, lazy enough, to wade across. He took off his boots and rolled his jeans up to his knees. He waded out until he could lean over and spit and hit another country.

Standing in midstream, Marcus watched the lowering sun redden high bluffs over in Mexico. Surely there was a way around them. He could go back to the truck, fetch a jacket for the cool nights of the desert, more water, what food he had stashed, start walking. He had left his money back in the hotel room, but what good had money ever done him? Wasn't it money that had led him to this boundary? Get stopped by the Mexican police, and from what he'd heard, the money was likely to disappear, anyway. Then he would be at the mercy of the infamously corrupt lawmen. He would rather be at the mercy of the desert, of the night, of rattlers and mountain lions, scorpions and tarantulas. Wind and cold. To starve or die of dehydration was preferable to torture, or worse, a slow lingering in a Mexican prison.

What kept him on this side of the border was the fact that no one knew where he was. He could not do that to his mother and Annie. Nor to Rebecca, though he had not spoken to her since the day she'd packed up her Honda and bumped up the two-track to the highway. He'd stopped answering the phone weeks before she left, had forbidden her to pick up as well, since it was always a creditor, always bad news. Rebecca had left a couple of messages on the cell phone she'd bought him in the three weeks between her leaving and his abandoning the farmhouse, her voice at once hesitant and plaintive, her words innocuous ("just wondering how you are"), her tone turning, just before she hung up, bitter with what seemed to be self-disgust for giving in, for calling, for caring. Marcus wanted to call her hourly, but he kept from it by telling himself — often aloud, because once she was gone, he spent days without leaving the farmhouse, talking to himself, eating out of the cupboards if at all — that she was the one who'd left.

And dying like this, estranged and incommunicado, in a foreign country, would seem like a choice, and everyone knew the aftereffects of such a choice on those left behind.

And so he turned around and headed back to the truck, thinking, as he hiked up the trail, of Rebecca still, of the last thing he had said to her: "Where is halfway?" Did she really expect him to abandon the center, even if he was on the brink of losing it? She should have seen the goodness in his dream, the altruism; she should have given him credit for mortgaging everything he had for a plant. Did he not deserve some credit for not squandering the money on drugs, or shady real estate, a Ponzi scheme? On other women?

Hiking up the trail in the gathering darkness, Marcus took the question away from her, away from them. No longer was it rhetorical, and no longer did it have to do with that line he'd fed fake-doctor Carrie Elwood in his kitchen all those years ago — "the capacity to merge your reality with someone else's version of same." "Halfway" referred now to distance, to *where*. And the answer — even as Marcus began to stumble a bit on the rocky trail as the batteries in his flashlight burned low, even though he'd underestimated the drop in temperature in the desert and wished he'd worn his T-shirt, even though he knew nothing, really, about the place—was right here where he had hesitated.

It was near dark when Marcus arrived back at the trailhead, but twilit enough to spot a white Ford pickup, had the truck still been there for him to find.

AFTER DINNER ON THE night they visited the restaurant, Maria's mother announced she was going back to the motel for a while. To check on things. She'd done that the night before as well. Checking on the motel was her television, her cross-word puzzle, her bridge club, church. She'd worked a full day already, and yet she gave the impression, sitting down to dinner with Maria, of someone on vacation who was not accustomed to being on vacation.

When her mother had made her announcement, Maria nod-ded. "Yes, of course, go," she said, thinking that perhaps with her mother out of the house the house might warm to her and vice versa, for after the initial shock of standing in those tight rooms she thought she'd never see again, the house had begun to turn on her. You left, it seemed to say, and you took your loud music and your giggly friends who'd come over after school and slouch and scream with laughter and sit on my floors eating cantaloupe and chasing it with Pepsi, and one day you were here with your warm feet on my walls and then it was just the man who preferred to sit out under the carport in a lawn chair grilling chilies stuffed with string cheese and wrapped in bacon and letting the smoke waft in through my screens and singing Roy Orbison songs to Sonny the dog, and the woman who swept and scrubbed and dusted and vacuumed in a manner so detached from the intimacy of my rooms, so devoid of any notion that I belonged to her, that it was here that she had brought you and your brother straight from the hospital, that she'd spent nearly every night of her adult life here, that she might as well have been cleaning just another of her motel rooms. For the house knew of the motel. How could it not, the way her mother sneaked off to be with it night and day? And perhaps, like her father and Ray, the house just had to live with her mother's ways, if the house wanted to live with her mother.

Maria went outside. There was enough moon to see her way down the drive to the cattle guard out by the highway. She traded her sandals for the pair of boots her mother kept out in the carport in case a snake lay stretched across the drive. It had been so long since she'd had to worry about stepping on a rattler; in her socked-in cities, walking at night had been dangerous in other ways. She did not care to study the ground on a night so clear, with a sky so bejeweled with star. Lift up your eyes. Her neck so extended she understood the derivation of the word *crane*. To the west the last of the light lit the high ridges, a twinkling here and there where lucky rich people had built houses with seventy-mile views. Or maybe they weren't lucky, just rich. She liked the way you could see the sunset slinging sidearm through high grass and scrub at dusk down here in the valley, dust and hovering bugs brilliantly backlit. And she liked being able to look up, to see always the wide sky, the widely possible sky with all its untrammeled darkness between millions of blinking stars, and who up there on those hills, with the long expanse of valley below, the stretch of ranchland and occasional cluster of lights marking a settlement, would ever be able to remember to look upward at the sky, when they assumed they were a part of it?

Sometimes Maria wanted to go back to college. Sometimes she wanted to know what it felt like to pull up into the parking lot of, say, some convenience store off an interstate with a man and two or three children and get out and extract the smallest of those children from the complicated car seat and hoist it on her hip and take it inside to the bathroom while the man whom she could not quite bring herself to call her husband would take the other two—they would be, like him, boys—inside and buy them something that she, with her strict ideas of proper snacks for developing bodies, would have preapproved.

That night—standing at the edge of the drive in her mother's boots, staring up at the stars, her arms crossed, her hooded sweatshirt riding up her rib cage, the thrum of trucks far away up the valley and the slow clang of train, the day declining, giving itself up to night, a sweet and willful surrender, nothing left to declare, nothing to talk or even think about, just a confidence that all would be there, in order, in the morning—Maria wanted just that, and only, forever, that.

The next morning at breakfast Maria said, "I'm thinking I'll stay awhile longer."

Her mother registered neither surprise nor glee. She seemed overly concerned with Maria's apartment back in Oregon, which Maria had already taken care of. The night before, after standing in the drive during the slow and lovely fade of day, she'd called her friend Beverly, owner of the restaurant where she cooked and mother to Matthias, who had been living at home since dropping out of college and was in Beverly's hair. Maria offered to let Matthias sublet her place for a song if Beverly would hold her job for her and box up some things from her apartment—mostly clothes—and ship them to her. All this she explained to her mother, who said, "You're going to let some boy live in your place? With your furnishings?"

"I don't have much stuff."

"What if he don't pay the rent?" her mother was saying, still preoccupied with the apartment. "Is it not your name on the paperwork?"

"Well, his mother's my best friend. We work together."

"Myself, I try to keep that separate."

"Keep what separate?"

"Business and friends."

Ray wasn't a friend, obviously. Her mother had no friends. Since Maria had been home, the phone had rung twice: once, it was Alberto asking if his cows were out, the other time it was someone at the motel. Her mother said she talked to Manny, Maria's brother, every Sunday, but something about the way she said it, or the way she turned away to say it, made Maria doubt her.

"Well, I'm doing her a favor, really. It's complicated. It'll work out, though."

"Don't you want to go back out there and put your things in order? You got the other half of your plane yet, don't you?"

She did not want to tell her mother what she feared: that if she got back to Oregon she would doubt her decision to stay in Texas, and she would have to call her mother and tell her she'd changed her mind. The silence that would fall between her statement and her mother's inevitable, Well, you know best what you need, would have killed Maria; each second of the pause would bear the weight of all she'd missed in her many years away. She had savings—she'd done well with a catering business on the side, which kept her busy when she wasn't cooking at Beverly's Bistro—and now that she was back here, and despite the fact that she thought of it as "here" still, instead of "home," it felt as if things she'd lost here could be, not found, but ordered. The night before, after squaring things away with Beverly, she'd shed her socks and stretched across the floor and rested her feet on the cool walls of the living room. Lying there until she heard her mother's car in the drive, she felt as if what she'd lost and the reason for the losing—not so much the event itself that had caused her to leave, but all the things that had led up to it, all the small desires and decisions that she had not let herself think about for years—could be arranged, if she stayed long enough, in some sort of order. This was exactly the way she would have written it were she the type to keep a journal: *I feel as if it can be put into order now* instead of *I feel I can put it into order,* for the passive construction of the former implied the power of some other force that would lead her, rather than her it.

"Beverly can handle it," she said.

"Well, you know best," said her mother. She had not yet asked a single question about Maria's life in Oregon or any of the other places she'd lived. How could Maria explain so many years of riding buses up and down hills in socked-in cities where seagulls circled vast parking lots? In some of those towns she could see her breath even in summer, which she took to be her heart, still smoking. To get by, she waited tables, developed photos at a drugstore, sold cigarettes to drunk students at a 7-Eleven across from a tony college; she lugged wing chairs abandoned curbside up flights to studio apartments. There were men, but they were chosen mostly for their indifference, and they treated her place like a motel room, bathroom floors puddled from showers taken with the curtain untucked from the tub. If pressed to name a staple of her diet in those first lean and consciously ascetic years of her exile, she would have to say toast. Scrape the burn away with a knife. The sound it made would echo against walls barren of cross-stitched homily and group portraits of rehearsal dinners and girls' weekends to Cancún.

Food had not yet become important to her because she could not afford to eat well or more than once a day. She was often hungry and nearly broke, but as hard up as she was, she never stole or borrowed and she never cried. She took classes at this college and that, but never toward any outcome save the experience of being in college, which, despite a few gratifying classes with interesting professors, she judged frustrating, owing to the entitled and lazy attitudes of her fellow students. Sometimes, on weekends, she saw college girls walking down the streets hugging pillows to their chests, and the sight of their brightly colored pillowcases, which Maria imagined them picking out with their mothers to brighten dorm rooms Maria had never seen the inside of, elicited both envy and derision.

But maybe it was not what Maria had been doing all those years that her mother didn't want to hear about, but any place she wasn't familiar with, which was any place but her corner of far West Texas. Her mother's lack of curiosity about anywhere else sometimes rankled Maria, but mostly she understood it as a kind of negotiation with all the things her mother had to take care of in her life. Ray was her Caribbean cruise, her trip to Vegas, her drive to the Grand Canyon. She could have chosen to travel but she would have had to give up something else. Ray was right there, three miles up the road. She chose Ray. It helped Maria to understand her mother if she summoned the ghost of Ray to explain both the things her mother would not talk about and the choices she'd made.

Even though she could tell her mother was antsy to get to work, she asked her to sit down at the table. Her mother had been unloading the dishwasher. As if she understood that Maria would never ask her to stop unless she had something to say, she took her apron off, hung it on the hook by the door, and sat. At least her mother understood when people had something to say.

"I've been thinking about that restaurant," she said.

Her mother did not have to say, And? Yes? What about it? She never said things like that. When you were telling her a story, she never made noises of assent or comprehension. She just waited for you to say what you had to say.

"I would be willing—if you would be interested, that is—in getting something started in that space."

"Getting something started?" her mother said.

"I mean I could try something out, see if it flies. I have a job back in Oregon and it's there for me whenever I want it, but I can also take some time off and it won't hurt me, Beverly will understand."

"What sort of food are you thinking it would serve?" her mother said, but it wasn't a question. What she meant was, I hope you're thinking you're going to serve something that people around here are going to want to eat.

"Well, I've not gotten that far yet."

"Might work best to serve the kind of food people around here like to eat," said her mother. "That way you'll make some money. And if people see it's busy, it's good for the motel."

"Right, but what if I want to serve something they don't yet know they like to eat but once they eat it they'll realize they like it?"

"Like egg rolls?" said her mother. Maria swallowed her laughter until her mother cracked the slightest smile, visible in the corners of that terminally tight mouth of hers.

"Wontons?" said Maria, giggling.

"What do you call it? Moo goo gai pan? I could not order anything started with *moo goo*. I'll feel the royal fool sitting up there saying, I'll take the moo goo."

"Sounds like someone's been to China Garden a time or two."

"Some of Ray's mess. Put a cashew, a cube of warm pineapple, and a piece of chicken on the same plate and that man would hand over his wallet."

"I was sort of thinking I'd find some way to incorporate fresh local ingredients from the area in the menu."

"You hear people talk about organic a lot these days," her mother said doubtfully. "Last time I was by the farmer's market they had them lined up to buy a bag of lettuce somebody fertilized with manure. I don't see how that's a better thing to put in your body than the next thing, but then again you said yourself how I am no cook."

This wasn't exactly a concession, but it was as close as her mother would come to one. And if she felt Maria did not cook her vegetables long enough, would she change her mind and insist Maria open a taqueria or a barbecue joint, and would Maria use the other half of her plane, as her mother had referred to it? How much would either of them give? So much of the strength of whatever bond they'd been able to reestablish depended on things as yet unsaid: Her father. Manny, whom her mother only talked about when Maria brought him up. Ray. Randy, of course, and the life Maria had led all those years away. But Maria did not have to fight, because her mother, after having expressed such ambivalence about the value of an organic diet, said finally, and with her characteristic air of finality—more a sign that she did not have all day to sit around the kitchen talking, she needed to get to the motel—"Well, I guess you can just try it and see. Where's the harm? There's already plates and saucers and all left over from Johnny Garcia's. I know for a fact that hood over the stove has hardly ever been used."

MARCUS HAD ONCE READ in a magazine that by age forty, men get the face they deserve. On his long walk back to civilization (he had no idea how far from town he was, he had paid no mind to the odometer, so distracted was he by the scenery), he wondered whether he was about to get the death he deserved. A couple of hours earlier, standing in the slow, sudsy Rio Grande, he'd fantasized about disappearing into Mexico, succumbing to the elements, his picked-clean rib cage discovered by men attempting to cross over. Such an indulgent thought, now that he was truckless. These border-lands had seemed the perfect place to pause when he still had the means to move on if he chose, but what would it feel like now that he was marooned here?

His flashlight died after thirty minutes of walking, though there was just moon enough to make out the road. The night was so alive with the click and buzz of grasshopper that each step created a disturbance worthy of scrutiny. He felt, with his truck gone, the arrival of comeuppance.

Surely these parts were frequented by the *narcotraficantes* he'd heard about, and the armed coyotes that ferried groups of the hopeful across in the night. At least if he died out here it would not be by his own hand, and he would have expired en route to some new stage of his life rather than been stricken in the farmhouse, rattling the ice in his tumbler of bourbon to quiet the mice in the walls. He imagined himself in twenty years, still hanging on to the center, a madman in the swamp-land, eccentric proprietor of a ragtag museum visited only by folklore graduate students more interested in vernacular oddi-ties than botany. His last-leg enterprise would be written up in blogs devoted to roadside kitsch, and the T-shirts Marcus reluctantly decided to sell in the gift shop would provide a substantial portion of his income. Someone he used to know would send him a photograph clipped from the pages of *Vanity Fair* of a faded rock star infamous for her stints in rehab sport-ing one of his shirts at some sort of urban gathering. Her shirt would be far too tight and the crude drawing of the flytrap and the ridiculous logo—"I Got Trapped at the Flytrap Educational Center, Silt, North Carolina"—would cause him to ignore the spike in requests from Japan for three dozen shirts, postage paid. He would ignore also the derelict state of the dome, stained by pine sap and crusted with leaves, though he would hold forth on the marvelous engineering principles of geodesic domes in general, held together by continuous tension and discontinuous compression, a metaphor he would apply to everything from consciousness itself to—blatantly, in the manner of a man too old to worry about offending anyone—copulation. Of far less focus in his monologues would be the flytrap itself, for which he would long ago have lost his passion. Or perhaps the flytrap would have thrown *him* over, weary of being exploited like some freak-show giant.

Pudgy, bald, breath so odiferous no amount of mouthwash or toothpaste could disguise it. Annie would long since have sold off all but the two acres housing the center and his equally run-down farmhouse to developers and loggers.

Better to be snakebit or shot for the laces in his shoes than wither like that. He stoked his wretched fantasy to distract himself from dangers present if not exactly clear until, after a mile or two of blacktop, he was swept up by the Border Patrol. A Mexican officer and a white one. They had him down on the pavement, spread-eagled, his pockets turned out, the useless flashlight confiscated.

"A late-model F-150?" said the Mexican officer when at last they allowed him to stand. "Two miles from the border? Keys under the seat?"

Both officers laughed. "You leave a plate of tamales steaming on the hood, too?" said the Mexican. "String a green card from the rearview?"

Marcus had no idea what they were talking about and it must have shown.

"Mexicans love a F-150," said the Mexican.

"Aren't you Mexican?" said Marcus, before he could stop himself.

"You think all brown people are Mexican?"

"I don't know," he said. "I just thought, us being right here on the border and all . . ."

"Let's say I *am* Mexican. That'd mean I'd be able to say shit like I just said."

Marcus nodded agreeably, even as he wondered how a Mexican, even one born in this country, even one hard up for a job where jobs seemed scarce, could sign up to catch people fleeing from unimaginable poverty and the threat of daily violence in order to live ten to a one-bedroom apartment in some shitty part of, say, Topeka or Charlotte, taking jobs so low paying even the American underclass would not stoop to take them. But this did not seem the right time or place to raise this question.

"What was in the truck?" asked the white officer.

After Marcus listed the contents, the Mexican officer said, "You might get some of that back. Might turn up in some draw, since it sounds like a load of junk. So what the fuck were you thinking?"

Unthinking was the only word Marcus could come up with for what led him to the backseat of the patrol car. Keys were easy to lose and hard to find if you had to tote them everywhere you went. He'd always left his keys in his truck at the farm. He'd not locked the doors to his truck or his house in years. He could not recall locking up even when he stopped for food and lodging on the way down. Since he could not remember consciously choosing one way or the other, maybe his unthinkingness was part of his dramatic surrender to the elements.

"I guess I wasn't," he said to the officers, who ignored him, having already made up their minds about him. Ferrying him back to town, they decided between them that the park ranger was to blame.

"Motherfucker set him up," said the white officer. "Sending him down there this time of day? Knowing what's kicking around out there just waiting on a chance?"

"Either that or Ranger Rick's still thinking like an Eagle Scout. 'Why, this is a delightful stroll through the natural habitat,'" the Mexican officer said in a girly falsetto.

For the rest of the trip, the agents ragged on the Park Service with a hatred Marcus suspected was common to government agencies with slightly overlapping jurisdictions. Hours later, after paperwork had been filed desultorily by a sleepy clerk, he walked the two miles from Border Patrol headquarters back to his hotel, stood in the rusty shower stall until all the hot water was gone, and fell into bed. He woke early to the music of a waking town indifferent to his straits. Beep of backing-up delivery trucks and Tejano music blaring from passing traffic. Just after nine he called the Border Patrol to check on his truck.

"No word," said the man on the other end of the line.

"What do you think the chances are it will turn up?"

"If it were me?" said the man, who had a lilting Hispanic accent, which made Marcus trust what he was about to say, even had he not started his sentence with "If it were me," which Marcus chose to believe implied sincerity rather than egotism. "If it were me I'd go ahead and file with the insurance."

"So you're saying basically no chance?" Marcus usually avoided the word "basically," which was both overused and obvious, but there was something basic about his situation that allowed him to make an exception.

"I'm saying if you need a ride somewhere, it would be best to get your insurance to pay for you a rental. Or go on ahead and buy you something new. If we'd've found it, it would have been within a couple hours of you reporting it, and you didn't report it for at least a couple hours after it got jacked, am I correct?"

"Well, see, I had to walk up to the road. My phone was in the truck."

"You might better get yourself a new phone, too."

"Wouldn't it be better to wait a few days?"

"If it were me I would not wait if it meant not having no truck and no phone."

"Well, I guess if it turns up I can always get my money back for my new phone and my new ride."

"I would not put too much into thinking what you are going to do when it turns up. That's just me, though. You can do what you want."

After Marcus thanked him and hung up, he had already decided he would like to be the man who answered the phone at the Border Patrol because the man had seemed so sure of what he would do if it were he. Marcus was never all that sure what to do in most circumstances, and he felt particularly anxious about what to do in his present circumstances. So he took another shower and sat naked on the couch making lists, the first of which was titled

All I Have in This World

- jeans × 2
- shorts I never wear because I read somewhere men over forty ought not to wear shorts or sandals
- work boots (one pair) and running shoes (one pair)
- several faded pocket tees and one button-down, frayed collar
- socks and underwear for three days
- my health, praise be
- bottle of passable zinfandel
- toiletries (I hate that word)
- a not insubstantial roll of purloined cash

And then on a separate but equally yellow page of legal pad:

Most Pressing Needs

- transportation
- warmer threads for high desert nights
- cheaper and maybe longer-term digs
- gainful employment
- redemption
- breakfast
- flytrap seeds locked in the glove compartment
- that song "Badge" by Cream, so I can crank up the part that goes, "I told you not to wander around in the dark / I told you 'bout the swans, that they live in the park / I told you 'bout our kid, now he's married to Mabel"
- because I do not deserve native cuisine, having behaved un-thinkingly, a greasy grilled cheese with chips and a Coke?
- call Annie?

Marcus got dressed and, in a diner down the street from the hotel, slightly revised his list by ticking off lunch first in the form of a BLT and cheddar, a tolerable substitute for grilled cheese, before moving on to "transportation."

WHEN MARIA SAID SHE needed a car, her mother said, "You can use the Cherokee." When Maria said that she needed her own car, that she did not want to have to depend on her mother, that her mother had far too much to do to taxi her around town, her mother said she wished she would have known, she let one of the girls at the motel who wrecked her car have Ray's truck.

"Good," said Maria. "I know she appreciated it."

"But here I gave it away and now you're needing it."

"I have some money saved up," said Maria, but she was wondering, again, was this the thing that would bring back the tensions of their past? That her mother had been so accommodating, in her terse way, about her plans for the restaurant only made Maria more anxious. More likely the falling-out would occur over something like a cereal bowl allowed to sit unwashed in the sink until supper, which her mother, scrubbing hardened flakes from the bottom of the bowl, would see as emblematic of Maria's unworthiness.

"Let me call one of the Keplers. They went to school with your daddy. They run a used lot off Presidio Street. Bobby, I believe, is the younger one. He'll do you a good deal, I bought the Cherokee from him."

Maria knew better than to turn down her mother's offer. This was the way it worked here. If you wanted something, you called someone you went to school with or married the cousin of or worked with at the Dairy Queen in high school. Besides, what did she know about buying a car? She'd never owned one. She'd always taken the bus or walked. Randy loved cars. He drove a Nova. Endless and incomprehensible was the list of modifications he'd made to the stock engine, and the fact that she even knew to say "modifications" or "stock" was shocking to her after so many years. But since she had been back, all sorts of details had shown up from somewhere she feared forever lost. She remembered the hours Randy and his cousins and his friends spent crawling around under cars on oily concrete slabs. She'd head over to his house after school and there he would be, in the drive, cut off to the waist, his head swallowed by the gaping hood. Good God, the hours wasted while Randy talked cars with her father. From her bedroom window she'd see Randy pull into the drive, and her father would be out watering or tinkering under the carport, and Randy would barely have the door open before her father would sweep up on him, and through the open window she'd hear her father say, "Okay, Rand, let's see what all you did to her last weekend." Then the pop of the hood latch, the creak the hood made as it rested its weight on the rod that propped it open, and she knew it would be thirty minutes before Randy would ever make it into the house, and most of the time he would not make it, she'd have to go out and stand around while Randy and her dad spoke a language made up entirely of car-part names and the histrionic verbs of sports writers, which they used to describe either the things their cars had done or the things they wanted them to do, along with sound effects that would have made her laugh had she not been so bored.

Later, alone in the car, she would make fun of him for caring so much about something so inconsequential and he would grin as if this was all he wanted in the world, a woman to stay on his case night and day for the next sixty years. But she did not want that. She did not want to nag, and so why couldn't he stop doing those things that caused her to nag?

"Just come over a half hour early," she said to him once. "Like, if we're supposed to be somewhere at seven, come at six thirty and talk your boring car talk with him until seven. That way we can be on time."

Randy said she was cracking him up, telling him when to show up and how long he could talk about the thing he loved besides her.

"But you love me more, don't you?"

"More than my ride?" Randy pretended to give it thirty seconds of thought. "It's in a different column, a car and a girl."

"What are you talking about, a column?"

"Like at school when they make you classify things in lists. And you have to put up top of the column what the category is."

"So you have a column for girls and one for cars?"

"Not *girls, girl*. *Girl* without an *s*. But yeah, *cars* plural because I like more than one car and I plan on owning way more than this one. Unlike in the girl column."

"Are you saying you own me?"

"Yeah, Maria. I purchased you at Dollar General. I still got the receipt, so maybe you better stop picking at me, trying to trap me into saying something stupid, like I want more than one girl or I own you or some shit like that."

They were pulling into the parking lot of Dairy Queen, where they would waste another night leaning on cars with their friends. Maria had wanted to go see a movie or something, anything but hang out for hours at Dairy Queen, and maybe her boredom was what caused her to be so prickly that night.

"I'm not trying to trap you. You were the one who started talking about columns. You know you love me more than all the items in your stupid car column. So why don't you show it?"

"By coming to pick you up a half hour early, you mean? By cutting your daddy off in the middle of a sentence just because you're ready to go?"

"For God's sake, don't you dare disrespect Daddy by not finishing a sentence y'all have already exchanged six thousand times. No telling what he might do."

"Your daddy is a good man."

"I wouldn't know. He hardly ever talks to me. Why should he? I couldn't point out a carburetor if my life depended."

"Good thing your life don't, then."

Maria got out of the car and went inside and sat in a booth with her friends, and Randy stayed outside in the parking lot, sitting on a lawn chair in the back of his best friend Johnny's pickup all night and glaring at her through the streaky plate glass. Finally Maria grew tired of her friends and their conversation and she went outside and announced to Randy that she was ready to go, and all his friends looked in another direction because it was obvious that Randy and Maria were "in a fight."

On the way home, Randy said, "Why do you have to be like this, you know I love you to pieces," but she did not say anything even when he pulled into the driveway. As she knew he would, he left what he called "some rubber" on the highway in front of her drive. The next day at school she pushed a note into the slot of his locker that read, "We broke up," and after the next class, she found a note in her locker that said, "No, WE didn't break up, YOU broke up." Both "WE" and "YOU" were underlined so angrily that the lines punctured the page. The next class, biology, they had together. She did not look at him but she could feel him in the back row with his friends, slumped in his desk chair, the anger coming off him like the flame under the Bunsen burners. After three days of this — Randy calling her house nightly, Maria telling her mother and father she did not want to speak to him, her mother telling Maria, "I'm not going to lie for you. If you want me to tell him you're not here you better go off somewhere," and her father asking her what was going on, why was she mad at Randy, what in the world had happened — Randy dispatched her best friend, Connie, to argue his case.

"He's acting crazy, Maria. He got so drunk last night he threw up this morning after history."

"That's supposed to be my fault?" said Maria.

"He told me to tell you he loves you," said Connie. "Since I don't got anybody telling me they love me, all I got is boys saying they want to do it to me, not even *with* me, *to* me, I would say you got it pretty good."

Maria said, "How does he even know what love is? He just misses being seen with me. All he's got now is his car. That's all he cares about, anyway."

"You don't love him?" said Connie.

"What do I know about love? I'm only fucking seventeen. I don't know, Connie, don't you think it's different?"

"Don't I think what's different?"

"The way we say we love each other in the parking lot of the Dairy Queen and the way people say they love each other, I don't know, in college? Or after college?"

"I wouldn't know," said Connie. "That's what I'm saying. Nobody's telling me they love me, and plus I am not in college and nobody is going to pay for me to go off to college, so I don't get to compare it."

"You could go to college," said Maria. "They have scholarships."

"Whatever, Maria, all I'm saying is, he looks so sad. He told me to tell you that you are his heart."

"Well, (a) what does that even mean? And (b) why does he have to send you to tell me?"

"Because you're ignoring him?"

"I'm not ignoring him. We broke up. I didn't realize that breaking up meant doing the same things you did when you weren't broken up."

"Everybody is jealous of y'all."

"Everybody?" said Maria.

"You're such a bitch sometimes," said Connie.

"Because I think everybody ought to be able to figure out that when they see me and Randy riding around town after school, that isn't, like, destiny?"

"What do you want me to tell him?" said Connie. "'Cause I'm not about to go telling him what you've said."

"Why not?"

"He couldn't take it."

"He's just being dramatic. Trying to get everybody to feel sorry for him. It's not your job to tell him anything."

"So will you talk to him?"

"When I'm ready."

By the weekend they were back together. The next week after school she took off her bra in the Airstream after fixing Randy a ham and cheese. But what she remembered most about that time was his telling her it was good that her life did not depend on her being able to recognize a carburetor.

She had thought about that a lot over the years, and she realized, when she learned to cook and discovered how much she loved doing it, that in a way, his life *did* depend on it, even more than he was allowed — or allowed himself — to realize. What she found in food was further proof that she really did not belong where she'd been born. Fennel made her feel worldly, and in time it no longer brought to mind the black braids of licorice her father used to buy her when they went to get gas at Stripes. She'd started out as a sous-chef, no culinary school, just endless hours on the line, heat and sweat and a surprisingly high tolerance for both the machismo and the irascibility of three-quarters of the chefs she encountered. She shrugged them off and met the mad pace of dinner rush. She was unflappable and efficient, and when she earned enough respect to move up the line, she proved inventive, even fearless with ingredient and variation. She learned a little French. The way it felt to feed an entire restaurant of hungry people and do it again the next night, to plan the menu and find the ingredients, the pleasure she got from it: Randy wasn't exaggerating.

And if she ever doubted it for herself, all Maria had to do was look to her mother and the motel.

On her way to buy a car, Maria decided that cars weren't even cars to Randy but a way to make himself feel a part of something, a way to keep moving forward, even if it meant dismantling things and coming home greasy and smelly. He took care to understand them, to know how they worked, and at such a young age, and was there anything that she understood, that she could take apart and put together again, anything in her life, whose mysteries she had the patience to spend hours attempting to demystify? Only her own feelings, and it turned out she knew them only in the way you know a hailstorm pelting a tin roof: thunderous as it is, it passes over quickly. There were so many things it turned out Randy knew that she never thought him capable of knowing. This did not mean she wanted to have his baby at seventeen. It meant that for all those years away, she had not even considered buying a car, because if anyone had asked her what kind of car she'd bought, she would have said, It's gray with four doors. She would not defile his passion with what she realized was snobbish indifference.

That there were no buses in Pinto Canyon was immaterial, and her mother was right, they could have gotten by with just her Cherokee, they could have made it work. But she was here and she had decided to linger here, and because she needed to, because so much depended on it, she was going to buy herself a car.

Cleveland, Ohio, 1984

Selling a car in a city known to the world for its flaming river called for tactics far beyond the slick skills Witherspoon had picked up from his father and uncles when he was a boy. Back then he'd worked on the lot daily, after school and on weekends, keeping even the antennas of the fleet of Buicks and Oldses so clean that the briefest glint of Cleveland sun would turn the slender rods into magic sparkling wands. The Cuyahoga on fire and then that boy-mayor Kucinich putting the city in default, GM and U.S. Steel pulling out: you would think the lot would be cleared weekly by people wanting the hell out of such a miserable city. But jobs were so scarce, money so tight, that anyone leaving the city—and according to an article Witherspoon had read in the *Plain Dealer,* nearly half the population had fled since 1950—would have to hoof it.

His father and uncles had relied on their pitch, and it was true that they had the skills, could gab you right inside the office and put a pen in your hand, but these days the hard sell was not enough. Witherspoon had a half dozen of the best salesmen in the city on the lot, handpicked not for their upright personalities. He was no saint himself, but he liked to think his mediocrity as a salesman stemmed less from his timidity than from his standards. He had a few principles left. It was hard to hold on to them in this business, in this economy. The crew he had out there now, good God: drunks, liars, philanderers. He couldn't keep a girl under fifty and even passably attractive, married or not, in the office. The boys—that's what they were, even though most of them were middle-aged and married with kids, put them together and they behaved like boys on a school yard—came back from lunch reeking sweetly of beer and could not keep their hands in their pockets, their filthy mouths clamped. He'd had to hire his girls based on a kind of reverse discrimination: only the homely and overweight were suitable.

Which got Witherspoon to thinking about the fact that half the city was black, and the blacks seemed to favor a Buick or an Olds. That he knew of, there was no black dealership selling new cars in the Midwest save for maybe in Chicago. Which is what led him to a used lot on a corner down in Glenville. He hadn't been over there since the shootings. He'd grown up playing in Rockefeller Park, but after the riots that part of the city was one a white man wouldn't want to find himself in, night or day.

So a white man showing up in a brand-new LeSabre (which he made sure to park directly in front of the lot, so no one would make off with his hubcaps) was obviously something of an event. For five or ten minutes the men inside the former gas station watched him through the wide, slanted plate glass, which was fair enough to Witherspoon's mind, since this is exactly what his boys would do if a black man turned up in their lot.

Finally a man in a gold suit and a wide green tie and well-shined boots emerged from the office. He whistled as he made his way over to where Witherspoon stood studying an Eldorado.

The man offered his hand. This took Witherspoon aback a little. He had not expected to be touched. While they shook, the man said his name. Ronald Stallings. Witherspoon said his name back but did not pay too close attention to this exchange, because he was studying the man's face, which was what they called open. Witherspoon was not expecting this, either, and he had never really thought what it mean to say someone had an open face. What it seemed to mean in this particular case was that Witherspoon was not in the least bit threatened by the way this man, this Ronald Stallings, looked him over.

Witherspoon studied this man's eyes. He was looking for mockery or distrust but what he saw was the desire to sell this Eldorado. This man did not even appear to note the strangeness of a white man in a neighborhood where two tow-truck drivers had been shot just because they wore uniforms that, if you were high on some kind of dope or were worn down to where you just didn't give a damn, might have resembled the police.

"In the market for a Caddy this sweet afternoon?"

"She's a boat, ain't she?" said Witherspoon, studying the sunken El D.

"Floats like the *QE Two*."

Witherspoon feigned uninterest as Stallings talked up product. Witherspoon nodded a lot, avoided eye contact.

"Witherspoon," Stallings said suddenly. He was looking beyond them, at the LeSabre parked snug against the curb. "That your ride?"

When Witherspoon conceded that the Buick was his, Stallings said, "Witherspoon Buick? I doubt you're down here checking out the competition."

"Straight up? I'm looking for a salesman."

"You mean you're straight-up looking for a black salesman."

"I'm looking for a good salesman."

"Who can sell to black people."

"Who can sell a car to a nun."

"Ain't that many black nuns."

"Proves my point."

Stallings cocked his head and pretended to be confused. "Your point?"

"I could care less about color."

"Oh, okay, uh-huh, right," said Stallings, as if he'd heard this before. "Which is why you're down in Glenville instead of over across on the East Side?"

"I used to play in the park over here when I was a kid. I have some fond memories of this part of town."

Stallings laughed. His laugh was open, too. He saw a lot in a little, this man. Swift on the size-up.

"Let me guess. You got a crew of Polish and Hungary boys and some flat-out O-hi-o rednecks working your lot who'd as soon go broke as sell a car to a Negro."

"They are a particular group of individuals."

"And black people, in your estimation, love a Buick."

Witherspoon shrugged. "We sell quality vehicles."

"Japanese invasion got your ass on the run," said Stallings. "Kamikaze sapsuckers taking a bite out of everybody's wallet these days."

"Desperate times."

"Desperate measures, too," said Stallings. "I imagine it would be kind of desperate, too, me trying to cop a customer on a all-white lot."

"Oh, I'd make sure you got your shot."

"With the Negroes?"

"You'd be selling cars to anyone who wanted to buy a car, and a whole lot who think they aren't ready to buy."

"Let's get down to it, Mr. Witherspoon," said Stallings.

"You can call me Spoon. All the others do, whether I say they can or not."

"Spoon," said Ronald, rolling it around in his mouth. "Nah, I think I'll pass on calling you what the others do without your permission. So what I am hearing you say is you're down here looking to add some affirmative action to your staff. But what I am hearing you mean is, this city's black and getting blacker and you need someone to move some units to the brothers and sisters."

Witherspoon slid his hand beneath the hood of the Eldorado. He found the latch and popped it, lifted the hood and propped it.

"You know my boss is having a high time watching this," said Stallings. "It's like a drive-in movie through that big glass. He had me swipe it down yesterday on account of we have not sold a vehicle in two weeks. My boss won't care too much to get poached by some East Side operation looking to prey on his staff. Especially a white man moving new units. I imagine you're going have to make things right for my man before I even think about leaving here."

"How much?"

"I'd say a thousand would ease his pain."

"What does he want for this crate?"

"Okay. I see. You'll be wanting something besides a salesman in the bargain."

"Lincoln freed the slaves, Mr. Stallings."

"Hold up, here," said Stallings, his face no longer open. He took a step closer to Witherspoon, which ought to have reminded Witherspoon of the neighborhood he was in, the fact that he had no friends down here, but instead made him worry he'd offended the man.

"You think I'm saying you get to *own* me for that? You don't get shit but me off this lot."

"That's not what I meant," said Witherspoon. "I meant, you got a contract with him? Otherwise, see, my paying him off might look like he's selling you off, that's all I was saying."

"Look like that to him or to you? If that man in there *could* sell me off, he'd do it. He'd tag on for these brand-new boots, though, and my tie, too. I don't have no contract with the man. Down here we don't sign contracts. I got a responsibility to him is all."

Witherspoon tried to imagine one of his salesmen displaying such loyalty.

"Crank it up," said Witherspoon.

Stallings pulled the key from his pocket. Witherspoon listened to the idle for thirty seconds before he drew his hand across his neck.

"Least you could do is replace the eggbeater somebody stuck in there in place of an engine," he said in the praise-be quiet following the ragged death of the engine. "How much does he want for it?"

"He's got it down for a grand. Though I believe he'd take eight hundred cash."

Witherspoon reached for his wallet. He had stashed it in his inside coat pocket instead of in his back pocket as usual, which open-faced Stallings took note of.

"You carrying that much cash on you? Myself, I lived down here all my life and I don't carry any more than lunch money."

"I anticipated a transaction."

"What you ought to anticipate is these dope fiends sticking a knife in your face. But I don't reckon you'll be back down here again."

"I'll send a man down here to pick it up later today," said Witherspoon, nodding at the Caddy. "Though I don't know what the hell I'm going to do with it."

"You don't sell used?"

"I don't sell crap."

"Well, I happen to be between vehicles right now. You float me a little advance on my first check and I'll make your money back on it."

"You know you're working on commission?"

"I'll make it up to you in a week."

"I don't think I've ever advanced a man on his check before he's even sold a car."

"We'll call it a signing bonus."

"This ain't the Cavaliers you're joining," said Witherspoon, though he felt his own face opening at the way Stallings worked. He had such a good feeling about this man, he would have handed him the keys to the LeSabre just to have him on the lot.

"Come by at noon tomorrow, I'll get you through the paperwork, show you around the lot."

First thing in the morning, Witherspoon called his boys into his office.

"You hired a spook" said Walenski. "To sell to spooks, right?"

"You only sell to Poles?" said Witherspoon.

"You think a white woman's going to buy a car from a black man, Spoon?"

"You know what I think? I think the fact that we are having this conversation is proof that it is not the economy or goddamn Toyota that's about to drive me out of business but the fact that I have packed my lot with idiots stupid enough, in such uncertain financial times, to talk back to the man who signs their checks."

Stallings appeared suddenly in the lot just before noon. The boys kept their distance, clumped up in the lot, smoking and looking occasionally at Witherspoon as he led Stallings through the stock.

"They'll ease up," said Witherspoon. "It'll take them some time."

"Don't make a bit of difference to me if they never say boo," said Stallings. "I'm here to make money, not friends."

That evening, on his way home, Witherspoon spotted Stallings waiting on the bus. He pulled over and waved him in.

"Where's your vehicle?"

"Funny thing, I took that Eldorado home last night, before I even pulled up in my drive, somebody took it off my hands."

"How much did you get for it?"

"Enough to pay my bus fare back across town. But you know I got to transfer twice? They don't make it easy on a black man to get over here."

"How much did you get for it?"

"I did okay."

"Well," said Witherspoon, trying to sound gruff, "I hope you play as hard on my court."

"I reckon I'll make it up to you by noon tomorrow."

"You reckon?"

"Got a fellow coming by first thing. He sings in the choir with my wife."

"Church, huh?" Witherspoon was thinking a churchgoing man had a far better constituency than a pack of drunks whose friends had to pool their money for cab fare after spending every night in a tavern.

"You a God-fearing man, Stallings?"

"Fear is not what gets me out of bed and up to the House of Prayer when the wind's coming off that lake at six below."

They were stopped at a light. Witherspoon looked over at his passenger. "So you attend church to sell cars?"

"Nah," said Stallings, "It's not like that at all. That wouldn't be right. See, I like the singing."

The next morning Witherspoon was standing with Stallings in the showroom, going over some features of the new models, when a rust-colored Datsun pulled into the lot.

"That's my man," said Stallings, but he made no move, nor did any of the others as they watched a black hand emerge from the window and palm the top of the car. The entire vehicle lifted as an obese man in a too-tight suit emerged.

"Whoever sold him that piece of plastic ought to be shot."

"Not near enough vehicle for his girth, you got that right," said Stallings.

None of his other salesmen would know a word like *girth*, Witherspoon thought as he watched Stallings greet his man with a shake. He wasn't sure himself he knew what it meant until Stallings put in into a sentence.

Witherspoon knew the entire staff was watching as Stallings led his customer right over to a sky-blue Electra. Stallings wasn't at it long enough for any of them to grow bored. Thirty minutes max and he had the big man sitting across from him at the desk. The showroom rang with laughter as the man signed the paperwork.

Witherspoon watched Stallings take the man out to the Electra. They stood alongside it talking, as if what they were saying was the most important thing in the world, as if the car were not the thing that mattered. But Witherspoon was staring at the car, not at the men. Maybe the car didn't matter at all. He loved a sell, and he felt confident that he'd made the right decision hiring Stallings, but he found it hard to get excited about the money he'd make off that Electra or the cars that Stallings would move for him in the future. And yet the longer the men lingered there, talking and laughing, as if the car could wait, the more Witherspoon focused on the car. He believed, after a time, that it sure did matter. He thought about the dollar bill framed by his grandfather hanging in his office, the first buck earned by Witherspoon Buick. The night before, after dropping Stallings off in his neighborhood and locking the doors before Stallings reached the stoop of his row house, Witherspoon felt as if he'd done something terrible, hiring this man. As if his motives were impure, as if everything he did these days, especially poaching Stallings, was done to line his pockets.

Stallings shook hands with the big man and held the door open for him. As the man climbed behind the wheel, the vehicle shifted only slightly under his girth. It was a good car, the right car for him. But it was more than that; it did matter. Maybe it was the most important car Witherspoon had ever sold. Cleveland was all to hell now. So much hate and fear and violence, so much poverty, so much distrust between the races. Witherspoon walked outside so he could better watch the Electra as it made its way out of the lot. For as long as he could, he kept the blue in his sights as the Electra turned onto the boulevard and entered the stream of other cars. When it stopped at the light, a rare slice of late spring Cleveland sun caused its window to glint. Then the light changed and Witherspoon watched the car drive away, off into the world, a sparkling symbol of something new, of some change in this city—in this country, hell, the whole world—that he had had a hand in creating.

Pinto Canyon, Texas, 2004

By three in the afternoon, on the lot of Kepler's Fantastic Deals!, Marcus had narrowed it down to a Ford Ranger pickup with 106,000 miles, an ancient and deeply suspect Volkswagen Thing with a sloppy backyard camouflage paint job whose mileage, given that it was nearly thirty years old, struck him as dubiously low at 173,000 miles, and a 1984 Buick Electra. The odometer on the Buick registered only 60K and Marcus believed it. It was a sweet, low block of a ride, light blue with a strip of black vinyl along the bottom of the doors, perfect for rumbling around town with the windows open.

Each vehicle had its perks. He'd loved his pickup and he had needed it, too — he wasn't the type to drive a truck around with nothing but autumn leaves in the bed — and the Ranger was a no-nonsense workhorse, a five-speed so stripped down — not even a radio — that it seemed like it would get him to Patagonia and back on a couple of tanks of gas.

The VW was butt-ass ugly, badly camouflaged, and capable at any minute of breaking down on the side of the road, but the fact that it was a damn lie made it fitting for a man deceiving his blood kin.

As for the Buick, Marcus saw himself steering that bad boy around town, the other hand out the window, drumming the side-view in time to the tunes or surfing stiff-fingered the fresh Texas breeze. He would not defile his vinyl tabernacle with Top 40 or talk radio; only deep southern soul or country old school and forlorn allowed. *Isaac Hayes at Wattstax, Dusty in Memphis,* that old silver fox Charlie Rich — when had he ever come up with a playlist just looking at a vehicle? And say Marcus got himself some companionship: She could start out on the passenger side, upside the window, but as soon as they got acquainted she could slide right across the seat and suction herself eventually, barnacle-like, to his side. Maybe put her head on his shoulder? No save-it-for-marriage bucket seats for the Buick. Yet it was a sensible ride, mature, dependable, more straight-and-narrow than bank-robbery getaway. Unless you wanted to lose a muffler, you'd be an idiot to take it off-road, say, on an ear-popping, downshifting descent through a series of gulches, bottoming out in a riverbed in the middle of which ran a trickle of suds demarcating one country from another.

While he was studying the Buick, a woman appeared suddenly from the rows of Fantastic Deals. Marcus had noticed her earlier, briefly, when he was checking out the VW, but the way she had been standing at the edge of the lot, looking not at the cars but at the plastic streamers fluttering in the wind kicked up by passing traffic, made him think she was either waiting for a ride or slightly crazy. But now she appeared to be looking, like him, for an automobile. *His* automobile, it seemed, since she had moved to the other side of it. Her hair was black and shoulder length and her skin was olive and later he would remember that the word *lithe* came to mind as he studied her, along with the word *lovely*, neither of which were common to the lexicon from which his adjectives to describe women were drawn. *Lovely*, too, was not a word he'd ever think to apply to someone so effortlessly attired, not that he went for the painted, put-together types. She was wearing a tank top, flip-flops. Worn jeans hung low and tight over her hips, and instead of a purse she'd slung the strap of a faded backpack over her shoulder like a schoolkid. Marcus knew jack about fashion but he could tell when a woman got up in the morning and yanked on whatever articles of clothing happened to be lying on the floor, and appeared more striking than if she had spent a half hour pulling clothes out of the closet, leaving behind on the bed a reject pile so high it resembled a body in slumber.

It had been weeks since Marcus had even noticed a woman, so bound up in his various miseries had he been, and so unwilling or unready to give up the wound licking set off by Rebecca's leaving. That this woman, standing just on the other side of the Buick, so close he might have smelled her perfume were she the type to wear same, seemed so entirely indifferent to his presence was maybe what made him so aware of *her*. But he wasn't about to say anything. He did not like that he was wasting time thinking of such things. "A lump of Lord have mercy" did not even make his list. This woman was distracting him from his purpose. Therefore she was not on his side. The way she stood so close, only the car between them, and ignored him was ample proof that she was not on his side in more ways than one. Maybe it was the night he'd had — the lack of sleep, grieving over his lost truck, the flytrap seeds he would never see again, the other useless items the Border Patrol claimed would turn up in some draw but he feared were lost to him forever—but Marcus did not want to lose anything else. He'd gotten there first. That Buick was his.

MARIA'S MOTHER HAD WANTED to come along with her to the car lot.

"I've known the Kepler boys for years, I've bought two vehicles from them," she said on the way into town.

"Thanks, but I know you have to get to work."

"Do you even know what to look for?"

"I can handle it," said Maria. She knew that with her mother along, she could not lose herself in what she had dubbed Rand-om: the kingdom of Randy not as he had been but as who he might have been. The sum of all the parts she had not recognized when he was with her. Occasionally she felt Randy's presence in a way that was free of guilt and regret. Mostly she felt him in a way that was black and heavy. Today she needed him to come lightly to her and to leave proud of her fearlessness. She believed he would be with her, guiding her, but she'd not be able to feel or hear him with her mother there asking questions and making decisions for her.

"Well, at least let me run in and introduce you," said her mother.

"It's only a half mile from the motel," said Maria. "I can walk."

"Okay," said her mother, as if she remembered that she had promised to stay out of Maria's way. "You just call me if you need me."

But obviously her mother had called Bobby Kepler, who was

deeply involved in a take-out feast of barbecued chicken, mac and cheese, and cole slaw when Maria walked into his tiny office. He knew exactly who she was. He stood up from his desk, barbecue sauce staining his fingers, and started right in on how well he'd known her father, played ball with him in high school, great guy, so sorely missed. Maria smiled and thanked him, said she did not want to disturb his lunch, and she was relieved—and a little surprised, for even though she had never bought a car before, she was aware of the stereotype of the officious and relentless used-car salesman—when Bobby Kepler said he'd be right out, feel free to look around and see if there's anything out there you fall in love with. Then he mentioned names—Astro, Saturn, Corolla—that reminded her of class field trips to a star party up at the McDonald Observatory. She smiled as if she knew what he was talking about and headed out on the lot.

What a strange feeling it was to go shopping for something so huge and have no idea what she wanted. Looking at the rows of cars, she felt unprepared and ashamed of her lack of planning. If buying a car was her attempt to honor Randy's passion, shouldn't she have at least gotten on the Internet and googled "how to buy a car"? Surely there was some book you could purchase called *Car Buying for Dummies*? She tried to summon those endless conversations between Randy and her father; she tried to remember the Nova in the drive, its hood propped open, exposing its complicated system of belts and points and plugs. Maria smiled at her recall of these terms she'd long forgotten. That such detail was lurking in her psyche made her feel a little less helpless.

Still, none of the cars seemed right to her. Too big, too flimsy, too high up, too green, too sporty. Only one drew her interest. It was squat and boxy and the slightly washed-out blue of the wide sky above. Randy would never think to buy such a car for himself, but he would approve of it for her. He would want, above all, for her to be safe. This car was safe. Runaway grocery carts in the parking lot of the Thriftway would alter their course rather than collide with its fearsome grill. There were nicks in the paint and she noticed a slight dent below the gas tank, but in her mind the car could fend off a bulldozer, none the worse for wear.

She read the name: Buick, it said up front, and along the back, in chrome cursive. Was Buick good? Any minute now Bobby Kepler would have cleaned the chicken to the bone and would emerge from his tiny office reinvigorated and full of questions for her. Randy, tell me now, quick, is this the one?

And then she noticed the man standing on the other side of the car. How had she missed him? He must have been hiding from her. When he was pretending not to look at her, she looked at him. He was of medium height and solidly built— well fed, she'd have said had she cared to say one way or the other—and his brown hair was thinning and graying a bit at the temples. Around here, white men of his age were either ranchers or hippies. He wasn't dressed like a hippie, really, nor did he look like a rancher, though it seemed from his skin that he was no stranger to the sun.

Even her notice of this stranger on the other side of the Buick threatened to keep Randy at bay. Yes, you loved cars, but I know you loved me more. So gone on her was he that she both feared his love and took it for granted. How is it even possible, she wondered now, to fear something you don't appreciate, something you don't even notice at times? He was kind to her father and she made him feel bad for that. He was passionate about his future and she ridiculed his passion. Even though she had only a vague idea of what she wanted to do with her life—a master's in deaf ed seemed, now, a schoolgirl fantasy—privileging her future over his is what tore them apart. What killed him. He knew what he wanted. Who knew what they wanted? He knew things she did not and she thought she was smarter and less provincial and she let him know it. No, God, Maria, don't think that way, especially here, now, in a place as sacred to him as an old-growth forest. Think of him now as he was so often in their Airstream: sweet tempered, big eared, vain about his hair. He always carried a tube of Chap Stick and applied it so liberally that when she poured him a Pepsi to go with his sandwiches, the rim of his glass would smudge with gloss. He loved Dwight Yoakam and he claimed to have a crush on Debra Winger based solely on one scene in the movie *Urban Cowboy*. She wished she could remember which scene, but she knew it had nothing to do with a mechanical bull, which Randy deemed ridiculous, suburban Texans getting thrown not from an animal riled up by their attempt to tame it but by a tangle of wires controlled by some wannabe cowboy with a lever.

Randy, do you know how sweet you were? How smart? It is so hard to know anything at all when you are that young, but it is far harder to look back on your youth and *think* you knew anything at all.

Maria looked up from the Buick. She saw the man looking at her and she saw him smile. To him it would appear, not that she was talking to her dead high school boyfriend, but that she was studying a car she was interested in buying. The man had a nice smile. His bottom lip was thinner than the top, which made his smile a little crooked and a lot nervous. For some reason his nervousness calmed her.

Over the hiss of cars on the boulevard she heard the door to the office slam. Maybe over time, Randy, you would have eased up or been ground down by my careless way of loving you back. And then I would have missed the way you always slipped your hand in the back pocket of my jeans when we were crossing the street, I would have missed the way you cared for me more than anyone I have let care for me since.

One of the Keplers, now she could not remember which one, would be upon her in seconds. How do you tell if a car is any good? Randy was not there and he was not coming.

Without even looking his way again, Maria said to the man on the other side of the car, "Excuse me, do you happen to know—I mean, I'm sorry to bother you, but is this a good car?"

"Looks decent from the outside," he said.

"Will you test-drive it for me?" she asked.

Two

Pinto Canyon, Texas, 2004

Standing in the car lot, the woman's question hovering unanswered in the space between them, Marcus remembered once having seen a man in a salvage yard where he had gone to buy a fuel pump for a tractor. The keeper of the salvage yard was mute, wiry, stingy with his gestures. He made Marcus wait while he stuck his head under the hood of a car, told a boy in the driver's seat to hit the gas, and listened to the engine rev as if contemplating an aria. Then he disappeared into a shed and emerged in seconds holding a lone socket wrench so resolutely the right choice that it appeared to be an extension of his hand.

The tool for the job, the names of things, the aloof cool of the present-tense drifter—what was it about the question that struck Marcus with the sudden want of all of the above, and at once? Nothing abstract or ambiguous about it. A yes was required, or a no.

What sort of place was this, anyway? A lithe and lovely woman, blown up from nowhere, had just asked him to test-drive a car for her. It happened to be the car he wanted for himself. Where, in America, could you not walk into a used-car

lot and purchase without impediment what looked to Marcus
to be at least a twenty-year-old Buick?

So open was this place, so wide its sky, so looming were
the craggy bluffs above town, so insanely tinted were they by
light the likes of which he'd seen only in coffee-table photog-
raphy books—more shades of brown, reddish brown, yellow-
ish brown, blondish brown, greenish brown, than he'd ever
thought possible—that Marcus worried his ability to reason
was overwhelmed.

Prudence was called for. He must keep from her, at least for
now, their mutual desire.

"Will I *what*?" he said, in a way that suggested he had not
heard her correctly as much as that he didn't understand.

"Well, see," she said, "I don't really know anything about cars."
She went on to explain that she had never owned one, that she
had always been able to get by without one, but that now she
needed a car because she had just started a new business.

"Even I know enough to know that you ought not to buy a
car before you drive it," she said.

"So you think there might be something wrong with it?" said
Marcus.

His question put her on the defensive. "No," she said. "I
didn't say that. But if you're suggesting I should just go ask the
guy whether there is anything wrong with the car, I mean . . ."

"I understand," said Marcus, when she failed to finish her
sentence. "I wouldn't recommend you do that."

"Not that he's not an honest man," she said.

"Right," said Marcus. "So you need someone who's more
objective?"

"Impartial," she said, as if she were correcting him. As if "objective" did not in this case imply "impartial." Still, her word rankled. So she assumed he was impartial when she came upon him studying the same car? Did she think he was out for a stroll? Was she arrogant or just oblivious? People sometimes found him arrogant, Rebecca told him once, and when he asked why—because he was truly shocked by this, he always thought he came across as modest and accessible—she said it was because he often seemed "unto himself." He had no idea what that meant—it did not sound bad to him or even noteworthy, for isn't everyone finally "unto themselves"?—but he decided that she meant oblivious.

Maybe arrogance always contained a dose of oblivion. He had about decided that the woman was equally both when he noticed that her expression was so pained, and she seemed so depleted, that she was obviously embarrassed. Marcus felt a little bad for her, and a little guilty for deceiving her, but only for a minute.

"Sure," he said. "I've owned a few cars in my time. I'll be happy to take it for a spin and tell you what I think."

The beginning of a lie is so sweetly delicious, for it seems not yet a lie but just a hidden desire, a secret rightfully kept. Though secrets can turn toxic, can thwart careers, ruin marriages, topple countries, there is such power in their incipient stage that the word *secret* is not yet applicable. For it is mostly just yearning; it has not yet taken the elevator up to the brain; it hovers somewhere between the heart and the groin.

Marcus was about to ask if he should go fetch the key when the salesman who earlier had come out of his tiny office to size

Marcus up and within seconds had obviously deemed him not worth leaving the comfort of his air-conditioning for came loping through the lot.

"Find something to love?" he said to the woman.

"This one," she said, pointing to the Buick between them, which elicited from the salesman such a hackneyed history—previous owner was an elderly lady, rancher's widow who'd moved into town after he died, hardly ever drove it, church, beauty parlor, grocery store, kept it serviced regularly, clean as a whistle—that despite its familiarity was delivered so passionately that it brought to Marcus's mind (even though he was sure it was a lie) a hunched-over grandma backing the car slowly down a driveway once or twice a week, on the seat beside her a shiny black patent-leather purse containing in a side pocket a folded plastic rain bonnet to protect her helmet of purplish hair.

"We'd like to test-drive it," said the woman when he was done. Marcus had looked at her once during the salesman's spiel and deduced from her frozen smile that she was not paying a bit of attention.

"We?" Only then did the salesman take note of him. Was Marcus, because he wasn't native, invisible? She'd not seemed to notice him, either, for a few minutes. "Oh, how you doing?" the salesman said to Marcus, and then he turned back to the woman. "I didn't realize y'all were together, your mama didn't mention . . ."

"No problem," said the woman, in a way that was sharp but not rude and that shut Mr. Fantastic Deals up and sent him off to fetch the key.

When he was gone, Marcus said his name was Marcus. She

said her name was Maria. After which, silence. No "Nice to meet you," no "Thank you for pretending to be my acquaintance if not something more than that."

"Hi," said Marcus, and when she smiled and looked away up the rows of cars, obviously impatient, he had a chance to study her a bit more closely. Her skin was unlined but there was something stark about her shoulder blades. Marcus was wearing sunglasses and she was not, but she did not blink in the full noon sun. Though the salesman was gone, there was still something formidable in her demeanor, which did not in fact make her less attractive to him, since he had not come to Kepler's Fantastic Deals! seeking the company of a soul mate or even a warm and lively chat with a stranger. She seemed a worthy opponent. She wanted what he wanted, and that made him want it all the more.

A couple of minutes later they were pulling out of the lot. Indeed the engine did smoothly purr. Marcus adjusted the rearview and when he checked the side mirrors he noticed how the seat belt sliced across her chest. Only momentarily did he allow himself to entertain this image, for it occurred to him that she and the salesman knew each other, and had he asked first to test-drive the car the salesman would never have allowed him to do so alone, to prevent him from taking off to, God knows, Mexico.

He drove. She said that she didn't want to drive, that she didn't even know enough to be able to tell by driving the car the things she needed to know.

"Fine," he said, "but I'm not really familiar with the area. Is there a specific route you had in mind?"

"No," she said. He wondered if it was his slightly formal diction—"a specific route," God, what a pretentious way to say it—or the notion that a specific route was necessary in this situation that made her sound clipped.

But once out of the lot and onto the boulevard, Marcus was happy not to have her issuing directions. It felt almost as if the car itself were choosing the turns: up the boulevard into town, hard right just past his hotel into a neighborhood backed up on a hill. Yards fenced with piecemeal plywood and sheet metal, small dogs wandering freely among chickens and a few goats tethered to trees, religious shrines elaborate and abundant and mostly devoted to the Virgin of Guadalupe, a tidiness even to the most weathered structures.

His passenger did not seem so enthralled by the world outside the windshield. She had made herself small against the door. From her backpack she had pulled a hooded sweatshirt. Her hands were swallowed by pocket. Marcus could tell by her shoulders, frozen in a shrug, that her fingers were balled into fists. Briefly he worried she'd grown scared of him, but later, much later, she would confess that she'd been freezing. Apparently Marcus had the AC blasting. He didn't feel it. He was just driving. It was the discovery not only of a part of town unknown to him but of the Buick—its low carriage, the slinky way it bounced over potholes, the wideness of its turning, the sunken seats—that contained him entirely.

Marcus said nothing at all when they pulled into the lot. He parked the Buick in its spot between a Saturn and a green Dodge Neon. He got out, opened the hood, stood listening to the tick of the cooling engine. He pretended to know things.

"Well?" said the woman from across the still-warm engine. "It's perfect," he said. "I'll take it."

THAT HE MADE NO effort at all to chat her up—that he barely even glanced at her during the entire ride—played a big part in Maria's decision, though it wasn't exactly a decision, since she never really decided as much as felt. And said what she felt.

It had been some time since she had said what she felt. Years. Who wanted to hear it? What value did it carry?

She had done so once, on a scenic overlook an hour or so from these very roads. A night so clear, a view so thrilling. "Crazy, right?" Randy had said when he parked the Nova and scooted closer to her and pointed to the valley twinkling and stretching away beneath them. He began to talk about what he wanted, as he often had, for he was a boy with a plan. He loved to think and talk about his future, his vision of which was meticulously detailed, right down to the color they'd paint their house, the breed of dogs they'd own, probably even what they would eat for Sunday dinner. And then she'd interrupted him with her news, and though what she revealed was a part of his plan (times three or four or even more, in fact, and it was true that he loved children and was good with them, she'd seen him at play with his little cousins), she could tell it took him out of his idyllic scenario. But only briefly. A few minutes later he had not scrapped his plan but merely moved it around a bit, as if this were only a minor convenience, a slight problem with the sequence.

This made Maria furious. To Randy it was no more a trifle

than if Rockfish needed a vocalist instead of a bass player. It was her life also, and her dreams had not been considered separate from his own. In fact, in his dream she was the lone aspect devoid of detail. Had it been a photograph she would have been blemished by shadow.

Thereafter she never much considered the future. Her menus were planned a day or two ahead. Perhaps this was why as a chef she'd gravitated toward all-local ingredients, for improvisation was the key; you made do not only with what was in season but with what was available in enough volume. Thereafter the very thought of frozen food—the staple of so many restaurants—reminded her of Randy's Plan.

And so she had said what she felt. She told him of her desires and she tried to explain to him how having this child now would render those desires (and his, too—she'd been convinced then that his life, too, would have been ruined by his sweet, innocent, but entirely wrongheaded and stubborn insistence on slightly rearranging things to accommodate a baby in the lives of two not much more than babies) impossible; she tried to explain to him that the things she wanted were different from what he wanted, and she tried, she really did try, to do this in a way that did not denigrate his love of the valley stretching beneath them, his love of hunting antelope and loading up ATVs on his uncle's trailer and heading down to Terlingua with his buddies to tear-ass around the sandy hills, his love of brisket and breakfast burritos, of Texas and Texan ways, all those things that her own father loved and that were probably what he loved about Randy.

But of course he felt judged. How could he not?

And so, after Randy died, she left off saying what she felt. She put more stock in the notion of considered decisions. Rather than offer her feelings to the world, she did her homework. She presented facts. It will work better for me this way and here are the reasons why. That her facts were often feelings manipulated or pitched in a way that appeared factual was not lost on those, mostly lovers, to whom these facts were presented. But she wasn't trying to fool her audience as much as she was trying to fool herself.

So when the man said to her over the heat of the ticking engine of the Buick, "It's perfect. I'll take it," she did not make a decision so much as entertain a feeling. Earlier, Randy's presence, his sweetness seeping through her rigid carriage, warming and maybe even melting her bones a little, softening her usual standoffishness, had led her to pretend to Bobby Kepler that she was *with* this guy and then to get in the car with him. She could have ended up murdered in the backcountry, her body discovered by Border Patrol in some gulch. But Randy whispered, Go with this guy. You can trust him. He's had hard times for sure. You can see it in his eyes and in his shoulders. Whatever he had, it ain't his anymore. Or he don't know how to get it back but he's not yet given up on the getting back.

In the car she felt Randy on the seat between them. He drives good, Randy said, got an easy way behind the wheel. And it felt after a time that the stranger was not in the car at all. She and Randy used to spend hours just riding around talking and looking at things. On weekends they'd head up to Balmorhea to spend the afternoon lying in the sun, their matching Budweiser beach towels coated with coconut tanning oil. Driving home still smelling of the sweet spring that fed the pool and slightly of algae and of the fish that pooled fearlessly just under the surface, they would watch the sun begin its slide down behind the mountains and the rock faces she'd seen so many times before, and the cottonwoods hugging the creek bank, the tassels topping the creosote—all would seem, in the newness of that particular sunset, painted by her and Randy's passage. For years when she wanted to calm her troubled mind, wanted sleep or even waking solace, she put herself in Randy's car, and in his hands, in his care.

So this man wanted the car and so did she. The woman who got out of her husband's shiny vehicle and unbuckled a half-asleep toddler from the backseat and took her to the bathroom while her husband, handsome even under the ratty baseball cap he liked to wear on road trips, took the boys inside the store for a healthy snack: Maria was not and would never be that woman. When the stranger said the car was perfect and he would take it, she honored what she felt, which was that she might just be able to pull off some risky but—if it worked—mutually satisfying arrangement. And it was worth the risk because Randy, who was there—she felt his sweet breath on her neck—approved.

"Well," she said, playing it cool, not acknowledging his vow to buy the car out from under her, "how much do you think it's worth?"

"How much do *you* think it's worth?"

"I don't know. If I knew these things I would not have asked you to test-drive it."

"I think we better find out what he wants for it."

"And then what?"

"And then I make him an offer," he said.

"And then I make him a better offer?"

"That's usually the way it goes."

"And you think he'll sell to the highest bidder?"

"I imagine he will."

"And that's how you want this to go?" Maria said.

"What other way might it go?"

"You strike me as a man with some imagination."

"And you're basing this on what, exactly? You don't know me. All you know is my name."

"I know that I got in a car with you three minutes after meeting you and you barely even looked at me. That tells me a lot."

"That tells you that I have some imagination?"

"Among other things," Maria said, though she had not bothered to consider what those other things might be.

"It seems if I had an imagination I might imagine that you and I could become friendly."

"Friendly? If 'friendly' means what I think you mean by it, I don't get the sense you're looking for a friend right now. Seemed more like you were so busy imagining yourself as sole owner of this car that you did not even notice my presence."

"Oh, I noticed your presence," he said. "I believe it was *I* who was invisible to *you* when you first walked up to this car."

"It's true I didn't see you, but in my defense I am a little intimidated by buying something I know absolutely nothing about. I'm a little distracted. So forgive me if I came across as rude."

"I don't know—I mean, rude? Isn't it rude of me to announce

that I'm about to buy this car when you asked me to test-drive it for you?"

"Yes," said Maria. "I'd say it was a little rude."

"And yet you seem to trust me?"

"Who says I trust you?"

"Okay, so you don't trust me. Why are you standing here talking to me? Why don't you go get the salesman and tell him what you want to pay for the car? He knows you, he mentioned your mother, so I am assuming you are a family friend, which suggests that he'll take your bid over mine no matter what I offer him."

"You think that's how small towns work?" Maria said.

"I know that's how they work, having spent the last ten years in one."

"Where?"

"North Carolina."

"On the ocean, right?"

"I lived less than an hour away."

"I lived on the coast for the last ten years myself. The Oregon coast."

"Yeah, well, I have nothing against sea otters and rocks and tide pools, but I'm a little spoiled by the Atlantic. What good is an ocean if you can't swim in it?"

"Maybe you *don't* have much of an imagination," she said.

"Let me guess. You like to sit around and look at it?"

"People pull fish out of it. They surf it."

"Wearing wet suits."

"It's just a thicker bathing suit."

He laughed. "A thicker bathing suit?"

"Let me guess. Everyone in South Carolina swims in the buff."

"North Carolina."

"Pardon?"

"You said 'South Carolina.' I'm from North Carolina."

"I assume from your tone there's a difference."

"Is West Texas the same as East Texas?"

"Actually they are in the same state," Maria said.

"Right, but are they the same place?"

"Not at all. East Texas is the South. West Texas is the West. I suppose North Carolina is not the South? Is that the North?"

"Have you ever been to the East Coast?"

"I've been to Washington, DC."

"What did you do there?"

"What you do there. Museums. Monuments. The Capitol. I saw a film shot from the cockpit of a glider."

"*To Fly!* National Air and Space Museum."

"It made me sick to my stomach," she said. "Ever since, I've hated to fly."

"How did you get here from Oregon? Surely you flew. You said you have never owned a car before. Do you even know how to drive?"

"Yes, I know how. I've driven a car. I just haven't owned one."

"How do you get around?"

"I walk. I have a bike."

"I had a bike. It was in my truck. It got stolen," the man said.

"Around here?"

"South of here. Down along the border."

"What were you doing down there?"

"Hiking."

"And someone stole your truck?"

"Yes. And everything I own except for what is in my hotel room."

"So you need a car," Maria said.

"I need *this* car, in fact."

"Where are you going?"

"I *was* going to Mexico."

"Were?"

"I like it here. I'm thinking I'll stay, for a while at least. But that doesn't mean I don't need a car."

"You need a car around here, it's true. People think nothing of driving three hours to get dental floss or a chaise longue."

"Not much out here in the way of goods and sundries," the man said.

"But you like it?"

"I do. Maybe because this landscape is the opposite of what I'm used to."

"In Carolina?"

"People don't say 'Carolina.' Well, people *from* there don't say that."

"I'm not from there."

"Okay, say it if you want. I'm just warning you, it makes you sound like a tourist."

"I don't have a problem with being a tourist," Maria said, "but *you* must."

"If I had a problem with it I would work harder to disguise the fact. So that you might have noticed me when you walked up to this car."

"You wanted me to see you? I thought you were my competition."

"I would like to be recognized as such."

"And yet you assume that Bobby Kepler will favor me in this deal?"

"I do assume that. I assume it even more now that I hear his name out of your mouth. I was just referring to him in my head as Mr. Fantastic Deals."

"Exclamation point," added Maria.

"Right. And I guess one of us should go fetch him?"

"And say what?"

"Find out how much he wants for this Buick."

"How much do you think it's worth?" she asked.

"WE'RE GOING IN CIRCLES," he said, and as he said it, he was damn near crippled by the truth of it, the repetitiousness of his life. For Marcus had failed at other things before he lost the farm. He had dropped out of college twice. When he finally finished, he decided to get his MA in history, but it took nearly five years to finish his thesis, since he resorted while writing it to low-paying and onerous jobs like delivering newspapers and grading standardized test essays for gas and rent money rather than teaching intro-level sections in his discipline to bored and increasingly insolent if not entitled undergraduates. He'd tried for a semester, but he was so transparently annoyed by the sorts of questions the students asked, which rarely had a thing to do with the content of the day's lecture—questions like "Are you going to curve the midterm?" and "Is this going to be on the final?" and "Is it okay if we share textbooks?"—that he himself came across in class as addled, insolent, detached, outright rude, as his mother would have said had she seen him shaking slightly behind the podium. He could not teach. He would not teach. It had not yet occurred to him to retreat to the family farm to raise flytraps, so he drifted for a few years. He sold time-shares for condos on the Outer Banks. He was an abysmal and abject wreck of a person during those days, the lone period of his life when he could honestly admit to drinking too much. He babysat a friend's art gallery in Richmond's Shockoe Slip, a job so low paying that he slept on a couch in the back room of the gallery and cooked ramen and chicken broth on a hot plate.

Then there were women. With them he had not only made the same mistakes but indulged in the same fantasies that disguised those mistakes. Central to the fantasy was that *this* time he might overcome whatever was within him that had led him to be described by one lover as a "split risk." Though he blamed Rebecca for packing up her Honda and disappearing down the canopied drive the last time he'd seen her, he knew that it was *he* who'd left by virtue of never fully showing up in the first place.

Here he was, still going in circles. Maybe losing his farm, Rebecca, his truck, maybe ending up marooned here, standing with this woman beside this Buick, was his last chance. Maybe he should *make* it his last chance. The nearby border might separate one country from another, but he did not need to go to Mexico in order to cross it.

"How much do you think it's worth?" she asked—of herself more than of the man who had so readily won Randy's approval.

She'd never sought Randy's approval of any man before, maybe because she had not found anyone she would open herself up to. Trust no one. You cannot fully trust yourself, either, for the last time you did so, the last time you honored and even insisted on carrying out what you felt, a boy died. A baby died, too. The baby would have been so beautiful. It would have been small. The town was small and so was the boy. Lying atop her, the crown of his head to the bottom of his feet, every inch of him covered every inch of her, a custom blanket of flesh, blood, bone, sweetness, Chap Stick. Why did this even matter, that Randy's dimensions were hers also? In the years since, she had dated men absurdly taller, men she'd comfortably made love to sitting in their laps. It had not destroyed or even dismayed her. But she did not trust them.

What if the baby had been born as small as those incubated children she'd seen pictures of, dangerously premature, dwarfed by a nurse's finger? Baby into infant, infant to toddler, toddler to preschooler, preschooler so comically stunted, picked last for dodgeball, given the part of a mouse in the third-grade play about Benjamin Franklin. No, its smallness would not diminish the precision of its features, the way it arrived in this world a melding of Randy and Maria. Its smallness would have become over the years unnoticeable. She supported the right of women to choose, she detested the sanctimony of those hateful zealots picketing clinics, and yet the beauty of that child, the undeniable fact that it would have carried forth none of her insecurities and all of Randy's decency, was undeniable. How could she forget his kindness to her father, her lonely father, abandoned by her mother, so lonely he sat out under the carport in a lawn chair waiting for the arrival of her high school boyfriend, who would announce his arrival by downshifting his souped-up Nova, which both Maria and her father would already have heard, so distinctive was its throaty rumble and the eventual cough of its muffler when Randy let off the gas, as if its speed was so precious that slacking off made the engine sick. Randy would pull into the drive and hop right out and talk cars with her daddy, or anything, it didn't have to be cars—the Cowboys, the Spurs, deer hunting, the burn ban in effect—it did not matter, Randy gave her father and everyone else he ever met the time of day, he was just that sweet, and their baby would grow into a child whose smile lit the waiting rooms of doctors' offices, whose attentiveness in class convinced student teachers that majoring in elementary ed instead of marketing was in fact the right choice.

Small beauty is bountiful. It blooms and spreads. Such deep inner sweetness as Randy possessed transcends scale. The town is small and it, too, is beautiful. Nature might have prescribed its smallness by positioning behind it a ridge of granite and on the other side high, grassy pasture and desert, but it was Maria's perception of it now that truly cherished its smallness. What was it worth to come back to this town and allow it, this time, to be real?

Tassels of roadside grasses blown in autumn breezes across the highway end up tufted in the fencing. What is it worth to be a witness to such wonder, to view the beauty of thatched fence in the last buttery light? To remember this about her small, lovely town instead of to see it colored by shame, not over what she had done so much as what it had led Randy to do—what was that worth to her?

But what he had done caused her to see what she had done as beyond shameful. It was worth everything to see it, and him, and her home, anew. *He's had hard times for sure. Whatever he had, it ain't his anymore. Or he don't know how to get it back but he's not yet given up on the getting back.*

"How much do you think it's worth?" she asked.

"We're going in circles," he said.

"Should I just go ask him?"

"It's a little weird that he's not out here trying to sell you this car. I mean, usually they're hounding you, you know?"

"No. I wouldn't know."

"Right. I forgot. Maybe he doesn't think we're going to buy it."

"We?"

"What?"

"You said *we're* going to buy it."

"As in either you or me."

"How about both of us?"

Now it was out there, in the world. In the car lot, at least. In the space between them.

Marcus wasn't sure he understood her at first. It caused him to sputter.

"I don't . . . what?"

"How about we go in on it? Buy it together and share it?"

"And why would we do such a thing?"

"Because we both like it and we both need it and because I have other reasons and something tells me you do, too."

"Something tells you? You mean something besides me tells you things about me?"

"You haven't told me very much. Where you come from, where you're going."

"But what besides me—something I said or didn't say, or the way I said something or the way I drove, whatever—could tell you something about me?"

"Do you really want to have a conversation like this in a used-car lot?" said Maria.

"I don't have certain places where and only where certain things can be talked about. And I don't go in on cars with women I meet in used-car lots in Texas."

"You mean as a rule you don't."

"What does that mean?" he asked.

"Do you have rules about such things?"

"I have a loose understanding of what is and what is not sensible behavior. For instance, I have known since I was able to walk and talk not to get in a car with some stranger."

"And yet you did," she said. "You didn't hesitate, either. Just hopped right in."

"I see what you're trying to do."

"What?"

"Make me out to be this rule-bound, uptight guy who misses out on life by playing it safe."

She laughed. Not in an entirely pleasant way. "What do you do when you're not driving to Mexico?"

"What do I *do*?"

"For a living?"

"Why does this matter to you?"

"Just curious. You sound sort of like a lawyer."

"Actually? I'm a farmer."

"Really? What do you farm?"

"Carnivorous plants."

She laughed again. This time with a bit more color and oxygen. But not out of delight; out of ignorance, he decided.

"Venus flytraps?" he said.

"Oh, right. We had one in our fourth-grade classroom. Johnny Rodriquez killed it."

"Gouged it with a pencil, trying to get it to bite the lead."

"How'd you know?"

"I know Johnny Rodriquez. I mean, I know the Johnny Rodriquezes of this world."

"So is your trip to Mexico work-related? Are you taking your business across the border, like everyone else in the States? Or are you trying to import Venus flytraps to, say, Chiapas?"

"I think Mexico has its hands full *exporting* plants."

"While we're sort of on the subject," Maria said, "it's maybe not too smart to leave your truck with everything you own in it a half mile from the border and go wandering off for a hike."

"Apparently not. Especially dumb if you happen to drive a F-150."

"I don't know anything about cars. What's so special about it?"

"Mexicans love a Ford F-150."

"Mexicans do?"

"Apparently."

"Before you say anything else about Mexicans, I should

tell you that my father was Mexican, which makes me half-Mexican. Just so you know."

"Before you go thinking I'm some cracker, I should tell you that a Mexican Border Patrol agent is the one who told me that Mexicans love a F-150."

"Did he also tell you that he is allowed to say such things but you aren't?"

"He did."

"Then he's an idiot. He's no more allowed to say them than some white Venus flytrap farmer from North Carolina."

"On the other hand, it's just a preference. It's not like saying all Chinese people are bad drivers. There is nothing wrong with loving a Ford F-150. It's an excellent vehicle for farmwork."

"And you think all Mexicans are farmworkers?"

"No," Marcus said. "Though the majority of Mexicans I have come in contact with where I live are engaged in some form of seasonal agriculture."

"You expect them to find work in banks?"

"God, no. I hate banks. The bank took my farm away from me."

"They just snatched it? For no reason?"

He said nothing.

"Sounds like something that might happen in Mexico. Not North Carolina."

He said nothing.

"So if you don't like banks, I am assuming you plan to pay for this car in cash?"

He said, "Yes."

"Good. Me, too. I mean, actually, I can write a check or

I can cash a check and bring him the cash later, either way, whatever he wants. I bet he'll take my check, though. So how much do you think we should offer him?"

Marcus was thinking about the bank. The bank did not take his farm away from him. Rebecca did not leave him. It was probably not even Mexicans who stole his truck. "Mistakes were made" is a phrase that made you feel slightly better for a while after you uttered it, for its passive construction put the onus on the mistake, as if the absent subject of the sentence — the implied "I" — were walking contentedly down the street, and out of the heavens dropped the net that was the mistake, scooping up the innocent "I" and dangling it above the sidewalk, trapped, foiled, ruined.

"The bank did not take away my farm. I fucked that up. I took it away from myself. And from my family. See, that land had been in my family for centuries."

"Family," she said after a silence, and she seemed about to elaborate but stopped herself, as if whatever she was going to say on the subject struck her as obvious, fatuous, or just plain wrong. Marcus so appreciated her decision not to finish this thought that later, looking back on this strange day, he decided this might well have been the moment when his resolve, his doubt, his instinct toward survival through fitness, crested its Continental Divide, after which the rain that was this woman's fierce desire to share, of all things, a Buick Electra with a man she had just met flowed toward a new — foreign, unfamiliar — ocean. Not his Atlantic. Not her Pacific. Somewhere equidistant: the muddy Gulf of Mexico.

"Offer him two."

"Two hundred?" Maria said.

"God, no. Even if it's twenty years old, it runs good and the mileage is low. He'll want more, but he'll come down. For you. Since he's a family friend, I mean. I did not figure on making a deal so quickly, so I don't have that much on me, but I can head back to my hotel and have it for you in an hour if that's okay."

"Of course," she said, so quickly that he wondered whether she was even listening, whether whatever desire was driving her to purchase a car with a stranger meant more to her than when she was repaid or even whether she was repaid at all.

That she trusted him so readily did not mean that he ought to treat the transaction so casually himself.

"Before you go, though, there are terms to go over."

"What terms? Can't I just write him a check and be done with it?"

"Not with him. Terms to discuss with *me*."

"Oh. Well. What terms?"

"Whose name will the title be in? What about maintenance? How will we share it? What sort of schedule? Three and a half days on, then we switch? Or every other day?"

"I'm pretty flexible," she said. "Can't we work all that out later?"

"Actually," he said, "I've changed my mind."

"Why?"

"Because you want it too bad. Because you've let desire cloud your reason. Because you're impatient, and impatience breeds sloppiness."

Instead of arguing with him, she looked away, at the multicolored plastic flags strung between telephone poles lining the lot. Marcus did not find her reaction encouraging.

"I think I need to know more," he said.

"About what?'

"About why you're doing this."

She nodded, as if she was about to tell him more. But she didn't. Instead she said, "I can see how you might think I am impatient. I get it. And I get why you'd want to know more. But if I have to tell you exactly? I couldn't. I can't do that. So if that is your deal breaker, if you need to know everything up front before you enter into this, I guess it's time for me to apologize."

"For what?"

"For taking up your time."

"It's okay," he said, because it felt okay. Marcus had time. He liked thinking of something besides his own failure, his shameful escape. He'd grown so defensive when she'd intimated that he was rigid, but in fact he had his list in his back pocket. That it included items like a song by Cream among his most pressing needs only meant that he wanted to be seen as a more interesting and less conventional person. Some woman named Maria with whom he might share a Buick was also not on his list, but maybe it was time he quit making lists of things he had and things he needed.

He was suddenly exhausted from the previous night's travails, the lack of sleep. The BLT and cheddar had long since been consumed by the effort it took to stand in a car lot in the hot sun circulating words and the ideas they suggested.

"Do you know that taco place just a few blocks from here? Across the street from that grocery store?

"Azteca?"

"See if he has two keys. We can work out the rest of the details over lunch. What are you drinking?"

"Dos Equis. Get a pitcher, with extra limes."

"Trying to get me drunk?"

"You don't strike me as much of a drinker."

"Well. it's a good thing I'm not," he said, "because one of us has to drive."

BOBBY KEPLER TALKED TO her about things she barely understood—titles and tags—and Maria might have paid more attention had there not been something in the way he spoke to her, and looked at her, and eventually did not look at her, that made her consider, instead of what buying a car with a strange ex–Venus flytrap farmer would do for her—how it might help her in ways she *felt* more than would ever be able to say, had she been forced to say it—how such a thing might look to others. But Bobby Kepler did not know that she'd just met Marcus that afternoon on the lot. Unless it was obvious?

Maria liked to think that she was beyond worrying about what people thought of her. All these years she had worked hard to cultivate an impervious air. She had convinced herself that she came across not as aloof but as confident and secure, but of course she cared. She'd never met Bobby Kepler or heard his name before that morning, but here she was, studying the corners of his mouth to see if they tightened with suspicion.

Well, it was her money. She'd wasted way more than twenty-five hundred bucks on rent money in the past six months. She wrote out a check, signed the paperwork.

"Any questions?" said Bobby Kepler.

"Only," said Maria, "I wonder if there are two keys?"

"Afraid you'll lose one? I hear you, I'm bad for that myself. Pre-owneds don't usually come with a spare but I can run down and get you an extra made and have it for you when you come back to pick up the vehicle."

Walking to the restaurant to meet Marcus, Maria decided that her father had cared too much what people thought of him. She had not seen it then, for she hadn't seen *him* then, had barely noticed him unless he was waylaying Randy with his talk of horsepower and Holley four-barrels. At the time she thought he'd abandoned her just as she reached puberty, as if the changes in her body and, far scarier, her personality were threatening to him somehow. His retreat, however, had nothing to do with her, her maturity or moods, for those changes happened to be timed to her mother's switch from first shift to third. Or, as Maria had come to think of it, her mother's long stint of double shifts, which now seemed synonymous with her two-timing, emphasizing her mother's most notable strength: her tireless devotion to the completion of the task at hand.

But her father just hurt. He lost one job, got another, quit that one; eventually he hardly ever left the house. Maria wondered whether he was so embarrassed by his wife's public abandonment that he put off going to the doctor until the cancer had spread to this lungs. From which she might deduce that caring too much about what others thought was potentially lethal. Though not caring—shrugging off entirely the opinions of others—might extend your life, but the years you'd gain would also be isolated, lonely.

There was always somewhere in between, a spot sweet with middleness, a compromise. You never hit it straight off, unless by accident. You worked to find it and you worked to keep it as you settled into that realm of not quite this and definitely not that, the slender but accommodating province of Somewhat.

When she arrived at the restaurant, Marcus was waiting for her on the patio, attempting to eat a taco, only he had no idea how, having obviously been brought up on the much less interesting but more manageable bread. Above his nose he held the taco, swooping it mouthward for a bite. She would have laughed had she not just bought a car with the man. But it wasn't as if she had to share meals with him, or political opinions or, for God's sake, bodily fluids. Just make this work. She could make it work, and regardless of how badly he handled a taco, she believed he could, too.

Coshocton, Ohio, 1985

Lawrence Simpson was a big man. When he went to buy a car, he'd had in mind a car that could handle his size up front—steering wheel needed to tilt, seat needed to move way on back. He'd picked a Buick because he had driven his mother around in her LeSabre growing up in Cleveland. Ronald Stallings, whose wife sung in the choir with him, had got on over at a Buick place owned by a white man out toward Bedford and had given Lawrence a fair deal on an Electra, light blue and brand new. He kept his car extra clean inside and out and he was careful at the high school where he taught math to park as far from the building as he could. There was no separate lot for faculty, and some of these students, seemed like they should never have been granted a license, the way, when classes got let out, they took to squealing up and down the street with their windshields shaking from the bass, to where babies a block away woke up crying out of their naps.

Lawrence had so far not suffered a scratch on his Buick, but he knew the kids would gather to watch him climb in or out of it and slap each other's hands, falling all out over how his car sank when he got in and sprung back up when he got out. He'd see them off to the side, falling out and high-fiving, but what could he do about it? Put them all in detention? Lawrence Simpson had been fat all his life. He had taken a job out here with these small-town folks and he had got to where he liked them. Nice folks mostly, and kids are going to make fun wherever they live, and around here there wasn't so much to do besides watch some fat somebody get in or out of a car. Kids are just going to make fun. Shoot, he did. He stopped acting ugly when he started going to church regular in college, but he still liked to cut up some with the women in the cafeteria and some of the other teachers. And at least those kids did not have to see him get out of his old car, that Nissan. Shocks on that car were so sprung the cops took to stopping him, acting like he was hauling drugs. Said one side of the car was leaning, and all it took for them to see why was to walk up to the car and see the way his stomach pushed up against the steering wheel even with the seat as far back as it would go. Being a black man in the United States of America, even up here in Ohio, where they like to act like all the racists are down south still, he was used to cops stopping him for not a thing in this world. Since he had owned his Buick, though, not one time had they yanked him off over to the shoulder.

Lawrence loved his Buick. It was the first new car he had owned. He didn't make all that much money teaching but he didn't have a whole lot to spend it on. He sent some every month to his mama, paid his bills. Rest he guess he ate up. He used to pray all the time for God to cut out whatever inside him made him so blessed hungry, but God said, Lawrence, I made you big for a purpose and you must not question that purpose. Lawrence didn't drink or chase women, which left him enough every month after he paid off his loan for the Buick to eat about what he wanted.

Lawrence was getting his classroom in order one morning when Althea Thompson stopped by. Althea was a pretty girl, and the way she moved down the hallway it was clear this fact had been pointed out to her.

"Hi, Mr. Simpson," said Althea in that cotton-candy voice of hers.

"Althea," said Lawrence. He did not believe in being garrulous with his students.

"Your room look good."

"Thank you, Althea." He used to try and correct the children's grammar, but he was so busy telling them what not to say, it just made them favor even more incorrect usage and slang. So he decided long ago to lead by example. He spoke in a voice clear and deep, and at church when he sang the old hymns and contemporary gospel that filled his heart with love for the Lord Jesus Christ our Savior, it felt sometimes to Lawrence as if all the humiliation he had endured on account of his size was worth the thunderous voice he lifted up in worshipful praise to the Almighty.

"Mr. Simpson, I know you're busy. I'm in the homecoming court? You know we getting ready to have our homecoming parade on Friday? Well, Miss Carruthers, she's in charge, she wanted me to ask you, could we use your car in the parade?"

"Miss Carruthers did?" Miss Carruthers was a white home-ec teacher with hair that looked to Lawrence like straw out of a scarecrow. He had hardly any more than spoken to that woman, and how did she come to know what he drove?

"Mr. Simpson, you got a *nice* car."

"Thank you, Althea. And what would be involved in this? There wouldn't be anything applied to the surface of the vehicle, would there?"

"Oh, no, sir, we're not going to mess with it. It'd just be, you know, all of us in the homecoming court, we get to ride in the parade."

"And the parade is Friday afternoon the day of the game, is that correct?"

"Yes, sir."

"And what time would you be needing me to show up?"

"Well, see, you could just give us the keys right after fourth-period bell rings 'cause, see, we got to go—"

"Hold up, child," said Mr. Simpson. "Who I'm going to give my keys to, now?"

"Well, you can just let Miss Carruthers have them if you want."

"Why would I do that?"

"Well, see, it's going to be—do you know Derek Lee?"

"Basketball?"

"Yes, sir, he on the team. See, he's my escort."

"Is he your boyfriend?"

"No, sir, I said he's my *ess*cort."

"And you're asking me to let that boy drive my Buick?"

"Just in the parade. He's not going to, like, drive it to Atlanta."

"And Miss Carruthers is going to oversee all this?"

"Yes, sir, but I mean, we're only going to be needing it for, like, one hour or two hours."

Mr. Simpson sighed. Was it vanity that made him say yes?

Pride that some white home-ec teacher with hair looked like it was pulled every morning out of a hay bale knew him as the owner of a sky-blue Buick Electra? Letting that basketball player drive his car made him so nervous that the night before the parade he stopped off at the bakery and ordered a German chocolate cheesecake with cherry topping and ate half when he got home and prayed to God for guidance because he had about decided he was going to take a taxi to school and say his Buick was in the shop, because he did not like the way that basketball boy walked around the halls after the bell had rung like he was the principal, and he could not believe he had agreed to let that boy drive his Buick, and then he ate another two slices and then he prayed some more over it and over his weight, and God never came back at him telling him to call a cab in the morning, so he had no choice but to go on ahead and let that boy drive his Buick.

The next afternoon when he found Miss Carruthers he said he hoped she understood how special his car was and how he kept his car clean and regularly serviced and it was not a play toy, and she said in her white countrywoman way, "You have a beautiful car." Took her ten seconds to get the world "beautiful" out of her mouth. Made him feel a little bit better, though. He asked her where the best place to watch the parade might be, and she told him right downtown by the bank because it turned onto Main off Elm right there next to the bank and that way you couldn't see any of it coming, so it just came around the corner and surprised you.

Mr. Simpson had arranged to watch the parade with some of the other teachers and he told them what Miss Carruthers said about where to watch the parade and they all said that sounded fine. The street was filling up with merchants who must have left their stores wide open and all the young ones were sitting up on the curbs waiting to fill their pockets with Jolly Ranchers and Tootsie Rolls, and because Mr. Simpson had grown up over in Hough, where junkies would run right out and stick a gun in your neck if you went rolling down there with all your windows open throwing stuff out in the street and for sure no merchants would leave their stores unattended to stand out and cheer on the football team, and because he was filled with something he guessed might have been pride in this commu-nity, which he had felt in his two years here only with members of his congregation, and because even those smart-mouthed, sassy children who lined up in the parking lot waiting to watch him get in or out of his car and laugh and clap and ridicule were of God and God was in them, Lawrence Simpson felt like reaching his arms out wide and gathering those he could encompass and pulling them to his chest.

He could hear the drums of the marching band for blocks, bouncing off the tops of the buildings, before the ambulance, its lights flashing and its siren singing, came around the corner. That Miss Carruthers had set them up right, for theirs was a fine spot to view the parade. First came the band playing that "Roller-coaster" song by the Ohio Players out of Dayton. Lawrence listened mostly to gospel but sometimes he switched the radio to a Top 40 station and he remembered liking that song back when it came out, and even though the band was squawky and the two boys on the tuba who were supposed to be laying down the bass could not keep time, the drums off the buildings and the trumpets stair-stepping up and down that funky riff had Lawrence swaying a little. Half the kids and some of the grown-ups were straight-out shaking it in a way that would have seemed to Lawrence shameful had there not been such pride in the air. Everybody clapped and hollered when a flat-bed truck carrying the football team swung around, the boys hanging all off the back and calling out to their friends and cutting up.

Then the first car carrying the homecoming court came around the corner, and Lord, it was a Corvette with that Debra Joyner he had tried to teach simple algebra stretched right out across the hood. Surely sweet Jesus Althea would not . . . but before he could even start to breathe hard, here came Althea atop his Buick. She was wearing some tight dress and black lacy stockings and had her high-heeled shoes splayed out right up by his ornament. Basketball Derek caught sight of Mr. Simpson in the crowd and, seeing the look on his face, raised a finger off the steering wheel at him and grinned, and the worst part of it all was not how that girl stretched out across the hood of his vehicle had lied in order to defile his Buick with her wanton posturing but the way the sunlight cut down off the roof of the bank and lit the side of the Buick and made the shape of its rear look to Lawrence *like* a woman.

It was then that Lawrence understood what he had to do: take that Buick back to Stallings even though he knew he'd take a big loss on it. He would not dare sell it local, because it would not do to have it anywhere here where he might run into it. Up the street the band had stopped to show off some stepping and the Buick was stuck right in front of him and he raised his eyes up to the blue above the buildings across the street rather than look at what had seemed to him when he bought it a heavenly hue.

He had loved that car. He had worshipped it in a way that he ought not to be worshipping some craven image cast not in the glow of godliness. He already had his food to say, God made me how I am and I'm not perfect, and he did not need any other thing to atone for when judgment came. He loved that car, loved it so much, too much, it had to go on away from here.

Pinto Canyon, Texas, 2004

When, in the night, as the trains rumbled past across the street and the Fina sign shone brightly through the thin curtains of his room, and Marcus lay awake filled with terror at the agreement into which he had so blithely entered, he consoled himself with thoughts of how sweet a ride was that Buick. On his disastrous excursion to the border, he had discovered that Texas roads were bumpy with gravel and in the F-150 he had felt the roughness of the macadam in his groin. Lying naked in bed thinking of the Buick also activated sensors down south, bringing not discomfort but a curious and somewhat embarrassing stirring. He could see getting it up over a truck, but a twenty-year-old Buick?

Certainly it was the car itself and not the woman, who was clearly no more interested in him than he in her. Marcus did check her finger for a ring but only out of reflex. He had long ago developed this habit with any woman he came into contact with, in the way he might, as an armchair botanist, categorize a plant by phylum and species. Of course her ringlessness did not mean she was without partner, especially these days. The word *partner* reminded him of his sister and it crossed his mind that this Maria whatever her last name was (she'd never said, and he'd responded in kind by withholding his own) might prefer her own tribe. You could not tell by looking. Annie was in no way what they called butch. Once, he had jokingly asked her if she was a lipstick lesbian, a term he had heard while selling condos in Nags Head with coworkers given to endless and graphic appraisal of every woman they saw, and applied liberally to any woman they deemed "fuckable" who did not respond to their come-ons.

"Do you see any stick on my lips?" she'd said. It was during one of her rare trips back home. They were sitting on the porch watching shadows claim the sandy drive.

"I don't believe it's supposed to be a literal term," he said.

"So, what, it's a metaphor?"

"Okay, sorry, Jesus, I didn't mean to offend you," he said.

"There are as many kinds of gay women as there are straight women."

"Got it," said Marcus, although he did not, having previously assumed that either you liked men or you liked women or sometimes both equally or even disproportionately, though this notion of crossing the border at whim seemed to be roundly discredited by both provinces.

What did he care what this woman did, or with whom? The only thing that might keep him awake again in the night was if she turned out to have been married more than thrice. He'd never understood the types who, having failed a second time (which was not in the least unconscionable, no more than was the pursuit of getting it right that had landed Marcus in this hotel room), insisted on repeating their mistakes. Such blind faith in an institution that, statistically, was unstable to begin with, was surely a sign of what the pop psychologists called codependency. Marcus wasn't sure he even believed in such a thing, given that its opposite would be total equality if not harmony in such a notoriously volatile arena as relationships. At forty-seven he had not once—unless he counted the earliest days of him and Rebecca, which were blurry with the headlong delirium of finding something wondrous when you had nearly given up on it—encountered such cohesion. And he had been married himself, but only once and at such an early age and so briefly he never even saw fit to tell Rebecca about it.

Marcus did not know why he was even thinking about such things, though his rumination had quickly quelled the sheet tenting. Still, welcome or not, the tangent touched off the slowly seeping blackness, and to sandbag the tide he thought of the car and only the car, a hulk of steel and chrome and vinyl devoid of the messiness of unhinged humans. When the light of morning tinted his curtains, he rose and, still naked, made a list on a long legal pad of things that might rival in sweetness the experience of navigating that low-slung Electra.

1. Round water bed, curvy woman, rainy afternoon.
2. Slow-dancing to "I'm Your Puppet" by Bobby Purify.
3. Sectional sofa in a sunken-ranch house living room circa 1972.
4. I am talking velour tracksuit.

His list making was so successful in holding off the water that he flipped to another page and got to work on a schedule. The day before, over lunch and a couple of beers, Maria had seemed reluctant to decide how to divide their time with the car until the car was in hand. Which left the task to him, for the sharing of that sweet chariot called for good fencing if he and Maria were to succeed even briefly at co-ownership.

Being a product of the American public school system, Marcus was an ace at chart making. The making of charts as educational tools had its detractors, but Marcus had never been one of them, as it was one of the few things he had learned in school that served him well later in life. One thing he had discovered was that women love a crazy homemade chart. Chart-as-aphrodisiac was not mentioned in fourth grade, but this was of course to Marcus's mind the true value of education, the way it served not those purposes for which it was intended but far more interesting ones that were inadvertently stumbled upon.

He decided to make a couple of charts: one in which Her Lowness (for first among the chores that fell to them was the naming of the vehicle) switched hands every other day, and another chart in which the exchange was made mid-week. The first chart went quickly; the latter raised some questions. Most people—perhaps 99 percent of Americans—did not seem to drive on Sunday mornings. Oh, they motored to and from church if they were churchers, and afterward drove over to put on the feed bag at some sneeze-guarded buffet, but in general, wherever you went in this country, the streets of Sunday morning resembled a B movie about a biological disaster. Marcus had always loved a Sunday morning ride. He went to bed early Saturday nights in anticipation. Through the empty streets he cruised, the world his and only his. Often he would stop for coffee in some brightly lit chain gas station and find no one behind the counter. Then through a steel door came the rush of water through pipes, and a sluggish employee in a red smock would emerge irritably from the back of the store, and Marcus would skedaddle rather than let small talk violate the sanctity of his Sunday mornings. Surely Maria would not mind if he helped himself, on the schedule, to this time every week, given her lack of interest in the details of their partnership. Though it took him away from his charting and was no more desirable a thought than how many times she had tied the knot, Marcus contemplated again the mysterious nature of her desire to share the car with him. He'd outright asked her why she was doing it and had been deflected with what at the time seemed to stem from a desire for privacy but now struck him as ominous. For she did not appear at all interested in the car itself. Was it the act of buying the car with a stranger that she desired?

Unnameable dread so paralyzed him that his pen bore a widening ink stain on the chart, as if black water were spilling out of it, drawn not from a cartridge hidden inside the pen but from the hand that held it. Marcus looked down at the soiled chart and recognized in its former orderliness that it was not the leap of faith involved in the act he craved but the back-and-forth of it, the compromise and sacrifice that results when you rise out of yourself into the wider world.

Into the wider world he went as soon as the sun rose, seeking relief from the forces that had ruined his beautiful chart. He'd counted out a thousand in tens and twenties from his stash and headed down the street to the branch of the

TransPecos, which he remembered from his encounter with the park ranger, for larger bills. The teller was pleasant enough when she waved him forward from the line, but once he stated his business, her demeanor shifted so noticeably that Marcus, still reeling from that blot of ink, asked if there was a problem.

"No, sir," said the teller, glancing over his head at a desk where sat an overweight Hispanic man who was obviously her superior. "Why would there be a problem?"

"I don't know," said Marcus, aware, too late, that his question only made things worse. Maybe the woman could tell that the money was not his to spend. The bills felt too rough or too polished to her touch, as if they had been printed up in the back of a tattoo parlor. Might as well be counterfeit, given that he was posing as a man who, by purchasing a car with a stranger, might somehow inch toward distant redemption.

It was only on the walk back to the hotel, his wallet so slim he did not feel it, that he realized the teller had suspected he was a drug dealer. Such operations were far more common in these parts, and involved, certainly, a steady conversion of small bills into big. That he felt better knowing that the woman took him for a criminal was not lost on Marcus, who returned to his room determined to create a chart suggesting in its spotlessness and clarity a conscience unsullied by second-guessing.

AT HOME MARIA'S MOTHER asked about the car, as Maria had known she would. What kind is it? How many miles? What was he asking for it? What did you offer? Was it Bobby or Pete you dealt with? Did it drive good? Did you remember to turn on the A/C to see did it work? Does it burn oil?

Maria answered those questions she knew how to answer and made up answers for the ones she did not. Yes, it burns oil, she said, and when her mother said, Why did you buy a car that burns oil, Maria said, What else would it burn, which made her mother quit scrubbing the stove top and study her daughter's face to see if she was joking. When she saw that Maria was not, she explained that by burning oil she meant, does it burn too much oil and she went on to explain exactly why that was bad, and Maria asked how you could tell by looking at a car how much oil it burned and her mother said you couldn't you had to drive it then check the engine, Didn't you even drive it and Maria said, Of course I drove it and after I drove it we looked at the hood and her mother said, You done what? and Maria said, I mean up under it and her mother said, Who's WE? And Maria said How do you know so much about cars anyway and her mother said, Well I've been driving one after another of them for thirty years so I guess I had to learn and then her mother said something she had said before more than once, which was that she did not understand how Maria had got on all these years without a car and Maria explained again that not everyone needs a car, that cars in fact are not all that good, that the emissions they give off are terrible for the environment and her mother said again, Back when I was coming up they didn't have any such thing as an environment, and Maria held her breath and her mother said, Nor cholesterol either, and Maria laughed and her mother said, First one day all of a sudden they're saying don't mess with it, it will kill you, you got to go get it checked at the doctor's and then the next day lo and behold seemed like overnight they went and took the cholesterol out of everything, and Maria shook her head and her mother said, Fat, too, woke up one morning went to the store and everything I picked up and put in my cart said fat free on the label, I would have hated to have that job, wouldn't you, whoever stayed up all night getting the cholesterol and fat out of nearly everything on God's earth must've worked their tailbone off and Maria thought that her mother was not dumb at all so why did she like to pretend she was and her mother said, Well what did you do on a day when the buses won't running and Maria said I waited until they *were* running and Maria's mother said that seemed like it'd be a pain having to depend on some schedule, did they run pretty much all night and Maria said she didn't usually take a bus anywhere in the middle of the night and her mother said something Maria did not hear because she was lost in a reverie about her mother coming to visit her dozens of times over the past ten years in all the various places she'd lived. Maria and her mother on a bus, her mother placing the coins in the tray by the driver and learning to keep moving down the aisle instead of standing there holding everything up watching her money drop into the receptacle beneath the tray and learning also not to stare at the other people on the bus who had been riding buses for so long that their faces reflected the pavement over which the bus traveled, and her mother relaxing out of her self-consciousness into easy conversation with Maria on a crowded bus, unconcerned that others around them might hear her discussing the movie they'd just seen—Maria and her mother at a movie!—and then, when they neared Maria's apartment, Maria's mother looking up and seeing the florist on the corner of her block and saying, This is us, right? and reaching up to lightly yank the cord signaling the driver to stop and talking on through the ding of the bell and rising as the bus lumbered up to the curb and talking, still talking, but not about the movie, about the car again: Who's WE? she was saying, and Maria said, What? and her mother said, You said WE looked up under the hood, who is we, By WE do you mean you and Bobby Kepler or you and Pete Kepler because even though those boys were good friends with your daddy back in high school and I am not saying they are not honest, still they're out to make something off those cars and I just hope when you say We looked under the hood you realize that even though those boys are not crooks, far from it, they still might just be telling you what you want to hear and Maria said That's like when men tell you that any other man who is nice to you is just being nice to you because he wants to sleep with you and Maria's mother said, Well, and Maria said, Why can't some men just be decent people and Maria's mother said, Maria, I don't know about all that, I haven't said anything to you about any of that, all I am saying to you is you said WE LOOKED UNDER THE HOOD and all I was asking you this whole time is Who is WE and Maria said Okay.

"VERY CREATIVE," MARIA SAID about the charts Marcus had slaved over, which depressed him, for *creative* was a threadbare term to his mind. They sat in a booth in the restaurant of his hotel, charts spread across the Formica. She had called his room when he had returned from the bank to tell him that the car was ready and asked if he'd like to come along to pick it up.

Something told him it would be best to decline, since the car salesman already assumed they were together, and Marcus did not care to propagate any lies here in this town where he had hesitated and been rewarded with what seemed to him a brand-new identity, as if he was a ward of the federal witness protection program. "Come by afterward and I will pay you and we can talk business over lunch," he'd said. She showed up wearing the same outfit—low-cut jeans and a tank top—though her black hair was pulled into a tight ponytail, which made more prominent and noticeable the fine bones of her face.

Not that he cared what she looked like. He'd hardly be seeing her from now on, only when they exchanged the vehicle, the key to which she presented him attached to a twist tie.

"Nice key chain," he said. "Very creative. Which reminds me, we've not yet discussed accessories."

"Excuse me?"

"What's your position on air fresheners—for instance, the ones shaped like Christmas trees?"

"Smelly."

"Ditto. Bumper stickers?"

"Keep it to yourself."

"Really? Across the board? What about 'Viva Terlingua'?"

"Terlingua is a place people go to drink themselves to death. In tiny trailers in the desert. So the saying makes no sense."

"'Somewhere in Texas, a Village Has Lost Its Idiot'?"

She sighed.

"Guess that one might get us pulled over, right?"

"Not likely. The cops around here are too busy trying to catch smugglers to worry about your politics."

"What's your position on smuggling?"

"My position is that you lost your last vehicle due to carelessness and you should maybe try harder to keep this one, especially since it's only half yours."

"So no hikes along the border?"

"What you do with that car on your own time is your business, so long as it doesn't end up impounded and sold to some dealer at the Border Patrol auction in Del Rio. Please remember to take the keys with you when you exit the vehicle. Do I need to paste a reminder on the dash?"

"I think I got it. What about my charts?"

She looked at them. She placed them side by side, then put one atop the other. She appeared to study them carefully.

"Very creative," she said.

"Well, thanks. Creative Individual is a term to which I have long aspired. But tell me, which plan do you favor?"

"I suppose we should just try one. See how it goes. And then, if problems arise, go for the other."

Marcus studied the charts to avoid looking at her. Was she affecting this casual attitude to appear easygoing, or was he correct in thinking that she was only after the kill and would leave the carcass to scavengers like him?

"Which do you want to try first?" he said, staring out the window, pretending that it mattered not a whit to him, either.

"I like the border on this one," she said, pointing to a block of hieroglyphic-like doodling running around the edge of the paper.

"Thanks, but I'm not really talking aesthetics."

"Doesn't it depend on your daily schedule? I mean, I haven't started working yet but I will this week and I'm sure I'll know more. As, I assume, you will also?"

He'd not given much thought to his work schedule. The items on his list were purposefully general so as not to limit his options. Buy some wheels. Secure gainful employment. Far easier to tick off—and it was the sight of that yellow paper stained with cross-outs that would make Marcus feel as if he was not merely marking time here—if his to-dos were open to all possibilities.

"I guess, sure."

"What kind of work are you looking for?"

"Oh, I'm flexible. What about you? I know you said you were starting a business, but what sort of business is it?"

"A successful one, we hope." Marcus wondered who 'we' was, but he did not feel he could ask, and she wasn't giving him time to ask. "Not much around here for Venus flytrap farmers. There's a hydroponic tomato farm outside Fort Davis."

"That's a pretty far drive, isn't it? I don't know how I would get there on the days you have Her Lowness."

"Her who?"

"I forgot to tell you I named it."

"Her Lowness?"

"Play on words. You know, instead of Her Highness?"

"Right, I get it. I was just wondering why guys always call their boats and cars 'she.'"

"Maybe to honor the women in their life?"

Why was it that, around Maria, he managed to say so many things wrong, or so many wrong things? The last thing he wanted was for her to think he was honoring her in some way.

"I mean, you know, women in general. Womanhood."

"Right. Back to the tomato plant. Every morning the vans from Presidio stop at the Fina for breakfast. I'm sure they could squeeze you in, and it's right across the street."

"I have some savings," he said, and he immediately regretted it, for what if Her Lowness threw a rod tomorrow and Maria turned out to have spent her last dime on her part of the car?

"Sorry, I wasn't trying to pry," she said, in a way that made him think his regret was noticeable and that made him feel a little less reckless for admitting he was flush. Though he wasn't flush, not at all—he was just about to hand over a tenth of what he'd counted on lasting him at least six months, and this hotel, though cheap by city standards, was eating away daily at his budget, and wasn't it strange that, because the money belonged to his sister, if not the Bank of America, he was even tighter with it than if it were rightfully his to spend? Shouldn't he be rolling up fifties to snort drugs through, leaving twenty-dollar tips for a breakfast taco, buying drinks for the whole of the Hitchin' Post Saloon? Isn't that the way embezzlers went about disposing of their evidence? Acting out a not-so-subconscious desire to get caught?

"One thing I notice about these charts," she was saying, "is that on both of them you seem to have reserved Sunday morning for yourself."

Marcus said, "Yes."

"Otherwise we each have the car every other weekend. But the weekend does not include Sunday morning. Are you a churchgoer?"

Sunday morning rides were his church, ergo he was not lying when he said yes.

"Huh. I wouldn't have pegged you, not that I have a thing against it. What flavor?"

"Oh, I like to try different denominations."

"Well, around here, it's mostly Catholic."

"That'll work."

She studied his eyes, the set of his mouth, for much longer than she ever had, as if she were trying to figure out, not whether, but why he was lying.

"I guess if I need to go anywhere on a Sunday morning I can borrow my mother's car."

"Do you live with your mother?"

"For now."

"And your father?"

"He passed away."

"Sorry to hear that," he said, but rotely, for as much as he was curious, he did not want to know details of her private life, lest he have to open up about his.

"Thanks. My father and I had not spoken in years when he died."

"Oh. Ouch."

"Yeah. It was bad. He was . . . I didn't . . ."

Marcus studied her while she searched her mind for what words might work next, but suddenly she grabbed the every-other-day schedule and said, "Let's go with this one."

Marcus had come to favor the half-week schedule. That he did not feel free to make his wishes known, even though he had asked *her* to choose, both surprised and worried him.

Was their every negotiation going to turn into a skirmish in his mind? He'd gone into this declaring that he had nothing at stake but the car itself, and he reminded himself that a car is all this was, and an ancient one at that.

"Where is the car?" Maria's mother had said when she came home from the motel to find Maria busy in the kitchen and the driveway empty. Just the day before, her mother had said, when Maria brought the Buick home from the lot, "Looks like a keeper." That was all. She'd looked it over in a way Maria felt was purposefully cursory, no doubt because she had just two days earlier hounded her with questions, and the only question her mother really seemed to want Maria to answer (who is WE?) Maria had ignored. So Maria assumed her mother's indifference was slightly vengeful, especially since "keeper," coming from her mother, was high praise, for her mother kept so little.

Considering how few things her mother kept led Maria to ponder her own need to travel light. She'd asked Beverly to ship her some things from her apartment, mostly clothes. Of the seven boxes that had arrived by UPS a few days earlier, six still sat taped and in the closet off the carport where her father had once kept his tools. Then there was her minimalist decorating aesthetic, which she had always claimed was a reaction to the tacky backdrops of the photos she had developed at the drugstore but which she was beginning to think she might have been born with. "Everything I have I give away and it goes away," Maria had once read in a poem in a magazine in the waiting room of her dentist. The lines so reminded Maria of her estranged mother that her hygienist, cleaning her teeth thirty minutes later, had asked her repeatedly if she was in pain.

She was in pain, but not from dentistry or even her mother's barren life. The line had reminded her of something her mother had said after Maria told her she was pregnant: "Do you not want to put it up?" Maria knew her mother was trying to be motherly, to present all options, though her choice of words, the way she left out the most important part of her sentence—"for adoption"—made Maria tearful and furious. "Put it up"? She might as well have said "give it away." And Maria had thought about it, giving the baby to someone who could not have one and would take better care of it than two kids not yet out of high school, but she knew two things: that Randy would not rest with that child in the world until he found it, and that giving it away would not make it go away.

"Would you like me to take you for a spin?" Maria had said to hide her hurt over her mother's dismissal of the Buick.

"Not now, I've got to run back up to the motel shortly," her mother had said. And when Maria was alone with the empty house and the empty car in the drive, she'd thought again about that line in that poem, which after all these years still haunted her. Maybe her mother was able to give things away and make them stay away because she had chosen to stay here, where everything that had ever happened to her had taken place within thirty square miles, rather than flee. Her mother's heart was so windswept, so uncluttered. Sometimes Maria saw next to no difference between her mother and this place where she'd been born and had lived out her whole life.

Maria wondered if her flight to the rain-soaked Northwest watered the part of her that dried up tragedy and swept it out of sight. It took her years to get used to the wetness, the lush and dripping foliage, the damp and ferny ground of the forests. She craved it and it terrified her. Depending on her mood, she saw it as either penance for sins committed in a place given only to dust and thorn, or a cleansing, an immersion, salvation. Sometimes the lack of sunlight, the shortness of the days, the fungus and the mold, holy Christ, the mushrooms and the giant slugs on the sidewalk, filled her with terror that was mostly longing for what she had forsaken, and at such times she had learned to convince herself that her sensitivity to climate and topography, her tendency to imbue landscape with mood, was but another indulgence, something to be shorn. Just get on the bus and go to work, Maria. Her new home was neither heaven nor asylum. It was just a place filled with more people in a square mile than lived in her entire county back home.

The day Maria brought the car home, her mother had ignored the car, but when it was not in the drive the next night, she was suddenly interested.

"Well, where is the car?" her mother said that evening when she came home from work. "Don't tell me it's already in the shop?"

Maria was at work on dinner. She'd begun to cook for them, trying out recipes on her mother that she thought she might introduce in her restaurant. Her mother was stingy with her reactions and would comment on a dish only if asked, and mostly she would say it was good, but in a way that made Maria think she preferred take-out brisket or enchiladas smothered in *queso.* That night she did not care what her mother thought of her meal—a risotto with squash and onions simmered in wine, and a salad of organic endive and heirloom tomatoes she'd found at the farmer's market the previous weekend—for she simply needed work to do, chopping and stirring, while she told her mother about the car.

"No, it's not in the shop. It runs fine. It hardly burns any oil."

Maria paused, and her mother, as always, did not ask her to continue but made clear with the pinch of her lips that she did not care for gaps in the conversation, as conversation was, like most things, a transaction, and there were other transactions imminent, and let's get on with it, shall we? I've got to run back to check on the motel here directly after we eat whatever in the world that is you're stirring the life out of on the stove top.

"Remember you asked me the other night who 'we' was?"

Her mother played dumb. Maria was so irritated that she vowed to speak into the pot of simmering rice from that point on.

"You know, when I said 'we looked under the hood' and you kept asking me who 'we' was?"

"Was it not one of the Kepler boys?"

"No. I met this man at the car lot. How I met him was, he wanted the same car. The Buick," she said, remembering to call it by name, as if this might make a difference in what she was about to reveal.

Maria took a deep breath. "Anyway," she said, "we went in on the car together."

"'Anyway'?" said her mother, as if this word—which did suggest that she was only continuing a casual conversation, one that so far had been understood by both parties — were the most befuddling part of her confession.

"We're going to share it," said Maria.

"What guy? Who?"

"He's really nice," said Maria, stirring the risotto, grateful for the risotto, for risotto must be stirred, as stirring creates friction, which releases the starch from the grains of rice and results in its necessary creaminess. Thank God for risotto, thought Maria as she poured more wine into the pot, and then she said, "He's a farmer from back east. He was moving to somewhere in Mexico but his truck got stolen somewhere down along the river, so he needed—"

"This man is Mexican?"

"No, he's from North Carolina. So he needed a car because—"

"And you met this man at Kepler's lot? You didn't already know him?"

"I'm trying to tell you what happened. I'm going to, if you would stop interrupting me."

"Good God Almighty, Maria. You went in on that car with a total stranger?"

Maria kept stirring. A wooden spoon would be preferable because it actually bruises the grains. But Maria's mother did not own a wooden spoon.

"Was it that you needed money? Why did you not just ask me for it?"

"It wasn't the money."

"You just wanted to share a car with some man who got his truck stolen at the border?"

"He was hiking, I think. It happens. You read about it in the paper."

"And here I thought you'd grown up."

"I know what I'm doing."

"Well, what? Tell me. What is this about?"

"I have to do it. I had this feeling about it and I had to do it because I guess it has to do with—"

"With what?"

"I was about to say. With what happened. Why I left."

Her mother sat down at the kitchen table. She had so rarely seen her mother sit down in her kitchen without being asked to—she often even ate standing up—that Maria gasped.

"I told you we could share the Cherokee," her mother said to the table. "If you're looking to share a vehicle."

"It's not the same. You're my mother."

"Meaning I'm not going to take off with it one night and sell it in El Paso for drinking money? Is that it? You need somebody to do you wrong? You need somebody to treat you bad so you can feel good about feeling bad?"

"No," she said, so shocked and hurt by her mother's shallow psychological explanation of her motivation that she dropped the spoon in the pot and gripped the edges of the stove.

"My God in heaven," her mother said. "I just had no idea."

"About what? What did you not have an idea about?" said Maria, immediately ashamed of the defensiveness and even hatefulness in her voice, for she knew her mother felt betrayed and she was beginning to understand why and at the same time it wasn't any of her mother's business. Her mother would rather rewire a lamp than have an intimate and uncomfortable conversation with her daughter about the past. Maria asked her mother again what she had no idea about, and her mother, looking as dejected as Maria had ever seen her, said, "I just did not see it, I just didn't, I ought to have, I ought to."

KNOWING NOTHING OF THE musical tastes of the co-owner of Her Lowness did not stop Marcus from spending his day with the car hitting all the thrift shops he could find in search of cassette tapes. The idea overtook him in the night, as did most of his ideas, lucid or not, and any idea solid enough to pierce his state of semiconsciousness struck him as more profound. So seized was he with his plan that he could not return to sleep. His task was essential, it could not be put off; hadn't he, looking over Her Lowness in the lot, planned the appropriate playlist? It wasn't as if the radio were much of an option. He'd switched it on once but a quick twist of the dial had turned up static, save for a couple of Norteño stations, some preaching, and the NPR affiliate he had listened to on his way.

It never occurred to him that his search would be less than successful. In an area where the past was much celebrated and commodified—there were fossil shops, gem shops, Wild West trading posts, Mexican blanket shops, and several joints devoted to the exploitation of the aboriginals, which trafficked in trinkets blatantly Taiwanese and baskets supposedly woven by local Comanches—Marcus thought it plausible that he might discover, in some dusty box alongside such thrift-shop staples as albums by the Ray Price Orchestra and the novels of Irving Stone, a box brimming with obsolete tapes.

Before he even got out of bed, Marcus had jotted down

treasures the likes of which, if he even came close to matching them, would usher in a gratification nearly equal to unexpected sex.

Anything by the Chi-Lites
Merle Haggard
The song slash sermons of Shirley Caesar, especially "Don't
  Drive Your Mama Away"
James Gang Rides Again

The list reached the bottom of a legal pad, after which his ink stained the yellow paper with double columns. Once he started on a wish list, he could not stop, which was ironic in that the making of lists had in fact originally been prescribed to him by a monosyllabic psychologist to cure the condition for which Marcus, as a last resort, had paid the man a visit: his life had become ungovernable owing to impulse. He'd visited the man only once, not long before Rebecca left, when it became clear that he would lose his business and his sister's inheritance. What drove him to it was the realization that his idea to build the Flytrap Educational Center had come to him in the middle of one sleepless night and had been put into action—without consulting a soul, not Rebecca or Annie, whose financial futures stood to be affected by his decision— as soon as the bank opened the next morning. He'd waited outside in his car for two hours, sipping coffee, like a drunk in line waiting for the OPEN sign to switch on at the liquor store.

This was not the first time he'd acted on such an impulse. At nineteen he had met a girl at an outdoor festival held at a defunct racetrack and married her three days later, fittingly in the state of South Carolina, where there was no blood test required to see if you were marrying your cousin and where bad decisions were encouraged once you crossed out of North Carolina and encountered the massive, cheesy South of the Border, the Mexican-themed tourist trap infamous for its racial insensitivity and overpriced gasoline. That you could buy fireworks legally and get married in a matter of hours in this wretched state was telling, but Marcus liked this girl, whose name was Monte Gale, because she had curly hair down to her shoulders, spoke with a mountain accent so foreign to his ears she might have been Nova Scotian, and wore a straw cowboy hat, which she took off only to shower. He told no one in his family—actually he had told no one at all until he told the bearded doctor—about his marriage, which was only slightly harder to annul than it was to commit.

Though he did not cotton to psychological evaluation, his fifty minutes were far from a waste. Thank you, Doc, for encouraging the supposedly prophylactic benefits of list making. Intended to temper his rashness with forethought, the tactic actually contributed to it. The lists he made made no distinction between impulsive and rational.

Armed with fifty bucks from his stash he could ill afford to part with, Marcus set out on his journey. He had a rule: he could not ask the clerks if they had any cassettes, for numerous and obvious reasons. Such queries would rid the process of serendipity, not to mention mystery. No one in thrift shops ever indulged in the "Can I help you find something?" obsequiousness that marred the shopping experience in venues hawking the brand new. You were left on your lonesome to wander and poke.

But lonesome was what he too often felt. He spent too much time in his head. He'd been accused of same all his life. Besides, the clerks he encountered were exclusively women sixty and upward with faces chapped and wrinkled from high desert wind and sun. Craggy wisdom of the stripe that would do him no good.

"Do you have any cassette tapes?" he asked one in a store.

"Lord, you're going backward, aren't you?" said the woman.

"The past is not even past," said Marcus.

The woman looked at him long and blankly enough for him to want back inside his head. Rules were in fact necessary.

"If you ask me, it better be. I'm well shy *of* it."

That beautiful phrase again: "if you ask me." Anywhere else—back home in particular—he would have found it vain if not redundant. But when people in this place said it, it sounded modest, and entirely generous.

"I hear you," he said, which was something people said to discourage further conversation. It was what it was not. But Marcus meant it. He, too, was well shy of the past.

"I believe there might be some on a shelf with the books," the woman said, and Marcus found marvelous the fact that not even the clerks knew the stock.

Because the reign of the cassette tape coincided with his late adolescence and early twenties, his purchases were a sound track from high school and college. How could, in pursuit of obsolete technology, the past not be past? Most of his finds were things he was too much of a music snob back in the day to admit to liking. The first thing he found was a copy of Pure Prairie League's *Bustin' Out,* the big hit of which—a syrupy ballad called "Amie," featuring a fingerpicked solo geared, in its two-measure brevity, to the attention span of commercial radio—was the only weak song on the album. Next he found a still factory-sealed copy of the sound track from *Saturday Night Fever,* a secret vanity for years. Now that he was old enough to admit that disco did not entirely suck, he had no problems confessing that he admired Yvonne Elliman's version of "Hello Stranger," almost as much as the phenomenal original by Barbara Lewis.

By early afternoon he had a bag of hits as heavy as a sack of potatoes. And then at his last stop he found a case, dusty and stained but made of a black and crackly vinyl that would look good against the deep blue upholstery of Her Lowness. He could leave them for Maria, a present. When he transferred the contents of the sack to the case, there were only three empty slots. Only then did Marcus remember that he had no idea what sort of music his co-owner preferred. Since she owned half the vehicle, his tapes should take up only half the box. Reluctantly did he subtract some of his treasures and return them to his bag. He could bring them along, though, when it was his turn. But that would be a pain. On impulse he popped open the trunk and hid the bag in the tire well.

The next morning Marcus arrived at the DQ forty-five minutes early. He backed Her Lowness into a spot near the rear of the lot and decided to sit for a while and drink a cup of coffee. He remembered a friend from grad school who was divorced telling him that the most stressful and awkward part of the rearrangement of his family life was the picking up and dropping off of his children: "If I just pull up in the drive and blow the horn, my ex accuses me of acting like a bloody cab driver. If I park the car and ring the bell and come in, there is the great risk that my children will be subjected to the tense and toxic silence — or worse, outright hatefulness — that led to my decision to leave in the first place." When Marcus naively inquired if some mutually agreed-upon system might be worked out for the sake of the children, his friend looked at him with a mix of pity and incredulity. "Would that it were so easily solved," said his friend, "but of course if it were, I would still be living with her and there would be nothing to solve."

The Buick was not a child and Marcus had no reason to assume that there would ever be any tension over its exchange, since Maria was very particular about when and where the drop-off should take place: Marcus was to leave it at the parking lot of the Dairy Queen by eight on her mornings and vice versa. When he offered to deliver it directly to her house in exchange for a ride back, there was, in the way that Maria smiled while declining, a rigidity that Marcus, whose first impression of her was of an easygoing copilot who would leave up to him the majority of the smaller details, found vaguely alarming. As trite as it sounded, people were apt to change after their desires were met.

Sitting in the parking lot of the DQ watching the ranchers in pickups roll in off the highway to fuel their morning with food fast and greasy, Marcus watched a boy in a paper hat and brown DQ-issue polyester uniform wheel a mop bucket out the back door, dump it into a drain in the pavement. The sudsy water spilled wildly out of the bucket and began its surge toward Her Lowness, a black tide rising. Monte Gale in her cowgirl hat stretched across the bed of a Mexican-themed motel nearly thirty years ago. And in *only* her hat, her skin reddened and sweaty from sex. Marcus had gotten up and fetched her a cigarette from his pants pocket and lit one for himself, which he smoked naked on the balcony at dusk. Just beyond a cockleburred patch of grass and a fence separating the motel from an access road, cars and trucks fled north and south on I-95. Miami to Maine, that highway stretched, and he'd never been to New York. Plastic bags aloft in the breeze kicked up by the traffic caught in the diamonds of the chain link. Marcus was nineteen and he was married. His parents had been married for a quarter century at this point, but Marcus had seen them in the same room only twice in the past five years: once for a funeral, again for Annie's graduation from Sweet Briar. He had tried hard with Rebecca, initially at least, to prove wrong their careless way with love, but now he imagined his presence in her life relegated to a photo album packed in a box, in which his image was no more significant than one of those strangers who crop up in the background of pictures, caught by timing and chance forever in the frame.

He had not thought of Monte Gale in years and years. "Come back," she'd called to him as he studied the flow of traffic on the interstate, and the sex they had next was rhythmically disappointing, as if they were in different time signatures. At first Marcus thought it was because they were married, until he remembered that this was the first time they'd as much as touched while sober.

Was it the sudden wind whirlpooling dust and straw wrappers in the parking lot of the Dairy Queen that ushered in his fear that he'd Monte Gale'd again? Or was it the thought of his legal pad defiled with a list of cheesy records from his youth, a list he chose over *the* list, the one he'd made the morning after his truck was stolen? That list was a recipe for survival; though it was padded with the trivial, most of its items were responsible ones. Again he had been sidetracked by the inconsequential. "Of making many books there is no end," was one of the few quotes he remembered from the Bible, and did it not distinguish between word and deed?

Oh sweet Jesus. To distract himself from the tide, he tried to determine, from the swinging of the DQ sign and the rock of the chassis beneath him in the stronger gusts, which way the wind was blowing. He decided it was shooting down from Canada, down across the plains, nothing for thousands of miles to slow or divert it. Monte Gale had gotten up and pulled on her tight jeans and her halter top and announced that she had to be at work at three at some drugstore in some town Marcus had never heard of. In the parking lot of the DQ, Marcus reached for his legal pad to rip out the offending list but realized he'd left it in his room. At Monte Gale's truck, which turned out to be her daddy's truck, borrowed without permission, Marcus had stood at the window and said, "You know what, I can hitch back to my car, it's not really on your way, I don't want to make you late," and she said, "Well, are you sure?" Out the window of Her Lowness a bag blew by and Marcus leaped out to chase it down, aware of the group of older Hispanic men drinking coffee at a table by the window, and all the ranchers eating their breakfast tacos in their high-idling extended-cab trucks, watching him. In the parking lot of

South of the Border, Marcus had watched Monte Gale drive away in her daddy's truck, and that was the last he had seen of her, but he had heard soon enough from her daddy, who said, "Son, I am going to send you some paperwork, and if you don't sign it and get it back to my office in three days, I am going to come and find you and you will wish you had never left whatever shit-hole swamp you come from down there."

Marcus snatched the bag from the wind and strolled back to the Buick. No one in this town knew who he was. They had no idea that liens had been slapped on him, that his assets were frozen. *Slapped, frozen:* the terms were so histrionic it was difficult for Marcus to believe they had anything to do with him. But that, according to Rebecca, was the problem: he never thought any of it had anything to do with him.

The bag was stained with ketchup, which made the note he wrote to Maria feel all the more desperate. He sat with the bag propped on the steering wheel, trying to figure out how to say why he had done what he'd done. He could not say it was because he sensed her deep need, though he had told her, in their negotiations or what passed for them (the crazy way they went at each other in the parking lot of Fantastic Deals! firing off questions and answers as if they'd known each other for years, as if the script had been written for them, still felt unbelievable to Marcus, who had never communicated so quickly or easily with anyone), that he could not do it because she wanted it so badly. And yet he had done it. Because he could talk to her so easily, as if he'd known her for years? He knew nothing about her. A gust of wind rocked Her Lowness, his pen slipping. Maybe it had nothing to do with Maria, his decision; maybe it was the car itself. He wanted it so bad he would split it to get it. Others had wanted it before him, and he wondered about them as he stared at what he had written so far, which was "Dear Maria." That the car had hardly been driven suggested its former owners did not feel its pull as he did. Or maybe they loved it so much they felt driving it would be a crime? More object of desire than method of transportation? Had any of those before him been seduced by it, allowed it to sidetrack them from their purpose?

You can love without vision, and desire is almost always blind. And deaf to caution and reason and, Marcus decided, real damn dumb.

Dear Maria,

I have decided to push on down the road. Much as I love this town of yours, I believe my hesitating here would, as the poet said, get me lost. There are other reasons more abstract in nature. And as we discussed, there seem to be scant employment opportunities in the area for former Venus flytrap farmers. Not that I am unwilling

"Fuck me," Marcus said aloud to the ridiculous note on the ketchup-stained bag. "Just get to the point. She doesn't need to know anything but 'Here's the extra key, I'm out.'" He crossed out his overly elaborate and tonally annoying false start. He thought of going back into the DQ and asking for another bag, for he liked a bag over, say, a napkin because it suggested in the empty but easily fillable space some pocket of hidden, deeper meaning. But he liked *this* particular bag. It bore the signs of his trying to get things right. The stain implied further reflection if not agonizing over his decision. I *bled* over this decision, said the bag as he turned it over and began anew.

Dear Maria:

I have decided to head down to Mexico after all. ~~That was the original plan and I guess I got distracted?~~ Please consider my stake in the vehicle my going-away present. I'm not sure it would have worked out so well, our arrangement. ~~Seemed like a good idea at the time, though.~~ Hey, I left you some tunes! Not all these tapes were ones I would have bought back when they came out, but there's something about the perfectly good things that people get rid of that increases their value, you know? Especially if there is a lot of use left in them and you are lucky enough to realize it.

Marcus stopped writing. He put the bag on the seat beside him. He cradled the steering wheel with both arms and rested his forehead on the still-soft vinyl. What was he talking about? Why could he not just get in and out of anything? Why did he have to get carried away educating the public about something anyone could learn all they needed to know about in a half hour on the Internet? He knew the difference, of course, between Wikipedia and nature, but what, finally, did it matter, his grandiose notions about truth and meaning, about the pocket of possibilities between the layers of a bag, the value of things thrown out with life left in them still?

And yet he could not toss it out. He was not going to go inside the DQ again, not this morning, not ever. He went over the crossed-out sentences with his pen until not even he, who had written them, could decipher them, and he folded the bag in half so it might at least resemble a missive, and he took the key with its twist-tie chain and laid it atop the bag.

He was almost to his hotel when he heard behind him a sound it shocked him to recognize: the high-idling tenor of the Electra. Her Lowness in motion, its hum a song in his head, though not at all the type described as "stuck." But then he realized that Maria had come to give him his money back. He would pretend not to see her, even if she called to him. No good could come from talking it over; his mind was made.

In the street alongside him she braked slowly. A few cars pulled out and passed her, their impatience obvious by the sound of their acceleration. The car rolled to a stop as if coasting. Horns blew. He looked over to see her staring straight ahead. She had taken her hands off the steering wheel, and without looking at him, she slid across the seat toward him. He knew, then, what she wanted, or what she needed: for him to drive.

Three

Pinto Canyon, Texas, 2004

Maria had never said his name aloud and she did not see why she needed to start now. She did not roll down the window and call to him when she stopped the car right in the middle of Pecos Street, morning traffic jamming up behind her. She did not ask him to drive. She just scooted across to the passenger's side and waited for him to get in.

He seemed to understand without one word from her that she wanted him to drive her out of town. First he had to drive her through it. The town was small and it quickly dwindled to lone campers surrounded by junk cars and cast-off appliances. Then it was the two of them, their car, wind-ruffled prairie.

Between them on the seat, tucked into the space between cushions, the bag remained where he had left it, except it was no longer folded over. She wanted him to know that she'd read it, but she would not mention it. But they could take a ride together before he left town. She understood that he was running from something and she understood that he had found her tiny town adequate cover from whatever or whoever it was he was fleeing. He understood things about her, too. Otherwise how would he have known to drive them out of town into the open emptiness she craved?

When, a half mile from town, the speed limit rose to seventy-five and Marcus only gradually accelerated, she decided he was driving slowly in deference to her mood. Certainly it was obvious, her mood. Transparent as a teenager in full-blown mope. Maria felt seventeen. She felt like she had on those evenings when Randy had made them late, yammering with her father on the subject of automobiles, and when she had finally gotten the two of them separated she had punished Randy with silence. Now, ten years later, she was riding in a car with another boy, not talking. No, it was not the same. She had only to look over at the driver to feel the difference, or consider the car itself. A Buick instead of a Nova. Light blue instead of the burnt orange that led Randy to nickname it Flamethrower. Not nearly so loud as the Nova, which was so loud you could not hear the radio, a loud that sounded sick to her, like the car was going to blow up, though Randy claimed it was only the sound of badassedness. The Buick was clean but it was not so clean that if you touched the dash you'd leave a thumbprint on the Armor All'd vinyl. The Buick rode low and absorbed the bumps of the backroads, while the Nova was high and bouncy. The Buick smelled kind of bad instead of fake citrus scented.

And the boy was not a boy. He was boyish in appearance, despite the fact that his torso showed the accumulated weight of middle age and within a year or so scalp would show beneath the thin, graying hair that he would comb over his forehead. Though he was perhaps not the most mature person—he tended to lose things, farms, trucks, more than likely women—

he was definitely not a boy. A boy would be so threatened by her silence that he would assume she was mad at him, assume her every thought was about him. The man beside her did not say, What's wrong? or, thank God, Do you want to talk about it? He could see she was upset and so he drove.

It felt wrong comparing riding in a car now to riding in a car so long ago with the boy. After all, it was the boy who, when she and the man test-drove the car, had seen something in the man that she could trust. *Not yet given up on the getting back,* the boy had said about the man, as if he knew that this would be a good fit for her, knew somehow that the man, too, had suffered some loss but was determined to move beyond the emptiness that follows you around for years if you let it. Preferring the ride with the man to the ride with the boy would be the worst sort of betrayal, since it was the boy who had vetted her union with this man; it had been the boy's hand atop her own that scratched the pen across the forms she'd signed in Bobby Kepler's office. Maria could not now say she preferred to ride with the boy instead of the man, for hadn't she hurt the boy enough when he was alive to keep on hurting him years after his death?

And now she had hurt her mother, too. The night before, after her mother had been so buckled by Maria's confession that she had sat down at the table, and after her mother had kept saying, "I just did not see it, I just didn't, I ought to have, I ought to," and Maria said finally, "See what, Mom, know what?" her mother did not answer. She did not even look up from the place mat, so plastic and so green, such a silly thing to stare at in order to demonstrate your indifference to someone who was just trying to be honest with you. So Maria had done what she had always done when her mother would not give her what she needed, which was so simple, only words — it did not really even matter *which* words. Maria just needed sentences sent her way so that she might send a sentence back until they had not so much reached an understanding as constructed, from their back-and-forth, some *attempt* at an understanding, something aside from her mother shutting down and Maria doing what she had always done, what she had done the night before: gone to bed.

But not to sleep. Even after all her years away, she had come quickly to relearn the train schedule and she heard and kept time by their passage until 4:00 a.m., alternately sorry and angry: sorry for not knowing how to communicate her needs to her mother, angry at her mother for acting as if, by buying a car with Marcus, Maria had committed some deep breach of loyalty, when her mother for years had carried on openly with Ray, driving her father from job to job and finally, humiliated, into idleness if not illness.

Guilt, anger, trains. Finally a few hours of sleep. She heard her mother get up and she heard her in the bathroom and then in the kitchen. Heard the coffee brewing, smelled it. She remembered lying in bed on those mornings so long ago and hearing her father's boots on the floor, his cough, the lower and longer cough of his truck in the drive as it stuttered to life. Her mother's movements were softer and she could tell she was trying to be quiet, and because Maria was angry and guilty and had lain awake telling time by the train whistle, she decided that there was something in the manner of her mother's quiet, the way she tiptoed around and opened and closed doors and cabinets with such care, that was slightly resentful; she decided that her mother was annoyed that she could not turn on talk radio or, for all Maria knew of her mother's life, belt out "Angel of the Morning" by Juice Newton, the only song Maria had ever heard her mother sort of halfway sing along to, off the only album her mother had ever owned, to Maria's knowledge.

The door sucked shut, followed by the whine of the Cherokee in reverse as her mother backed it down the drive. Maria was halfway through her cup of coffee when she discovered the note. It was on the same place mat her mother had spent so long studying the night before. Same ancient stationery—the floral-bordered stock her mother had written her on all those years ago—and the same careful penmanship.

Dear Maria,

I have been thinking and I am not so sure this restaurant idea is a good idea. I just do not think the type food you are wanting to fix would go here. I believe if I am going to put something in that space well I have to think first of the motel. Whatever goes in that space, would it have an effect on business? That is what I will have to keep in mind. As you know that motel is the only thing I have got to live on, your daddy did not have any pension, he had not worked in years. So I have been thinking about it and I believe you ought to think what else you might do while you are here if you decide to stay.

She signed it "Your mother." No "With love" in quotation marks this time for Maria to interpret as her mother's misunderstood notion that quotation marks embodied emphasis.

Maria left the note where she found it. She went to her room and got her suitcase out of the closet and stuffed it with clothes and she went into the bathroom and grabbed her toothbrush and her lotions and her hairbrush and she fetched her jacket and her car keys. It was 7:40. If she hurried she could be at the Dairy Queen when Marcus dropped the car off. She wanted Marcus to drive her out of town and let her look at things. Maybe they would happen upon a pack of javelinas, or see, racing alongside the car, pacing it, a pronghorn antelope, or glimpse, across far grasslands rippling in wind, the silver glint of a train on its run to El Paso. She could not remember ever having desired so totally a man she was not sleeping with. In their previous conversations they had asked each other many questions and the answers were not the sort that raised more questions. Instead they were words that filled in blanks, as if on a test. They were the right answers only in that they took up space where once was a gap. What she desired now was for his presence to fill a blank.

And then she arrived at the Dairy Queen to find him gone already, the car backed into a space near the drive-through. Inside she found another rejection letter, her second in as many hours. Written on a Dairy Queen bag, but a dirty one. She stared at it a long time — his jerky handwriting, the stain she realized was ketchup, the words crossed out as if he was the sort who writes before he thinks and then thinks better of what he has written — before she read it.

Now, in the car with Marcus, Maria studied the red-rock cliffs outside her window for hawks, or a cave, something to distract her from the thing that had led her to pull over to the curb on Pecos Street, slide over when she found him, and ask him without words to drive her out of town into open air. She hoped being in Her Lowness with Marcus would keep her from thinking about her mother's note. Did she want Maria to pack up and leave? Was that what the note was trying to tell her? *If you decide to stay.* Sweet Jesus, it's only a car. Her mother knew that Maria cared more about her jeans than she did a car. Even had the man taken off with the car, it was only, to her, a thousand-dollar car.

And yet Maria knew, too, that it was far more than a car. When she was living in San Luis Obispo, she had gotten into a spat with a lover over whether to dine alfresco. The night was busy with flies and she got tired of shooing them from her salmon and he did not want to go inside—"I like fresh air," he kept saying, as if Maria did not—and the next day they had broken up. But not over flies. Like the car, the flies were singled out. Upon their fragile wings were heaped months of suppressed infractions.

Maybe her mother really *was* worried about her running the restaurant and the effect it might have on her occupancy rate. And she was so thrilled at first to have her daughter home that she had said yes despite her misgivings about the menu, but then Maria went out and bought a car with a perfect stranger, and her mother saw something in her daughter that she assumed had been beaten out of her by years of surviving on her own, no family, no support—for this is how her mother got over things, by working herself to the bone—or maybe she thought this thing in Maria that she ought to have seen would have been leached out of her by the unyielding accretion of time. But obviously it had not. It was still there, whatever it was that her mother saw, and its presence made her mother want Maria to go back where she had come from and all because of a car.

"I wonder if you will do me a favor," she said after twenty-three minutes of silence.

"Sure," he said, and she knew he would not ask what the favor was or say, as so many men would have, Depends on what it is.

"I want you to keep the car."

"So you read my letter?"

"You mean your bag? Yes, I read it. And I appreciate your offer, but you know I could never do that."

"I don't want the car."

"How are you planning on getting to Mexico?"

"They have buses that cross over all the time."

"You used to like the car." He had liked it enough to claim it out from under her, after she asked him to take it for a test-drive. He had liked it enough to pretend he was not interested in it, which meant he had liked it enough to lie. He desired it so much that he was willing to split it with her. Maybe that was all that drove him to share it in the first place: he had to have it at any cost. Maybe her notion that he, too, was hiding something was wrong. Just another man who loved another car.

"So did you."

"I still like it," she said. And it was true; she liked it as much as it was possible to like something you knew nothing about. "It's just that I don't need it now."

"Why not? I thought you were starting your restaurant."

"My mother's buying a truck and giving me her Jeep," she lied. She wasn't ready to say she was leaving to herself, much less to Marcus.

"Oh. Well, it's none of my business, but how come—"

"Her timing's never been all that great. So you're going to take a bus across the border, but how are you going to get around once you're there?"

"My friend has a car. I'll buy a bike. It's not that big, the place I'm headed. Apparently you can walk everywhere. I'll get a job on a farm within walking distance of the village."

"A white guy working the fields in Mexico?"

"Maybe they have affirmative action."

"Have you ever been to Mexico?"

"In fact, I have," he said. "To the Yucatán. My ex-girlfriend ate a salad the first night we were there and she got so sick she was in bed for the next three days, and I went off to see the ruins but I felt so guilty for leaving Rebecca that I confess I did not enjoy myself."

"Typical Mexican vacation narrative. You were staying in Cancún?"

"Playa Del Carmen. Same difference, I guess."

"I wouldn't know. I've never been to either of those places. Mainly I know Chihuahua. Or knew. My father had cousins in Ojinaga. He didn't cross over much because he was Tejano— his people were living in Texas before there was a Texas. He said people treated him differently even just across the border in Ojinaga. Still, because my father is Mexican and because I grew up so close to Mexico, I know a little about it. One thing I know is that they have not heard of affirmative action. They have no need for it, because the white people who go there are either retired or run the maquiladoras."

Marcus was silent. Before, she had craved his silence, but now she wanted him to talk to her. Had she said something to upset him?

"I kind of got the feeling you liked it here," she said.

"Oh, I do. I really like it. I like Texas, what I've seen of it."

"What have you seen of it?"

"Just what you see from I-10."

"Like Houston? San Antonio?"

"I didn't see much. I mean, I didn't stop. The interstate loops around them. All I saw were warehouses and apartment complexes."

"What would you *like* to see in Texas?"

"I don't know. The Hill Country? The Alamo?"

"The Alamo would disappoint you. It's tiny. And crowded. Not to mention a lie."

"How is it a lie?"

"Well, I would say that the view of history you learn there is definitely skewed."

"That's not surprising. History is always skewed. I can't be disappointed by something I expect. Plus, hagiography is the modus operandi of shrines. I know this because I built a shrine myself. It wasn't like I was going to emphasize the negative qualities of carnivorous plants in the exhibits."

"What are the negative qualities?"

"One could argue that they're cold-blooded killers," he said. "Sitting around with jaws open waiting for unsuspecting insects to light on them and then eating them for lunch."

"That's what's cool about it, though, right?"

"It is what's *unique* about it," Marcus said, in a way that made her feel foolish for using the word "cool."

"There's nothing unique about the Alamo. But if that's what you want to see, you should see it before you leave Texas. You should see Texas before you leave Texas."

"I guess you're right. I wasn't really in the position to stop a lot on my way down."

When he did not elaborate, Maria did not ask him to. She figured he'd talk when he wanted to talk.

"Once I open my place, I'll be working eighty-hour weeks," she said. "I haven't been anywhere in this state for years. Since you're leaving and you won't have a car, we could take a short trip. See a little Texas."

"You mean now?"

"I do mean now. I can drop you off at your hotel and you can get what you need for a few days. That is, if you think the car will make it that far."

Marcus pushed a button and water sprayed the windshield. Wipers obscured her view of the black line of highway ahead. Though there were, as always in West Texas, bugs crusting the windshield, she decided he was only feigning deliberation. She decided he did not really want to go to Mexico today, for otherwise he would have said, immediately, No, thank you, I'm headed south instead of east.

"Long as we keep her topped off with oil and don't run her off-road, we could drive this crate to Alberta and back."

"This is a hovercraft, not a crate," said Maria. "And we don't want to go to Alberta. We want to go to San Antonio."

Austin, Texas, 1986

Dr. Brock bought the Buick because his father had played golf with the owner of the Buick dealership and Dr. Brock had always worked hard to please his father, who before his death had worked in the physical plant of the University of Kansas in Lawrence. His father had bought Buicks from this man because he had known him all his life. His father was a townie and the Buick dealer was also a townie and for this reason Dr. Brock's father drove Buicks.

Despite the fact that his family had been in Lawrence for generations, most of them within a square mile of the university, Dr. Brock was the first in his family to attend college. He lived at home and rode his bike the two blocks to the university and he worked summers in the physical plant and saved his money for med school. After a residency in Ann Arbor, Dr. Brock came home and married and bought the first of his Buicks, a LeSabre that, after he and his wife had three children in five years, took on the ragged and vaguely odiferous air of a car used to haul around toddlers. Dr. Brock bought his wife a Volvo and kept the LeSabre for himself until he traded it in for a slightly used Electra.

The Electra was light blue and clean and he was perplexed as to why anyone would want to part with it, seeing as how there were only sixteen thousand miles on the odometer. His father's friend the car dealer had tried to sell him a new Buick, but Dr. Brock had wandered over to the Electra, as he was drawn to its sky blueness and its general cleanliness. He assumed at first it was brand new. Because Myron Brock, the doctor's father, had been such a good customer, and because the Buick had been so long on the lot that he had twice reduced the price, the Buick dealer had quickly conceded to selling him the used Electra, though of course he would have preferred to sell him a new vehicle. He told Dr. Brock that the car had come from a dealer in Cleveland who had trouble moving it since that area of the country had suffered much during the recent economic downturn. When Dr. Brock, during the test-drive, asked the dealer why anyone would opt to sell such a car, there must be something wrong with it, the dealer assured him that all his pre-owned vehicles were subject to rigorous examinations. "Just like you'd do on me, Doc," he added, laughing. "Just think of it this way: all the bugs have been worked out, the car's broken in good now."

Dr. Brock lived only six blocks from his office and on all but the wintriest or rainiest days he walked to work. The Buick sat in the drive. His children were getting older — he had two boys and a girl — and in a year his oldest son, Matthew, would have his license. He was not about to give Matthew a car. He himself had not owned a car until he got out of med school, and he felt it prudent to wait and see how the boy handled himself before conferring on him even the occasional use of the car.

But Matthew was a good boy. He'd always been good, if
quiet, the type who read on long car trips and could be counted
on to entertain his younger siblings if need be. His fresh-
man year he had gone out for the track team at his father's
suggestion—his father had run some in high school but
worked after school at a downtown hotel and was not able to
join the team—but it was not until Matthew gravitated toward cross-country that his talent emerged. Dr. Brock took off
a couple of afternoons when the meets were in town, for he
loved to watch his son run, and he was impressed by the boy's
training regimen, which included long runs in the early morning, well before breakfast, out past the river onto the levee that
ran above the misty, moonlit fields.

And then something happened. Dr. Brock was never sure
what it was. It might have been nothing, for even though Dr.
Brock was by nature and training a scientist, and diagnosing
even the most niggling illness involved isolating symptoms
and ascertaining, through questioning the patient, how long
the symptoms had been noticeable, he also knew, from dealing with the depressed and anxious, for which he was only
minimally trained, that there is not always a single event that
causes someone to plummet. And yet he would always wonder
if something had happened to cause his boy to retreat. He was
so busy that he barely noticed how withdrawn the boy had
become, and he did not even remember his wife's alarm, nor
did he remember trying to calm her alarm with rote banali-
ties about the moodiness of teenagers, hormones, burgeoning
emotions.

Matthew's grades slipped. He stopped going out with his

friends. He kept his door closed, and from that closed door, walking down the hallway at night, his father heard music he did not like the sound of, music so slow and thick it reminded him of a morphine drip. No more morning runs. In fact, it was hard—according to his wife, for Dr. Brock was up and out of the house early—to get Matthew out of bed.

Dr. Brock was reading the paper one Saturday morning when Matthew emerged sullen and disheveled, smelling of sleep and stale bedroom. He sat down at the table, his arms crossed, his eyes glassy and trained on his lap. Dr. Brock was reading the sports page. He came upon the results of the cross-country invitational held the week before and did not see his son's name. He assumed the boy had had a bad day—inevitable, given how sporadically his son had been training—so he asked what had happened.

"I quit the team."

"When?"

"Weeks ago, Dad."

Then it was Dr. Brock's time to snap. He was not like the boy—he needed for something to happen before he felt one way or the other—and this was enough of an event for him to yell at his son in a way he never had before. And when his son said nothing at all in his defense, when he just sat there, looking so glum, as if he had not a roof over his head nor parents who bought him clothes and fed him, as if he had reason to feel sad about something, Dr. Brock yanked the boy out of his seat and told him to get his act together and quit feeling sorry for himself.

Matthew fled to his room. Dr. Brock's wife came in the

kitchen, looked at Dr. Brock for a while, waiting for an explanation. Finally she said she was taking the younger kids shopping with her. Dr. Brock took a shower and walked down to his
office to catch up on paperwork. For the first hour he was too
anxious and distracted by what had happened with Matthew
to get much done, but he was unused to second-guessing his
actions, especially at home, and in time he grew sluggish, as
the emotional energy he'd spent worrying over what had happened had depleted him physically as well. He dozed in his
chair. Around five his wife called him from home. The Buick
was gone, she said, and so was Matthew.

Thereafter followed the hardest five weeks of Dr. Brock's
life. He felt as if there were fans inside him, one where his
heart ought to be, a couple of smaller ones in his head, just
behind his forehead, down near the nape of his neck. Their
blades whirred unceasingly, operating not unlike the fan in
an engine, designed to switch on automatically to cool things
down.

Everywhere Dr. Brock searched for answers. He spoke to
Matthew's classmates, his former teammates, his teachers, the
neighbor kids. Late one night he convinced himself that the
Buick was to blame. He ought never to have bought a used
vehicle. Someone else's misery seeped out of it.

He knew this was not rational. He was a man of science.
Yet as he entertained the idea, the fans slowed to a chop and
finally to a point where each blade was singly distinguishable.
It helped to imagine the previous owner as someone too ir-
responsible to keep up the payments. Probably a drug addict
or someone on welfare. Someone who did not learn from his

mistakes and who had probably gone out and purchased another vehicle he could ill afford. Now his boy had taken off in
a vehicle cursed by indolence and greed.

The police turned up nothing. Dr. Brock was outraged by
their response, which ran from condescending to indifferent.
How, he asked them, could a boy in a light blue Buick, a boy
with only his learner's permit, disappear? Likely he switched
the tags, said the detective in charge, or had the car repainted.
But Dr. Brock said this was ludicrous. His son was not a criminal, he would not steal someone else's plates, and it was doubt-
ful that he even knew how to unscrew the plates. And how
could he afford to have the car repainted? Nothing was missing
from his room, according to Dr. Brock's wife, but some clothes.
He did not even have a job, his afternoons and weekends having been taken up with training. It made no sense that he had
managed to hide out for five weeks.

Then Dr. Brock got a call from a detective with the Austin,
Texas, police department. The Buick had been pulled over in
the middle of the night for running a stop sign and the driver
had fled the scene on foot and had evaded capture. Dr. Brock
got off the phone and made a reservation and flew out the next
morning, spare key to the Buick in his pocket. He would find
his son and bring him home.

The car was impounded. Dr. Brock took a cab from the
airport to the police station, assuming that the car would be
nearby or that a policeman might drive him to fetch it, but
in fact it was across town, on the outskirts of the city, which
required another cab ride, a long wait, more money. At the lot
he was met by a detective who looked at him with contempt.

Why? Because his son ran away? Had he not encountered in his line of work children who do things their parents would rather they not? Were his days not filled with people who did not conform to the laws and statutes of the republic? Dr. Brock explained as best he could what had happened, which was difficult, as he had no idea what had happened. His son was fine, then Dr. Brock bought a used Buick, then his son became sullen and withdrawn, then he was gone. Five weeks passed. The car turned up in Austin. As a story it made no sense. But Dr. Brock could not elaborate, even though the detective stood in silence waiting for him to continue.

Dr. Brock decided he hated Austin, Texas. It was a little too pleased with itself for his taste. He had noticed scores of young people and perhaps this is why Matthew was here. He knew it was a college town and the state capital, but coming in from the airport, he had driven through neighborhoods of squat, low, ramshackle houses with badly fenced yards and stores peddling piñatas and Mexican food. What he saw seemed more like a struggling city than a college town. Beyond the lot where the car was impounded, the land flattened out and an unseasonably hot wind kicked up dust, and Dr. Brock found it deeply unappealing.

The detective was asking him for a description of his son. Dr. Brock did his best to comply, but it was not easy to describe someone you see every day of your life for fourteen years.

The detective was checking his details against a report on a clipboard.

"I will say this for your boy," he said. "He sure can run. The officers who pulled him over said they'd never seen anything like that boy running."

Dr. Brock never cried and he had never even come close to crying in public. The fans in his chest and head ran so high that it was hard to hear what the detective was saying to him. Something about some magazines? Dr. Brock nodded. The detective said, "Okay, but I'm just saying, we left them where we found them. Some deeply nasty shit."

The detective led Dr. Brock to the car. Dr. Brock pulled out the spare key and was about to unlock the door when he noticed the back window was rolled down. The car was filthy, inside and out. The back floorboards were invisible beneath plastic bags and pop and beer bottles and across the seat stretched a couple of ratty blankets. Dr. Brock said to the detective, "Is it okay if I . . .?" and the detective shrugged and walked away to a nearby pickup. He turned and leaned against the truck bed and crossed his arms and studied Dr. Brock as he climbed into the back of the Buick. In the backseat Dr. Brock rummaged beneath the trash and found a backpack that seemed familiar, out of which he pulled a gray T-shirt he recognized and some socks and underwear. He reached under the seat and pulled out a stack of magazines. They had names like *Honcho* and *Mandate*. He opened one. He closed it. He was horrified but the horrified part of him was almost immediately blotted out by a voice faint but swiftly growing broken and loud. Is that all, Mattie? Goodness, Son, is that it? I would have learned to live with that in a matter of days. No, hours. That is nothing, Matthew. That is just . . . Matthew, why did you not just . . . ?

Dr. Brock sat in the car though he hated the car. He thought that he might never see his son again and he thought that it was not his fault. When he got out of the car he walked past the detective, whom he also hated. The detective said, "You're not going to take your car?" Dr. Brock said, "No. I never want to see it again. I don't care what you do with it. When you find my son, I want my son. You call me when you find my son. I want my son. I don't want that car. I don't want to ever see that car again."

Pinto Canyon, Texas, 2004

During Maria's silence, after she stopped in the middle of the street and slid across the seat, leaving Her Lowness unmanned, Marcus, driving them out of town, went from one hand to the other. On the one hand, dirty mop water rose beneath the streets and would any minute bubble up from the grates and career the Buick into a thirsty wash. Marcus must have summoned the surge, even though he had taken action to redress not only his present predicament but a deep rent in his psyche long in need of repair: He had testified on the back of a bloodstained bag in order to avoid another folly. He had rejected impulse and the present tense for forethought and prudence. He had outwitted stasis, only to have it swamp him less than a half mile from the scene of the crime.

The other hand wasn't so much a hand as a finger that he could not quite put on the way he felt, driving into the country, Maria riding shotgun. It had to be Her Lowness because Marcus, when out for a ride, had always preferred male company to female. Men just put their elbows out the window and either smoked or didn't. It never occurred to them to switch on the radio and waste good wayside scenery mashing buttons that made different voices and instruments spill tinny from the speakers. The countryside flashing past was enough to occupy their minds. No need to talk small or wag chin.

Women — whose company Marcus in all other respects preferred overwhelmingly — did not understand the concept of an aimless drive. When he said to a woman, Let's go to ride (for that is how they said it back in Silt, not, Let's go *for* a ride) she would say, Why? Where are we going? How long will it take?

Driving around with Maria was different. Maybe coming from a place so vast and open and unpopulated, where one had to travel more than a hundred miles to attend a high school football game at the home field of the closest rival, had made Maria so uncharacteristically talented at going to ride.

That was what Marcus was thinking during the first few miles out of town: that it was the car plus the girl that made the ride so pleasurable. Curiously, her lack of explanation — for it was a little odd, her pulling over in the street and abandoning the wheel to him after he had left her a note relinquishing his rights to the Buick — did not make him anxious or impatient. Clearly she needed him in a way that she both had not before and could not yet articulate.

Then, twenty minutes into it, Maria asked him for a favor. "Sure," said Marcus, as was his wont when asked for favors. He had not been raised to ascertain the nature of the favor before agreeing to it. In this case Maria's request for him to keep the car annoyed him. He found it rote and insincere. He had relinquished his rights, and here she was, responding in kind. You go. No, you go. Was this what passed for partnership? For co-ownership? Theirs was not a democracy; how could it ever be equitable? He'd claimed Sunday mornings because of his love of a Sunday morning cruise, but he had lied to her when she asked if he was a churchgoer. Therefore the partnership was tainted from the get-go.

Marcus was distressed by the notion that, having taken the great risk of buying the car together, they were now fighting to give it away. That a part of him wanted to take her up on her offer distressed him even further. He tried to remember how he'd felt just an hour ago in the parking lot of the Dairy Queen. Monte Gale was a mistake, but it took only his signature to redress his error. Was it even plausible for him to think that he would never again act on impulse?

As for their partnership, the equality of it: no relationships, business or romantic, were free from the manipulations of desire. So when, so quickly after offering him the Buick, she suggested a sightseeing trip around Texas, Marcus did not allow himself to say what he was thinking: that she offered the car only so he would refuse it again and she could, with impunity, ask him to turn around and then dump him in front of his hotel and take off to wherever it was she really wanted to go.

When he was a kid, Marcus had favored, above comic strips and the sports page, the district court docket of the local newspaper. Only documented trouble engaged his eleven-year-old interest. He had no idea what many of the charges were, and he did not want to reveal his secret passion to his parents, so he came up with his own definitions. *Uttering* he confused at first with muttering, mumbling. He imagined a sheriff's deputy leading him handcuffed from his social studies class, his mouth trembling with muffled oath and supplication. Though he was old enough to know better, when he saw someone charged with *check kiting* he imagined wings of checks Scotch-taped to a stick, soaring skyward, and a criminal dangling one-armed from the line, laughing at the cops in hot pursuit on the ground below. *Breaking and entering,* though less metaphorical, scared Marcus no less, for it seemed every place he wanted to be was locked, and he possessed neither key nor combination.

What was in his heart that drew him to such fascination with broken law and due punishment? He understood even then that his sin was not original, that it was a cliché, that he was born with it like the rest of the world, and that he would live with it always. And yet there was one phrase that seemed to apply specifically to Marcus and that kept him up nights: *failure to appear.* How it terrified him, as all he wanted then and had wanted his whole life was the one thing he thought himself incapable of: to be present, to show up, to participate.

Maybe she wanted him to say, Okay, you win, you can have the car. But it felt just as likely, as they took the ramp onto the interstate, that she needed him to show up.

"That is, if you think the car will make it that far," Maria said, and Marcus, one hand outweighing the other, understood that walking away from the Buick and its co-owner was far worse than committing another Monte Gale. When Marcus replied that, with proper maintenance, Her Lowness could get them to Alberta, Maria did not say that *she* wanted to go to San Antonio, not Alberta. Marcus relaxed his grip on the wheel of what seemed not a car but a pronoun made plural so that he might remain present, if not a willing participant.

THEY WERE IN OZONA, three hours east of home, before the guilt Maria felt for not telling Marcus the truth about this trip outweighed all the rationalizations she'd concocted to keep it a secret. Showing him Texas—especially the Alamo—would never have motivated her to leave town. Offering him the car was also calculated, for she had read his note and she knew he would refuse her, but she banked on her offer making him more inclined to go along.

Yet telling him to take the car after he had tried to give it to her seemed almost obligatory; she would have taken the car had she not been keeping something from him. Pretending to be some sort of tour guide for the state of Texas, however, was ludicrous. She lacked both the knowledge and the enthusiasm, having been gone for so long and having missed not the state itself but *her* corner of it, the only part that was real. Sand, rock, creosote, agave, and sunsets so brilliant, due to much dust and little humidity, that she used to make Randy pull onto the shoulder so they could watch them as they would a drive-in movie, the horizon their own endless screen. The way the train sounded in the night, no trees or towns for miles to mute its whistle. The things that were real to her, that were hers, would not be real to Marcus, for they were images, not facts. He had said he had his degree in history. He would depend on her for dates and the names of things.

She knew nothing about the rest of the state. She'd only been to Austin twice, once with her parents when she was too young to remember, and another time with her classmates on their senior trip. They had stopped on their way from San Antonio to Austin in New Braunfels to spend the day at a water park. It was just weeks before Randy died, and they had sneaked away while everyone was eating pizza and fooled around on the bus. What was she thinking? What if they'd been caught by the chaperones? Later she would wish that someone had noticed them gone and seen their shadows through the tinted windows of the bus, for based on math done months later, that was when she got pregnant.

What a thing for her to want to nail down, given what happened. Who cares which time it was, for it could have been any of a couple of dozen times, and in effect it was all one time. But back then it had helped her to think of a specific instance where they might have refrained, for it made it easier in her mind to justify all the times when everything worked out.

She had no good memories of New Braunfels, but this was where her brother lived. What she had not yet told Marcus was that they were on their way to see her brother. She had decided this after finding her mother's letter. It had been longer than ten years since she'd seen him, as he was away in the Coast Guard when she left town, and did not often come home on leave. She could not say she much missed him, because she could not say she knew him. To her mind there were two sorts of families: those so close they seemed to share the same tastes if not convictions, who talked on the phone and spent holidays together and took common vacations; and her stripe, for whom kinship was a fact and not some sacrosanct bond, and blood was something drawn by nick or cut, not a substance shared in the manner of royalty.

But after reading her mother's letter and feeling at once

saddened and annoyed by the way her mother, when confronted with the slightest breach of "common sense," withdrew, Maria wanted Manny to explain to her why he never visited or even called home. She wanted to know why her mother had claimed, after Maria returned from an errand, that she had just missed Manny, he had called while she was out. Her mother would, not looking at Maria, consumed in some task or other, deliver news that *sounded* like lies: how his kids were enjoying soccer, how much he liked driving a truck for H-E-B, how he was planning a trip home this summer when he could stay longer than a weekend.

Of course she did not need Marcus to come along, but she wanted him to. It was seven hours to New Braunfels, most of it on interstate. She had never driven on an interstate. Marcus hadn't found work yet. What else did he do with his days? They could split the driving. She would feel safer with him along. The Buick, after all, was twenty years old. Fine vehicle for around town, said Bobby Kepler. Randy always drove. She only knew how to ride in a car with Randy, and Randy would not want her to drive all that way alone in a quarter-century-old car.

But it wasn't just practical. There were other reasons, less selfish ones. He was good company. His presence filled a blank. Even if she could not narrate their sightseeing with the appropriate authority, wouldn't he still see some of the world he would not otherwise have seen? And the car was half his.

As agreeable as he was, she did not look forward to telling him they were going to interrupt their sightseeing to visit her brother, or rather asking him if they might. But first she had to call her mother and let her know she'd be gone for a while. She owed her that much, at least.

In Junction she asked Marcus to stop at a gas station. In the bathroom she locked the door and called her mother. Her mother did not own a cell phone. Maria knew she would be at the motel, so she left a message on her landline. "Hi, it's Maria," she said, trying to sound as if nothing was wrong, as if she'd read the note and was fine with it. She said she was going to San Antonio but she did not say why. She said she'd be back in a few days, and because some part of her she was not proud of but could not quite control wanted to punish her mother, she said, instead of good-bye, "Take care."

They ate dinner in a Thai place Maria spotted on a service road just off the interstate. Neither had eaten since breakfast and so they double-ordered fresh spring rolls and tasted each other's entrées and split a bottle of wine.

Marcus, offering her a taste of his chicken with lemongrass curry, said, "My mother says about every other thing she eats, 'This is the best thing I ever in my whole life tasted.'"

"Does she mean it?"

"I'm no linguist, but I would wager that a close examination of her syntax would prove her sincerity."

"So you're saying she means it?"

"Yep."

Maria took a bite of chicken.

"It's pretty damn good," she said.

While he ate, she found herself studying his eyes, which were a blue that seemed washed out but which flashed and sparkled, and his lips, which were oddly attractive, given their unevenness—the top one was plump, the bottom only a slight line. She wondered why he was alone still, for other than the few extra pounds, which women almost expected on a man his age (men past forty with flat stomachs and definition in their arms were, in Maria's experience, trouble), he was attractive. He was in pretty good shape, considering his diet—he'd told her at lunch that first day how much he'd taken to breakfast tacos, and he professed a love of the deep-fat-fried jalapeños called poppers, which he ate at Dairy Queen. And he was interesting. He did not talk about himself too much; he was curious about other people. Best of all, he knew, when he saw a woman stop her car in the middle of the street and slide over, to get in and drive her out of town and not ask her what or why.

But surely it was more complicated, and none of her business, why he was alone, and not even something she cared to discuss with him, especially now that they'd arrived in San Antonio and she needed to reveal the true purpose of their visit. They finished the wine, and the wine made it slightly easier for her to ask, in the car on the way back to the motel, if they might rearrange their itinerary a bit.

"I wasn't aware we had one," he said, which was exactly what she wanted him to say.

"I know you wanted to see the Alamo, and while we're here we should take a stroll along the River Walk and go see a mission or two. But I'm wondering if you'd mind if tomorrow I could stop by to see my brother. He lives less than an hour from here, in a town called New Braunfels."

"Well, I'm dying to see the Alamo after your glowing

endorsement." He smiled to let her know he was joking. "Of course I don't mind. Family comes first, always."

Instead of comforting her, this made her feel even more guilty for deceiving him.

"You can drop me off and take the car and go exploring, or I can get my brother to meet me somewhere. I promise I will not subject you to the awkwardness of meeting someone else's relatives."

"I don't have a problem with *other people's* families," he said. "How long has it been since you've seen your brother?"

"Do you have siblings?" she asked Marcus, aware that she was answering his question by posing another, but fully intending to answer his question after gathering some knowledge of how he might interpret the story of Manny.

"One sister," he said, studying her face as they stopped at a light.

"Are you close?"

"We see each other a couple times a year."

"Talk on the phone?"

"Only if something's up with my mom."

"Does she have children?"

"She's gay."

"Gay people have kids, Marcus."

"She told me once she was just pretending to be gay so she wouldn't have to have kids. But she was just playing with me. Or maybe she was just trying to make me feel better for not having kids myself."

"Does she have a partner?"

"If by 'partner' you mean girlfriend, it seems she switches

them out every six months or so. Like you're supposed to do with batteries in your smoke alarm."

"You mean she breaks up with them when the time changes?"

"Seems like word would get around, right? I find it hard to believe there is an unlimited supply of lesbians in Asheville, North Carolina. Sooner or later she's going to run out."

"Actually I've had smoke alarms go for years without switching batteries. She might have to just learn to go until it gives out."

"Or else move to another town when Asheville runs dry. I'll put my money on the latter."

"I'm going to answer your question."

"Oh, I know you are."

"You do?"

"You're stalling," he said, "but I'm patient."

He *was* patient. They were back at the motel but neither had made a move to get out of the car. The Buick had contained them all day and they were not yet sick of its space. And it had performed brilliantly, holding its own on the interstate among tractor trailers and pickups pulling campers. Now it sat ticking, settling down for a night's rest under the protective eye of streetlights busy with swarming bugs.

"I have not seen my brother in over ten years," she said. "Nor talked to him."

"So tomorrow's going to be tough?"

"I don't even know if he'll see me."

"He'll see you," said Marcus.

She almost told him not to say things like that, for she had enough of her mother in her to feel, when confronted by cheerful optimism, annoyed rather than comforted. But she'd bought a car with this man and it had worked out so far and maybe there was something he knew about how to make things right.

"I guess I'll find out in a minute," she said, and she told him to sleep well and she'd meet him for breakfast.

Alone in her room, dialing the number she'd copied off the list her mother posted on the wall of the kitchen, Maria came close to hyperventilating. Her voice cracked as she told the woman who answered the phone who she was and asked if her brother was around.

"Manny's got a sister?"

She should have seen this coming, but it made it even harder to draw a breath. "I've been living out west."

"Still," said the woman. "I got sisters in Corpus and Round Rock and one in Mexico, and Manny has not met all my sisters but he at least *knows* about them."

"Right," said Maria. What else could she say? The woman said nothing and there was a silence long enough to make Maria think she'd hung up, but then Mannie's voice came on the line.

"Maria?"

"Hey, Manny," she said. "Blast from the past."

When he said nothing, she felt foolish for trying to sound casual.

"I know it's been forever," she said. More silence, even louder this time.

"I'm back in Texas," she said. "For a while. I've been staying with Mom."

"I heard that."

"From Mom? You talked to her?"

"She sent me one of her notes. She never calls me. Nor writes me, really, except at Christmas and on my birthday."

She did not say, on the telephone, Why is that? Instead she asked how he liked living in New Braunfels and he said it was okay, and then, as if he were nervous to talk to her, he went on about the rivers, the Comal and the Guadalupe, about how his youngest daughter worked for one of the tubing outfits, how much fun she had, how much of a pain it was to live here in the summer, how he was thinking of buying a place out past Boerne, away from all the tubers.

"Actually, I'm in San Antonio," she said. "I was wondering if I could come by and visit for a while."

"Well, I got to work tomorrow. You mean tomorrow? I have to go to work."

"Tomorrow evening? I could take you out to dinner."

The pause lasted so long that she was about to tell him it was okay, she understood, she was sorry to bother him, when he said, "I guess we could meet at Rudy's. They got good barbecue. Not the best I've ever ate but it's pretty good for a chain. You eat meat?"

"Living at home, with Mom? She doesn't really do vegetables. I'd starve to death if I didn't."

"I wouldn't know," he said, as if he had no memories of the meals their mother had cooked for them before he left home, as if she'd turned carnivore after he left.

"I'll see you there at six," he said.

"Rudy's," she said, but Manny had already hung up.

THE NIGHT BEFORE, AT dinner, Maria had told Marcus about the water park with the crazy Teutonic title, and about the rivers, the Guadalupe and the Comal, one of which flowed smack through town, the other of which skirted it, where people from all over central Texas came to float on inner tubes and so when he met her for breakfast and saw in her face a rigidity so severe her lips would barely part to make words, he said, You know, where I come from we have rivers but the water moccasins hide in the Spanish moss and wait for boats and kayaks and canoes to come by so they can drop in for lunch, I'd no more sink my fat ass through a circle of rubber and into that evil black water than I would leave the keys in Her Lowness while I take a hike down the Rio Grande so do you think since we have a whole day to kill here before you see your brother, do you think we could go by the Dollar General and get ourselves some cheap bathing suits and maybe a cheap cooler and a couple of beers, all on me of course, you paid for the rooms and the gas, I'll pay for everything today, and while Marcus was laying out his plan, Maria's face did not so much relax as slightly brighten and in that barely perceptible shift he sensed that she saw right through his plan to take her mind off what she faced later that day (and even though it was not the same thing, for Maria's estrangement from her brother did not seem to him to have anything to do with money, he knew he would welcome the same from her if at the end of the day he faced a reunion with Annie) and obviously Maria did not care if he was only trying to distract her because an hour and ten minutes later they were putting their tubes into the Comal River and a few minutes after that Marcus had lashed his to

Maria's and to the extra tube for the cooler and was freestyl-
ing down the sweet green river, its water so clean and clear
he wanted to eat it, and overhead stretched a canopy so full it
made him realize how long it had been since he'd been underneath a tree, a real tree, one even slightly reminiscent of the
thick forest surrounding the farm, and because he did not want
to think about the farm, he was glad when the grackles along
the bank, not native to his part of the world, screeched their
windup-toy noises to each other, and soon the river thickened
near the tube chutes with huge knots of folks whose inner
tubes were connected by rope or in some cases arms and even
legs, everyone laughing and somehow attractive in the slashes
of sunlight that penetrated the lushness above, and sometimes
on the river bottom a blemish of aluminum and the sacrilege
of beer cans in such purity antagonized him until he dived for
trash, and in forty-five minutes of their four-hour float he had
collected so much trash that Maria (who was at first stiff in
the floral bikini she had finally decided to purchase despite
the fact that she would never in any other circumstance wear
such a thing, it's only because it's six bucks and I have to have
something to swim in, she said) after a mile or so afloat leaned
back with her eyes closed, her hair dipping into the river, her
skin shiny with lotion (and okay, yes, she was beautiful and yes
Marcus liked it when other people — men, some women —
noticed her and assumed she was with him in a way that she
was not and that he did not really want her to be, not that he
did not find her attractive, but there just seemed far more at
stake here than whether he slept alone or not), and said to
him, Okay, Al Gore, You have to can it now, The garbage barge

is about to tank, and he dived down and swam over to the
other side of her and popped up and said, But who will save
mother earth? and she laughed at his silliness and said, Future
generations, and Marcus was so pleased to see her smile and
hear her laugh that for the next mile of the river he hung on
the side of her tube and they talked or they didn't and when
they did their talk was slow and idle and perfect as the water
beneath them and when they did not talk Marcus thought,
well, I may have lost the farm and my truck and my birthright
and my dignity and it is possible that I am into something crazy
destructive with this woman and there may well be something
lurking under these waters that I cannot see, say under the
docks of those houses perched above the river, or among the
rocks lining the banks, maybe a snake, harbinger of unrest, or
maybe not even a harbinger, just unrest itself, and I may well
soon be broke and homeless, it seems almost certain, since I
am jobless and barely employable and spent a good portion of
my savings on a by-God Buick with this woman who might be
using me, though I'm not quite sure what for, her chauffeur
maybe or maybe just someone to drag along for kicks while she
cavorts through her mysterious past trying to make right whatever happened back there, but you know what, if she *is* using
me I can't say I really am ready for her to stop because here I
am wearing a pair of Jams I got at the Dollar General for $4.99
floating down a sweet green river with a woman with whom I
bought a low silky ride and the water I'm going to say it again is
so pure and green it must be bubbling up from someone's fantasy and in the cooler are a couple of cans of ice-cold Beck's,
tallboys too, waiting for me should I get thirsty and here he was

in Texas, of all places Texas, who would have predicted how much he loved it here, loved its rivers and deserts and shimmery grasslands, its taquerias and dance halls, and also to his mild alarm loved Texans, all of them, even the drunkest ones on this river, hell, even the ones who stole his truck, though they might have been Mexicans, but he loved Mexicans too, and Mexico, and he was glad Maria had ignored his bag letter and taken him along to see this river, and he was thankful also to the Buick for not overheating or throwing a rod and to Earth, Wind and Fire for writing "That's the Way of the World," which he had played over and over for the last hour of their trip, singing to the highway ahead and the trucks alongside and Maria beside him the lines "You will find peace of mind / If you look way down in your heart and soul" as if he believed such a platitude, as if by singing it even badly he might make it true, until Maria threatened to toss the tape out the window, and owing to some crazy Texan variety of religious experience, some miracle equal almost to a Ruffles potato chip in which Jesus on the cross is discernible if you look way down in your heart and soul, Marcus even loved, for a glorious sunburst, in the sweet green current, most of all—for making it down here, for purchasing a sky-blue chariot so that he might have reason to stick around, for failing to *dis*appear—himself.

MANNY'S HUG WAS STIFF and he sounded as if he was still on the phone, distant, suspicious, but Maria was too startled by how he had aged into a likeness of their father to take offense. His hair had receded in the same spots, and the bulge of his stomach, just like their father's, appeared disproportionate to the rest of his body. She had remembered him taller. Was it guilt over her loss of him that led her to grow him in memory? People, books—people *in* books—claimed that everything from childhood revisited after years away appeared absurdly small, but Maria had not found this to be true. Her town felt larger, even though her mother claimed it had lost a quarter of its population in the past ten years.

Her father was short—five feet six at the most—but he had, at least when he was still working, carried himself so stoutly that she never thought of him as below average height. Manny, standing by the hostess station at Rudy's when she first walked in, was her father, in nicer jeans, an inch or two taller in his thick-heeled boots.

No, Manny was not her father. He knew the waitress by name. They sat at a booth by the window. Manny ordered a Bud Light, Maria stuck to water. "So" was the first word of the first five sentences she asked him. Waitress that my brother knows by a name I have already forgotten, if I was even paying attention in the first place, please hurry back. Bring me food I am too nervous to eat and probably would not eat, anyway. Maria needed somewhere for her hands to go instead of her lap, where they sat clasped and clammy. Chips came, with salsa, but Manny stopped eating after the third or fourth, noticing, she was sure, that she had not once reached for the basket.

"So, I came here once before. In high school."

"New Braunfels?" He said it in a way she knew was the way of natives.

"The water park. Schlitterbahn? I can't believe I still remember the name of it."

"Hard to forget," said Manny. "I'd say that's what most people know us by."

Us. As in, he'd found a home here. Why did this bother her, given how long she'd been gone?

"Also we went to see these tiny houses. I guess the Germans built them when they settled here?"

"Sunday houses. Ranchers would come into town and stay over on the weekends so they wouldn't miss church."

"Are they still around?" asked Maria, thinking of the car ride back from El Paso with her mother, talking about abbreviations. Tiny houses, what *gym* was short for: Did everyone, after years away, have to push through talk so small? Or was it only her?

"Some. They rent them out now, to people who come for the tubing."

"I went down the river this afternoon," she said.

"By yourself?" he said, as if this was a violation of some local ordinance, or dangerous, or flat-out pathetic. It might *have* been pathetic had she floated it alone, which she would never have done. She would, instead, have paced around her hotel room, or taken a magazine down to the tiny pool and tried to read it, or tried to watch the Food Channel, tried to nap. Tried everything, been engaged by nothing. When Marcus first suggested tubing, Maria felt like it was just another thing she'd have to try to involve herself in. She saw through it—his attempt to distract her, which she thought sweet but unnecessary—and bumping up against flotillas of drunks was likely to make her even more anxious.

But Marcus was so excited by it. First by the idea of it, which he referred to as "an adventure." His enthusiasm made her slightly nervous, as she worried that he was in a similar state when he drove down to the border for a hike and got his truck stolen. Once he stepped foot in the Dollar General, though, he turned so goofy, pretending to want everything he saw, marveling over flip-flops and calendars and a rack of personalized key chains as if he had no idea such ephemera existed, threatening to buy a burnt-orange bathing suit emblazoned with the longhorn insignia of UT athletics, that she realized, once on the river, that he *did* think of it as an adventure.

"I have a friend with me," said Maria. Maybe she should have pretended she went down alone — maybe it would have been easier if he thought her pathetic — but Marcus *was* her friend.

"Boyfriend?"

"Just a friend."

"He come with you from out west?"

"He's just here for a visit." This was neither a lie nor a denial. Hadn't he left her a note stating his intention to move on? He was passing through, slower than a train, faster than a drought. She wasn't about to explain all this, much less how she knew Marcus, to Manny. Manny's obvious lack of interest made it easy to leave things out. She had asked ten questions to his one, and the few questions he did ask were delivered so declaratively they hardly seemed to require an answer.

The one thing she wanted to ask him was when he'd been home last, but she was worried it would sound hypocritical, given her years away. A lot more recent than you, that's for sure: he had every right to say it. But she had not come all this way (and it seemed, sitting across from him in the booth, that she had come, not from far across the state, but all the way from Oregon, across valley and mountain and endless treeless plain) to *not* ask.

It didn't seem possible to provoke his ire, given that he had about as much emotional stake in the conversation as he did in his Bud Light. The food came: roast turkey for her, brisket for Manny. Without a word he rose and she followed him to the condiment bar, marveling at the oddity of the choices: pickles, peppers, onions, brown sugar, slices of white bread. Following him as he threaded his way back to their booth reminded her of how much she'd worshipped him once, how she used to sit by the window before she went to school and wait for the bus to deliver him home.

Manny might have passed on the chips because he did not want to be the only one eating them, but he did not wait to see if she put her napkin in her lap before he started in on the three-bean salad. He ate as if he were starving, as if he'd come here not to see his sister again after twelve years. She was hurt, but also annoyed, and it was her annoyance that allowed her to say, "Have you been back there lately?"

Manny pointed to his cheek. He chewed awhile, cleared his throat, swallowed some beer, and said, "Back where?"

"Home," she said, though she knew this was the wrong word for it.

The way Manny looked above her head, as if someone behind her, someone besides her, had asked him such a silly question, was the first hint of their mother she'd found in him.

"I used to go pretty regular when I was just out of the Coast

Guard and living in Midland for a while. But it got to be, why even bother? She'd stay gone when I was there. I'd just see her for a few minutes, she'd make a big fuss like she was glad to see me, and then she'd say she had to get back to work. It was always like that. And *he* never left the house. He'd just sit there telling me how she was going to quit her foolishness, they were about to get right, and he was going to go back to work, start his own grading business, or it was going to be repairing drill bits, or he was going to go in with Alberto and run cows. But nothing ever happened. He got sick and died. But you knew that part."

Of course you were too busy to come home for your own daddy's funeral, was what she heard him say. What she wanted to say to him, even though it didn't exactly explain why she stayed away from the funeral, was that it was her father who would not let her go to *Randy's* funeral. Through the cracked door of her bedroom, where she lay unwashed and distraught three days after Randy died, she had overheard her parents fighting about it in the kitchen.

"She knew him as good as anyone," her mother had said.

"Doesn't mean Randy's parents want her anywhere near that church."

"Well, a funeral, last time I went to one, it wasn't like a wedding, they don't send out invites." Maria was slow to realize that her mother, who had said nothing at all to her about Randy, who had dealt with her daughter's grief by boiling her canned soup and bringing her ginger ale, was taking her side.

"Be hard for a person to send out invites from the grave," said her father, in his I-don't-want-to-hear-any-more-about-this voice.

"Well, you're as good as saying she ought to go, then. Randy would have wanted her there, but Randy's not the one gets to—"

"It's about some respect, Harriet. Randy's not going to be there. It's his family that stands to be riled. If Maria turned up in her Sunday dress and sat up by the grave carrying on . . . What has got into you, anyway? Why would you even think it would be okay for Maria to attend that boy's funeral?"

"Well, she loved him," her mother said, which caused Maria to gasp. Other than "I'd love a Coke about now," it might well have been the first time in her life Maria had heard her mother say that word.

"You ought to have told me," her father said. "You drove her to El Paso, so you must have known about it for a while, and you never said one word. She's my daughter, too."

Her mother said something she could not hear that caused her father to start shouting, and even though his words echoed tinny through the heat grate and she could have made them out, she did not care to hear, because she had realized that they were no longer talking about her, that what had happened between her and Randy was, to both of her parents, mostly about what was happening between them.

Maria started to tell her brother about this conversation, but he was nearly done with his food and she had had only a few bites of turkey and she had not even buttered her corn and there wasn't time to say everything. There would not be enough time.

"Why didn't he leave?" said Maria.

"He couldn't," Manny said, in a way that made it clear to her that he thought they'd all have been better off if he had.

"Why didn't she leave him?"

"Why don't you ask her? You're the one staying with her."

That he seemed annoyed by her questions did not displease her, for at least now he had a stake in the conversation.

"She won't talk about stuff like that with me. Especially Daddy. She's said a few things about Ray. I didn't realize he was sick the same time Daddy was. I guess he had Alzheimer's?"

Manny shrugged, as if he knew little and cared less about Ray or what killed him.

"You married?" said Manny.

"No."

"Never have been?"

"No."

"Not easy to walk out. Especially if you got kids. It's got to get real bad."

"You don't think it got bad for Mom and Dad?"

"Well," he said, "every time I asked why didn't he just leave, he would say, 'I wouldn't know what to do without that woman.' He called her 'that woman.' Like he didn't even know who she was anymore and didn't even care, he just didn't want to be alone. Last time I was out there before he got real sick, I went out there once to see him just before he died, but the time before that I was out there and he said to me, 'If I'm not good enough for her, then at least some of me does her some good. Otherwise she'd have left me a long time ago.'"

Manny looked out the window at the steady traffic coming in from Canyon Lake. Maria looked where he looked. The cars backed up in a long line at the intersection were not cars to her, nor people on their way somewhere, but lights in the quickly falling night.

"It was a mess," he said. "He was a mess, and she wouldn't give anybody the time of day. I don't know, I just could not see why . . ." He stopped and took a sip of beer. "Anyway," he said.

She wanted him to finish but she could not ask. There was no end to what they were talking about. She followed his gaze again. Outside, the light had switched to green. Traffic was moving again.

What she wanted to know from him he could not tell her because he did not know himself. She needed them to figure it out together, for soon Manny would be a truck pulling out of the parking lot, which she would watch turn into a trail of light.

But she didn't know what else to ask. She picked up her fork and tried to eat. Finally Manny said, "Want to see a picture of the girls?"

"Of course. I was about to ask."

Manny pulled out his wallet and showed her several pictures of the oldest, who was a sophomore at Texas State, and the youngest, who was sixteen. Inez and Iris. Iris in her photo wore a pink gown and held a bouquet and was posed in front of a blue velvet backdrop. Maria was about to ask if it was her prom when she remembered that Manny's ex-wife was Mexican, and she said, "Her Quinceañera?"

Manny told her all about it—how all Iris's friends were there, how some of his ex-wife Alicia's people came up from Mexico to attend.

"I'm still paying for that party a year later. But it was worth it, to see the look on Iris's face that day. Even now when Gloria—that's my girlfriend, she's close to both the girls—when Gloria'll get the photo album out and they start going through it and telling all the stories, Iris just beams."

"Gloria sounds great," said Maria.

"She's got me speaking Spanish. Dad told me once the schoolteachers would beat him if he didn't speak English, so I can see why we never learned growing up. But I guess being with Mexican women and living away from Mom all these years, whatever West Texas redneck was in me has about gone by now."

She heard him but not really, for she was staring at the photo of Iris, who might have grown to know her cousin. She started to stop herself from crying but couldn't. Why shouldn't she show Manny what still needled her awake some nights? He was her brother. He ought to know, even if he did not care to know, why she stayed away from funerals.

Manny said, "You all right?"

"I was thinking, I don't know. It's been so long since all that happened with Randy. You know, I'm always—well, I guess anybody in my situation would always be aware of how old they'd be."

"How old who would be?"

"You know," she said, drying her eyes with her napkin. "If we'd had the baby."

Manny moved his beer mug around on the table. He studied the ring it had left.

"Me and Randy. That's what started all this."

"Started all what?"

"That's why I left," she said. I thought you knew that, she almost said, for of course he knew it, and the way he would not acknowledge what he knew, the way he made her say everything out loud, words she did not think she needed to say—"baby," "Randy"—was the second thing that evening that made Maria see her mother in Manny.

"You running off didn't start any of what we've been talking about."

"What do you mean?"

"Nothing," he said.

"No, what? What do you mean, Manny?"

"Just, I thought we were talking about Mom. And Dad. Why he never left her."

"We were," she said. "Then we were talking about your daughter. And then I said—"

"I know what you said." Manny looked at her until she wished he'd look out the window again.

"I'm sorry," she said. "I shouldn't have brought it up."

"I didn't really . . . I mean, since I was gone I wasn't all that up on what was happening," Manny said. "Dad told me about it, but way later."

Maria started to shrug. It was true, she realized, what he'd said earlier: her leaving did not start, or stop, the things that had taken place whether she was there or not.

"No," she said. "No, Manny, look, even had you known about it, there's nothing you could have done. I know I didn't handle it well. I ought not to have brought it up."

She waited for him to tell her it was okay—she thought he might say more so that she could say more, she thought they were just starting to talk—but Manny said, "Well, I better be getting back to Gloria."

She tucked her bottom lip in her mouth and clamped it with her teeth to keep it from quivering. His leaving so abruptly, when the conversation turned difficult, would be the last thing that reminded her of her mother, the third thing, the charm. Obviously he did not see it. *Whatever West Texas redneck was in me has about gone by now.* But it wasn't as if she ever understood, or even considered, how she might be acting like either one of her parents. What did it matter now? Manny was not leaving because he had been overtaken by some slim remnant of the mother he'd tried so hard to get away from. Manny was Manny. He was leaving because he had somewhere to get back to, people waiting for him to return.

In the parking lot his hug was looser but still reserved. Maria said, swallowing, "Do you think sometime I could bring Mom out here? We could stay in one of those Sunday houses. They'd be the right size for us."

It wasn't that she could not leave well enough alone, since there was nothing well, or enough, and certainly nothing that could be understood, ever, as alone.

"I'm glad she's got you there," Manny said. "I hope you're planning on staying with her awhile." What kept her from registering her disappointment was her understanding that the way he'd said, *No, I don't want her around me,* was exactly the way her mother would have put it. Their way of saying no—evasive but unequivocal if you knew how to translate their language—was strangely reassuring, as it reminded Maria that she could not fix whatever was broken between Manny and her mother.

"Which is your car?" he said, gesturing to the parking lot, and she said, "Oh, you don't have to—" and he did not let her finish.

"I'm not going to leave my baby sister out in the parking lot of Rudy's, bunch of drunks coming in off the river. Which is it?"

That she didn't need his help did not stop her from wanting to pull him close to her again, link her arm in his, and lead him to the Buick. This is my brother, Manny, she imagined saying to Marcus, saw the two of them shaking hands, exchanging comments about the Buick. Two men talking about cars was not something she had ever desired. But when they approached the Buick, she stopped. She'd made a promise to Marcus: no awkward conversations with family.

Marcus had the windows down. His left hand tapped the side-view, and she could hear music, and she realized the car was running, as if he was her getaway driver.

"It's the Buick," she said.

"Damn, Maria," said Manny. "How old is that boat? I bet it don't even have a catalytic converter?"

"Of course it does," she said, amazed that he'd brought up the one thing Marcus had explained to her about the car that she remembered: that the government started requiring all cars to have catalytic converters a couple of years before their Buick was made. "It's only an 'eighty-four."

Manny looked at her as if he'd never seen her before. Then he looked back at the car and said, "Only?" and laughed. "Looks like it hasn't been washed since 1984."

"West Texas," she said.

"Dust and bugs," he agreed.

"You miss it ever?"

"I don't put a whole lot of time into missing stuff," he said.

"Driving a truck, it's something new every day, you never know where they're going to send you."

"You know it's to a grocery store, though, right?"

"Yeah, and say I get hungry, I can just pull over and chow down," he said, patting his belly. And then the awkwardness that had made the first minutes so painful and sluggish returned only because they both seemed to realize how easily they'd fallen into a jokey rhythm. She wanted to go home with him. She wanted to meet his family, who obviously had filled in any blank space left by the absence of his father, his mother, the sister he'd never even mentioned to his girlfriend. He seemed so devoted to this town, with its tiny houses and its tubers, and even more devoted to Gloria and the girls. Cling hard, she wanted to say, they're all you've got. I'll take care of Mom, you just cling.

"Well, I better let you go," he said, "so y'all can get over to Desert Rain before it closes and get that car cleaned up."

"I promise you next time you see that car it will sparkle," she said. He did not acknowledge her hint, which sounded, once it was out of her mouth, more like a plea, but at least when he turned away he was smiling.

Shafter, Texas, 1986 – 2003

The day that the Buick Cord bought for her showed up in the driveway, Evelyn had taken the pickup into town. They had been down to one vehicle since Evelyn had hit a pronghorn coming home from church one night four months earlier.

All Evelyn said about the Buick when she got home was, "It's a mighty pretty blue."

"I know you never cared to drive this thing into town," Cord said, helping her unload groceries from the extended cab of his truck, but of course what he meant was, I want my truck back and I will be goddamned if I am going to hang around town waiting on you to practice choir.

A month later Cord had a heart attack. He died alone, out penning cows. He was just sixty-six, but he hated doctors and hospitals, even though his father and one of his brothers had died young with bad hearts. Evelyn buried him and came home to the cries of mother cows calling for their babies. It was time to separate the calves from their mothers, and her husband's friends and neighbors had skipped the funeral to take calves away from their mothers because this is what her husband would have expected them to do. This is how they should pay their respects. In all her years out here she had never gotten used to the wails of cattle mourning their taken-away calves. Sometimes it would last three or four days. She'd run fans and sometimes even turn up the radio to drown it out, but it lingered even after the cows had given up on ever seeing their babies again and then it was their silence that got to her. How could any of God's creatures put up with the loss of a child and go right on eating and sleeping? She didn't see how that was possible. She had wanted children and her husband had not. Cord was from a large family and had nothing to do with any of his siblings. Two of his sisters up in Fort Worth she had never even seen since their wedding forty-four years earlier. The few times Evelyn brought up wanting children, Cord said, "Once you start, you have to keep on going. You can't have just one, because they'd need someone to play with and they say one is just as much work as five. More work, because the older ones will raise the youngest and let you do your chores. Fill a house up with young'uns and they'll grow up hating how you made 'em share everything from toys to oatmeal to dungarees."

Evelyn thought this was either the strangest reason she'd ever heard of for not having children or the saddest. Because he did not want his children to have to share? She knew Cord had grown up in a house where nothing ever got talked about. He said to her once when they first started dating that his parents acted like two kids in a contest to see who could hold their breath the longest. About purple in the face and bug-eyed three-quarters of the time. He only mentioned this the one time, but she never forgot it because she had grown up in a house not too far off from what he described. Her father, home from work at the sawmill he ran, sat in his chair next to the radio asleep with his mouth open, and her mother sat knitting across the room from him. The whole house filled with flies that Evelyn went around swatting just to exercise something so deep and buried in her she favored it, something a little cruel and a lot desperate, maybe what made her marry whom she married when she married and surely what made her—still in the dress she wore to the funeral, her house filled with women of the church come to comfort her with rectangles of Pyrex they all knew she would give to the Mexican girl who came twice a week to help her around the house, or feed untouched to her dogs—climb into the Buick he had bought her and drive the six miles of two-track out to where the men were loading up the calves to the cries of mothers and tell them she wanted every last cow off the ranch as soon as they could move them, cow and calf and bull, all of them, and when they opened their mouths to tell her what she knew would be what her husband would have said to this, she got back in the Buick and backed it the six miles to the house, getting within the first half mile a crick in her neck so awful she welcomed it, for this sort of pain was far preferable to what she felt listening to the cows keep up their vigil for the calves who were not coming back.

The Buick went backward as good as it drove forward. She winced at the pain in her neck as she remembered a time when her older brother was driving her to a friend's house in town and they came to a fork, and she said, "Go straight," and her brother taunted her, saying, "You mean forward, dummy, not straight." Her life had been straight but not forward. A path with no forks, but she *stood* in it more than traveled up or down it. She'd never thought to notice a difference between straight and forward until her smart-alecky brother claimed there was one.

The crying cattle were gone, but she still heard their cries in the wind whipped up in the winter night. After a year she sold the ranch and bought a small green cottage in town with a patch of grass and three oak trees. First shade she'd been able to savor other than a porch in nearly forty years. She was sixty-four years old. She pulled the Buick up under the carport and rolled the windows up tight against the dust, and there it sat. She was six blocks from church and only two to the market and she hardly ate anything but cottage cheese and Pepperidge Farm cookies and did not cook more than a sweet potato.

Her sister Edith and her husband came down from Amarillo when Evelyn turned seventy-two. They had meant to come when she turned seventy but something came up and then it was two years before they could make the drive. They were sitting out on the porch when her brother-in-law Herb got up and walked over to the Buick and started poking around it. He had already tried to put a washer in her kitchen faucet and it leaked worse than before, and here he was, about to act like he knew something about cars even though he sold insurance. Evelyn supposed this was his idea about what he ought to do when he visited a widow. She thought it was kind of sweet, but she didn't like it when he started asking her questions about the Buick.

"How long has it been since you drove this car?"

"I drive it to the store some, but when it's nice out, I'd rather walk."

"That's a classic right there," he said. Then he said he was going off to the library to do some research. When he was gone, Evelyn said to Edith, "What is Herb wanting to do research on exactly?" and Edith told Evelyn what she already knew, that Herb didn't have one iota what to do with himself when he was a guest in someone else's home and the reason they hadn't come on her seventieth was that Herb acted like he was sick. "Let's just let him go on acting like he's going to take care of everything," Edith said. "That way he'll be out of our hair."

Herb came back in an hour and told Evelyn that she owned a mint specimen of the last Electra they manufactured.

"You could get top dollar for that car," said Herb.

"How's she going to get around if she sells her car?" Edith asked her husband.

"She said herself she hardly ever uses it." He turned to Evelyn and said he would be happy to take it off her hands.

Edith said, "Herb, come inside for a minute, I want to talk to you." They went inside the house and Edith tried to whisper but it came out like a scream strained through a towel. Evelyn heard every word. Her sister lit into her husband, accusing him of trying to take advantage. Herb said he was going to pay her what it was worth, he liked the car, he'd drive it himself, and Edith said, "You got two trucks, Herb, and one of them sits in the yard," and no.

While they were in the kitchen arguing, Evelyn studied the Buick. It struck her as funny that it would turn out to be worth a dime. But she didn't need another dime. She was set from selling the ranch and even if she were about to starve she would never try and make money off that vehicle. How could she admit to her sister and Herb the real reason she had let that car sit, even when she would have saved time or stayed warmer by driving it? How could she admit that she had never even turned on the radio because every time she got in that car she heard the cries of all those mother cows sounding out their loss night and day?

But that wasn't the worst of it. It took her moving into town and living alone for the first time in her life and not minding it at all to realize her husband had bought her that Buick for the same reason he claimed he did not want children. He was tired of sharing his vehicle. Had he not wanted children because he did not want to share *her*? Was that out-and-out selfish or was there somewhere in it a sweetness? Was it straight or forward? Her brother had claimed there was a difference, but even if there was, she did not see how, at this point in her life, it mattered.

San Antonio, Texas, 2004

The Alamo was, as Maria had warned, not all that memorable, but it made Marcus remember things he'd gotten decent at forgetting, namely his education center, and in particular the crudely lettered and badly framed placards, with bullet points, that he had ended up designing himself after his disastrous and costly session with Dr. Elwood.

INSIDE THE VENUS FLYTRAP

CARNIVOROUS PLANTS MUST BE ABLE TO

- ATTRACT INSECTS
- CAPTURE BUGS
- DISCRIMINATE BETWEEN FOOD AND NOT FOOD
- DIGEST THEIR PREY

Despite his rudimentary skill with "visualizing the narrative," as Dr. Elwood had referred to it, it was hard for Marcus not to feel a little envious of the line to get into the Alamo. After breakfast and a quick stroll along the River Walk, Maria had suggested hitting the Alamo early so that they could avoid the midday heat. The Alamo at nine in the morning had more visitors than Marcus had drawn in his first month. Though a part of him understood that a standoff ending in bloody annihilation was a bigger draw than some oddity of nature, Marcus still considered the flytrap to be — as Dr. Elwood had claimed he needed to "make" it — sexy. What was sexy about slaughter, about bullets ricocheting off adobe? The flytrap was the very definition of sex: attract, capture, discriminate, devour.

"Remember that scene in *Giant* where Elizabeth Taylor tells Rock Hudson at the breakfast table that she'd stayed up all night reading about Texas and it was clear to her that Texas was stolen from Mexico?" Marcus asked Maria when they were back in the Buick headed west on I-10. Maria was driving. She had insisted. "We share the car, we share the driving," she had said, but he could tell she was not accustomed to — and there were signs she was in fact deeply terrified of — driving on the interstate.

"I've never seen *Giant*," she said.

"Can't much blame you," he said. "I've never seen *To Kill a Mockingbird*."

"Did you expect what you learned at the Alamo to agree with Elizabeth Taylor?"

What I Learned at the Alamo, by Marcus Banks. Floating down a central Texas river, I fell in love with Texas, Texans, and Texana, yet on the sacred grounds of its Bastille, all that consumed me was thoughts of my own failures, past but obviously not passed.

"I was just thinking about how the Alamo's success depends on its manipulation of what happened, which is very different from a science museum. Not much room for revisionist history when you're talking plants."

"What are you talking about, Marcus?"

It was her use of his name—the first time he could remember hearing her say it aloud—that brought Marcus back into the Buick. The interstate was eight-laned and clogged with lunch-hour traffic. Maria's hands gripped the wheel in a manner that seemed less steering than holding course in a treacherous current. Terra-cotta-topped haciendas crowned the far hills. Subdivisions of snow-weary refugees, gated against the undesirables who only a few generations back owned this land. A landscape ravaged by money. Surely the bank had taken San Antonio from the Mexicans and made it safe for pharmaceutical sales reps on the run from the windchill of lakes great and frigid.

"Sorry. I forget what I have told you and what I haven't." He'd had the sense, ever since coming off the river, that he was still hanging off her tube, talking or not, but moving slowly forward at a pace all the more perfect for the fact that it had taken them a while to calibrate. The night before, when he'd picked her up in the parking lot of the restaurant, he'd watched her in the rearview as she said good-bye to her brother, and it was clear to Marcus that it was good-bye, that she would not climb into the car and order Marcus to follow her brother home to share dessert with his family. Yet she wasn't unhappy, really, or as distant as she'd been when she stopped in the middle of the street and scooted over to be driven away. *Tentative* seemed the word to describe her affect. She talked some, joked a bit, but she mostly went away. And he'd let her. Let her know that he was alongside still, keeping the tube from pooling in an eddy, but said nothing.

Perhaps he had become so adept at not asking, at listening, waiting, because he had something to hide. And so did she. If her long estrangement from her brother were all she was seeking to remedy, there would have been nothing tentative about her after leaving that parking lot. And she would not have asked if they could skip Austin this trip and then head back, which he agreed to immediately because, as much as he enjoyed seeing Texas, he had no business being on vacation, he had no job from which to vacate, and it seemed idiotic to be wasting his loot on a pair of bathing trunks he'd never wear again.

"It wasn't just my failure at farming flytraps that did me in. I also built a flytrap educational center," he said.

"Like a nature center?" Her response seemed reflexive, as if she could not fully converse while navigating the interstate. Just as well; it was more about the confession, for Marcus, than about her reaction.

"Sort of like that," he said.

"Can we after viewing this object, hesitate a moment to confess, that vegetable beings are endued with some sensible faculties or attributes, similar to those that dignify animal nature," wrote Bartram in that phrase Marcus had paid dearly to have cast in bronze and set in a block of Pennsylvania limestone placed at the entrance to the center. To this moment, Marcus had believed every word of it. His flytrap had no mind and no heart and yet in some ways it behaved the same as those equipped with such organs. Say a small twig or baby acorn fell from the skies into its clutches. Such inanimate prey would not fire the trigger hairs, but the flytrap would remain closed for business for hours until the leaves spread apart and the unwanted prey was blown away or fell out. Carnivorous plants must be able to discriminate between food and not food. Who among us with heart and mind has not failed to distinguish between the two?

"So I'm assuming the flytrap center failed as well?"

A rapturous Bartram wrote, "We see here, in this plant, motion and volition."

Where did Marcus want to go now, and why did he want to go there? Though commerce took you away from me, nature will always bring me back, my sweet Venus, and from your example have I fashioned my own adaptive strategies: silence, exile, and cunning.

"Apparently a scientific mystery ceases to be mysterious once you break it down into bullet points," he said. "Also," he said, desperate to get it all out in the hallowed and forgiving sanctuary of Her Lowness, "I never told my sister about the bank taking the farm."

"Oh. But I thought you said you were in touch with her."

"Some. But never about this."

"Do you think she would not be supportive?"

"I imagine not, since we co-owned the property."

"Oh," said Maria. "Okay."

"Yeah," said Marcus.

"Well, I don't know anything about it, but if she's co-owner of the land and the bank takes the land, surely the bank would have notified her. I mean, how could she *not* know?"

"Yeah, the thing there is, see, Annie has a tendency to move quite a bit, usually a couple times a year, and so because she's just not that great about details like change-of-address notices, at some point I just thought it best that she just have all the financial stuff related to the property sent to the farmhouse. I mean, I told her I was going to do it and she was fine with it. And I was planning on telling her about what was going on but I kept thinking that somehow something would happen that might bail me out, which is maybe the most embarrassing thing about it now. I mean, what, I'm going to find a buyer for a carnivorous plant museum? Maybe some venture capitalist was going to hear about my plight and charter a jet and airdrop bundles of cash in the swamp? Or maybe the state would finally realize the incredible resource they had growing on their native ground and maybe it would dawn on someone in Raleigh that these plants are far more valuable things to be known for than barbecue and basketball and the fucking Lost Colony. I used to sit on the porch and fantasize about getting the call from the gov himself. Not only would I get a fat pension, but they'd give me a slew of state vehicles, including a golf cart or two to tool around in, and some research associates, who I would get to hand-choose among the dozens of earnest young grad students in botany clamoring to lead groups of schoolkids around the center while I busied myself cultivating *fructus naturales*.

"That's Latin," Marcus said, and because he knew he had just said too much and he could not find a way to stop talking and to get the taste of his pipe-dream diatribe out of his mouth, he translated the phrase for Maria, who said, "Right."

"Sorry, I guess you knew that."

"Not that hard to figure out. Anyway, back to your sister."

"Yeah. Annie. So all the overdue notices and the warnings and the foreclosure letter came to Route One, Box Nine-A, Silt, North Carolina, and from there the lot of it went into a Dumpster in an alley behind a place called Love Wigs in what passes for downtown Silt."

"Okay," she said again, and her saying it was starting to irritate Marcus, as there was nothing okay about it, any of it, and yet he did not mind being irritated at Maria, for it took the heat off him, if briefly. "Wasn't she in on the flytrap thing?"

"The flytrap thing," Marcus repeated, and not in a nice way.

"She must have known what you were doing with the land, right? It must have taken years for you to start your flytrap farm and this museum?"

"She knew I was raising flytraps. I did not tell her about the educational center. I meant to, but we don't really talk that much. And you don't need to keep saying 'okay,' okay?"

"I'm sorry," she said. "None of my business, and you don't have to answer, but just so I understand, um, the gravity here, was the land worth a lot of money?"

"The initial loan was for nine hundred thousand. Since the bank had no problem lending me that amount against the value of the land, I'd say it's worth a good deal more. Some of it is swamp, but there's so much cypress back in there that the logging rights alone could have paid for the center had I been inclined to cut down a single tree. And there's a good deal of river footage. Even though the river is nothing like the one we floated down, they're starting to develop down there now."

"Would you sell to developers?"

"Not if I had made a go of it selling traps and running the

center. But I certainly thought about it. And I probably ought to have. As banal as it sounds, sometimes you have to do things you swore you'd never do."

"Like thank the town fathers of Fort Stockton for that hideous display?" she said, pointing to a roadrunner constructed of painted rocks on the bank of the overpass, signal for their exit onto back roads.

"Sort of like that, but way worse. Anyway, stop at a gas station. I want some beef jerky and also I want to drive."

When he got back into the car he offered her a stick of jerky, and for once she did not deride his awful diet and catalog, as she had several times before, all the awful things lurking in a solitary serving of beef jerky. "I'm not hungry, thanks," she said from far away, against the passenger-side door. Her demeanor, suddenly, was the same as when she'd stopped Her Lowness in the middle of Pecos Street and waited for him to drive them out of town.

He did not say, Did something happen while I was gone? even though he thought it. Whatever had put her where she was had nothing to do with his presence or absence. He figured that whatever had made her want to leave town in the first place had settled in again upon their return. As if they had not left? This made Marcus feel worse than he'd felt when confessing that he had squandered his sister's inheritance and hadn't gotten around to notifying her. He remembered wondering, afloat on the river, suddenly blissful, whether Maria was another Monte Gale, the beginning of some impending unrest. For the first time since they'd left town, Marcus fought off the fast black tide.

After five silent minutes she began to talk. She started with the day she'd first spoken to Randy in the cafeteria her junior year and ended with the note her mother had left two days earlier on the place mat. Her story covered the distance from the interstate back to town. Marcus did not so much as nod. She would not have noticed if he had. She spoke not to him nor to the highway shimmering ahead but to the desolate miles outside. Her story took place along these roads and it was as barren a story as he'd heard in his life, but the words out of her mouth made this place she'd returned to make even more sense. It explained a lot, her faraway and unfading loss, her years of displacement, but one thing it did not explain—at least not in a way that was instantaneous and total, like that thing he'd heard described as an epiphany—was why Maria had chosen him to share the Buick. There seemed to Marcus, after listening to her tale, as many reasons why she wouldn't do it as would. The obvious reasons—taking a risk, trusting a man back in this place she'd had to flee because she'd insisted on both motion and volition—seemed far too obvious. He wasn't about to ask her, What does all this have to do with me? He wasn't about to ask her anything. The questions she had posed about his story trafficked in facts: Did the bank notify your sister? How much was the land worth? But her story did not seem made of fact. It wasn't so much what had happened as how she had let it linger.

Marcus would stop short of a reaction. He had no idea what it would be like to be a young, smart girl and return home with your mother from the clinic to find your boyfriend dead behind a camper. He would not offer any platitudes. You do what makes sense, and if it does not make sense, you make it make sense. This seemed the only advice (and reassurance) he could dispense. What did he know? He was wrong about so many things. The Alamo was no different from the Flytrap Educational Center. Science was as easily skewed as history. It was not the product he was selling, the so-called narrative he had to offer; he had spent too much money. The note came due. He was no businessman. If he had any business sense he would not have gone in on a used Buick with a woman who stopped said Buick in the middle of the street, oblivious to traffic backing up behind her. The plant was not animal. Rebecca did not leave him. Marcus was not going to disappear into Mexico. There was life and there was the "visualized narrative" of his life.

All he said to Maria was, "I am so sorry." But he knew it was inadequate and what he was apologizing for was how he had started out sympathizing with *her* tragic past and ended up obsessing over his own.

Maria was silent all the way back to town and through it, until he pulled into the parking lot of the Dairy Queen.

"Why are you stopping here?" she said.

"I can walk back to the hotel from here."

"But it's your day," she said.

Marcus counted back to prove it wasn't.

"We can't use one of your days on *my* trip," she said.

"But I was on the trip, too, remember? You were showing me Texas."

"I should be apologizing to you for even suggesting I was some kind of tour guide. You know why I wanted to go to San

Antonio. Take the car. It's your day. In fact, I owe you a few days. I owe you a week. Take it for as long as you need it."

Marcus thought about what he should say. What he wanted to say was, I can't believe we're back here arguing about who should take the car. Why even leave if we're going to act the same way the moment we roll back into town? But he did not say that, because he could not say it. After what she had told him about the boy she loved and the baby they made and the boy dying and her leaving, he could not assume, ever again, that the way she acted had anything to do with him. And it wasn't as if nothing had changed. He wondered whether he would ever have gotten to hear her story had he not written that note on the dirty bag, and if his note had not followed so closely her mother's. His own response, after not one but two rejections, would have been to blow everyone off and head to Mexico. He did what made sense to him, but if it did not make sense he did not try too hard to make it make sense.

"Okay, I'll take the car today. But I'm going to drive you home."

"Fine," she said. Before she would have said no. But now she did not seem to care if he saw where she lived. He did not let himself wonder whether this was a good thing or a bad thing, because it was just a thing and water rose from the gutters and she was giving him directions now to her house, where she lived with her mother. The storm drains were clogged was the problem. The town was not used to rain and the black water had nowhere to run off.

"Right on Pecos to San Jacinto, left on Nueces, right on One Eighteen," she said. "It's a couple of miles out."

As he pulled into Maria's drive, Marcus tried not to stare at the Airstream. He would have thought they'd have gotten rid of it years ago, but there it was, alongside the drive. He tried to look away but the sun hit the edge of it and turned it into a mirror flashing a semaphore indecipherable but impossible to ignore. When he realized he was trying to decipher it, he turned quickly and in shame to Maria, but she was looking where he'd looked.

"I'm sorry," he said.

"Don't be," she said. "It's your day."

Four

Pinto Canyon, Texas, 2004

The way Marcus apologized for looking at the Airstream—as if her story, the details of what happened behind it, had turned it into something he ought not even glance at—was what led Maria, her bag still in the drive, Marcus and Her Lowness just out of sight, to climb the steps and open the door and peer in.

Trapped air, and everywhere dust so thick the wood paneling—once cleaned weekly by her father and reeking of Murphy oil soap, an odor that ever after put Maria in this camper—was the wan gray of lint.

Only twice did she remember the Airstream leaving the yard: Once, the family went to Balmorhea, where she and Manny splashed around in the roped-off shallow end under their father's care while their mother did God knows what a quarter mile away in the RV park. Another time her father took them down to Big Bend. Her mother stayed home. Manny had been allowed to bring a friend, which meant Maria slept in a sleeping bag on the floor, the two older boys whispering and giggling into the night on the foldout sofa above her, her father snoring, then not snoring, then snoring so wildly she feared he was dying, in the double bed at the other end of the camper.

Not until she left home did Maria understand the camper
as an emblem of her parents' stalled marriage. Her father had
bought the camper from a coworker before Manny was born.
They were going to hitch it to his truck and take off every summer for two or three weeks. Her father thumbtacked a map of
the country on the wall above the double bed, and Maria knew
that if she made it farther than the threshold, she would find
the map there still, yellowed, its edges curled, looking like a
relic, a newspaper from another era. Careful circles faint but
still visible around the places her father had planned on taking
them: Yosemite, Mount Rushmore, Yellowstone, Great Smoky
Mountains. The usual destinations for middle-class families
for whom hotels or even motor courts were held in suspicion
because they belonged to another rung. The leisure class. Leisure, to her father, turned out to be sitting under the carport
grilling chilies, or burning trash with a six-pack and a buddy
who saw the smoke and stopped by to bum a beer, or leaning
against a souped-up Nova talking cars with his daughter's boyfriend. I like to sleep in my own bed, she imagined her father
saying to her mother in defense of his purchase, for surely her
mother had put up a fight, as she was finally the reason the Airstream came to rest in the yard. But her father had also bought
it *for* her mother, for she certainly wasn't going to stay in any
motel. "Why would I want to spend one minute on vacation in
a damn motel when all I do every day is cater to people who
expect, because they've rented a room, for everything to be
like it is back at home, except better?" her mother would say.
"Because in a motel they don't have to pick up after themselves
or straighten up at all, and my land, the way people will mess

up a motel room, it's nasty. No, thank you, I know way too much about what goes on in those rooms to ever sleep in one." And so her father, in an attempt to satisfy his curiosity about somewhere other than West Texas (or maybe it had nothing to do with actual places, for Maria doubted that had they ever actually made it to the Great Smokies, they would have done much but set up in some campsite and eat what they would have eaten at home, and their father would have burned trash in the campfire and her mother would have scrubbed the tiny shower, which was actually the entire bathroom, or cleaned the tiny oven or gotten down on her knees and scrubbed the linoleum floor while Maria and Manny played the same games they might have played at home), knowing that his wife would not stay in a motel, saved his money and bought the Airstream and brought it home one day and announced his plans to do something different from the day-to-day that had overtaken each of them, singly, as well as their marriage, that abstract union they had celebrated in a simple ceremony in a small Methodist church in Valentine, and—Maria was just now realizing this, as seeing the inside of this camper after all these years, breathing its stale air, opened up to her the se-cret, shadowy spaces of her parents' early marriage, the things they wanted for their union and they things they wanted for themselves—the camper was maybe his most ambitious and perhaps final shot at fulfilling his fantasy of a future with this ranch hand's daughter, this white girl he met at a dance and courted for six months and married and loved even when he knew he ought to have found someone else to love.

The camper, like her father, ended up hanging around the

house long after it should have, long after it ought to have belonged to someone who would have taken it somewhere, slept in it, cooked on its tiny two-burner stove.

Maria had been the last to set foot in it. She did not know this until she opened the door and stood so tentatively a few steps inside.

But before she let herself think of that, of Randy, of the last time she'd inhabited this space, of ham thick and gelatinous and equally thick cheese, tasteless but chewy, of mayonnaise and spongy white bread, of what had happened behind the camper, she thought of campers in backyards all across West Texas, of how she'd seen them all her life and never seen them for what they were, mobile living spaces marooned permanently in backyards. Maybe it wasn't just here but in certain neighborhoods and small towns all across the country. Bought to pull behind pickups, to *go* (places different from home, beautiful places, mountains, beaches, lakes, parks) and to *stay* (sleep in my own bed, cook my own food), symbol of the hopes of newlyweds, the wishes of young married couples, of people who fall in love and think love is always going to feel the way it *did,* first flush, can't sleep or eat for want of you, *more* of you, I don't even feel like I am in my own skin when I am with you, it's like we're sharing the same space and every night is so new and different and so like a motel room in another city, the air-conditioning cranked up without a thought of how we're going to pay the bill, and all those channels on the television, and here is a hair dryer, let's take a bath and point this gun of hot air at each other's skin and then let's jump still wet in the bed and let's take all the shampoo and lotion and let's wear shower caps and nothing else. And so the trucks were trailer-hitched and the campers were outfitted and their tiny cabinets were filled with extra blankets, board games, bug spray, sparklers, and let's just take off and go, it's us — me, you, the children we made together who are each of us and us together, our future, the gift we give to the world — against the rest of them. Driving along the interstate at dusk, they watched the sun set behind the mountains of America, and the sky striped with yellows and pinks causes the father to say to his wife and children, My God, will you look at that! and life intersects with the dream you had about what life would be like for you and the one you chose to spend your life with. But after a time, maybe two or three years, five at the most, of occasional trips, you outgrow the camper, it feels cramped, the kids get older, there's no privacy, you can hear everything, and who wants to lie awake at night, ten feet away from their mother and father sharing a bed, and listen in the dark to their parents breathing and shifting in sleep, and what parents want to sleep in pajamas and nightgowns after so many years of slipping naked under the sheets? The kids get older, they want to stay home with their friends, they want to hang out at the pool, they can't miss this game or that dance, they have lessons, or practice, and who wants to have to deal with kids so sullen and brooding in such tight quarters when it is supposed to be, after all, a vacation, which is supposed to be fun and filled with discoveries? Weeds reach the bottom of the camper; the tires go flat. Maybe an errant teenager or an ailing grandparent moves into the camper. Mostly their surfaces gather dust and the carcasses of expired insects.

Maria stepped farther inside the camper. For years she did

not cry. She never asked people for anything. Everything she had, she earned. Kids get older, she said to Randy, starting to sob. They change, and when they do, everything changes. Or everything has already changed and the way the kids change makes it all the more obvious how we might have changed. Randy loved this camper. "I want to go to the Grand Canyon," he said. "After I build our house, we can get a camper like this one and park it wherever we want." He might have tried to buy this very camper. And Randy would have been the only person her father would have considered selling it to. In the afternoons when her parents were at work they would come here after school and eat sandwiches and drink Pepsi. She pushed farther into the camper and there was the bed still made with the awful orange-and-green polyester comforter. She walked to it and sat down on it. In the afternoons when her parents were at work she and Randy would lie in this bed and practice being grown up. I want this part of life to be over, they said to each other with their young bodies. It will always be like this, Randy said to her with his hips as he moved inside her, and she said, Like this, as she wrestled him over on his back and made him sit up with his head against the map of the United States of America and sat in his lap and lifted herself up and down and grabbed his head and brought his lips to her breasts, and there were so many ways to say to each other, I want this part to be over, I want to move on to the next part, and she said it back to him every time, she never said no with her body, she only said it afterward in the car high up in the mountains overlooking the twinkling valley.

"Maria?" her mother called. Had she said, instead of Maria's name, "balloon" or "pencil," her voice would have registered the same amount of shock and confusion. How had Maria not heard the Cherokee in the drive? Where had she been?

Her mother stood in the tight hallway. Maria wiped her nose. It ran when she cried.

"Maria?"

"I saw Manny."

"You went there? I thought you said you were in San Antonio."

"Manny said you never call him. He said you never talk on the phone."

"Seems like Manny has taken up more with his father's side."

"What does that mean?"

"If he wants to be Mexican I can't stop him. He's half me, though. There was nothing wrong with my people."

"I think Manny just fell in love, Mom."

"Both of them Mexicans."

"You married a Mexican."

"Not because he was Mexican."

She wanted to know why her parents got married and she wanted to know why her parents stayed married, and yet instead of asking, she said, "I want this camper."

"You want what with it?"

"I want to live in it."

"This nasty thing?"

"I can clean it up."

Her mother crossed her arms. She tightened her jaw. She said something Maria knew it nearly killed her to say. She said, "You're mad about that note I left you. You're mad I said that about the restaurant."

"Actually I'm not. You were right. People want blooming on-ions. If the restaurant didn't make it, I'd just go back to Oregon and work for Beverly, and business-wise, as you keep on saying, it would hurt you more than me."

"You don't want to live in this camper. It's not even hooked up."

"I want to move it."

"Where to?"

"It was Dad's, right?"

"Your father bought it without asking me. But you know when you're married your money all comes out of the same pot."

"You never liked it."

Her mother looked around as if seeing the place for the first time. The look she gave it seemed to Maria the look she probably gave it when her father brought it home. She bet her father was crushed. He had so wanted his bride to feel, step-ping up into the camper, something she had gone past ever feeling again.

"Too small," said her mother.

It was easier to take her father's side because he was dead. It was easier to take Randy's side because he was dead. The child was not dead because it was never born. But that did not mean that it did not have a side.

"I want it. I want something of him. Daddy would have wanted me to have it."

"Well. Maria. I did not mean when I wrote that note that you—"

"I'm not leaving. But I am too old to live with my mother in my old bedroom. We're too old to act like we're acting."

"How are *we* acting?" her mother said, but Maria ignored the spin she put on the word "we."

"Like I am still in high school. Like I just went away for the weekend. Like I haven't been gone so long. Like I haven't changed and you haven't changed."

"Well, I know you're grown," her mother said. "I said when I wrote you the first time I would stay out of your way. I just didn't see why you would go and do a thing like that with someone you don't know from Adam. I just did not want you to get cheated. I do not want to see you get hurt."

Maria started to say, You're worried about someone hurting because they got cheated? But she stopped herself because she had changed even if her mother had not. If she moved into the Airstream, would it honor Randy's memory, or would it desecrate all that had happened here? Marcus had built a shrine. "History is always skewed," he had said about the Alamo, but he had also said that hagiography was the modus operandi of shrines. About his own shrine he claimed it was not possible to revise history. Because it was a plant he idolized, not a person. Yet sometimes he spoke of the plant as if it were someone he could never quite get over.

What was the Airstream? Alamo or flytrap? It stayed and it went. Randy loved it because it had wheels. But it never went anywhere. It would have been easy enough for her mother to call one of those Keplers and tell them to come get it, but she did not. She let it sit.

She ran her finger along a windowsill and wondered how much of the dust she picked up had accumulated since she'd been back home. "There's just not as much time as I thought there was," said Maria.

"It never is, is it," said her mother.

• • •

PRETTY MUCH EVERYONE IN town knew where Bobby and Pete Kepler got the brunt of their cars. Drive by the lot on any given day, and chances were high a good 60 percent of the vehicles would have come through the Border Patrol. Kepler's kept them whistle-clean, but those cars had some history. Secret stash in tire well, double gas tanks stuffed with drugs. Best if they were hauling bodies over drugs or money, because there would be no factory upholstery to try and match, no danger to the undercarriage caused by agents with welding torches gone greedy for a find by the boredom of stop, ask, look, stop, ask, look, all day long. Bobby himself did a stint with Border Patrol when he was younger, but they tried to transfer him to McAllen and he told them, "No, sir, no farther than Del Rio, no, thank you," and that was when he went in with Pete on the lot.

Had it not been for his time with the agency, though, the lot would not be half what it was. He was always telling Pete it was owing to his connections they got the vehicles they did. Anybody could show up at auction and buy a seized vehicle, but some dealers got a preview, and having friends to tell you what was coming up meant saving a whole lot of sitting around listening to some auctioneer stutter. Sometimes you got lucky and got an early trip, beat the vehicle to the auction. Pete wouldn't listen to any of it. Since he was the older brother, to him it was his lot and would always be, though half the time he did not even show up. He had another lot up in Monahans and he pretended like he was needed up there three or four days a week, but Bobby knew he hardly moved anything off that lot, he was shacking up with some bank teller from Pecos.

Bobby wasn't all that upset about Pete not being around.

He guessed Pete, being his brother, being family, ought to have been somebody he didn't need to think about how he felt about, but when his brother was around, telling him what to do and how to do it, asking for stuff Bobby would have had a chance to get around to had he not been the only one moving any vehicles, all Bobby felt was like he wanted to hit his brother in the neck. Then he had to *think* about why he *felt* such a thing. Go away, Big Brother, and let me peddle my cars in peace. Bobby could hardly even eat when his brother was around, or that was about all he could focus on, where he was going to get lunch at that day.

Bobby had a lot of peace most days his brother was gone, for other than washing the vehicles and keeping the little strip of grass by the street mowed, there wasn't much to do. Some days he did not have a customer at all. Back a few weeks ago he had had two people show up on the lot at the same time. That was like Black Friday for Kepler's Fantastic Deals! Or would have been, had not one of them been Harriet's—Harriett who ran the Mountain View, took up with Ray Menton, used to be married to Luis who Bobby had gone to school with—daughter. Harriet had called ahead and said that the girl was on her way and that she did not have a clue what she needed and that she hadn't even ever owned a vehicle before, and Bobby had said, "Well, I'm pretty stocked right now, so she's got a decent choice at least," and Harriet said for him to call her and run it by her what vehicle the girl chose, and Bobby thought back to when all that had happened with that boy who killed himself behind their camper when the daughter was in high school, and he decided that was the last time he had seen that girl, Maria was her name, she'd took off and been God knows where for God knows how long.

"You're wanting me to call you while she's here?" said Bobby. He did not understand what Harriet was asking, nor did he care for it. If Harriet cared so much what kind of vehicle the girl purchased, why didn't Harriet come to the lot with her?

"Not so she'll know it," said Harriet. "Can't you just, after she picks one out, sneak off and call me up? Let me know what the situation is?"

"I guess," said Bobby.

"What all have you got out there, anyway?" said Harriet.

Good God, woman, I have not got time to go through my whole inventory for you on the telephone right now. He had just gotten back from May's Place and his lunch was getting cold and Pete had taken the microwave up to Monahans or to his girlfriend's house one. But Bobby was a little scared of Harriet. He had always been. He liked her well enough and remembered when she showed up in town from up around Van Horn. She was a pretty girl and at that time a lot of people wondered why she married a Mexican, but it was into the seventies then and she wasn't the only white girl mixing it up. Besides, it was Luis she took up with, and Bobby didn't know a soul who would have held being Mexican against Luis. Not out loud, anyway. Laid-Back Luis, they called him. He was about as easygoing as they come. Bobby could see why Luis went with Harriet, but as pretty as she'd been back then, there was always something thorny about her. She didn't laugh much or even smile. Bobby remembered thinking whoever had named her either pegged or cursed her. She sure wasn't a Luanne. She wasn't even a Hilary.

Bobby went through about half the lot for Harriet on the phone. Harriet hummed if he mentioned something might work for her girl. She hummed twice—Honda Civic and Ford Ranger—but the Civic hum might have been something on the line, it was so faint, nothing like the Ranger hum. The pickup Bobby figured out she wanted for herself. He'd sold her a Cherokee a year earlier and she'd said when she bought it that what she really wanted was a four-wheel-drive Silverado. "Didn't anybody anymore run drugs with a Chevy?" she asked and Bobby said, "Well, it's not *all* these cars have been involved in illegal activities," and Harriet laughed in his face and said, "Bobby Kepler, who do you think you are talking to?"

Later Bobby would wonder why she did not hum at the mention of Miss Evelyn's Buick. Maybe because she was thinking she wanted something she could drive some, and Harriet was not a Buick-driving type of woman.

But the Buick was the only one her girl even acted interested in. The other person on the lot that crowded day was interested in it, too, turned out. Bobby did not recognize the man. Later when Harriet asked what he looked like, all Bobby could remember was how in-between he was. He wasn't skinny and he was not fat. He wasn't young but he wasn't all that old. He wasn't bald but he didn't have the hair he probably had once. Because it was lunch time and because Bobby knew that Harriet's daughter was on her way and that he had a car sold, all he had to do was let Harriet know which car and type up the paperwork, and because it had been a year at least since he had moved more than one car in a day, and because he did not particularly care for it when the man said, "Any Fantastic

Deals to be had today?" acting like he was the first one clever enough to say that or something like it, Bobby did not fool with that fellow. "Let me know if you see something you want to test out," he said, and that was it, he went back to his chicken.

And then it turned out the guy was with Harriet's daughter. Or so Bobby thought. Actually he did not know what to think. It didn't seem like he ought to think too much about it. Either way, whether this Maria was with him or not, Bobby had a sale.

"Find something to love?" he asked Maria later when he found her out by Miss Evelyn's Buick. He did not see the man at first until she said, "This one. We'd like to test-drive it," and Bobby meant to *think*, We? but instead he *said*, "We," like "We?" And then he saw the fellow standing on the other side of the vehicle and he went to apologizing, "I didn't realize y'all were together," and then he screwed up and said, "Your mama didn't mention . . . ," and then Maria cut him off. "No problem," she said, and he decided it damn sure wasn't a problem because what was the point in worrying over it? He was getting ready to sell a car. He let the two of them take the Buick out alone because truth be told, he had his doubts about that vehicle. The mileage was just too low, given the age on it, even if Miss Evelyn had let it sit up under her carport for over ten years. He had known Miss Evelyn's late husband, Cord, and not to speak ill, but Cord was one hard-bargain crusty old fucker and tight as a tick and he would not put it past the man to—well, Bobby didn't need to worry about it because he had the paperwork on it and he had in his day sold worse.

When Maria came into the office and said she wanted the Buick, she was alone. He sold her the car for two grand even though he had put twenty-five hundred on it. He didn't have all that much in it because Miss Evelyn, he guess because she had done so well selling off the ranch, didn't care much what he gave her for it. Bobby, though, figured he gave her a fair deal, given her husband and his overall shadiness and the fact that she seemed to want that car out of her drive that very day.

Every time Bobby Kepler sold a car he would knock off early and go home and wait for Sherry to get off work. He'd stop by the store and buy her some flowers and some wine and him some scotch or beer and they would grill steaks. Last time, when he'd sold that Winnebago, they were in bed ten minutes after she got home. She still had her hose on, pulled down to her knees. She pinched his big stomach and said, "You only want to do it when you're flush, buster," and he said, "Bulge in the wallet equals a bulge in—" and she cut right in and beat him to his punch line, squeezed what she called old Belly Roll Morton again, and both of them laughing crazy naked in the daylight and right on since high school still in love.

It was a week after he sold that vehicle that Harriet came storming into his office. He happened to, thank God, see her Cherokee tear into the lot spraying dust all over the vehicles he had just hosed off. He saw her little stick figure hop out. *What in the world does she want?* He pictured that Buick hood up on the side of the highway, but it wasn't anything as simple as that.

"How come you let her buy that car with him?"

"Harriet, I don't know what you're talking about. Buy that car with who?"

"That's what I want to know. Who was he?"

"I just got through telling you I don't know who you're talking about."

"You never seen him before?"

"You mean the fellow was up here the day your daughter bought the Buick?"

"Mexican?"

"No," he said. "White guy."

"So you *do* know who I mean."

"I do *now*. I didn't when you came dusting my fresh-washed cars and asking me all kinds of questions before you even said good evening."

"She said he wasn't Mexican but I didn't know."

"He wasn't Mexican," said Bobby, thinking, What does Harriet care? Last time I checked she married a Mexican. "Unless he's one of those Mennonites. He didn't sound Mexican."

"She said his truck got stolen down along the river somewhere."

"I don't know the first thing about any of this."

"You got the paperwork?"

"I sent it to the DMV, Harriet. It's in the pipe. She ought to be getting her registration this week."

"His name's not on it?"

"Hers is."

"Not his?"

"I would not know his name if you said it."

"How am I going to say his name? I don't even know what the man looks like, you haven't even said yet what he looks like." Harriet was breathing big and she was trembling. She was wearing a Spurs T-shirt that was too big for her and jeans from the Dollar General, he knew the brand, his sister-in-law wore them, they came up to your rib cage. Also she was wearing a red visor that made her hair bush out below her ears.

"She told me she had never even laid eyes on him before," she said.

Then Bobby saw in her eyes and in the twitch of every nerve in her body that she had said something she did not want to have said. She looked around the office and saw the desk chair and she took it. Bobby got some SunnyD out of the fridge and poured her a cup. She drank some of it and he watched her stare at the floor. They said she was happy with Ray. Bobby felt bad for Harriet but he did not understand her. Why did she care what he or anyone else thought about her daughter buying a car with some man when she carried on with that Ray for years living at home with Luis, who half the time was dying of cancer? Then Ray died of Alzheimer's back-to-back, and on top of that what happened years ago with her daughter and that boy behind the camper. It was a lot for a person. But he still did not understand her because she acted like none of it ever happened. She got up in the morning and pulled her jeans on up to her ribs and went out into the world expecting everything would be just so, even though, how could she?

"You want a little more juice in there?" he said, pointing to her cup. He couldn't remember when he had been this uncomfortable. Then Harriet said, "You won't say anything, will you?"

"Say about what?" he said, but he knew what she did not want him to say anything about, and the only reason he said something was that seeing her like that, Harriet, all crumpled and sipping SunnyD, it nearly choked him up. He never in his life thought Harriet would make him feel like he was about to cry.

"What happens at Fantastic Deals stays at Fantastic Deals," he said.

Harriet lifted her cup in the air for him to fill. "What happens what, now?"

He explained that this was the name of the lot, though most people just called it Kepler's.

She said, "Well, I bet there's a lot you don't want to get out goes on around here."

Bobby could not help his grinning. He splashed some SunnyD in her cup. He sat down in his desk chair and rolled it a little closer to her. That's okay, Harriet. Go on acting like you don't care. I saw it. I know it's there. In you like it's in me and everyone. Even my brother, who half the time I want to hit in the neck. And in that girl of yours and the one she bought the car with. There and waiting, all of us have it, got it to burn.

AS HE DIALED HIS sister's number, Marcus pictured that camper, sun-struck silver as tin foil. Nobody died, it helped to remember, for he knew how long Annie had been banking on one day coming into big-time money. One ought not ever employ the word *bank* as a verb, or at all. Foul and four-letter word. But neither ought one to be taking consolation from the vision of an Airstream where tragedy lingered still.

But it was his day. The phone was ringing. As it rang, he thought of the time he had said to Rebecca, one night near the end of them, "Something is wrong with me," and Rebecca, lying next to him in bed, against him (her softness still warm and chiding him in memory for forsaking all that was good and sweet and kind in her for all that was rapacious and prideful and greedy in himself), but as far away, at that point, as Minneapolis, said, "Something is *wrong* with everyone," her emphasis placed so rightly on the word "wrong" designed—and just now successful in its designation—to make Marcus realize how utterly unoriginal were his sins.

If everyone is wrong, might as well call upon the present-tense drifter to join hands with the mute and wiry man and provide me the right tools to deliver this confession I ought to have made months ago.

"Marcus?" said Annie, when Marcus said his sister's name into the phone.

Marcus said, "I lost the farm."

"At least you didn't buy it," she said, which meant, he knew, "die." Which meant she thought he was kidding.

"Somebody did die," he said.

"Who?"

"You don't know him," said Marcus. "I don't even know him." Why was he even talking or thinking about him when he was supposed to be confessing his wrongs?

"Are you drunk?"

"No," he said, "I'm in Texas. And I mean it. I lost the farm."

"Well, maybe you ought to get the hell out of Texas and go find it," she said. "If you're even in Texas. Why would you be?"

"It hasn't gone anywhere. I just . . . we just don't own it anymore."

Then came the lag between what he said and what she said back that he had so dreaded.

"Well, who did you sell it to?" she said finally.

"No one. The Bank of America took it."

Marcus heard trees fall in forests. Mosquitoes, their unison buzz nearly mechanized, in the Great Dismal Swamp. The squeak of sneakers in a gymnatorium in rural Kansas. Vee of geese honking over the ancient and storied silt of the Mississippi Delta.

"I'll get a job and pay you back, Annie, I promise," he said into the quiet. "I will go without everything until I have made things right with you."

"What kind of job?" said Annie. Her voice after the hours of silence was wet and raw, as if she had already been crying, or yelling. "Where are you even calling from?"

"I told you. I'm in Texas."

"You're living in Texas now?"

"Yes."

"Jesus. Who moves to Texas? So, what, you're going to go drill an oil well and pay me back five hundred grand?"

"That's a little high, don't you think? I'd say at the most I owe you three hundred grand. And I said I would pay you back. Maybe we can work out a payment plan?"

"Maybe you can pay me what half of that land was worth instead of trying to tell me what you think you owe me. What are you living off, by the way?"

"I sold my truck."

"That Ford? And what are you living in, a tent?"

"I'll send you what I got for the truck."

"So you can be homeless and I will have to feel sorry for you, living under an underpass in, like, Houston? I cannot believe this. I cannot believe you. You think I don't know about your fucking museum? In a place you'd have to get lost in to find? Two hours off the interstate?"

"Lots of people came, Annie. I had Canadians and some Japanese and a couple who invited me to their chalet outside Zurich. It wasn't just that people didn't come, it was more, I just got in over my head."

"Yeah, if it were only *your* head you got in over, that would be one thing. You don't even sound that upset about it."

"Lots of families fall out over money late in life."

"What, so, this is like a thing? So you're like *normal*?"

"I'm just saying." The mute and wiry man, having handed off his tools, was gone, but the drifter was waiting for him in the present tense. He had the Buick pulled up to the curb outside the hotel. Rising water lifted tire-flattened beer cans from the gutter underneath Her Lowness. I'm just saying I got to go now.

"Don't call me again, Marcus. If you get in trouble down there, don't bother Mom. We're not going to bail you out."

"I know," said Marcus, but he wasn't worried about it because he had someone waiting on him downstairs and he had another someone else waiting for him, someone to whom he could tell things, someone he did not owe a dime.

But when he hung up the phone he did not move from the bed. What paralyzed him was first a feeling and then the feeling that he could not tolerate what he felt. He could not stomach feeling hated, despised, pitied, reviled, regretted. Marcus had known people who spoke of others who, for this reason or that, held them in low regard, and it no more bothered them than did an airplane passing high above them in the clouds, just barely visible, then gone. What can you do about it? I can no more control what people think of me than I can make that airplane up there turn around and fly back to wherever it took off from, and how do I ever even really know what goes on in somebody else's head? I don't know any more than I know where that plane is headed or who is on it or whether they seek in the city of their final destination business or pleasure. Who knows?

Well, Marcus knew. He knew what other people were thinking; he always had. He could tell whether they liked him or not, and if they did not, he did everything he could to make them change their minds about him. It is okay to lie sometimes. It is fine to lie if it means people otherwise would hate you. He said to his sister when she asked him how he was supporting himself, "I sold my truck." He did not tell his sister that someone stole his truck, that in fact he was living off money hidden from the bank and from her; she would have been hurt and also she would have hated him more than she already did. She hated him. She would never forgive him.

It is easy to pretend that people love you instead of hate you. Just go to ride. You can go to ride in your head. You can say to yourself, Now you get out of this hotel room you cannot afford, and you get in the car you cannot afford, and you drive across the street to the Fina station and buy a paper. It's only a dollar. You can afford that because in the back of the paper are the help-wanted ads. And you want help. You need it. Getting a job and paying back your sister is the only thing you can afford to do because then she won't hate you as much. Every time you send her a check, maybe she will hate you a little less.

Pay down the hate. But it wasn't as if he had just now figured out that she would hate him for what he had done to her future. See, from the beginning he had found a way to pretend otherwise. He could, for instance, forget the land was half hers. Which half? He would stand on his porch at dusk and stare off into the sunken scrub, already claimed by shadow, alit with fireflies, and holler, "Who do you belong to? Speak up, I can't hear you." The land lay there like a recalcitrant truant refusing to rise in time to meet the school bus.

Or he could, rather than forget that it was half hers, hold that against her. If it is half yours, why aren't you down here trying to turn a profit or at least half a profit? Why did you leave it all up to me?

See, you can find rooms in your head that are empty. You can dress them up however you want. Marcus found an empty one and he filled it with mirrors. Fine ones with gilded frames and funky oval ones with no frames and the long rectangular ones you buy for dorm rooms. Every time he would go inside that room he would look in the mirrors, and there looking back at him was a man who tried to do right by everyone. All you can do is try. Only assholic coaches and preachers whose faith has no doubt don't recognize the single most recognizable sign of life, which is the good old try. Holding a mirror to the mouth is less effective than checking to see whether they at least tried. But some people still hate you for not succeeding, so they decide you never even tried. They hate you for not trying because it is easier than hating you for failing. People started their sentences with "From where I stand" and "To my mind" and "Looks like to me." From where they stood to their minds it looked like to them that Marcus had not even tried, but people had no idea how elaborate had been his vision for the transformation of a piece of swampland into an oddball but wildly seductive temple of scientific lore that no less than *National Geographic, Smithsonian,* and even the *New York Times* would have featured in their slick pages. Every frame of every mirror in that room in his head flashed with the image of the man who could have made this happen had they just given him more time.

Marcus sat in the parking lot of the Fina station accusing himself of the crime of attempted living. He paged through the newspaper, searching for his name in the court docket, but there were only want ads. He searched the ads for wants that even slightly matched his needs. But everyone wanted Creative Individuals. To drive trucks, to serve food in cafeterias, to take X-rays, to pick tomatoes. Marcus was not a creative individual. The only thing he could create was a right fucking mess. If you get into trouble down there, don't call us, we're not going to bail you out. That's okay, I got someone I can call. I got a ride, thank you very much. But when he looked out the window at the street below, Her Lowness sat empty. No one is waiting for you, Marcus. There was no present tense. Just his sister's hate blowing through the ventilation in his room. Her hate fluttered curtains. It lifted the pages of a magazine. It drove him out of his room and downstairs and into Her Lowness and across the street to buy the paper.

Now he had the paper spread open and all the world wanted was creative individuals. He was neither. I am no different from anyone else, Marcus said to the black water pooling in the parking lot of the gas station. In seconds it had reached the bottom of the Buick. This was not his car; it was only half his car, just like the farm had been half his. But the problem was he acted like it was his and his alone. "You do exactly what you want, *when* you want," Rebecca had claimed. The trick is to share all the world, and time. To merge, not to divvy.

But it was not his car it was only half his just like the farm. Maria's half must stay dry because two people in one day wrote her hurtful letters and all because of the car. But she kept the car and the car took her to a river where she was baptized in a bathing suit from the Dollar General. The car took her to see her brother so long lost to her who maybe hated her for what she had done and they ate some barbecue from some chain place by a busy highway and now the brother did not hate her.

This car could save him too. But water covered his lap. The car would save him and his sister would no longer hate him only if he could keep the water from rising. Rebecca would not come back but she would forgive him his sins. At the very top of the Buick there was a pocket of air but that air belonged to Maria because his half was swamped. He said it was her day but she had given her day to him. A chart to keep these things straight lay soaked and ruined on the floorboard. Ink from the pen he had used to do the divvying bled the water even blacker. Marcus would rather succumb than float up to breathe big from Maria's half. He felt the newspaper lifted off his lap and he watched it float away. He put the car in gear and he pulled out of the parking lot into traffic, because he did not want to owe Maria a dime.

BECAUSE SHE HAD A project at home — helping Maria clean out the Airstream — Maria's mother did not go back to the motel that evening. Neither of them was hungry, and

Maria, having decided to move into the camper, wanted to get to work cleaning it up, so they skipped dinner and filled buckets with soap and water. For a while they worked quietly until Maria, thinking of Manny—of how, when she had quizzed him about their parents' marriage, he'd said, "Why don't you ask her? You're the one staying with her"—said, "Why did you not leave Dad?"

Her mother had been cleaning the tiny stove. She looked up at Maria, who was washing the walls. "I couldn't leave him," she said after a while.

"Why not?"

"Because I married him. Maria, you'll maybe say it's old fashioned, but what is old fashioned about keeping your word? Or I guess I know the answer to that. Doing what you said you're going to do, that's *been* old fashioned."

"I guess being miserable has been around a long time, too."

"Well, I don't know," said her mother, putting down her sponge. "Now you're going to stand there and tell me how I felt inside? I never once told you how *you* felt after that boy killed himself."

"You never said anything about it at all."

"What was it to say? I did what I could, I guess. Anyway I can change it now, well, I can't figure it out."

Maria said nothing. For ten minutes she scrubbed and listened to her mother work. But it did not seem right to her that she should be in her father's space, this camper he had bought with such hope for some renewal, and not try to honor his memory in ways other than dusting and scrubbing.

"Did you ever *try* to leave Dad?"

Her mother was in the bathroom. But she could hear her. Maria heard the toilet seat slam down. "Maria, I swear."

"I just need to know. I'm not trying to make things harder than they already are. I just need to know these things."

Her mother came out of the bathroom. She leaned against the stove. She said, "Your father, he'd fall apart. I would say, I'm leaving, I'm going to go be with Ray, and he'd cry and he'd beg me not to. He'd just—he was, I don't know, fragile maybe. He couldn't stand the thought of being alone. He just wanted to be around me even when I told him I wanted to be with Ray. He'd cry and he'd say things."

"What things?"

"That's all been over so long, I don't see the sense in—"

"No," said Maria. "Tell me, what did he say?"

"Maria," said her mother, "had your daddy made good on his crazy, half-drunk claims and done to me what that boy done to you—"

"He didn't do it to *me*," Maria said.

"But he did, child. Look at you."

"What? I hurt still? How could I not?"

"How can you keep it? How can you live and hurt over all that right on?"

"You're asking me how I can live?"

"Yes. I guess I am."

A car pulled up in the drive. Alberto come to check on his water tank, most likely. Maria looked out the window and saw the Buick. She said to her mother, "Just a minute."

"Who is it?"

"Marcus."

"Who?"

"The man I share the car with."

"Lord God. What does he want?"

"I don't know. I'll see. I'm not through talking about this."

Maria went out to the car. Marcus was sitting behind the wheel, the car idling, as if he were waiting for her to come out. As if he had come to pick her up, as if this was the plan.

"Marcus?"

"I wondered if you have a moment to talk."

"Can you give me a few minutes? I'm kind of in the middle of something."

"Sure," he said. Of course he would say that. He was always so agreeable. She had asked him to buy a car with her and he had said yes. She'd chosen the schedule where they alternated days and he had said fine, even though she could tell that he preferred his other chart. He told her he was leaving town, take the car, time for me to go, and she'd stopped the car in the middle of the street and slid over and he'd gotten in and driven her east to see Manny. She had begun to wonder, well before she got his note, what made him so accommodating. Surely indulging her was not just a way of redressing his wrongs to his sister and his family and his ancestors and the land he had lost. That would make her just a line on a list that needed to be ticked off so he might live his life with somewhat less shame.

But of course that was all she was to him. It had nothing to do with her, with her needs, just as what she needed from him had nothing to do with him as a person distinct from a stranger in a car lot upon whose mercy she had placed her trust in others. Just seconds ago, when he asked her for a moment to talk, her first reaction was to send him away. He looked haggard and needy, sitting in her drive, and she had other things to attend to. She was in the middle of something she had been in the middle of for years and years, and now finally she was talking to her mother about things her mother would never talk about, and here came Marcus in their car. He needed her, obviously. But she needed her mother now.

She said, "Just a few minutes."

"What does he want?" her mother said when Maria came back into the camper. Maria had seen her looking out the window.

"You said Randy did it to me. He didn't do it to *me*. He did it because he could not see past his own hurt."

Her mother had been looking out the window at Marcus. She said, still staring at him, or at the Buick, "Well then, you need to honor his memory by seeing past yours."

"You make it sound so easy. You don't think I've tried to get past it? How am I supposed to—"

"Not by buying a car with some man you've known all of five minutes. What does he want?"

"I don't know what he wants. I told him I was in the middle of something, he'd have to wait."

"You ought to just go out there and buy him out. Send him on to Mexico or wherever it is he was on his way to. I'll loan you the money, I got plenty saved. What in the world was he wanting in Mexico, anyway?"

"We're not talking about him. We're talking about me. You were about to tell me how I am supposed to see past my hurt in order to honor Randy's memory? Remember? We were talking about Randy?"

"You already said this business with the Buick had to do with what happened back then. I am just saying, I never even laid eyes on that man out there until now and I don't like him sitting in my drive spewing exhaust all over the yard for Alberto's cows to breathe. Why does he not just cut the car off? If you ask me, it's not a good sign that he just shows up without calling first. He's probably wanting money. I don't have any good reason to care one way or the other, but does he know why he's even driving that car? Did you tell him?"

Maria said, "I don't think any of this is any of your business, really, but yes, I did tell him."

"When?"

"What does it matter when?"

"I'd say it matters a lot. I don't guess you had time to tell him before you marched into Bobby Kepler's office and paid for that car with half his money, did you?"

"No."

"Well then, would you not say you are using him?"

Maria had her back to the window, but she saw the stricken expression Marcus wore when she left him to come back into the Airstream. Something was wrong with him, but she did not want to think about Marcus and what he was doing there on his day, in her drive, when she was trying to talk to her mother.

"Do you want me to go out there and tell him to get lost?" Maria said. "Take his keys away and pay him off and tell him to get off your property? Will that make you feel better?"

"We're not talking about me feeling better."

"Right. You were about to tell me what to do to make myself feel better and honor Randy's memory in the process. So what is it, Mom?"

"Well, what is it you still feel bad about?"

Maria said, "You're kidding, right? Have you even been listening?"

"I'm just saying, is it what you done in El Paso? Or what happened when you got home?"

Maria was quiet. It was so hot in the Airstream. I want this part to be over, they said in as many ways as they could think of; I want to move on to the next part. She tasted Pepsi. Seemed like she was always crying now.

"What I did in El Paso is what I had to do. But I never got to go to his funeral. And I know you thought I ought to go, I heard you tell Dad so, but I didn't get to go and because I did not get to go to Randy's funeral, I did not feel like I ought to go to Dad's funeral."

Maria's mother sighed. "A funeral, Maria—I've been to quite a few in my time, I buried both Ray and your daddy within weeks of each other. A funeral, all it is, you sit on a hard chair up under a tent and some preacher says some words you can't even hardly hear for the wind. They claim it's about sending somebody off proper and letting everybody and their brother pay their respects, but some hymns on an organ isn't about to heal how you hurt after somebody close to you's gone."

"Don't you think that's easy for you to say? Since nobody was telling you you could not go to one?"

Maria's mother said, "You got a lot of your daddy in you, you know that?"

"Jesus, Mom."

"What? I'm just saying, your daddy—"

"You mean I'm fragile? Isn't that what you said he was? He was fragile for loving you, for not giving up hope that you'd fucking love him back?"

"You need to watch your mouth."

"Let's say I am like Dad. Why don't you tell me how to be like you? Tell me how to do it."

Her mother looked at her as if she were just now recognizing her. As if for all these weeks, since she met Maria in Baggage Claim, it had not been her daughter sharing this house with her but someone she could not quite place. Now she blinked and there was Maria, come back home. Maria was wondering what she had said to make her mother see her, when her mother said, "Come inside."

"Why?"

"Just follow me," she said, and she pushed past her, and Maria followed her mother inside without even looking at Marcus in the Buick. In the kitchen her mother already had the phone book out.

"What are you doing?" Maria asked as her mother paged through the thin book. Her mother picked up the phone and dialed. Maria said, "Who are you calling?"

Maria's mother said Randy's mother's name.

Maria said, "Why?" and then, louder, "What are you doing?" She crossed the room and grabbed the phone out of her mother's hand and hung it up.

"This has got to stop," her mother said. "You said we have to quit acting like this, and there isn't but one way for us and it won't happen until you get on the phone and tell that woman you're sorry you did not get to go to that boy's funeral or whatever it is you have to tell her. And you can tell her you're sorry her son's dead even though you aren't responsible for what happened to him, and when she tells you you're going to burn in hell for what you done to her child and her grandchild, you hold on to that phone and say you're sorry again and you say it louder. Don't you dare ask for her forgiveness, for she won't give it to you, just like your daddy would not ever forgive me. I know how they are. They aren't going to give you what you want. You got to find your own way past it. You can't have any say over how they take it but you still got to give it."

Maria's mother's hand was on hers. They both shook. Marcus was waiting in the car. He was behind the wheel. If he drove her to Randy's house he would wait for her in the car. I'll just be a minute, she would say to him, and he would say, Okay, and he would not turn on the radio or get out and lean against the car and smoke. He would not pull out a cell phone and call someone and laugh and yell and curse in the manner of people who could not for one second be alone without distraction. He would watch to see she was inside Randy's mother's house and when she came back down the walk he would lean over and open the door for her. Then she would listen to whatever it was that had him in such a state. She hated to make him wait but she had faith in the chart she'd chosen. It was his day and then hers. They had made it work.

Maria said, pulling her mother into her embrace, "I can't do that over the phone. It wouldn't be right. And it wouldn't accomplish anything. She'd just hang up on me."

"You want me to go over there with you?" her mother said into her ear.

"No," she said. "I want Marcus to take me."

"You wait right here, baby," said her mother. "I'm going to go ask him."

MARCUS WAS IDLING HER Lowness in the drive, waiting for Maria to finish whatever she was in the middle of (and whatever it was, it had started inside the camper, which, had Marcus not been so desperate to keep dry, he might have taken as a sign that this was really not a good time for him to be coming around asking for whatever it was he was there to ask her, he wasn't even sure what that was, he just knew he needed to see her, needed her to come out of that trailer and motion him over to the passenger side and drive them someplace safe from the coming tide), when the woman who minutes earlier had come out of the Airstream — *busted* out was more like it — walked out of the house and right up to the Buick.

Marcus had the window rolled up tight because he deserved to drown. He had seen, in the way that Maria had followed that woman, obviously her mother, into the house without looking his way, that only vanity and pride — those same failings that had delivered the farm and the center to the bank — had allowed him to hang up the phone with his sister feeling as if someone would bail him out. The water flooding the Buick had followed him from home, for it was tannin-laced, the color of whiskey, reeking of sulfur, black crappie, and catfish. There wasn't any water anywhere around here that looked or smelled like that. Wasn't hardly any water around here at all.

He had rolled up the window. Maria would find him afloat and bloated. She had given him this day. He thought it meant—

Here came Maria's mother up to the car and he could not finish a thought. It had been this way since he'd gotten off the phone with Annie. Half thoughts abandoned like cars in a blizzard. Treadless tires spinning out into ditches. Nor could he gain traction on feeling. Soon as he felt he had some sense of what was in his heart, here came another wave, one atop the other. Maria had only been humoring him when she came out of the camper to tell him, "Can you give me a few minutes? I'm kind of in the middle of something." So stuck in the middle was she that she'd forgotten about him idling just outside the Airstream. And now she had sent her mother to deal with him. Too timid herself to tell him to hand over the key and get lost, it was over, she could not help him, she never could.

Well, he wasn't much better. He'd left her a letter. Dear Maria, take the car, it's yours, see you later, I'm gone.

Maria's mother stood by the car. She was thin in the manner of someone for whom food is consumed only as fuel for the task ahead. Maria, too, was thin, but not the same kind of thin. In no other way did she favor her mother, who was fair-skinned, sun-spotted. The sleeves of her shirt were rolled up past her elbows, and the knees of her jeans were dirty. Everything about the woman—especially the set of her mouth—said she meant business.

Carefully did Marcus roll the window down; mercifully did the tide refrain from slamming Maria's mother into the camper.

"Maria needs to go somewhere," she said. She was breathing heavy and talking fast. Her voice was just throaty enough to suggest she'd stuck a cigarette to her lips a time or two. Although Maria had no accent, there was a slight twang in the way the mother said "somewhar" that reminded Marcus of people from up in the Blue Ridge back home, though Maria's mother clipped her words, as if she had too much to do to waste breath drawing them out.

"She's getting ready. She's got to go see somebody. Can you take her over there?"

"Yes, ma'am," said Marcus.

"This isn't going to be anything easy. I mean, it's, she's got to do something and it's going to be hard on her. She asked me to ask you to drive her over there and I just want to know she's going to be safe."

"Yes, ma'am," he said. "She'll be safe."

The woman studied him. She said, "You look to be about as old as I am. You can skip the 'ma'am.'"

"You haven't said your name."

"That's because it's Harriet."

"Oh, okay," said Marcus, as if this were reason to withhold her name. Now she would hate him. He'd just met her and she hated him. But here she was trusting him, with an errand she said wasn't going to be anything easy. She trusted him but he needed her to like him.

"What would you have *chosen* to go by, if it were up to you?"

The look on Maria's mother's face suggested she was appalled by his question, as if it were wholly inappropriate. Oh God, what have I gone and said now? For he did not plan on saying it; he would never have planned on saying such a thing to a woman asking him to perform an important task. They weren't at a lawn party. Surely she was about to ask him to leave. But when he looked up at her she had started to blink. Her eyes grew wet, and he realized that she was crying. Very lightly at first, the way he imagined it rained sometimes in this place so unaccustomed to moisture, a soft and ephemeral tease of a rain. It seemed to Marcus that Maria's mother had been holding off crying for a very long time.

"I guess Juice," she said. "Like Juice Newton?"

Marcus didn't say anything. He did not even nod. Maria's mother's face was soaked with her tears. Maria came out of the house. She had changed into a skirt and she carried a sweater. When she saw her mother crying she hurried over and pulled her close. They held each other. Maria looked at him over her mother's shoulder. She did not want him to leave; she needed him to drive. While Maria and her mother sobbed into each other's necks, the water drained away. The car dried out, but it didn't make Marcus feel any better knowing that his pain had subsided only in the mounting presence of someone else's.

The hugging and crying lasted for what felt to Marcus like five minutes until Maria's mother pulled away from Maria and said, "I'm going to call her and tell her you're coming and that you won't take up more than a few minutes and will she please see you," and Maria nodded and then she got into the car. Maria's mother squatted beside Marcus. She held on to the door with both hands and said in a softer way than before, "Thank you. You just took me by surprise asking me that. You can call me Harriet." Marcus said it was nice to meet her and said his name. Harriet nodded and stood and wrapped her arms around her rib cage as if she were alone now, walking through pasture into a frigid wind. "Bring her straight on back here," she said, and he said he would.

He would not have disturbed Maria's silence had he known where they were going, but on the way into town she said nothing at all. He put off asking as long as he could. "Take a right by the Thriftway," Maria said, and then, "Go left here." Two more turns before they were in a neighborhood over near the high school. She told him to pull up in front of a ranch house. A basketball hoop above a garage, a conversion van parked in the drive, a satellite dish titled skyward in the side yard.

Marcus switched off the Buick. They sat in its sanctuary. Maria did not move. He reached across her and rolled her window down. She said, "Now I don't know why I'm doing this. What is it I am apologizing for, again? What am I doing in front of Randy's house?"

"It's going to be okay," said Marcus.

"How do you know?"

Marcus did not know. He only really knew what *he* was in the middle of. But we're always in the middle of something. Never does it begin the way we choose to isolate it in memory, and never, ever does it end with our actions. But he could not say this. She had asked him to drive her over here. In order to help, he had to lie.

"Why do you have to know what you're sorry for? Can't you just say you're sorry and then come back to the Buick and we'll leave?"

"Except she might think . . . I mean, I don't want her to think I have spent all these years feeling guilty about what I did in El Paso."

"She won't think that."

"How do you know?"

"I don't know," said Marcus. "I don't know the lady. But from what you've said about her, it seems like if she thought you were capable of feeling guilty about the choice you made, wouldn't that mean she'd have to forgive you? And isn't it easier for her not to forgive you?"

"Why is it easier?"

"Just makes the world smaller. She can understand it better that way," said Marcus.

Maria was quiet. She'd stopped crying but it felt to Marcus like the moment when a storm passed and the sun has not yet emerged to wash everything brilliant and clean. "You're right," she said. "She won't forgive me."

"Are you here for her forgiveness?" he asked, but he was thinking about his sister, of how he could never pay down her hate. A hundred dollars a month. His wages garnered until he keeled over making change at a Whataburger. The thought of money ushered in the tide.

"I want to come with you," he said.

"What?" said Maria. "Why? No."

"I'm not just being nice. I'm not all that nice. I need to."

"But why?" she said. "Why do you need to go with me?"

It was not a competition, what each of them had lost; it wasn't something to tally up on one of his little lists. Her losses were not quantifiable in the way of greenhouses, geodesic domes, slabs of limestone imported from Pennsylvania, tools he never learned to use. Even land, no matter its history or its mystical aura cultivated by sentimental agrarians, a club into which he had been born, was something you could auction off, a minimum bid firmly in mind.

She had started to cry again. She looked at the house and he looked also. A curtain parted behind a bay window.

"I'll stay with the car, then," he said. Not *in* the car but *with* it. As if it were more than vinyl and metal. Something to be minded, tended to, never left alone. His preposition rattled him. He remembered that look on Maria's mother's face when she said, "Juice," as if she had been carrying this around for years and had never let herself think it, much less say it.

Maria did not appear to have heard. She'd gone off somewhere. Finally she said, "Randy used to do that. Leave me in the car. He'd say, 'I've got to stop by Johnny's house for a minute and pick something up, I'll just be a sec,' and he'd hop out and leave me in the car with the motor running. There was something so lonely about that. It made me so anxious sitting there, the car running but not moving. There was never the right song on the radio."

She went away again. While she was gone, Marcus thought, You could have just switched the station. But then he remembered how it is when you are a teenager, especially one of a certain sensitive stripe, how there is only one station, and usually only one song. If he stayed with the car, he would only be able to tune in to the slosh and gurgle of rising water.

"I won't say anything, I promise," he said. "I'll just stand beside you."

"It's going to be awful."

"For five minutes maybe. Then it will be over."

"Why should I do this?"

"Because you told your mother you would."

"It's for her, then," said Maria. "For us."

Marcus heard "us" and thought she meant *them*. But Marcus and Maria were only a chart. From now on they would adhere strictly to that chart. He would, like Maria's mother, mean business.

"Someone is watching us," he said. "We should either leave or go to the door. I say, just do it. Later you can make it make sense."

Maria wiped her nose with the sleeve of her sweater. She nodded, sniffling. The hinges creaked as she pushed open the door. She stood in the street pulling on her sweater. The fabric bunched up on her back; Marcus plucked it loose and smoothed it out as he followed her up to the front porch.

The woman who came in time to the door was shorter than Maria but plump. Her hair was long in the back and she wore bangs. Her haircut made her look even more angry and severe.

"Your mother told me you were on your way over here. She asked would I give you five minutes of my time. I told her I would give you three."

The woman looked at Marcus.

"Is he your husband?"

"No," said Maria. "This is Marcus." Randy's mother looked him over and said, "Why is he here?"

"He's my friend," said Maria.

"Well, why are *you* here?"

Maria said she was there to say that she was sorry and that she never got the chance to say it because her daddy would not let her go to the funeral, and Randy's mother interrupted her to say, "You were not wanted at the funeral."

"But Randy . . .," Maria started to say, and Marcus wanted to somehow let Maria know that she ought not to be telling Randy's mother what Randy had wanted. But he was not there to talk for her or tell her what to say. He was in the middle of a slow black river.

"Then I moved away," Maria was saying. "But now I'm back."

"I heard."

"And so I came over here to say I'm sorry and to say also that I wish —"

"I cannot forgive you, Maria."

"I know," said Maria. She nodded but just barely.

"I wish I could. It makes me feel terrible not to. God wants me to but I can't. I am not at peace with him over this because I know he wants me to forgive you but I can't. That's all I can say to you. I'm sure it's not what you came over here for."

"No," said Maria. "That's enough. I didn't come —"

The woman closed the door in the middle of Maria's sentence. They carried it with them, unfinished, up the walkway to the car. Maria was in front and she got in on the driver's side. Her mother had asked him to take her over here, and what would her mother think of him if they pulled up in the drive and he was riding shotgun? But Maria wanted to drive. It was her day now. Maria's mother would just have to hate him.

On the drive she was quiet except sometimes she cried. They caught two lights just as they turned from yellow to red, and at both lights Marcus almost said, I'll get out here. But he didn't and he was glad because as they were passing the Thriftway, Maria started to talk.

"Because Randy is dead I get to make him up. He is more

alive to me because he is dead. But if he were still alive, he might be, I don't know, my dad. Grilling his venison steaks in the drive, working on his car under the carport. Or we'd be divorced and I would still live here and I would run into him in the Thriftway and he'd be with his new wife and she'd be someone I sort of knew from school and she'd hate me because I had been with him first. She would talk for him, as if he had laryngitis. He would look at the rows of pinto beans or cereal boxes while she said what they'd been up to. Or probably I would move away and never think too much about him."

Now she turned to Marcus. "Thank you for going over there with me, Marcus. Thanks for taking me and for going to the door with me. I don't think that what I said to Randy's mother and what she said back to me changed anything. But I told my mother I would go, and thanks to you I went through with it."

"Credit due Her Lowness," said Marcus, patting the dashboard. He had noticed, while idling in Maria's driveway, that they needed gas. He was about to ask Maria to stop by the Fina station when she braked and pulled over to the side of the road as if she were letting him out.

"Oh my God. You came over to my house because you needed to talk and I totally took you off on my thing. Now it's been hours. I'm so sorry. What is it you wanted to talk about? What's wrong?"

Marcus stared out the window. He remembered leaving the gas station knowing he had somewhere to go, someone he could call. But now he did not want to show his face to Maria because something in her tone suggested that the look on *her* face would resemble her I-mean-business mother

"You have a lot of your mother in you, you know that?" he said.

"That's it?" said Maria. "That's what you came over to tell me?"

When Marcus did not answer, she said, "You met my mother for, what, two minutes?"

"She makes an impression."

"Oh God."

"No, she's great. You know what she said while you were inside getting ready?"

Maria hunched her shoulders and sat up in her seat. Would he always say the wrong thing?

"What did she say?"

"I kept calling her 'ma'am' and she finally told me to stop and I said I would but I didn't know what else to call her because she had not told me her name. So she said, 'That's because it's Harriet.'"

Maria eased back into the seat. She swabbed her cheek with a bit of sweater she'd pulled like a glove over her hand. "She said that?"

"I haven't gotten to the good part. Because your mother is pretty intimidating and I wanted her to like me — I mean, actually I really *needed* her to like me — I asked her, even though it was hardly the time or place for such a question, I don't even know where it came from, I said, Well, what would you have *liked* to be named?"

"You asked my mom that?"

"Sometimes I blurt. You might have noticed."

"I can't imagine asking her that."

"Well, me neither, now," he said, worried again that he'd ruined things, but she seemed more shocked than angry.

"Nor can I imagine what her answer would be," she said. When Marcus did not reply, Maria said, "Am I supposed to guess?"

"If you want."

Maria looked over the steering wheel. Above town there were clouds dappling the folds of the mountains ahead.

"I have no idea," she said. She shook her head slowly. "Not a clue."

"Juice," said Marcus.

Maria squinted as if she hadn't heard him. "Juice?"

"Yep."

"Like Juice Newton?"

"Exactly. That's what she said. 'Like Juice Newton.'"

At first Maria looked stricken. But then she started to laugh. Her laughter was of the sort you try to squelch and your failure to do so makes it all the more impossible to control. Back-pew church laughter, terrible-elementary-school-orchestra-recital laughter. Maria draped her arms around the steering column and touched her forehead to the wheel, and Marcus, when he was certain she was in fact laughing and not having an asthma attack, succumbed himself. Hicuppy gasps dead-ending in snorts. Maria laughed at the deep offensiveness of his bray. The Buick filled with the air of their lungs unburdened. They would try to stop but they kept failing until finally Maria gained enough control to say, "I don't know, God, it's not that funny, it's actually really sad but it's also crazy, and in a way—in *her* way, I mean—it's so, so sweet."

They were quiet for a while, and then Maria said, "You never talk about *your* parents," and Marcus said, "That's because they're named Harriet," and this started them off again. When this round died they were breathless and Marcus craved quiet until he didn't anymore.

"You want me to get out here?" he said.

"No," said Maria. "Let's go for a drive."

"We need gas," said Marcus.

"I'm on it," said Maria, and she pulled into traffic and drove them to the station.

"I can pump my own gas," said Maria when Marcus opened the door to get out, but Marcus said no, she got gas last, it was his turn. He opened the gas tank and reached for his wallet and found that he had left it back in his room. He went around to her side and motioned for her to roll down the window.

"Let me guess," she said. "You're a little short."

Marcus allowed that he was a lot short.

"And that's what you were coming to tell me?" said Maria.

"I wasn't really coming to tell you anything," said Marcus.

Pinto Canyon, Texas, June 2004

Harriet loved a map, and even though she made it clear to both parties her feelings about their plan for the Buick, thought it wasteful, not to mention dangerous, liable to land them in trouble with Border Patrol, she knew the area as good as about anyone around. So when Maria and Marcus told her about what they were referring to as their "ceremony," she suggested the far-back, broken country between Van Horn and Valentine, where she'd grown up.

"My daddy used to work that land. Wasn't his but he knew it better than the man who owned it, or any other hand. He used to take me along on horseback when he was checking fence and I can't imagine anything's changed out there in the last forty years."

She started to give them directions to the spot she had in mind, but it did not appear to Harriet that either of them (a) were listening too good or (b) would be able to locate the place without a map even if they were listening. They were sitting at her kitchen table one Sunday morning. Sunday was when they did stuff together because it was the only day the three of them had off in common. Maria had paid Alberto and a couple of his friends to gut the Airstream and put in a stove and a window counter and on Thursday, Friday, and Saturday nights she and Marcus towed it to a lot across from the train station and sold tamales and raspas to the tourists. The rest of the week Maria fixed food for special parties—*catered,* Harriet guessed was the word for it—out of the kitchen in what used to be Johnny Garcia's. A couple of weeks after all that mess with Randy's mother, Marcus had got on out at the Desert Research Center. He put in forty hours a week there. Harriet could not for the life of her figure out what there was to do out there in the desert for forty hours a week. He said he cleared brush and tended to the plants, but she didn't see what brush there was out there to clear, nor how you could waste more than a couple of hours a week tending to twenty acres of prickly pear and sotol and agave. She guessed she could pay a visit out there and see, but that place was for the tourists.

Maria had fixed some kind of fruit pie for breakfast, only it wasn't a fried fruit pie but some dough with fruit laid out on top of it. It tasted pretty good. Harriet wouldn't have picked it, but she had gotten to where she'd eat anything put in front of her when it was the three of them, for she liked it when they did stuff together. Ate dinner, drove to the True Value to pick up some railroad ties she wanted so she could plant something in that space where the camper had sat for so long. Now that Maria had turned that camper into something you might see someone selling popcorn out of at a rodeo, Harriet had told her she had to park it behind the motel. She didn't want that thing in her yard anymore. Luis had wanted it gone the week after

Maria left. He had wanted it gone *before* she left. But Harriet had not lost that fight.

Maria and Marcus had got to where they carried on like they'd known each other for years. They'd argue, too, almost like they were married. But Harriet knew there wasn't anything between them. She was glad, too, that it wasn't going in that direction. If it had, she doubted they'd have wanted her around.

When Maria told her she was going to take the camper out to Austin, explained how there were more people and more money and more of what she called options (which Harriet took to mean she could serve what she damn well wanted to serve), Harriet said, "Well, that sounds like a plan." She would never have said anything but. Sometimes it amazed her that she ever asked Maria to come back home and help with the motel. Now here Maria was, leaving again not six months later, but at least she would still be in Texas. Sometimes, still, the weight of all those years apart—the not knowing where her child was, then the knowing and the not knowing whether to go after her or even if she ought to write to her, and then the knowing finally that she'd let the girl go, that she did not write because she didn't know how to say it, what she ought to have said to the girl before she ran off, and then the not standing herself for letting her girl go like she did, and then the not letting herself hate herself anymore over it because what was she supposed to do, climb in some airplane and go flying across the country to bring back a girl who wasn't a girl but grown and not likely to be talked back onto an airplane by a mother of the type Harriet had been to her?—sometimes the burden of it all came upon her still. She'd be remaking a poorly made bed or revacuuming a room and she'd have to stop and go to the room she kept open, where she and Ray had met for years, their room, 117, and just sit there on the double and think about all her years lying next to Luis by night and poor sweet Ray by day and most of the night too, and now both of them gone and her daughter back but so many years with her lost and her son gone she guessed for good. She thought about how, when Manny did come home, it had seemed he was just there to visit Luis. She knew she ought not to have just given up like she did, but a bigger part of her than she could now stomach saw Manny sitting there with his daddy consumed with talk chosen because she could not share it. Just like Luis done with that boy Randy and she could tell Maria too hated it when they went on about cars and ball games as if these subjects were something safe between them instead of just, she realized now, common interests, not interesting ones but ones they shared, and she just said, Well, I'll leave them to it. Told Manny she had to get back to work, hugged his neck, and said, "Bring your wife next time," even after he had got rid of that wife, she knew it, he'd told her, she just slipped up.

Maria was back but now here she was leaving. Harriet didn't understand a lot of what she did and some of what she said. For instance, what she said she was going to do with that Buick.

Maybe it was the sharing part of what they did with that car that got to her. Or scared her. You could say that parents share their children, that this is what a marriage was supposed to be, a partnership where everything—a house, a car, and even children— was supposed to be jointly tended to and appreciated. Not that it had ever been this way with her and Luis. It was more like they took turns with the kids but not in the way you're supposed to—one looking after them when the other one was off doing something else, spelling each other until they could all be together. Luis would take Manny off with him and they'd come back and she'd want to get the boy back in her corner, so she'd take him into town and buy him a Blizzard at Dairy Queen. Harriet and Luis were nearly over by the time Maria was old enough to go to school. So then it was sharing her with school, then with whatever she had going on after school, friends and lessons and clubs, and eventually with Randy. But Luis was so keen on Randy that he just let Maria go when Randy came along. Just turned her over to him. Harriet couldn't fault him, though, because she'd already let go.

She had always thought that she had learned to share when she got with Ray. They came together at first over making a go of the motel. But after they started up with each other, it stopped being a motel or a business or even a building. It was something different, a part of them, the part that never did—because they never could—admit even to each other what they were doing, right out in public practically. So they took it day by day, just like the rooms in the motel, turning over, everybody out by eleven sharp or you'll get charged, and Lord knows she and Ray didn't run up any bills. Pay as you go, that's what they were. Or thought they were.

Was she supposed to see in Maria's choices all the things she'd done wrong? She didn't know where that would get her. She told Maria, "Well, that sounds like a plan." She could see this town wasn't the place for her daughter anymore, if it ever was. She'd outgrown it, and good for her. She'd be in Texas. Harriet had this idea—more like a dream—that she'd go visit Maria in Austin and they'd drive down to New Braunfels and she could get to know her grandchildren and maybe she'd sell the motel and get a place near her children and her grandchildren. But she knew it was a dream. Wouldn't take a train whistle in her ear to wake her up out of it.

"I'll draw you how to get there," she said about the place she had in mind for what they were wanting to do with that Buick. She got a pen out of the drawer and started marking up the back of a bill. She had already paid it but she pretended she hadn't.

"Y'all can pay this bill, too, when you're done with the map."

"Check's in the mail," said Marcus. He was eating more of Maria's fruit pie, and good for him, because he'd gone a little thin. Maria had probably been feeding him organic. Harriet had a plan to put some pounds back on him after Maria left. She knew Marcus favored more her kind of diet than Maria's and she'd gotten to where she hated eating alone now, that was the loneliest part of it, she'd nearly rather starve than sit behind her desk at the motel stabbing Styrofoam with a plastic fork.

"Good a place as you're going to find for what y'all want, though if you ask me . . . ," said Harriet, and Maria said, "We didn't ask you," and Harriet said, "Well, I guess it makes sense you didn't ask me, since you did not ask me the first thing about going in on it," and Maria pointed at the map and said, "Your maps resemble Marcus's charts."

Harriet knew when a subject was being changed. She knew

better than to say one more word about what they were planning on doing with that car. She'd said too much already. Still, it seemed like to her a waste, even though she never did much care for that vehicle. She didn't see what they saw in it. It was too long to park and rode too low for her taste. You couldn't haul anything in it. She never did see why they chose it, much less why they got in it and drove it around like it was something special.

"You like a chart, Marcus?" she said.

"I do love a chart."

"I wish you'd make one for me, then. I could use a chart to give out to my help so they'd know when to show up and when not to. And what time they ought to get there, because some of them don't know what a watch is."

Valentine, Texas, October 2004

The ranch hand out searching for stray cattle found, hidden under piles of cut brush, a sky-blue Buick Electra. He did not see at first that despite having no battery and no tags, the car was in relatively good shape and perhaps salvageable if you were inclined to drive a Buick. He did not know anyone in the area, save some of the older couples he had seen in town driving slowly down the streets toward church or the grocery store, who might drive a car like this. It wasn't a very good car for the terrain.

He wondered how in the devil it got down here in the draw. It had rained some in the past few weeks, so it wasn't possible to track it. He didn't carry a cell phone. He couldn't call the sheriff, so he poked around a bit, trying to figure out why someone would leave this car out here.

Someone went to some trouble to hide this Buick. Opening doors and glove compartments and looking up under seats did not enlighten him as to why. In fact the longer he stuck around out there, the more he felt like it wasn't any of his business, this abandoned Buick. Could be any number of things led to it being left out here, and none of them, to his mind, called for him to meddle or squeal. He had parked his ATV over on the rise and someone might come up on his tracks, but if he told his boss man, Sure, I saw it but I didn't feel like it was any of mine, his boss man, who had been known to lie to the Border Patrol because they had gotten to be more and more a nuisance, would take up for him. But the hand did not think it would come to that. He had this feeling he'd be the last to see the Buick.

The last human. Antelope came to poke. And javelina, set on something to eat. Coyotes came down out of the mountains. The ranch hand in his examination of the Buick had left its right rear door cracked open enough for anything smaller than a burro to squeeze in wanting shelter from a wind. Grasshoppers, tarantulas, snakes—all the crafty species adapted to survival in a place not known for its bounty. Tumbleweeds in time added to the brush piled atop it, some of which blew away, only to be replenished by the wind. Rust came slowly in this thirsty draw but dust was so thick across it that within weeks the Buick blended with the desert but for a patch on the hood as clear blue and startling as cloudless sky.

Acknowledgments

The author wishes to acknowledge the help and expert guidance of Peter Steinberg, all of the good people at Algonquin Books (especially Lauren Moseley, Kathy Pories, and Craig Popelars), my generous and attentive first readers (you know who you are, and please know this book would be so much less without you), Balmorhea State Park, Jesse Donaldson and Kevin Jones, and B.K.W., who always kept my seat warm at the Table.